The Jones-Imboden Raid

The Jones-Imboden Raid

The Confederate Attempt to Destroy the Baltimore & Ohio Railroad and Retake West Virginia

DARRELL L. COLLINS

McFarland & Company, Inc., Publishers

Jefferson, North Carolina, and London

LIBRARY OF CONGRESS CATALOGUING-IN-PUBLICATION DATA

Collins, Darrell L.
The Jones-Imboden raid : the Confederate attempt
to destroy the Baltimore & Ohio Railroad
and retake West Virginia / Darrell L. Collins.
p.   cm.
Includes bibliographical references and index.

ISBN-13: 978-0-7864-3070-3
softcover : 50# alkaline paper ∞

1. West Virginia — History — Civil War, 1861–1865 — Campaigns.
2. West Virginia — History — Civil War, 1861–1865 — Transportation.
3. United States. Army — Supplies and stores — History —19th century.
4. Baltimore and Ohio Railroad Company — History —19th century.
5. Raids (Military science) — History —19th century.
6. Jones, William E., 1824–1864.   7. Imboden, John D. (John Daniel), 1823–1895.
8. Confederate States of America. Army — History.
9. United — History — Civil War, 1861–1865 — Campaigns.
10. United — History — Civil War, 1861–1865 — Transportation.   I. Title.
E475.3.C68 2007   973.7'454 — dc22   2007021186

British Library cataloguing data are available

On the cover: (left) Major General Samuel Jones and
(right) Brigadier General John D. Imboden (U.S. Army Military History Institute);
(background) Baltimore & Ohio Railroad map (Library of Congress)

Manufactured in the United States of America

*McFarland & Company, Inc., Publishers
Box 611, Jefferson, North Carolina 28640
www.mcfarlandpub.com*

To the memory of one of the raiders,
my great-great-grandfather
Private Nicholas Stulting
of Company I, Nineteenth Virginia Cavalry

Table of Contents

List of Maps

Preface

This book is about the dramatic spring 1863 Confederate raid into the new state of West Virginia. The raid was two-pronged, one column led by Brigadier General William E. "Grumble" Jones and the other by Brigadier General John D. Imboden. Their stated purpose, fully and enthusiastically sanctioned by General Robert E. Lee and the Davis administration, was the destruction of the Baltimore & Ohio Railroad at certain critical points, the defeat of Union troops in the area, and the gathering in of much needed supplies and manpower for the Army of Northern Virginia. But the great raid was much more than that. It was a pivotal moment in the momentous struggle between the counties of the trans–Allegheny and those of the Tidewater and Piedmont, with the former seeking freedom from perceived irreconcilable political, economic, and cultural differences, and the latter trying to prevent "secession" from within Virginia's borders.

In this book I have tried to follow the raiders on their remarkable month-long journey of suffering and sacrifice. During a grand sweep of the western counties they brought down mighty bridges, tore up miles of track, burned oil fields, scattered their foes, reaped a great harvest of horses and cattle, and returned triumphantly to the Shenandoah Valley. They left behind, however, a wake of death, destruction, and bitterness that ultimately proved self-defeating.

Although I have drawn on many sources including unpublished documents, other books, written accounts, and various scholarly studies, the ultimate source of inspiration for this, my fifth book on Civil War subjects, is something I find far more fascinating and moving: the oral tradition. The captivating stories I learned as a boy from my parents, grandparents, and other relations about the experiences of their West Virginia grandparents during the Civil War set me on a wondrous lifelong journey of inquiry into the nature of that great conflict in general and its effect on West Virginia in particular. Among several ancestors who served in the war was my great-great-grandfather Nicholas Stulting, an immigrant from the city of Utrecht in the Netherlands, a silversmith and carpenter who in 1846 settled in the tiny hamlet of Hillsboro in Pocahontas County, (West) Virginia. When in early 1863 the Confederate government, increasingly desperate for soldiers, extended the military age limit from 35 to 45, forty-two-year-old Nicholas promptly enlisted in a new regiment then forming in the area, the Nineteenth Virginia Cavalry (some twenty years before, the Dutch army had rejected him for being too small). Barely a month later, Private Stulting found himself taken up by a great adventure like nothing he had ever known, an adventure that nearly killed him, an adventure that is the subject of this book.

It is often said, with great truth, that no one writes a book alone. My thanks are due for the invaluable assistance provided by the excellent staffs at the Virginia Military Institute Archives in Lexington, the National Archives and the Library of Congress in Washington, D.C., the West Virginia University Library in Morgantown, the University of Virginia Library in Charlottesville, the United States Army Military History Institute in Carlisle Barracks, Pa., Marshall University Library in Huntington, W. Va., the West Virginia Department of Culture and History in Charleston, the Virginia State Library and the Virginia Historical Society in Richmond.

And a special thanks for the support and encouragement given by my sweet wife, Judy, who always will remain my love and my life.

CHAPTER ONE

The Setup

The Temptation

On the cool, crisp day before Christmas in 1852, a large, enthusiastic crowd gathered in the still mostly unpaved streets of the growing and soon to be immensely more prosperous town of Wheeling, Virginia. Fully aware of the historic significance of the occasion, the people had come to witness the ceremonial driving of the last spike, a joyous, festive event that honored the completion of a twenty-three year startlingly visionary project for its time: the Baltimore & Ohio Railroad. That line now stretched 379 unbroken miles, crossing numerous mountains, rivers, streams and chasms, from the great Maryland city in the east to Wheeling on the Ohio River in the west.[1]

On the following day, most of the 100 or so citizens of the tiny hamlet of Rowelsburg, Virginia, located on the B&O line some eighty-five miles southeast of Wheeling, turned out to receive with child-like excitement a very special Christmas gift when a steam locomotive came chugging into town for the first time after having crossed over three recently completed nearby engineering marvels. Rising twenty-seven feet above the water, the two-span iron and wood Cheat River Bridge stretched 312 feet from shore to shore. Resting on stone bases along the side of a steep ridge about a mile west of the bridge, the cast iron Buckeye Hollow Viaduct reached 340 feet across a forty-six foot deep ravine. Six tenths of a mile further on stood the crown jewel (costing $36,049) of the entire line, the beautiful, cast iron, 445 foot long Trey Run Viaduct, spanning a chasm fifty-eight feet deep, and which today is proudly depicted on the reverse of the Seal of the State of West Virginia. These last two, designed by Benjamin H. Latrobe and Albert Fink, were America's first iron railroad viaducts.[2]

A product of the "railroad mania" that swept across the eastern United States in the 1850s, the B&O, with its growing number of branches, including the Northwestern Virginia 100 mile link from Grafton to Parkersburg, Virginia, in 1857, became one of the busiest commercial roadways in the nation. With the coming of the Civil War in 1861, the B&O took on the added status of being one of the North's most important military lines. As the shortest route between the Ohio River and the Potomac, it connected Washington with the Midwest's vast wealth of men, supplies, rations, and much of the timber and coal that built and sustained the Federal fleet blockading Southern ports. And it became the primary base and supply line for military operations in both the Trans-Allegheny and the Lower Shenandoah Valley. "It is the great artery that nourishes the country," loyalist Virginia Senator Waitman T. Wiley accurately observed. "We cannot do without it."[3]

All this in turn made the B&O a constant, great thorn in the side of the Confederacy, being especially harmful, and humiliating, to Virginia, the line running 188 miles (including the trunk line from Grafton to Parkersburg) through the state's mountainous, thickly forested, and mostly "disloyal" counties of the northwest. "The Baltimore and Ohio Railroad has been a [great] nuisance to this state, from the opening of this war to the present time," Governor John Letcher warned the Virginia Legislature in late 1862, "and unless its management shall hereafter be in friendly hands, and the government under which it exists be a part of our Confederacy, it must be abated."[4]

In lieu of the difficult and perhaps impossible task of placing the B&O in "friendly hands," particularly that portion of it stretching from Baltimore to Harper's Ferry, Confederate military planners readily understood that the best way to inflict on it severe, long lasting damage was to bring down its bridges and viaducts. With its three grand and seemingly accessible spans, Rowelsburg easily stood out as one of the most tempting targets on the line. "The rupture of the railroad at Cheat River," General Robert E. Lee had written as early as the summer of 1861, "would be worth to us an army." In early March of 1863, Lee received for consideration the outline of a daring proposal to do just that.[5]

The Planners

Born February 16, 1823 at Christian's Creek near Fisherville, a small community some five miles east of the Augusta County seat of Staunton, Virginia, John Daniel Imboden was the eldest of eleven children. From local institutions he received a good education for the times, the dark haired, dark complexioned boy, who grew to a height of just over six feet, eventually choosing law as his profession. Practicing in Staunton, he prospered, became a slave owner and served two terms in the Virginia Legislature. In matters of love, however, Imboden was not so fortunate, being married five times during his life and made a widower four, losing to disease several children along the way.

During the secession crisis of early 1861, he took the unusual stance of hoping that Virginia might remain neutral and thereby negotiate a compromise settlement between the North and the Gulf States that would result in a new union. When that did not happen he became an ardent secessionist and supporter of the Confederacy.

In the wake of the John Brown raid at Harper's Ferry, Imboden used his own funds to help raise and equip the Staunton Artillery, which elected him their captain on November 28, 1859. Despite having no military training or experience, the Virginia lawyer proved to be a capable, intelligent, and natural leader. Attached to Barnard Bee's brigade, he won distinction at First Manassas when the battery stood and fought alone for a full half hour on Henry House Hill.

Returning to his beloved Shenandoah Valley, Imboden raised the First Regiment of Virginia Partisan Rangers, which in the spring of 1862 served with Stonewall Jackson in the Valley Campaign, seeing action at the battles of Cross Keys and Port Republic. In August and September 1862, he cooperated with Albert Jenkins in a moderately successful supply-gathering raid into western Virginia, and on September 15 of that year he lent support to Jackson's seizure of Harper's Ferry.[6]

In recognition of his valuable services, Secretary of War James Seddon offered on January 28, 1863 to make the dark-haired colonel a brigadier general, provided he raised sufficient forces to constitute a brigade, all of whom then would be incorporated into

Brigadier General John D. Imboden (Massachusetts Commandery Military Order of the Loyal Legion, U.S. Army Military History Institute, Carlisle Barracks, Pennsylvania).

Confederate service. Highly gratified by this inducement, Imboden quickly put the finishing organizing touches on the Sixty-second Virginia Infantry, 792 officers and men commanded by Colonel George H. Smith, and the Eighteenth Virginia Cavalry, 706 officers and men commanded by his twenty-seven-year-old brother (one of five serving in the Confederate army) Colonel George Imboden (1836–1922), and Captain John H. McClanahan's battery of ninety-four men. Thus with the establishment of the Northwestern Virginia Brigade, as it came to be called, Imboden received his commission on April 13, 1863.[7]

Also under the nominal command of Imboden, but not part of his brigade, was a small (its roster rarely exceeded 100 men) partisan company popularly known as McNeill's Rangers. It was their commander, Captain John H. McNeill, who came to the new brigadier with a daring proposal to strike the Cheat River Bridge at Rowelsburg.

Born in Moorefield, Virginia, on June 12, 1815, John Hanson "Hanse" McNeill had led a hard life as a farmer in both Virginia and Kentucky before moving in 1848 to near Columbia, Missouri, where he achieved national renown as a breeder of Shorthorn cattle. When the war inconsiderately disrupted that successful enterprise he became captain of a local militia company that wasted no time in getting into several hot scrapes with the Yankees. In one of those scrapes, McNeill was wounded and captured, his burgeoning military career apparently at an end. In late 1861, however, he carried off a dramatic escape from a St. Louis prison, then, not wanting to risk the fatal consequences that might attend recapture, he gathered his three grown sons and made his way back to Virginia. In the South Branch Valley surrounding his boyhood home in Moorefield, McNeill, slightly built with a thick head

Captain John H. McNeill (Massachusetts Commandery Military Order of the Loyal Legion, U.S. Army Military History Institute, Carlisle Barracks, Pennsylvania).

of hair carefully parted on one side, and a full, salt and pepper beard that somewhat obscured a handsome face featuring sympathetic eyes, helped raise and became captain of the volunteer company that bore his name. After conducting several successful hit-and-run raids on Union camps and supplies, during which time his reputation soared into notoriety, McNeill felt confident enough in the early weeks of 1863 to approach Imboden with a fresh and daring plan to strike at Rowelsburg.[8]

The Plan

With the ardent backing of President Jefferson Davis, several attempts already had been made against Rowelsburg. All had failed because the place had had ample warning, and time, to be reinforced by Union troops.

The first attempt came as early as June 1861, when Colonel George A. Porterfield, by order of General Lee, led 750 poorly armed men from Harper's Ferry to Grafton with the intention of hitting Rowelsburg along the way. Porterfield burned two bridges at nearby Mannington, but turned back when he learned that the Federal troops at Rowelsburg vastly outnumbered him.[9]

After Robert Garnett replaced Porterfield later that year, he too received orders from Lee to destroy the Cheat River Bridge. And like Porterfield, Garnett turned back after Federal reinforcements reached Rowelsburg, though not before achieving the mild satisfaction of throwing enough timber into the Cheat to temporarily block river traffic.[10]

On August 14, 1862, Imboden and 300 of his Partisan Rangers set out from Franklin in Pendleton County. Hoping to sneak up on Rowelsburg, he avoided the main roads, relying on local sympathizer Zeke Harper to guide him from Mouth of Seneca six miles over Allegheny Front Mountain, cutting new paths through the dense forest as they went. The careful plan came apart, however, when the struggling column unexpectedly came within sight of the home of John Snyder, a staunch Union man. Correctly surmising the intentions of the Confederates, Snyder's nineteen-year-old daughter, Mary Jane, bravely made a twenty-five mile all-night ride to warn the Union garrison at Parson's Mill, which then pulled back to Rowelsburg. When Imboden reached St. George in Tucker County, about fifteen miles from his target destination, he thereby learned that the Federals at Rowelsburg knew he was coming. With the game up, he turned around and went back to Pendleton.[11]

Undaunted, Imboden tried again three months later. On November 7, with a new guide, William Harper, he and 310 Rangers rode out of their camp on the South Branch, just north of the Pendleton-Hardy county line. After crossing Allegheny Front Mountain in a most unwelcome snowstorm, they successfully surprised and captured the thirty-man garrison at St. George on the ninth. They did not, however, capture the entire garrison. One Yankee got away and made it to Rowelsburg to warn the garrison, leaving Imboden no choice but to once again turn back.[12]

Sometime during the ensuing winter months, Captain "Hanse" McNeill hit upon the reasonable notion, drawn from his vast experience in such matters, that the task required a more efficient and balanced combination of stealth and strength — a force not so large as to be slow and unwieldy, nor too small to deal with an alerted enemy. Give me 600 or 700 men, McNeill confidently told Imboden, and I will make a lightening, powerful strike against Rowelsburg and bring down its bridge and trestle works.[13]

Imboden liked the idea, so much so that he sent its author to Richmond for the purpose of making a face-to-face presentation to the Secretary of War, James A. Seddon. The clever tactic worked far better than any official, impersonal dispatch or telegram, for McNeill's confidence and enthusiasm readily persuaded the secretary. But since the proposed operation fell within the military jurisdiction of the Department of Western Virginia, from where troopers for the raid might need to be drawn, Seddon refused to sanction the enterprise until the department commander had reviewed it. This proved to be the first step in the unraveling of the simple plan.[14]

Born in Powhatan County, Virginia, December 17, 1819, Samuel Jones graduated from West Point in 1841, after which he led a rather undistinguished military career that included twenty years of service at various posts from Maine to Texas. In April

Major General Samuel Jones became the Commander of the Department of Western Virginia in 1862 (Massachusetts Commandery Military Order of the Loyal Legion, U.S. Army Military History Institute, Carlisle Barracks, Pennsylvania).

1861, he resigned from the U.S. army and entered Confederate service as a major of artillery. For his commendable work as General Beauregard's chief of artillery and ordnance at First Manassas, Colonel Jones received promotion to brigadier general. Despite this promising start, Jones for the most part was denied field command, being relegated to various administrative duties in different departments. Upon replacing Braxton Bragg as commander of the Department of Alabama and West Florida, Jones received promotion to major general. From there he bounced around from post to post, generally turning in mediocre or unsatisfactory performances, until November 1862, when he landed the assignment as commander of the Department of Western Virginia. On December 10, he established his headquarters in southwest Virginia at Dublin Depot in Pulaski County.[15]

The command originally had been formed May 8, 1862, as the Department of Southwestern Virginia, comprising the area of Virginia extending "west to the eastern boundary of Kentucky and as far west of that boundary as circumstances may allow." Major General William W. Loring commanded the department until John Echols replaced him on October 16, 1862. Four weeks later Echols gave way to Brigadier General John S. Williams, who in turn stepped aside for Jones, the fourth commander of the now renamed Trans-Allegheny Department, more commonly called the Department of Western Virginia.[16]

Jones's responsibilities included providing protection for the Virginia & Tennessee Railroad, which may arguably have been as important to the Confederacy as the B&O was to the Union. Moving eastward from Bristol, the 204-mile line passed near numerous important salt and lead mines in southwestern Virginia before connecting at Lynchburg with equally vital supply lines coming up from the Deep South. Jones also held the rather nebulous responsibility of offering protection to the loyal citizens of Virginia's western and southwestern counties.[17]

For this great task, the beleaguered department commander had but four small brigades of infantry and one of cavalry, plus five batteries of artillery, all totaling barely 7,000 men. Moreover, the nature of the assignment required that these commands be scattered over a vast area. The First Brigade of about 1700 men, under John Echols, was headquartered at the Narrows on New River in Giles County. John S. Williams's Second Brigade of only 600 men was stationed at Saltville and Salt Sulphur Springs in Smyth County. The Third Brigade, 1100 men under Colonel Gabriel C. Wharton, was based at Glade Springs in Washington County. John McCausland's Fourth Brigade of 1500 men was centered at Princeton in Mercer County. And Albert Jenkins's Cavalry Brigade of about 1500 men was based at Salem in Roanoke County, Virginia. Various other small, unattached commands floated in between these main brigades.[18]

Jones believed, perhaps justifiably, that he had been given an impossible task. Much to the annoyance of Lee and the War Department, he persistently complained of having too few men and resources to hold and protect an area he considered "cursed with intrigue and political plotters."[19]

On March 6, 1863, the disgruntled department commander received from Secretary Seddon a telegram that informed him of McNeill's plan and of the impending visit of its author. "He is perfectly confident of his ability to accomplish the enterprise," the impressed secretary wrote of the captain. "I am inclined to think the enterprise very likely to prove successful. I have long thought the best mode of accomplishing it was by a sudden and unexpected dash of a small force rather than by the movement of a larger, which must necessarily be known, and probably induce preparations and defense."[20]

"Hanse" arrived at Dublin Depot two days later. Jones never liked to provide his own troops for others to use, no matter how urgent the need or important the reason, and this time proved no exception. Though ostensibly supportive of the enterprising captain's proposal, he felt sufficient wariness to beg off providing for it any of his own cavalry, giving as reasons the broken down condition of his mounted arm and the great distance between it and the intended target. To avoid the appearance of being totally uncooperative, however, he did not send McNeill away empty handed. "The destruction of the bridge and trestle, even if we had quiet possession of it," the department commander explained to Seddon in a letter written March 8, "will require skill and proper tools. I have, therefore, arranged with Captain McNeill to send with him an engineering officer [Lt. Hart] and 8 or 10 men-mechanics — who have been instructed for this particular work, provided with necessary implements and materials for the destruction of the bridge and trestle." Jones then passed McNeill on to beg for troops and support from the commander of the Valley District.[21]

Born near Glade Springs in Washington County, Virginia, on May 9, 1824, William Edmondson Jones received a Master of Arts degree from Emory and Henry College before graduating from West Point in 1848, too late to participate in the Mexican War. After serving briefly in Missouri and Kansas, he went to Oregon in 1849. Two years later he left Washington Territory for duty with the Mounted Rifles in Texas. In early 1852, he returned home on furlough to marry Eliza Dunn. From Virginia, the newlyweds made their way to New Orleans, where they left by ship for Jones's return to duty. Off the coast of Texas, however, the vessel foundered in a storm wherein Eliza slipped from her husband's arms and perished. Broken hearted, Jones never fully recovered from the devastating loss. After five more years of drudgery in the service, mainly in Texas, he resigned from the army on January 26, 1857, and became a reclusive farmer near his hometown of Glade Springs.[22]

The war that came four years later proved a tonic for the despondent Jones by giving his life new meaning and purpose. He helped organize and became captain of the Washington Mounted Rifles, which subsequently became Company D in the First Virginia Cavalry. Exemplary service in the First Manassas campaign received the gratifying attention of the army commander, General Joseph E. Johnston, who proclaimed the company the strongest in the First Virginia, "not surpassed in discipline and spirit by any in the army." Johnston in turn recommended that Jones, "skillful, brave and zealous in a very high degree," be made commander of the regiment to replace its first colonel, J.E.B. Stuart, who had been promoted to brigadier general. Thus as part of Stuart's new brigade, Colonel Jones and the First Virginia went on that fall and winter to perform excellent service in keeping a watchful eye on the enemy from the Blue Ridge to the Potomac. For various reasons, however, Jones's relationship with Stuart turned bitterly sour, degenerating to the point of irreconcilable hatred. This in turn produced a negative affect on the men of the First, who still held "Jeb" with a regard bordering on adulation. That and Jones's irascible, profanity laced temper that exploded without warning from behind a perpetual scowl (framed by a full beard and a balding head) made it rather easy for those troopers to turn "Old Grumble" out of office at the reorganization of the command in April 1862.[23]

On June 20 of the same year, however, Jones took over Turner Ashby's old regiment, the Seventh Virginia Cavalry in Beverly Robertson's famed "Laurel Brigade," the renowned Ashby two weeks before having been killed at Harrisonburg during Stonewall Jackson's Shenandoah Valley Campaign. Though once again succeeding a beloved commander, Jones did much better with the Seventh, vastly improving its discipline and efficiency, while readily identifying with the men by wearing "a home spun suit and a broad yellow hat," and riding an "old yellow mare," all of which produced "a rough, seedy-looking individual, without any insignia of his rank."[24]

Though Jones continued to despise Stuart, he developed a close and cordial relationship with Jackson, under whom he rendered commendable service at Brandy Station, the Second Manassas Campaign, and the Maryland Campaign. Largely at Jackson's insistence, Jones received promotion to brigadier general on October 3, 1862, to rank from September 19. Jackson's influence also helped secure the Laurel Brigade for Jones, as well as command of the Valley District on December 29, an important subdivision of General Lee's Department of Northern Virginia.[25]

"This will be handed to you by Capt. J.H. McNeill," began a note from Seddon to Jones at his headquarters in Lacey Springs near Harrisonburg and dated March 10, "who has proved himself by past service a gallant and enterprising soldier. He has submitted to me, with the commendation of General Imboden, a plan of gallant dash, with some 600 or 800 men, to accomplish the destruction of the trestle-work on the Baltimore and Ohio Railroad and the bridge over the Cheat River. These are objects of great importance, and their successful accomplishment has long engaged the attention and special interest of the President. Several efforts heretofore have been, from special causes, frustrated, but the practicability of the enterprise, especially by the sudden dash of a small force, is believed to be by no means doubtful. The plan of Captain McNeill meets the concurrence of the Department, and after consultation with General Samuel Jones, whose approval (as the enterprise was to be attempted in a district of his department) was desired, has secured his sanction. I hope, when explained to you by Captain McNeill, it will likewise have your approval and co-operation. You will be expected to afford a portion, at least, of the force required for the enterprise, and by any contemporaneous operation you may deem judicious to favor and promote the scheme."[26]

Though "the scheme" offered no real opportunity, for which he remained ever vigilant, to seek personal glory, Old Grumble, perhaps somewhat begrudgingly, gave it his approval. At last, it seemed, the much-traveled McNeill had gained the support he needed and the plan was on go.

Imboden Offers More

All this delay, however, gave time for thought among those who, through a combination of motives that included both personal ambition and patriotic service, began to consider even greater possibilities. The first to succumb to this urge was Imboden, who now wanted to dramatically expand the scope of the plan, taking it from the quick dash of a small force of cavalry that had so appealed to Seddon, to a grander, more cumbersome and thus riskier venture. With this idea he appealed directly to the commander of the Department of Northern Virginia, Robert E. Lee.

"General:" began Imboden's letter dated March 2, written at Camp Washington, his headquarters near the base of Shenandoah Mountain some ten miles northwest of Staunton. "In a recent letter I stated that I would shortly submit to your superior military judgment a plan of operations in the northwest that I thought would be successful in accomplishing some important results. I beg leave now most respectfully to lay the matter before you, and request your approval. The objects aimed at are, first, the destruction of all the bridges and trestling on the Baltimore and Ohio Railroad, from the bridge across the Youghiogheny, at Oakland [Maryland], as far west as Grafton, and, secondly, the defeat and capture of the enemy's forces at Beverly, Philippi, and Buckhannon, and then to enlist in our army the young men of the northwest, and endeavor, if possible, to hold that section of country long enough to overthrow the local government, of which four-fifths of the people are heartily tired, and would joyfully unite in our State elections in May."[27]

Imboden's more expansive plan called for Grumble Jones to divert the attention of the enemy by a demonstration toward Romney, located between two main Federal outposts at Winchester and New Creek. "Simultaneously with that demonstration," he went on, "I will send 500 well-mounted men from Moorefield to Oakland, leaving the former place, without baggage of any kind, and reaching Oakland by a forced night march over a country road but little traveled, till they strike the Northwestern turnpike. I know this can be done without the enemy having the slightest intimation of it till the bridge at Oakland, which is wood, is in flames."[28]

With the Federals in the lower Shenandoah Valley prevented from pursuing both because of Jones's demonstration and the destroyed B&O bridge over the Youghiogheny

River at Oakland, Imboden's cavalry then would be free to rush west on to Rowelsburg and bring down its bridge and trestle works. To keep enemy forces already in western Virginia from interfering, Imboden intended to march from Staunton with his infantry and artillery and attack the Federal garrison at Beverly. This in turn would allow the two Confederate forces to reunite. "Being joined by my cavalry at Buckhannon or Weston," Imboden continued, "much of the Northwestern Railroad might be destroyed in a few days, and with a general destruction of these roads and bridges will end, I believe, the occupation of the northwest by the enemy, at least for some months to come, and even its temporary occupation by us will be of immense advantage. I am satisfied that I should receive several thousand recruits, and large numbers of cattle and horses could be collected; and, again, I would be in good position to operate in conjunction with General Williams against Charleston later in the spring."[29]

Since heavy snowfalls in the mountains had swollen many low-lying streams beyond fording, Imboden believed the expedition should not start before the first of April. Moreover, his thorough considerations convinced him of the necessity of borrowing from Lee the Twenty-fifth and Thirty-first Virginia Infantries. "These two old regiments are from the northwest," he explained, "and would fight like tigers the vandals who have so long domineered over their helpless families."[30]

Thus, it seemed, Imboden's restless, furtive mind now envisioned not simply the destruction of B&O property but nothing less than the "liberation" of the western counties from Yankee oppression. "These expectations may seem wild," he concluded in his letter to Lee, "but I assure you, general, that at no period since the war commenced has the opportunity ever been so good to gain a foothold in the northwest. The weakness of the enemy there, the disaffection of the people toward their rulers, and the unexpectedness of the movement, all give promise of success."[31]

If there is going to be a raid into the western counties, Imboden must have reasoned, why limit its possibilities? And if his planned expedition achieved the success he envisioned, he stood to reap a great harvest of glory. This does not, however, explain completely the motives of a man, who, though like most of his species, craved favorable recognition, but who also still retained enough humility to resist the urgings of friends to seek a major generalcy. "I do not desire it," he explained, "I really feel that I have as high a military rank as I am qualified for." Something more drove him.[32]

The constant flood of reports, rumors, and refugees arriving in the Shenandoah convinced the former lawyer that in the western counties Southern sympathizers, particularly those suspected of aiding Confederate raiders, lived in constant fear of harassment, confiscation, arrest, and even death. Imboden's November 1862 failed raid toward Rowelsburg that went as far as Tucker County proved to be a particularly galling case in point when local Union authorities sent a company of Ohio troops into the area to collect assessments from Southern sympathizers in compensation for the damage done by the raiders. Those refusing to cooperate and pay the fines faced the threat of having their homes burned or of being shot. "This is only one of a thousand barbarities," Imboden angrily protested in a December 7 letter to President Davis, "practiced here in these distant mountains of which I have almost daily heard for the last few months," adding emphatically, "Oh, for a day of retribution!" (Lee protested to Union general-in-chief Henry Halleck, who revoked General Robert Milroy's order, but not before some $6,000 had been collected from about a dozen Tucker County citizens, including one man who supposedly sold his pants to make the payment.) [33]

The Plan Expands

"I think if carried out with your energy and promptness," Lee wrote Imboden on March 11 after giving careful consideration to the new plan, while Hanse McNeill was about to sell the old one to Grumble Jones, "it will succeed." What especially appealed to the general was the possibility of greatly adding to the manpower and supplies of both Imboden's command and the Army of Northern Virginia.

"I will endeavor to give you the two regiments you ask," Lee added, "[the] Twenty-fifth and Thirty-first [Virginia], if I can replace them temporarily in this army, otherwise I shall not be able to spare them, as I have been obliged to send three divisions [under Lt. Gen. James Longstreet to Suffolk] on other service. If I cannot spare the regiments named, I will endeavor to get you two from General Samuel Jones.... I am expecting General Hooker's army to move against me as soon as the roads will permit, and I do not feel that I ought to diminish this army by a single man. By the 1st of April, or before that time, I expect this army to be engaged in active operations."[34]

Imboden's desire for the Twenty-fifth Virginia Infantry and Thirty-first Virginia Infantry was a measure of his thorough consideration of the new plan. The two regiments indeed had been raised primarily from trans–Alleghany counties, and after fighting well under Stonewall Jackson in the Shenandoah Valley, during the Seven Days Battles around Richmond, at Second Manassas, in the Maryland Campaign, and at Fredericksburg, the men of these tough old units now yearned for a chance to liberate and defend their homelands.[35]

Lee was willing to accommodate these deserving veterans, provided he received prompt compensation by way of two regiments from Sam Jones, whom he also ordered to be prepared to make a diversion toward the Kanawha in favor of Imboden. Now that the expedition had taken on a much grander scale, however, Jones regretted not having included himself in it. He told Lee as much on the 17th, using as a face saving argument the wish that he had been informed earlier so that he might have contributed more than two regiments. One day later he told Imboden the same thing, while also reminding him that during the coming operations, which would take place within the Department of Western Virginia, he wanted the dark-haired general to report to him.[36]

Preparations now picked up steam. On March 21, Lee wrote Imboden that he had arranged to provide him with twenty wagons and teams as requested. Imboden's other request, however, seemed at this point to be in jeopardy. Sam Jones, characteristically, was hedging on his pledge to send two regiments to Lee, arguing that he had been waiting for two of his own regiments to return from North Carolina, and that even when they did he might need them to protect the salt works. Lee assured Imboden, however, that Jones's anticipated demonstrations in the Kanawha might be enough to secure success. Lee then offered one final caution: "You must send no dispatches by telegraph relative to your movements, or they will become known."[37]

On March 26, Lee informed Grumble Jones about the modified plan and of the district commander's part to create a diversionary threat against Romney. "No period has occurred since the commencement of the war so favorable, in my opinion," the commanding general wrote enthusiastically, "for dealing a blow against the enemy's possession of the northwest as now. The paucity of their numbers and the disaffection of our citizens combine in our favor, and if the movement can be made unexpectedly and simultaneously, it must be successful, if rapidly and boldly executed. Their active force, as far as I can learn [based on estimates given him by Imboden], distributed from New Creek to the Kanawha, except the garrisons at Beverly, Philippi, and Buckhannon, does not exceed three regiments, say 1500 men."[38]

Lee's growing enthusiasm for the plan inevitably carried with it a touch of impatience. "I am anxious to know how you progress in your preparation for your expedition west of the Alleghany, the strength and composition of your forces, &c.," he wrote Imboden on March 26. "The season is now at hand when it should be executed." Then after telling Imboden of the arrangements to forward from Richmond to Staunton rifled pieces, arms, ammunition, and supplies, Lee expressed a growing confidence in the diversionary movements of Grumble Jones against Romney and Sam Jones in the Kanawha. "If the different columns move with precision and act rapidly and boldly," the commanding general concluded, "success appears certain." Yet even without that total success, Lee finally reasoned, at least the bridges at Oakland and Rowelsburg will be destroyed, and men, horses and cattle obtained. "Leave your feeble men and horses with your 6-pounders to guard the pass at your camp," he cautioned in closing, "and keep you entire march a secret, even from your own men."[39]

Two days later, on Friday, March 28, Imboden arrived at Sam Jones's headquarters in Dublin, presumably to work out the details of providing troops for the expedition. Despite the impatience of President Davis, who in reaction that day to news of the movement west by rail of Ambrose Burnside's IX Corps to reinforce General William Rosecrans in Kentucky had wired Lee, "Now is the time to destroy ... the Cheat River Bridge, if possible," Jones and Imboden both agreed that the recent week-long heavy rains had rendered April 1 impractical as a starting date for the expedition. The one advantage to this, however, was the added time to more thoroughly prepare. The next day, the 29th, Sam Jones ordered Colonel George Patton at Lewisburg to make ready his Twenty-second Virginia Infantry for a march north to a rendezvous with Imboden. Four days later, on April 2, Jones finally started for Richmond the Fiftieth Virginia, 648 strong, to thereby effect the release to Imboden of about the same number of men in the Twenty-fifth and Thirty-first Virginia regiments combined.[40]

Further Modification

But delay, this time caused by the rains, again allowed too much time for thought. Never happy with the diversionary role assigned to him, Grumble Jones now made a grab for a greater share of the expedition and its glory. On March 31, he proposed to Lee that instead of marching on Romney he assume the role planned for Imboden's cavalry by taking the entire brigade to Moorefield and thence on to Oakland and Rowelsburg. His tough, experienced cavalry, he must have reasoned with some justification, had a much better chance of success than did Imboden's relatively new regiments. Retaining his own cavalry then, Imboden still would move against Beverly, but he also could hit the B&O at Grafton and eventually unite with Jones. Under this third version of the original plan, the entire expedition thus would possess much greater strength, thereby hopefully assuring a corresponding greater chance of success. To cover his district while he was away from the Shenandoah, Jones suggested that Lee send Wade Hampton's cavalry brigade into the Valley.[41]

After pondering the proposal for an entire week, or at least giving it what attention he could spare while preparing for the expected onslaught from General Joe Hooker, commander of the Army of the Potomac, Lee opted for the stronger strike force. On April 7, Old Grumble received the gratifying news, along with orders to start the expedition on the 15th. "Two simultaneous attacks on the Baltimore and Ohio Railroad, at the points proposed," the commanding general concluded, "will certainly increase the probabilities of success, and facilitate a more complete destruction of the road." Lee's enthusiasm grew as the plan expanded and appealed to his daring nature. "You must make the best disposition in your power to conceal your departure from the Valley and to prevent the inroads of the enemy," he cautioned Jones. "You must leave your pickets as heretofore, but they can be kept up by your weaker men and horses, allowing you to take the strongest for your expedition. An inspection should be made of every man, horse, and arm carried with you, and none must be allowed to go except those found every way competent for the hardships that may be incurred."[42]

Lee, however, declined to move Hampton into the Shenandoah, arguing that the swiftness of the strike should be sufficient to keep the enemy off balance long enough to protect the Valley. Moreover, in lieu of the diversionary movement originally assigned to Grumble, Lee promised to make some move against the enemy east of the mountains about the time of Jones's departure, "which may serve to fix his attention upon his lines of communication, and thus give you time to make your blow." Lee then added one final word of caution. "I feel it unnecessary to advise you that your movement must be expeditious and bold; but that you must take every precaution against discovery and failure. You must keep intelligent scouts in your front, flanks, and rear, who will give you accurate information and not mislead you by false reports. The utmost secrecy in regard to your expedition must be observed, and I consider that the collection of cattle, horses, and provisions will be of as much importance to us, and under certain contingencies, even more, than the destruction of the railroad.... I will send Lieut. William [G.] Williamson, who was employed in the destruction of the Monocacy Bridge, to report to you. You will have to supply the implements he may require, as he will not know for what purpose he joins you."[43]

The same day, Tuesday, April 7, Lee informed Imboden of these important changes in the plan, which eliminated the necessity of sending off any of his cavalry. "You will, therefore, have with you your whole command," said Lee, "and can push your cavalry on to Grafton while attacking Beverly." Lee then gave Imboden the same pep talk about secrecy, boldness, and good intelligence. If the former Staunton lawyer felt at all disheartened by these new arrangements, which lessened his role in favor of that given to Grumble Jones, he gave no outward indication of it.[44]

Also on the 7th, Lee wrote Sam Jones that, with the new target date of April 15, it now was too late to exchange the Fiftieth Virginia for the Twenty-fifth and Thirty-first. When Jones wired the next day, however, that the Fiftieth already was on its way, Lee on the 9th issued Special Order 99, directing the two regiments (the 25th belonged to John Jones's Brigade, Isaac Trimble's Division, and the 31st belonged to Jubal Early's old brigade of Early's Division), to proceed by rail to Staunton and report to Imboden.[45]

Early on Friday morning of April 10, the Twenty-fifth marched from its camp near Buckner's Neck southeast of Fredericksburg to Guiney's Station, where it took the cars that afternoon for Hanover Junction. From there it went some 125 miles by rail to Staunton, the last of the regiment arriving about midnight the next day. "It is conjectured," the regiment's thirty-three-year-old Doctor Abram Miller wrote in his diary on the 13th, "that we will go out to Beverly or in that direction." In the afternoon of the 15th they reached Camp Washington. "The present indications are," Miller wrote three days later, "that we will remain here several days or perhaps several weeks." The Thirty-first arrived about the same time after following a similar route, all its officers having prophetically signed a petition in late March to have the regiment transferred to service in northwest Virginia.[46]

Slowly, the pieces fell into place. On April 11, Sam Jones informed Imboden that after receiving 500 new rifles, Lt. Colonel Ambrose C. Dunn's dismounted Thirty-seventh Virginia Battalion, about 450 men, would depart Salem by foot on the 12th, march north some eighty miles and report to Colonel William L. Jackson at Hightown on the 18th, and that Colonel George S. Patton's 650 men of the Twenty-second Virginia Infantry would leave Lewisburg for the same place on the 13th.[47]

Accompanied by the acting commissary of subsistence, Major John W. Mitchell, a native of Wheeling who carried $100,000 for the purpose of buying provisions in western Virginia, the Twenty-second on April 13 marched about fifteen miles east from Lewisburg to White Sulphur Springs. It then headed twenty-five miles north through Greenbrier County to arrive at Greenbrier Bridge (Marlinton) in Pocahontas County on the 15th, where it camped for four days. It then went on to Hightown in Highland County, on the Parkersburg-Staunton Pike, about six miles west of the county seat of Monterey, arriving there on the 20th. There it met up with the Thirty-seventh Battalion.[48]

Daily, it seemed, the expedition took on increasing complexity. After urging Imboden to send his cavalry on from Beverly to cut the rail line at Grafton in order to prevent enemy reinforcements from coming in from Parkersburg or Wheeling, Sam Jones reassured him about the diversion in the Kanawha. Jenkins's cavalry, he wrote, would be near the mouth of that river, and McCausland was to move to Fayetteville when Imboden reached Beverly.[49]

Imboden's cavalry force was to include a new regiment, the Nineteenth Virginia, which only recently had begun recruiting in Pocahontas and other border counties, and was designated for assignment to Jenkins's Cavalry Brigade. "Col. W[illiam] L. Jackson has a regiment collected," Jones wrote Imboden on the 4th, "and the field officers will be elected and the organization completed before you start. Something over 200 of his men are now in the lower end of Pocahontas; most of them are of the Virginia State Line, are armed, and have seen service. I will direct Colonel Jackson to join you and act under your orders." That same day Jones instructed Jackson to try to have at least 300 men join Imboden at Hightown before the April 15 scheduled start of the expedition.[50]

Born in Clarksburg, (West) Virginia on February 3, 1825, William Lowther Jackson before the war had been a successful attorney, state politician and circuit court judge, elected in 1859, of the Twenty-first Judicial District of Virginia [which included the counties of Taylor, Preston, Upshur, Harrison, Barbour, Tucker, Randolph and Marion]. Over the years Jackson, a redhead who parted his hair low on the side to affect a swoop designed to conceal a growing baldness, became well known in the area as a man "devoted to the interests of Virginia to the last extremity." With the outbreak of war in 1861, political connections gave command of the Thirty-first Virginia Infantry to "Judge Jackson." Near year's end he accepted a position on the staff of his second cousin, Stonewall Jackson, with whom he served through all the major campaigns of 1862. When the Virginia Legislature determined to disband the Virginia State Line and the Virginia

Colonel William L. Jackson (Boyd B. Stutler Collection, West Virginia State Archives).

State Rangers, which operated behind Federal lines in western Virginia, it recommended to Richmond that Colonel Jackson take control of these men. On February 13, 1863, the War Department authorized him to raise a cavalry regiment from the disbanded units. On April 11, at Warm Springs in Bath County, Jackson completed the organization of the Nineteenth Virginia Cavalry, with enough companies left over to form the nucleus of what would become the Twentieth Virginia Cavalry. For the most part, however, though the men had been enlisted and the muster rolls properly formed, the new companies lacked mounts. (Having thus acquired a new command, Jackson before the end of the year also would acquire a new nickname, "Mudwall," provided by contemptuous Yankees when the cousin of the renowned Stonewall stepped aside to let them pass on a raid through the Greenbrier Valley.)[51]

Meanwhile, just when everything finally seemed to be falling into place for the raid to begin, another delay occurred when intelligence convinced Lee that a large body of Federal cavalry was moving toward the Shenandoah. "Collect your forces and be on guard," Lee warned Grumble Jones, who in turn wired Sam Jones to cancel the movement of troops from his department. Soon, however, it became apparent that the Yankees had not crossed the Blue Ridge. The movement turned out to be a ruse, resulting from a false rumor planted to disguise the true, southern destination of Hooker's cavalry under George Stoneman. "There is no sign of the enemy in the Valley," Grumble wired Imboden on the 16th. "I would be glad to see you in a few days to arrange our affairs."[52]

At last, the expedition was about to begin, an expedition that had grown considerably in scope from the now almost forgotten and much simpler one proposed barely two months before by the now almost equally forgotten Captain John H. McNeill.

West Virginia

"[F]our-fifths of the people" of western Virginia, Imboden brashly had declared in his March 2 letter to General Lee, "are heartily tired" of the Federal government, and if given the chance they "would joyfully unite in our State." Lee agreed. "The disaffection of our people," he had written Grumble Jones, made this an opportune time "for dealing a blow against the enemy's possession of the northwest." The two Southern generals could not have been more wrong.[53]

According to the census of 1860, of Virginia's 1,596,318 people, only 376,677 lived in counties that would form the new state of West Virginia. Of Virginia's 490,865 slaves, the western counties possessed but 18,371, three-fourths of which lived in only four counties: Kanawha, Putnam, Greenbrier, and Monroe. While the slaveholding plantation society of the Tidewater and Piedmont thus generally guaranteed the loyalty of those regions to the new republic, the trans–Alleghany, with few slaves, and an economy and culture oriented northward by the region's major rivers and highways, had strongly opposed the state's Ordinance of Secession, passed April 17, 1861. Mass Unionist meetings immediately sprang up all over the region, and at Wheeling on June 11, delegates representing twenty-six counties convened to form a new "loyal" state government. Within two months, during which time Union forces rather easily secured much of the region by a series of small victories at Laurel Hill, Rich Mountain, and Corrick's Ford, the delegates established a reorganized legislature and selected Francis H. Pierpont "Governor of Virginia," with the capitol at Wheeling. (Born June 25, 1814 in a small log cabin in Union District, about four miles from Morgantown, Pierpont moved with his parents a year later to Harrison County, and at sixteen he moved to near Fairmont, where he became a successful lawyer and industrialist.)[54]

In November, another convention drafted a constitution for the state of West Virginia, which voters who had taken the oath of allegiance to the Union ratified on April 3, 1862. Convening May 13, the new state legislature immediately requested admission to the Federal Union. On December 13, 1862, Congress finally approved the bill, with the proviso that the new state gradually abolish slavery within its borders. After some hesitation, President Lincoln signed the proclamation on April 20, 1863, and on June 20, West Virginia formally entered the Union as its thirty-fifth state. Arthur I. Boreman of Parkersburg became its first elected governor.[55]

Created by the war, the new state suffered terribly from it, as regular and irregular troops, bushwhackers, guerillas, partisans, rangers, and local home guards engaged in a bitter, deadly contest throughout its many rugged mountains and valleys. Pillag-

MAJ. GEN. ROBERT C. SCHENCK

Major General Robert Schenck (Collection 2027, Ohio Historical Society, Columbus, Ohio).

ing, marauding, oppression and fear became common, quickly removing from the new state any romantic notions about war. Some 25,000 West Virginians served in the Unions ranks, while at least 16,000 took up arms for the Confederacy.[56]

In March 1863, meanwhile, the proposed new state had been added to the Middle Department, a military jurisdiction created one year before to embrace New Jersey, Pennsylvania, Delaware and the eastern shores of Maryland and Virginia. This vast area came under the protection of the VIII Corps, commanded by Major General Robert Schenck, with headquarters in Baltimore.[57]

Born in Franklin, Ohio, October 4, 1809, Schenck before the war had been a lawyer, a state legislator in his native Ohio, a four-term U.S. Congressman and a diplomat to Brazil. When the war broke out, he earned a brigadier's star, in part, as reward for working to help elect Lincoln. He capably commanded a brigade during the Valley campaign of 1862, and a division at Second Bull Run, where he received a disabling wound that left him fit only for administrative duty. He thereupon succeeded to command of the Middle Department, which contained some 35,000 men in garrisons scattered over a vast area, from Philadelphia to Wheeling. (On April 30, 1863, Schenck reported the strength of the Middle Department as 34,297 men present for duty.)[58]

Those troops of Schenck's VIII Corps that most concerned Jones and Imboden included Major General Robert H. Milroy's Second Division, about 8100 men, stationed at Winchester and Berryville to protect the Lower Valley of the Shenandoah, and the 4500 men of Major General Eliakim P. Scammon's Third Division, located in Charleston and the Kanawha Valley. Of more immediate concern, however, was Major General Benjamin F. Kelley's 12,000 strong First Division.[59]

Born in New Hampshire in 1807, Kelley had lived in Wheeling since the age of nineteen. There on the banks of the Ohio he had built up a successful mercantile business before becoming a freight agent for the B&O Railroad in 1851. By the time the Civil War broke out a decade later, Kelley's popularity and influence in the Wheeling area were such that he was largely responsible for raising the loyal, ninety-day First Virginia Infantry, for which deed he was made the regiment's colonel. He led the First at the war's first land battle, Philippi, where he sustained a severe chest wound. Thus his status as an early hero in the war, combined with his strong pro-union activities in western Virginia, made Kelley the natural choice to take over the newly formed Cheat Mountain District. On April 1, 1863, he assumed command of the First Division, with headquarters at New Creek on the Potomac River.[60]

Kelley held two main responsibilities: the protection of that portion of the B&O line that stretched from Harper's Ferry to the Ohio River, and the defense of that part of West Virginia not under the jurisdiction of Scammon in the Kanawha Valley. The first job he gave to Brigadier General John R. Kenly's Maryland Brigade and Colonel James Mulligan's Fifth Brigade, their troops being scattered in small garrisons all along the line. Benjamin Roberts's Fourth Separate Brigade, whose main base was at Clarksburg, with small detachments at Beverly, Buckhannon, Birch, Sutton, Weston, and Bulltown, held the second job.[61]

Born in Vermont on November 18, 1810, Benjamin Stone Roberts ranked fifty-third in the West Point class of 1835. A highly intelligent man of varied interests, he resigned his commission in 1839 to become the chief civil engineer of a New York railroad company, and two years later he received an appointment as geologist for the state of New York. In 1842, he went to Russia to help with the construction of the St. Petersburg to Moscow railroad line. Returning to the U.S. the following year, he earned a law degree and began practicing in Des Moines, Iowa. With the outbreak of war with Mexico in 1846, Roberts returned to the army as a First Lieutenant of the Mounted Rifles. He distinguished himself in the conflict, earning promotion to the regular rank of captain and the brevet ranks of major and lieutenant colonel, after which he received an honorary sword from his adopted state of Iowa.

Sustained by these accolades, Roberts chose to remain in the service after the war, performing frontier duty in the southwest until his May 13, 1861 promotion to major of the Third U.S. Cavalry, with command of the Southern District in New Mexico Territory. In December, he became colonel of the Fifth New Mexico Volunteers, which the following spring served with Edward Canby's force in opposition to Henry Sibley's Confederate invasion of the territory. Though now fifty-one years old, Roberts's heroic role in the battle of Valverde, New Mexico, on May 16, 1862, brought attention to him as a man of great promise. He was brought east, promoted to brigadier general, and made inspector general and chief of cavalry on the staff of Major General John Pope, commander of the newly formed Army of Virginia. At Cedar Mountain on August 9, 1862, Roberts suffered a severe contusion on the left arm and breast. From there, however, his military career began to spiral downward. After the disastrous campaign of Second Bull Run, he became embroiled in the celebrated case of Fitz John Porter, officially preferring against him Pope's charges of disloyalty, disobedience, and misconduct in the face of the enemy (subsequently found guilty and dismissed from the service, Porter spent years trying to clear his name, finally succeeding in 1886). With Pope's fall, Roberts went down with him, both being sent to the wilds of Minnesota. Roberts then was exiled to the military backwater of western Virginia, where on March 11, 1863, he assumed command of the newly formed Fourth Separate Brigade. Clean-shaven except for lengthy thick sideburns extending down from a balding head to frame a face of thin lips and pleading eyes, the Iowa general now looked much older than his fifty-two years.[62]

Responsible for the security of most of West Virginia outside the Kanawha Valley, Roberts, appalled by the extent and influence of disloyalty within his jurisdiction, and by way of extending his reputation for controversy, lost no time in antagonizing much of the local population by the use of harsh measures against those suspected of having Southern sympathies. "A determined will on the part of the people," he wired Governor Pierpont on April 7, "in destroying the outlaws now busy in planning their system of brigandage, will have a great moral effect. If the pretending neutrals see that the people are rising and organizing to make war upon them, I am undoubting in my convictions that their atrocious schemes will at once be abandoned, and comparative quiet will be restored to your new State."[63]

The same day, Roberts informed department commander Schenck of his radical proposal. Those in West Virginia who favor secession and the rebellion are "very much more numerous than I had expected to find them," he wired, "and are much more dangerous here than they could possibly be in open rebellion and in arms within the rebel lines. They harbor and give shelter to the guerillas, and to rebel soldiers who, in disguise, pass into our lines, bringing information, and returning with intelligence for our enemies, and carry off horses and other property they steal from Union citizens. They are especially active at this time, and prompt and severe measures must be adopted to strike down this great mischief. The character of this country favors this kind of brigandage, and the disloyal portions of the citizens who claim to be neutrals can, as a general thing, escape detection.

"I propose to compel this class to go beyond our lines, making few exceptions, if any, and to take with them their families, old and young, but not their property, or anything that could aid the rebels. I see neither humanity, justice, nor any wisdom in permitting them to live under the protection of the new State government of Western Virginia, or the Federal Government, while they withhold their allegiance to either, and covertly aid the rebellion, vexing the loyal citizens, inflaming resentments, and encouraging the raids of the guerillas in the destruction of their property, and in continuing the system of brigandage, planned by Governor Letcher at Richmond, for the overthrow of the new State government at Wheeling."

Roberts, his blood up, had not finished. "There is another class that should be sent at once into the enemy's lines," he went on. "They are the wives and families of officers and soldiers in the Confederate service. They carry information and supplies from point to point in these mountains, where they meet their friends, and thus keep up a channel of communication that can only be broken up by expelling them from the country."[64]

From his headquarters at Buckhannon in Upshur County, Roberts thus promoted what many regarded as nothing less than a campaign of terror. Often upon the flimsiest evidence, he forced the "disloyal," including many women, children and old men, to abandon their homes and pass through the lines to the South. Though Pierpont and Schenck did little to discourage him from implementing these drastic steps, many of Roberts's own men considered the measures too extreme. "This indiscrimination touched the chivalric sense of justice and right of our soldiers," wrote Major Theodore Lang of the Third West Virginia Infantry, "and Roberts was charged with making war on women and children instead of going after those who were in armed rebellion."[65]

The reports coming into his headquarters, however, convinced the Iowan of the correctness of his policy. "This is to inform you that I have found out the plans of the Secesh at Beverly," Colonel Nathan Wilkinson wired him on April 10. "Learn they have frequently conveyed news to General Imboden by letters every week. The Beverly ladies say that if they knew the time when the Secesh would make an attack on Beverly, and if they would send them the materials, they would spike their cannons."[66]

Aroused Suspicions

Despite Lee's careful admonitions about protecting the secrecy of the plan, by early April the Yankees on the other side of the Alleghenies knew something was up. Reports, derived mostly from local civilians, indicated that the rebels in the Shenandoah were gathering strength, presumably in preparation for carrying out something big.

Indeed, as early as February, before plans for the expedition even had been finalized, rumors began to spread. "Mr. King says Imboden is camping on Shenandoah Mountain and says he'll quarter in Philippi after the first of April," Isabella Woods wrote on February 7 to her husband Samuel, "but I have no such hopes." The Woods, staunch secessionists, had lived in Philippi until the summer of 1861. In June of that year, Samuel, a judge and a delegate to the secession convention, joined the Confederate army at Richmond, whereupon Isabel took their six children some 100 miles southeast to live in Waynesboro, Virginia, a town of unquestionable Southern loyalty. In the ensuing months, Samuel and Isabella kept each other informed about events in and around Philippi. "It is perfect folly," she continued in her February 7 letter, "to talk of holding that country while the railroad is in possession of the enemy." Samuel, however, put more stock in the rumor. "We've heard Imboden has gone down the valley," Isabella wrote her husband on April 19, "just as you supposed."[67]

To investigate the rumors arriving with increasing frequency at his headquarters, Roberts ordered two regiments to do a reconnaissance toward the Shenandoah. On or about April 6, some 250 men of the Second West Virginia Infantry under Colonel George Latham left Beverly and marched about seventy-five miles east to Franklin in Pendleton County. Six days later, Colonel John Oley pulled out of Beverly with 250 men of the Eighth West Virginia Infantry and marched about thirty miles southeast to the Greenbrier River in Pocahontas County, where he met up with "Kelley's Lancers," under thirty-six-year-old Lieutenant Nimrod N. Hoffman, a printer before the war in his native Morgantown. Named after local hero Benjamin F. Kelley, the Lancers had been formed in Morgantown in July 1861. (It remained an independent company until the expiration of its three-year enlistment in 1864, whereupon it would be reorganized as Company A of the Sixth West Virginia Cavalry.)[68]

"After throwing ourselves on the outside of our coffee, crackers & such," a Lancer recalled a few days later in a letter to the Wheeling *Intelligencer*, "and smoking one of Mitch's Wheeling regalias vulgarly known as stogies, we laid ourselves out at full length on terra firma, supposing that we were to have the privilege of a good night's rest; but no! some busybody — not having the love of the Lord nor the fear of the devil in his sacred conscience — reported to Col. Oley that there were a few bushwhackers at Greenbank. The Lancers were ordered out at 12½ midnight to ride 13 miles over one of the roads merely 'for the novelty of the thing,' as Corporal Street used to say, and when they arrived there, not a rebel — in arms — was to be found."[69]

The following morning (14th), the Lancers led the Eighth twenty-one miles east to Hightown in the vicinity of Crab Bottom in Highland County, across the newly established border between West Virginia and the Old Dominion. Though they again saw no armed rebels, from many of the locals along the way they received confirmation of the Confederate build-up in the Shenandoah. In very unpleasant weather, Oley, satisfied with the success of his mission, then fell back into the mountains a few miles and encamped. "The storm of snow, hail and rain," continued the Lancer in his letter to the newspaper, "penetrating every nook and corner that a soldier could find, so you may imagine that we had a rough night of it. A storm in the Alleghanies," he added, "is not to be sneezed at without a prime article of Scotch snuff."[70]

Starting at 6 a.m. the following morning (15th), the command made their old camp on the Greenbrier River that evening, and the next day, Thursday the 16th, they reached Beverly, shortly after the arrival of Latham and the Second West Virginia.[71]

Though no one actually had seen any rebels during the expedition, the enemy nonetheless had kept a close eye on them. While bringing up the rear on the way to Beverly, Lieutenant Hoffman and fifteen Lancers came under fire from as many as forty bushwhackers, shooting from behind trees near the Greenbrier. The lieutenant took three balls, one in the leg, another in the ankle, and a third that struck his hip. An orderly sergeant (T.H. Lemley) took a ball that broke a rib, and two other men (C.W. Conn and Charles Star) had horses killed from under them. Incredibly, Hoffman remained mounted and led all his men safely on to Beverly, while a gun from Ewing's battery came up and shelled the woods from where the shots came, no doubt with little effect. (Despite the severity of his wounds, Hoffman would return to duty within two months, and continue to serve until the end of the war.)[72]

Though neither Latham nor Oley directly observed the enemy on their respective scouting missions, they did acquire valuable information. The rebels, Latham wired Roberts, have three regiments of infantry and five of cavalry in the vicinity of Crab Bottom, "and all the indications are a move by them in this direction.... Colonel Oley reports indications of an advance, and says the citizens along the route were expecting it. All Imboden's force was reported under marching orders." Moreover, later that same day, Latham's scouts confirmed Oley's report that the Twenty-fifth and Thirty-first Virginia "have been secretly sent from the east." Despite all this evidence, Latham drew a remarkable conclusion: "I do not consider Beverly in danger."

Roberts promptly sent these reports on to department commander Schenck in Baltimore. "It is beyond doubt the intention of the rebels to attempt an attack upon my forces," the Iowan wired, "but it seems to me improbable that they have gathered in so large a force, yet it is possible, and preparations should be made to meet it. I need artillery and cavalry," he added correctly, the entire region woefully lacking either. "My quartermaster has not a dollar of funds to pay spies and scouts, or for any other purpose."

Schenck in turn consulted with general-in-chief Henry Halleck, both of whom remained skeptical about the intentions and size of the rebel force. At any rate, because of Hooker's impending move against Lee and the diversionary support it was to receive from the divisions of both Milroy and Kelley, Halleck forbade the transfer of any troops to Roberts. "I do not believe they [the rebels] have any such strength," Schenck wired Kelley the morning of April 19. "I can send no re-enforcements to Roberts, who is asking for more cavalry and artillery. You must support him as far as practicable, from the railroad, and give instructions to Colonel Wilkinson, at Clarksburg, accordingly."

Thus despite an excellent job of intelligence gathering, the Union commands in western Virginia, Baltimore, and Washington did virtually nothing to prepare for the expected attack.

Ironically, many citizens in the area wisely heeded the warnings and took better precautions. "As early as March," Roy Bird Cook wrote in his 1924 history of Lewis County, "rumors were on every hand that an invasion was contemplated by the Confederate authorities."

Understandably alarmed by these rumors, officials of the Exchange Bank in Weston invested $15,000 of the institution's money in U.S. government bonds, which they prudently deposited for safe keeping in the Metropolitan Bank of New York. Later they removed all of their own and the bank's valuables to Wheeling, giving rise to further rumor that the bank president, Richard P. Camden, had been tipped off by one or more of several nephews currently serving with Imboden.

So much for secrecy.

CHAPTER TWO

Beverly

The Expedition Begins

In Washington on Monday, April 20, President Lincoln signed the proclamation that gave his formal approval to the admission of West Virginia as the thirty-fifth state of the union. Out in the Shenandoah Valley soon after dawn on the same day, John Imboden, officially a brigadier general now for one full week, received word that all was ready to begin the invasion of the "so-called" new commonwealth. He promptly gave the signal, and his Northwestern Virginia Brigade, 1825 men, began to move out from "Camp Washington," some ten miles northwest of the Augusta County seat of Staunton, which stood on the eastern terminus of the Staunton-Parkersburg pike (present route U.S. 250). "[I]t was an ideal spring morning," Paul McNeil recalled forty-two years later in The Richmond *Times Dispatch*.[1]

A seventeen-year-old boy in 1863, McNeil lived in nearby Pocahontas County and was the son of John McNeil, captain of the newly formed Company F, Nineteenth Virginia Cavalry. Though not yet an enlisted soldier, young McNeil was determined to tag along on this expedition, hoping for adventure as well as the opportunity to be of some use while visiting his many friends and relatives in the Twenty-fifth and Thirty-first Virginia Infantries. Moreover, the lad held the wild notion that he might be able to recover some of the more than 200 head of cattle and a number of fine horses taken from his father's farm in the past year by Federal raiders.[2]

Proudly astride "Billie," his newly acquired five-year-old, blood bay swift mount, who stood fifteen-and-a-half hands tall with a white star on his forehead, young McNeil rapturously watched the long column as it moved out. "The soldiers were still bewildered as to their movements," he remembered, "but when the command began to move west over the Staunton and Parkersburg Turnpike you could see joy in their faces." The boys of the Twenty-fifth and Thirty-first quickly surmised that at last they were heading over the mountains and into their home country.[3]

Imboden and his aides led the way. "The Sixty-second regiment, a large regiment then," recalled McNeil, "was immediately behind General Imboden's staff, and with fife and drum they moved out." Commanded by Colonel George H. Smith, an 1853 graduate of the Virginia Military Institute, the Sixty-second Virginia had been formed the previous September from a diverse mixture of infantry and cavalry companies. In December, most of the companies transferred to the newly formed Eighteenth Virginia Cavalry, being replenished in turn by companies transferred over from the Twenty-fifth Virginia Infantry. The regiment saw its first action during Imboden's expedition into Tucker County in November. (In late 1863, the Sixty-second would become a mounted regiment.)[4]

With growing pride, McNeil watched the rest of the column pass. "Colonel John Higginbotham, at the head of the Twenty-fifth Virginia Infantry — and what a soldier this man was!" Barely a man, having turned twenty the previous November. While a student at Lynchburg College, John Carlton Higginbotham became captain of Company A of the Twenty-fifth in May 1861. A year later he made major. Always in the thick of his regiment's fights, he received a wound in the leg at McDowell and another in the thigh at Second Manassas. On January 28, 1863, he became the Twenty-fifth's colonel.[5]

"Next came that war-worn veteran, Colonel John S. Hoffman," McNeil went on, "at the head of 'the old Thirty-first,' as the members of that regiment delighted to call it." By now McNeil was overcome with emotion. "The scene was too much for my young rebel heart," he confessed. "I was visibly affected." Born in Weston, Virginia, in 1821, John Stringer Hoffman now possessed a "grand physique," the majesty of which was somewhat offset by a pair of thick spectacles worn to correct acute nearsightedness. Starting out as a sergeant in the Thirty-first in May 1861, Hoffman a year later became the regiment's colonel.[6]

After not seeing the Twenty-fifth and Thirty-first for nearly two years, McNeil now was struck by the present contrast. "The ranks of those two regiments had been fairly depleted at that time," he sadly recalled, "and what a change had come over the living. Their faces had grown old and careworn and while they looked strong and healthy, still their limbs were so stiff that not one of them I tried could mount 'Billie' from the ground."[7]

Along with the column came John McClanahan's six guns and Colonel George Imboden's Eighteenth Virginia Cavalry, both units formed from the recent successful recruiting efforts of Imboden in the western counties of Virginia. Like his older brother, twenty-six year old George William Imboden had been a lawyer in Staunton. He had been a sergeant and a lieutenant in the Staunton Artillery, a captain and a major in the Sixty-second Virginia, and, since December 15, 1862, Colonel of the Eighteenth Virginia Cavalry.[8]

"[T]he 25th, 31st, and the 62nd in good condition," Captain Frank Imboden told his diary, adding about his own regiment, "18th OK." The third oldest of the five brothers in Confederate service, twenty-two-year-old Captain Francis Marion (Frank) Imboden (1841–1922), had gone with his company of Virginia militia to maintain order in Harper's Ferry following John Brown's raid, then resumed his studies at the Virginia Military Institute until the war broke out. While with the "Wise Legion," commanded by former Virginia governor Henry A. Wise, young Frank had been captured on Roanoke Island off the coast of North Carolina in February 1862, and later was exchanged with the help of a letter written by his older brother John to President Davis. Eventually joining the Eighteenth Virginia Cavalry, Frank now commanded the regiment's Company H.[9]

On the pleasant 20th, the Northwestern Virginia Brigade made an impressive twenty miles on the Staunton-Parkersburg Pike, passing through Buffalo Gap and camping along Bull Pasture River near the village of McDowell in Highland County, the scene of Stonewall Jackson's great victory the year before. The following day, the command marched sixteen miles northwest to Hightown, where they met with reinforcements sent up from Sam Jones. These welcome additions included Colonel William L. Jackson's newly formed and still mostly dismounted Nineteenth Virginia Cavalry, and Lieutenant Colonel Ambrose C. Dunn's Thirty-seventh Battalion Virginia Cavalry, both units nominally members of Jenkins's Cavalry Brigade. And from John Echols's First Brigade came the Twenty-second Virginia Infantry under Colonel George S. Patton. These three units added to Imboden's command 1,540 men, giving him 3,365 altogether, of which only about 700 were mounted. Not included in these figures were a number of civilians who somehow had got wind of the expedition and now were vengefully determined to tag along and regain the homes from which the despised General Roberts had driven them.[10]

When young McNeil went to have a look at the new arrivals, he was quite surprised, and a bit annoyed, when several men of the Twenty-second Virginia began crowding around him. "It's Billie, it's Billie," they called out in obvious recognition of McNeil's mount. Presently, along came the regiment's Lieutenant Colonel Andrew Barbee, who seemed most delighted to see old Billie. To puzzled young McNeil the lieutenant colonel explained that he once had owned the horse, and had ridden him for a year until it developed a sore back, whereupon he sold it to someone who then evidently sold it to McNeil's father.[11]

General Imboden, meanwhile, his column supplied with thirteen days' rations of flour and thirty of salt "while relying upon the country to furnish meat," had intended to cross the mountains and fall upon the Union stronghold at Beverly on the 23rd, then head northwest for the B&O and a junction with Jones. On Wednesday, April 22, however, the weather turned bad, drenching the men with cold rain and converting the road into a quagmire. Following renowned local guide Zeke Harper, the same who had led Imboden through the wilderness over Allegheny Front Mountain on the failed attempt to strike at Rowelsburg eight months before, the column struggled across the mountain into Pocahontas County and the new state of West Virginia.[12]

Rather reluctantly had Pocahontas been taken into the new commonwealth, the overwhelming majority of eligible voters among the county's 4,000 citizens having in the recent presidential election cast their ballots for states' rights advocate John C. Breckinridge, and later they decidedly approved secession, all of which meant that in this region, at least, the rebel invaders might still feel welcome.[13]

At 5 p.m., Imboden stopped for the night at Camp Bartow, three miles east of the Greenbrier River. Here on October 3, 1861, 1500 Confederates stubbornly threw back the attacks of the 5,000 Federals who had pushed the rebels off Cheat Mountain two weeks earlier. "A very different scene is presented to the eye now," Private James Hall of the Thirty-first Virginia, a veteran of the fight, noted in his diary that night. "The hard, baked earth has given way to luxurious vegetation, and all over that broad camp a dead silence reigns, following the hum and stir of busy camp life. The graves of our soldiers who fell in that battle are all sodded over, and the green grass waves in beauty over those fallen heroes, as if it were enjoying the genial air of spring. As we stood around their graves we could almost envy their quiet, peaceful lot, when we remembered what we had undergone, between that time and the present, and also thought of the probability of a still harder life to come."[14]

At Bartow, Imboden learned from a picket he had sent there two days before that the "notorious Yankee scout" John Slayton and a squad of seven men had passed by around sunrise that morning. After rebels killed his brother early in the war, Slayton, a member of the Pocahontas County Home Guard, became "notorious" in these mountain regions as someone who carried his duties to the vengeful extreme of mercilessly raiding the farms of known Southern sympathizers.[15]

Fearing Slayton now might warn the Federals at Beverly, and hopeful of catching this local villain, Imboden sent twenty men riding after him. He also set up a picket line that ran from Pocahontas County to the Greenbrier River at the foot of Cheat Mountain. Though the twenty pursuers did not catch the "notorious" scout, the picket line forced him to swing north of the pike to where he got tangled up in the dense forests of Cheat Mountain, thereby preventing him from reaching Beverly in time to warn his comrades. Unaware of Slayton's delay, however, Imboden assumed the Yankees now knew he was coming.[16]

From Bartow on the 23rd, the command marched three miles west to the Greenbrier River, now full of slush ice from the spring thaw. James H. Mays of the Twenty-second Virginia later recalled that the soldiers' feet, "which were but poorly clad at best, were almost frozen" before they got across, some forty men in the regiment having no shoes at all. They then climbed to the top of Cheat Mountain, where six inches of snow had fallen the night before, and which now threw in their faces a cold, driving sleet. The men, many scantily clad in anticipation of warm spring weather, suffered miserably before descending the mountain into Randolph County.[17]

The Fight for Beverly

As they had in Pocahontas County, Imboden and his men could expect to be among friends in Randolph, the voters among its 5,000 citizens having clearly supported the Ordinance of Secession. The command stopped that night at Huttonsville on the Tygarts River, near the western foot of Cheat Mountain, where the men collapsed in camp after having gone seventy miles in four days.[18]

Upon regaining his strength after a decent night's rest, William McCarty (regiment unknown) slipped out of camp the next morning to go back up on Cheat Mountain to find a broken down horse he left there the day before and had worried about since. Before finding the poor animal, however, bushwhackers got him. They killed him, emptied his pockets and left his body on the road, making McCarty the first combat casualty of the expedition. His grisly death hereafter served as an effective warning to those with notions of wandering off from the safety of their commands.[19]

Though now only twelve miles south of his primary objective, Imboden was dismayed to learn that a Federal picket of thirty men had been recalled from Huttonsville to Beverly at 11 a.m. that morning (23rd), thereby convincing him that the notorious Slayton had done his work. That conviction strengthened when about midnight he received a report of an enemy force moving up the east side of the Tygarts River to apparently climb Cheat Mountain, from where they obviously meant to gain a clear view of the Confederate camps. Though the Yankees mysteriously turned around before reaching the mountain, Imboden remained convinced that they knew of his presence in Huttonsville.[20]

Having learned that twenty-four year old Captain Joseph French Harding of the Thirty-first Virginia's Company F (a wounded veteran of Chantilly) was a Huttonsville area native, Imboden that night sought out the man and asked him to lead a scouting party toward Beverly in order to learn more about the enemies' strength. "The boys were tired from a hard day's march," Harding later recalled, "but George [62 Va. Inf., later killed at Berry's Ferry] and Squire [Edward H., Co. F, later killed at Mine Run, brother of George] Kittle and J[ames] R. Apperson [Co. F, 31 Va.] volunteered to go with me. We started at once, reached the homes of some friends near Beverly without trouble, ascertained from reliable sources the desired information, and, late in the night, started on our return."[21]

Before Harding and his men got back to Huttonsville, however, Imboden, not wishing to risk further delay, set off for Beverly. Friday, April 24, dawned as "one of the most gloomy and inclement I ever saw," he reported. A thick fog hung over the landscape, obscuring visibility. "As soon after daylight as possible," young McNeil later recalled, "General Imboden had his army in motion and every man believed that there was work ahead of us that day."[22]

The village of Beverly lay at the junction of the Grafton Turnpike and the Staunton-Parkersburg pike, just east of Rich Mountain, the scene of General George McClellan's 1861 victory that catapulted him into national prominence. The town now was held by a detachment of the Fourth Separate Brigade under thirty-one-year-old native Virginian (born near Haymarket in Prince William County) Colonel George R. Latham (1832–1917), a pre-war lawyer and Wheeling Convention delegate who had entered the service in May 1861 as a captain (Co. B) in the Second (West) Virginia Infantry, rising to regimental command one year later, seeing action along the way at McDowell and Second Bull Run. His force now consisted of seven companies of his own Second West Virginia Infantry, 400 men, five companies of Lt. Colonel John Polsley's Eighth West Virginia Infantry, 289 men, Captain Frank Smith's Independent Company of Ohio Cavalry, ninety-eight men, Captain Harrison H. Hagan's Company A, First West Virginia Cavalry, fifty-nine men, and one section — a ten pound Parrott and a six pound brass smoothbore — of Captain Thomas Ewing's battery, thirty-two men, making for a total of 878. Incredibly, in stark contrast to Imboden's conviction, and despite the successful intelligence-gathering missions carried out earlier that month, none of these men knew the Confederates now were anywhere near them.[23]

Captain Harding and his three tired companions, meanwhile, continued heading south. "We had, so far, kept to the east side of the river," he later recalled, "but now crossed it, reached the pike near where Daily is now located, and proceeded on our southward way just at dawn." Harding knew the area well, so well in fact, that when

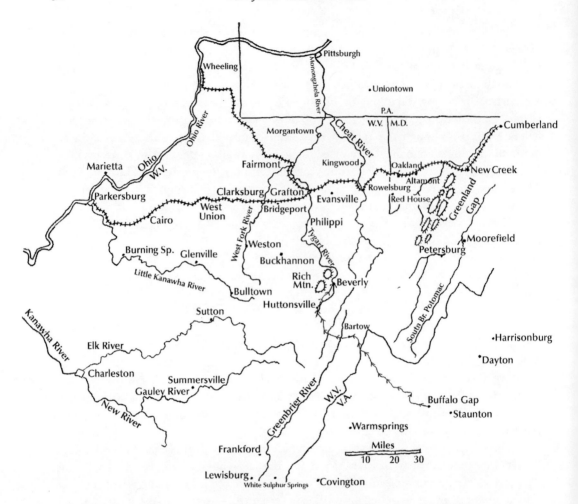

1. Imboden's movement from Buffalo Gap, Va., to Beverly, W. Va., April 20–25, 1863.

the four men came within sight of a house by the side of the pike the captain put up his hand and motioned for the men to stop and be silent. That was the home of "a rabid Union man," he whispered, and they accordingly set off on a hidden detour through a nearby field. Soon afterwards, they saw a lone man riding hard up the road toward Beverly. Harding and his companions were close enough for one of them to recognize the rider as Jesse Phares, the sheriff of Randolph County. To stop Phares from reaching Beverly and spreading the alarm, the men loudly called out for him to halt. The sheriff obviously heard them but kept riding. Three of the men then fired at him, two shots missing and one knocking off his hat. Harding then stepped out into the road, took careful aim and pulled the trigger.

The bullet tore into Phares's back and entered his lung. The sheriff staggered but did not fall. "We knew at the time that he was wounded," Harding recounted in utter amazement, "but he pluckily kept his saddle until reaching the Federal pickets at the bridge about two miles distant."

Harding and his men now made speed. "Keeping the pike," he went on, "we now proceeded on our return." Along the way, they encountered two more fast-riding, armed civilians (George Bradley and James McCall), evidently intent on reaching Beverly to spread the alarm. The rebels blocked the road, pulled the surprised men down from their horses, disarmed them, and took them along as prisoners. Finally, the small band reached Imboden, who "seemed satisfied with our report that there were but 1,100 of the enemy at Beverly." They also told the general about their encounter with Sheriff Phares, which left no doubt now that the enemy knew they were coming.[24]

Upon arriving at the site of where the tiny hamlet of Dailey is now located, Imboden split his force in two in order to proceed north up both sides of Tygart's River. For a direct assault on the town, he went up the east side with the infantry, the dismounted cavalry and four guns. Captain McNeil's Company F, "the best mounted," led the column. Up the mail road on the west side of the river went the cavalry, with the Eighteenth Virginia out front, under Colonel George Imboden. They were to cut off the enemy's retreat by gaining the Buckhannon road to the west of town.[25]

After advancing a short distance on the east side, General Imboden instructed Captain McNeil to send forward his five swiftest mounts to scout the road ahead and act as an alarm of an enemy approach. They were not to fire a shot unless fired upon. No doubt influenced by the fervent pleas of his son, the captain included Paul among the five chosen riders. "Billie was in all his glory that day," the young McNeil later recalled.

Soon after the five excited riders set out on their great adventure, they came upon a small foraging party of a few wagons and mules sent out that morning by Latham to collect corn and hay. "We rode right into them before they knew our presence," recalled McNeil, "and the guard of a dozen or so men surrendered without a shot. Not a man or mule escaped." (Despite McNeil's claim, the records show that the rebels captured only two or three men.)

Riding on a little further, the five Confederates came upon a quartermaster. "He was a big, fat Dutchman," remembered McNeil, "and was mounted on one of the most beautiful sorrel mares I ever saw." In the thick fog, the Yankee quartermaster mistook the rebels for his own men out foraging and he accordingly began to "verbally abuse" them upon noticing that they were returning empty handed. Cleverly playing along, the rebels told the "Dutchman" that the party behind them had had better luck. With barely a glance at McNeil and his friends, the quartermaster rode by them. "This is the last, and first, time that I ever saw the [militia] major," McNeil later recalled, "but, as I saw one of General Imboden's aids (sic) riding the major's mare the next day, I know what had become of the major."

McNeil and his comrades cautiously rode on toward Beverly. A few minutes after passing the unsuspecting major they came upon a squad of cavalry. This time there was no mistaken identity. The Yankees promptly turned and fled, the five rebels giving a hot chase for more than a mile before giving up and turning back.[26]

In Beverly, meanwhile, Latham decided to get direct personal confirmation of the startling report brought in by the wounded Sheriff Phares. At 9 a.m., he rode out of town with his two cavalry companies, Smith's and Hagan's, one company on each side of the river. After riding about five miles, they encountered Imboden's oncoming columns.[27]

Though unable to see clearly through the thick fog, Latham quickly realized that he faced a superior force and slowly pulled back, the men taking occasional but generally ineffective shots at each other. When about two-and-a-half miles from Beverly, the colonel at noon posted skirmishers and sped back into town to deploy his forces against what clearly was going to be a determined effort to take the place. "I do not consider Beverly in danger," he had wired Roberts less than a week before.[28]

He took up a strong position south of town on a plateau fifty to sixty feet above the river bottom, thereby giving him a one-mile command of the main road of approach. In this forward position he placed the Parrott gun and his own Second West Virginia, now under Lt. Colonel Alexander Scott. In reserve near the town church he placed the brass gun and Colonel Polsley's Eighth West Virginia.[29]

About 1 p.m., the sun broke through and the fog quickly lifted to finally give each commander the opportunity to observe the strength of his enemy. Latham overestimated his at about 4500 men in five regiments of infantry, two of cavalry, and one six-gun battery. Likewise, Imboden judged the Federals to have about 1500 men. Moreover, the Southern commander also now wisely determined that a frontal assault on the enemy's obviously strong position might cost "hundreds" of men. He therefore decided that, in addition to gaining the Buckhannon road, he would send another force on a two-mile swing north of town to cut off the retreat to Philippi, thereby both turning and surrounding the Federal position. By way of a diversion, he ordered McClanahan at 2 p.m. to open fire with his rifled gun at 1200 yards, and for the infantry to intensify their long range skirmishing, much to the discomfort of an unfortunate local farmer caught between the lines with his herd of cattle.[30]

Not far from the skirmish line, French Harding was enjoying, with Imboden's permission, a well-earned breakfast at the home of a friend named Washington Long. "While at first an occasional bullet struck the house," Harding later recalled, "I was fearlessly and kindly entertained and sumptuously breakfasted by Mrs. Long and one of her daughters, who appeared to be the only persons about the dwelling."[31]

When the first shot boomed out from McClanahan's gun, fully five hours after learning that Confederates in strength were approaching Beverly, Latham finally wired General Roberts in Buckhannon. The enemy in large force had driven in his pickets, he told his brigade commander, and was advancing on the post in two directions. Latham asked for orders. Roberts, only some twenty-five miles away with several hundred men of the Twenty-eighth Ohio Infantry, did nothing more than tell him to hold, if possible, keep communications open and fall back if overpowered.[32]

For two hours, while Imboden's flanking movements struggled to gain their positions, both sides south of town maintained a general fire that ranged in intensity but did little damage, except on the men's nerves, especially those in the Twenty-second Virginia. Stuck in a ravine between the two lines, the regiment anxiously watched artillery shells arch overhead from both directions, genuinely fearing their own had a better chance of hitting them. Intending perhaps to distract them from the danger, Captain William Bahlman ordered his Company E to fix bayonets, whereupon some men went so far as to wrap paper around their muzzles to make the bayonets fit more securely.[33]

When Latham, meanwhile, got word about 4 p.m. that Confederate cavalry had been seen approaching the Buckhannon road on the town's western outskirts, he finally perceived the danger to his right flank. He called on his reserves, bringing up a detachment of the Eighth under Captain William L. Gardner (later killed at Droop Mountain) to support the Second and sending the remainder to the west side of town. A fight for the Buckhannon road now seemed certain.[34]

Colonel George Imboden of the Eighteenth Virginia Cavalry ordered twenty-six year old Lieutenant David Poe to bring forward his men, recent enlistees recruited mostly by Poe into an unattached company, the nucleus of the future Company A of the Twentieth Virginia Cavalry. Apparently impressed with what he had seen thus far of their toughness and discipline, despite their inexperience, Imboden had in mind a special mission for Poe and his men. He told the young lieutenant to report to Captain John Righter of Company D, Nineteenth Cavalry. Righter, who had enlisted only six weeks before, told Poe to form his company and charge the enemy, estimated to be from seventy to 150 men hiding behind houses, barns and buildings on the west side of town. "There I was," Poe proudly recalled years later, "occupying the post of honor, with untried soldiers whom I had led through the mountains and the enemies' lines, to go with me, in front of a veteran foe, double in number and sheltered behind buildings."[35]

Poe rode out in front of his green recruits. "You have followed me through the mountains," he called out, "now, when I tell you to close up, raise a yell and follow me!" With that, the lieutenant "saw every face brighten." He gave the signal and the advance began. Almost immediately, they saw in the distance numerous muzzle flashes, followed by the terrifying sound of bullets angrily whizzing by. Poe called out for the men to close up. The young troopers dutifully tightened their formation, gave a deafening yell and broke into a charge. The frightened Federals promptly fled.[36]

With barely a shot fired, Imboden had gained control of the Buckhannon road and put the Yankees in a desperate fix. Latham wired Roberts. "If overpowered," the general counseled, "destroy your stores, and fall back on Philippi."[37]

Latham immediately started his train north and he ordered Polsley to pull together the Eighth and take the lead of the infantry column. Fortunately, the road to Philippi remained open; Imboden's force sent to take it got bogged down on a rough road and would not reach its destination until sunset (Lt. Poe contended that the flanking party got lost). With the Confederates so close now that their officer commands "could be distinctly heard," Latham set fire to his stores and at 5 p.m. he pulled out.[38]

The Confederate cavalry, led by the Eighteenth Virginia, tore after the retreating column. At Leading Creek (near present day Elkins) they hit the rear regiment, the Second West Virginia, as it was crossing the stream. Private Henry Barnhart of Company C received a mortal wound (he died on the 28th) and a few men were captured before the rebels pulled back under heavy fire.[39]

About four miles up the road, the Confederate cavalry again charged and again they were driven off, this time "with such vigor and dash," declared the Second West Virginia's Frank Reader, "that they then let us alone, not deeming it prudent to follow us so closely." (Latham reported three Confederate charges.)[40]

"There was no confusion," Latham proudly reported of the retreat, "no hurry, no independent haste. His [the enemy] cavalry charges were handsomely repulsed, and he learned to follow at a respectful distance."[41]

After marching about nine miles, the colonel stopped the column and put it into camp for the night. Altogether for the day, he had lost only two men wounded (one mortally) and fourteen captured (ten from the Second West Virginia, two from the Eighth West Virginia, and two from Smith's company of Ohio cavalry).[42]

It might have been much worse, and the Eighth West Virginia's Colonel John Polsley, for one, knew it. "Our safe retreat with so little loss," he concluded in his report, "was entirely owing to the dispositions made by the colonel commanding."[43]

The losses also included five men (Sgt. George Jones, Privates Martin Walters, Hugh Smith, William Weible, and Thomas B. Richardson) missing from Company F of the Second West Virginia, who somehow had been cut off from the regiment during the Confederate cavalry charge at Leading Creek. Believing their situation hopeless, the five stranded infantrymen at first considered surrendering, but eventually they talked themselves into hiding until the Confederates had left. For two agonizing days with no food and one sleep-deprived night they lay quietly in the bushes, the enemy apparently still all around them. Unwilling to endure the torture any longer, they quietly held a "council of war" after sunset of the second evening, whereupon they decided to split up, make a break for it, and reunite at a designated place. The daring tactic worked. After eluding the Confederates around them, they met up and headed west, carefully keeping to the woods and hiding in caves in order to remain undetected. After two weeks of this rough travel, which once included dodging Confederate picket fire, the five adventurers finally, much to the happy amazement of their astonished comrades, reunited with their regiment at West Union.[44]

The Occupation

"The general kept us moving most of the time," Private L.G. Potts of the Eighteenth Virginia Cavalry recalled sixty years later about this part of the raid, "but the Yankees that we went to see were [not] home. They had gone to see neighbors they thought more of than they did of us."[45]

Imboden thus triumphantly entered Beverly, having paid a relatively small price — only one man killed (Pvt. John Smith of Co. A, 22nd Virginia), and three men wounded (who would be left behind and captured when the Federals retook the town), for a primary objective of the entire operation. Undoubtedly, he felt very pleased. "Marched to Beverly," younger brother Captain Frank Imboden happily told his diary on the night of April 24, "and drove the Yankees like dogs." According to at least one member of Imboden's command, in Beverly the men were "kindly received by the ladies," among whom, no doubt, were those who supposedly had offered Imboden, through his spies, to spike the Yankee cannons upon receipt of "the proper materials."[46]

The entire command was in high spirits. "The Confederates were pretty well worn out when we reached Beverly," Paul McNeil remembered "and especially was this true of the infantry, that had come from Lewisburg, Staunton and Harrisonburg, all of them having tramped over one hundred miles, but they were greatly rejoiced at the thought of capturing so easily the old town of Beverly, that had been in the hands of the Federals since the 11th day of July, 1861."[47]

Imboden's first order of business was to set his men to work putting out the fires begun by Latham, which had gone out of control and spread to about one third of the town's buildings. The quick action of the Confederates saved most of the town as well as about $100,000 worth of abandoned Federal supplies (Imboden later estimated that about $40,000 worth had gone up in flames), much of which, to the delight of the men, went into private haversacks. James H. Mays of the Twenty-second Virginia declared that his regiment "captured as much government provisions and cattle as it could eat." Perhaps it was at Beverly that the Twenty-second also found three kegs of whiskey, which Colonel Patton judiciously decided to jigger out to his companies alphabetically, an arrangement the impatient men of Company K considered so unfair that they refused to take their share.[48]

"I captured five new army wagons," the May 2 issue of the Richmond *Whig* quoted Imboden, "thirty odd fine horses and mules, thirty-four new Enfield rifles, a number of good tents, a quantity of grain, a bogus militia major, and a number of prisoners. I learn I will procure over 1,000 head of fine cattle in this and Barbour county, and a large quantity of bacon. The people are rejoicing at their deliverance from the oppressor."[49]

Unaware of what Imboden's men had saved from the flames, Latham claimed in his report that "nothing of value fell into the hands of the enemy." Polsley said as much in his report when he stated that he had destroyed 3000 rations, 2000 pounds of forage, 30,000 rounds of ammunition, fifty Enfield rifles, 100 sets of infantry equipment, and "all camp and garrison equipage." Likewise, Frank Smith, captain of the independent company of Ohio cavalry, reported a loss of eleven tents, five sabers, and 4000 pounds of forage.[50]

In Beverly, the Confederates also "saved" the "bogus" sheriff, twenty-seven-year-old Jesse T. Phares, who could not be moved because of his agonizing bullet wound. "We found him almost in a dying condition," Imboden reported, adding regretfully, "though he will probably recover." (Phares lived till 1903.)[51]

Oddly enough, one of the few persons to show genuine concern for Phares was the man who shot him. French Harding, after visiting his mother near Leadsville, where he "found all well, and Mother's table and downy bed proved a complete requital for any inconvenience I had undergone in the last twenty-four hours," paid a visit to the wounded sheriff. Surprisingly, the captain "found him doing quite well."

In the meantime, Harding and his companions had rifled through Phares's saddlebags, which were stuffed with unpaid tax notices. As county sheriff, Phares held the responsibility of collecting personal property taxes from county residents. He could not do that without those notices. Knowing this, Harding and his friends conscientiously delivered a few "and carelessly lost the rest." After the war, the county brought suit against Phares for being unable to account for the missing tax money. Phares brought Harding into court as a witness for the defense. Before Judge Woods, the former captain testified that on April 24, 1863, he had indeed shot Phares, wounding him severely and thus rendering him incapable of collecting the taxes, making no mention, however, of how the notices became lost. Though the testimony helped exonerate him, Phares understandably remained "slightly offish with [Harding] for some time thereafter." After later relying on him again, however, this time to verify a pension application that sought compensation for his wound, Phares softened toward Harding and the two men became friends.[52]

Imboden initially had wanted to arrest Phares and send him, along with several other citizens holding strong Union sympathies, to Richmond. Harding strongly opposed this and he let the general know it. "My policy was not only right but best, as the sequel proved," he subsequently explained. "The Federal authorities made reprisal upon our innocent sympathizers." Those reprisals included the arrest later that summer of thirteen citizens in and around Randolph County, who were sent as prisoners to Fort Delaware. Ironically, Sheriff Phares intervened on their behalf by way of a "contract" he entered into with the victims' families, whereby, for example, it is known that Rebecca Ward paid him thirty dollars to negotiate the release of her husband. In a presumably like manner, Phares secured the release of the other twelve captives.[53]

This had not been the first time Imboden wanted to arrest as a traitor a county sheriff loyal to the "Pierpont government." In retaliation for Milroy's attempt the previous fall to levy fines on Southern sympathizers in Tucker County, General Lee suggested that the office of sheriff should be rendered "as dangerous a position as possible." Heartily supporting the notion, Imboden in January arranged for the kidnapping of James Trayhern (or Trayhorn), the sheriff of Barbour County, and carted him off to Richmond. Not surprisingly, this in turn brought swift reprisal. Two Southern sympathizers in Barbour were killed and Pierpont ordered that eight others be taken hostage and held until Trahern's safe release. Outraged, Imboden on January 20 openly declared his intention to "arrest and imprison as dangerous enemies of my state and country every man I can lay my hands upon, who holds any office under the usurped State of West Virginia." Pierpont at first wanted to arrest another fifty civilians, but cooler heads finally prevailed and he released two of the hostages (one being Dr. Abraham Hershman) and sent them to Richmond to negotiate for Trayhern's release. In late January Trayhern was let go, vowing, however, "if he ever gets home he'll never act as sheriff again."[54]

In connection with the Trayhern affair, Pierpont also ordered the arrest of George W. Thompson of Wheeling, judge of the Circuit Court of the Twelfth Judicial District of Virginia, a vociferous Confederate sympathizer and father of Lt. Colonel William P. Thompson of the Nineteenth Virginia Cavalry, now with Imboden's command. The local court, however, ordered the release of Thompson "on the ground that he had been deprived of liberty without due process of law." But when Thompson then refused to take an oath of allegiance to the United States Government, the court forced him to give bond and leave the new state.[55]

This war against the "Pierpont governments," both county and municipal, made special targets of not only the county sheriffs, but also the courthouses and records. The Confederates, whether regulars or guerillas, tried to destroy them on sight. This in turn left for sometimes long periods of time many southern and central counties in West Virginia without sheriffs, Union or Confederate.[56]

In addition to his bitter war on the "Pierpont governments," Imboden now was free to pursue other important objectives. He sent out special squads to recruit new soldiers, and he began the exploitation of the surrounding rich farming area. Horses, cattle and foodstuffs his patrols secured in abundance, having paid for them with Confederate funds taken from the $100,000 reserve brought along for the purpose.[57]

Inevitably, however, the "appropriations" occasionally got out of hand and outright looting occurred. The problem became serious enough for an outraged Imboden to issue General Order No. 20: "I. The Commanding General regrets that occurrences at Beverly and in the neighborhood on yesterday have developed the fact that to some extent the idea prevails or at least is acted upon that individuals in the command have the right to seize and appropriate to their own use the property of Union citizens in this part of the State of Virginia. It is now distinctly announced that any seizure or appropriation to private uses of the property of any citizen, will be treated and punished as robbery. In respect to the property of Union citizens useful & necessary to the army, impressments will be made by the proper officers in legal form, and certificates given under General Orders from the Hd. Qrts. II. To prevent the lawlessness of a few men from bringing discredit on the fair name of this command, it is ordered that hereafter, whenever the command enters any town or village, the Col. or other officer in command of the first Regiment arriving, shall immediately detail a company to guard every store & home in the place, and the Captain of such guard will be held responsible for the protection of all property in the place, till (sic) he is relieved. As a general rule it is the stragglers & skulkers, who profit by plunder, while the faithful soldier is performing his duty. This fact of itself, if there were no higher consideration, requires the suppression of all plundering—and it shall be suppressed."[58]

And so the "liberators," at least to some inevitable extent, had become the oppressors.

CHAPTER THREE

Buckhannon

Union Response to the Fall of Beverly

The fall of Beverly sent General Roberts into an anxious frenzy. "Re-enforcements should be thrown into Grafton without delay," he pleaded by wire from Buckhannon to general-in-chief Halleck in Washington on the 24th, "or the enemy will reach the Baltimore and Ohio Railroad and do great damage. The roads in this region are impassable."[1]

Halleck had little patience, or use, for Roberts. General Hooker was only days away from throwing at Lee the well trained, well-supplied 130,000 men of the Army of the Potomac. The prospects for success never seemed better, perhaps good enough to win the war. The backwater of West Virginia at this time therefore was little more than an irritant to the general-in-chief. "Collect your forces, defend the railroad, and drive the enemy back," he scolded Roberts by telegram sent that night at 8 p.m. "You are strong enough to do it if you try. Do not call for re-enforcements from here. You have no need of them, and we have none to give you if you had. I do not understand how the roads there are impassable to you, when, by your own account, they are passable enough to the enemy. If you cannot drive the enemy out, we will seek someone who can."[2]

Clearly offended by this stiff rebuke, Roberts lost no time in offering excuses by way of a reply. "Colonel Latham, with half of my command, has allowed himself to be surprised," he sheepishly told Halleck that evening (9:40 p.m.) in a less than noble attempt to shift blame, "and has been compelled to retreat in the direction of Philippi, where he cannot reach me. The enemy has five regiments of cavalry. I have but four companies. The roads the enemy has passed over are the mountain roads. Those I must move over are in the valley, and I have never seen any in so impassable a condition. I shall fail in nothing that is possible."[3]

To this Old Brains contemptuously refused to respond. He turned the matter over to department commander Schenck in Baltimore, from whom Roberts finally received a modicum of sympathy. Like Halleck, Schenck strongly advised Roberts to concentrate his forces, but he also authorized Kelley to begin shifting troops westward from Harper's Ferry.[4]

Though still skeptical about Confederate strength and intentions, Kelley in turn reluctantly promised Roberts "to carry out your suggestions if necessary. Think, however, that Latham will be able to repel Imboden." He nonetheless started by rail for Grafton, distant some 140 miles, Colonel James Mulligan with the Twenty-third Illinois Infantry (Lt. Col. James Quirk), the 106 New York Infantry (Col. Frederick E. Embick), and Battery L, First Illinois Artillery (Captain John Rourke).[5]

Schenck also sent warnings to Scammon in Charleston. "The rebels, Imboden and Jackson, with combined forces," he wired on the 25th, "are pressing General Roberts. Keep yourself on the watch toward Summersville."[6]

Roberts had not finished. The following day (25th), he pleaded by wire with Governor Pierpont to send to Grafton "All the troops in and about Wheeling." Then, finally satisfied that he had accomplished all that was possible with the telegraph line, he dutifully set about trying to concentrate his own widely scattered forces. He ordered the small commands at Birch, Sutton (the Third West Virginia Infantry under Lt. Colonel Thompson, and Captain Lot Bowen's Company E under Lieutenant Timothy F. Roane of the Third West Virginia Cavalry), and Bulltown (Eighth West Virginia Infantry) to send all wagons and supplies that could be moved north through Weston to Clarksburg, to destroy that which could not be moved, and then to march with three days' rations to join him at Buckhannon.[7]

Then Roberts waited. He used the time to arrange for twenty-seven rebel prisoners, mostly rounded up deserters held in his custody for some time, to be transported to Wheeling. Not willing to spare any of his own troops for the job, he called upon the Union League of Upshur County to furnish fifteen men. Dr. D.S. Haseldon, president of the League, easily secured the volunteers, and, under Dr. D.M. Gibson, they promptly set off for Wheeling.[8]

As the hours passed with no word regarding the receipt or execution of his orders, anxiety overcame Roberts and he turned once more to the telegraph. He had heard nothing from Latham since 6 p.m. the day before, he nervously wired Schenck that evening (25th), quite as though he hoped the department commander might do something about it. He therefore did not know if the colonel had made it to Philippi. Moreover, with the telegraph lines down between Bulltown and Buckhannon, he did not know if his other forces were complying with the order to concentrate at Buckhannon.[9]

In this case, ignorance, for Roberts, was just the opposite of bliss.

The Plan to Strike Back

"On Friday the 24th," twenty-eight-year-old Maria Louise Sumner Phillips recorded in her journal, "the news arrived here just at night, that a fight was going on at Beverly, between our troops and the Confederates." She was the wife of thirty-three-year-old Sylvester Phillips, former captain of Company E of the Third West Virginia Infantry, who had resigned from the army the past November after serving nearly a year-and-a-half. The young couple originally had lived as farmers with her parents at French Creek, nine miles south of Buckhannon, but they recently had moved into a house of their own in town with their two young children, ten-year-old Leonard and five-year-old Clara. Mrs. Phillips proved to be a keen and sensitive observer of the momentous events about to unfold in her town. She derived great comfort from recording her feelings and observations in a journal, which fortunately survived the war.[10]

The Phillips' currently had residing with them, probably as a temporary boarder, Claude See, a friend and former lieutenant in the Third (West) Virginia. The following morning, See went over to General Roberts's headquarters to find out about the situation in Beverly, whereupon he returned to the Phillips house for breakfast.

"What news?" Mrs. Phillips anxiously inquired. "Nothing," the captain solemnly replied, though the look on his face said otherwise. "I have news that was told me in confidence by one of the officers," he suddenly blurted out by way of releasing the stress building up inside him. "Beverly is taken by the Rebels, the telegraph ceased operating at six o'clock last night, and our men were retreating to Philippi."[11]

Such dire news could not be contained for long. It raced through the town like wildfire, everyone realizing that Buckhannon, defended by just one regiment, now lay helpless before a powerful enemy only some twenty-five miles away.

General Roberts put the Twenty-eighth Ohio Infantry to work fortifying the place. Under the direction of their officers and the engineers, the men frantically set about digging trenches, erecting breastworks and planting batteries. They placed one gun on Leonard Hill (Water Tank Hill) overlooking the southern approach to the town along French Creek road, and another on Middleton Hill (Blair Hill) to command the road coming in from Weston in the west and protect the regiment's encampment. The remaining few pieces they positioned out on the Beverly road coming in from the east, near the river.[12]

"The shifting of the artillery kept up a great excitement all day," observed Mrs. Phillips. "At night every one was afraid to sleep, for we were expecting an attack every minute. I made a fire in the front room, in the second story and put the children to bed, but dared not undress or go to bed myself, till quite late." Earlier that day her husband, Sylvester, had volunteered to serve as a lookout south of town on the French Creek road, which also conveniently gave him the opportunity to check on his in-laws living there. Though Maria took some measure of comfort from her husband's gesture, his absence only increased her anxiety.[13]

For Mrs. Phillips and many others in town, nerves finally calmed considerably around midnight. "A noise of tramping in the streets," she recorded, "attracted me to the window," where she happily witnessed the arrival from Bulltown of that part of the Eighth West Virginia Infantry that had not been at Beverly. Her elation, however, quickly became mixed with sympathy for the exhausted soldiers dragging themselves through town at the end of a thirty-mile forced march. "If I can only get a place where I can lie down," she overheard one of them mutter, "it is all I want." After struggling to set up camp at the Northern Methodist Church at the end of the street, the dusty, blue-clad soldiers soon were fast asleep.[14]

Meanwhile, from his camp nine miles north of Beverly, Colonel Latham on the 25th had marched a "leisurely 8 miles to Belington," east of Tygart River, arriving there at 10 a.m. With no enemy in sight, he rested his men till noon, when he received Roberts's order to concentrate at Buckhannon. He started immediately, marching thirteen miles to arrive that night at Philippi, the seat of Barbour County, population about 9,000 and decidedly pro-southern.[15]

"But darling, my own darling wife," the Eighth West Virginia's Lt. Colonel John Polsley tenderly wrote from Philippi on the 25th, "I have scarcely eaten or slept for two days and nights — have been busy all the time and on horse back nearly all the time." Like several other officers (including Capt. William L. Gardner, Lt. Alonzo Wilson, and Lt. Jacob Rife) whose wives had joined them (Mrs. Rife being pregnant), Polsley had hoped that his dear Nellie (Ellen nee Donnally) might also come to Beverly. Now he was grateful she hadn't. "For, my own darling," he explained, "it would have killed me nearly to have had you here. These folks were nearly all distracted and would very probably have left their wives had it not been for me." Polsley took credit for arranging to evacuate the officers' spouses to Philippi. "I do not think any of these ladies," he wrote Nellie, "will want to visit the seat of war again."[16]

On the 26th, Polsley and the rest of Latham's command marched seventeen miles to Buckhannon. "They were welcomed with great joy by all of us," wrote Mrs. Phillips, who expressed her feelings by vigorously swinging the stars and stripes from her window as the men marched past. "We never saw that flag displayed by any one of the Beverly people," a grateful soldier called out to her, receiving in turn a smile from the happy matron of the house.[17]

With many of the nearby rural residents having come in to check on the rumors swirling about the countryside, the town now was filled with people, clogging the streets, blocking the sidewalks, and generally adding to the overall excitement. With the reassuring arrival of Latham's command, the town took on something of a festive air, and in that high spirit Mrs. Phillips and a few of her lady friends decided to visit some of the new fortifications. "We chased each other over the long bridges and along the delightful shaded walk by the riverside," she wrote by way of expressing how they now felt more like happy, carefree children than worried adults. "Lieut. Smith's wife charged bayonets upon us, with a long pole, and put us to flight." She added, "We girls jumped over into the trenches and chased each other and then climbed over the breastworks to the other side, where soldiers were."

The "girls" then quickly matured somewhat when they looked out over the landscape in front of them. "From the elevated ground," wrote Maria Louise, "we could see far over the hills and vales where the Beverly road moved along like a white serpent, now and then hid from sight by the trees and the rising ground."[18]

Before noon the following day, Monday the 27th, the revelry in town quickly reverted to alarm when a messenger rode in to excitedly report that the enemy in large number was approaching, being now only five miles south of French Creek. Before panic could set in, however, calmness not only returned but confidence and relief redoubled when the truth soon became known that the troops were not Confederates but the Third West Virginia Infantry arriving after an all night march from Sutton and Birch, the men, having tramped some sixty miles since early Saturday morning, suffering terribly from swollen and blistered feet.[19]

"My spirits were raised very high at the sight of our old Third," wrote Mrs. Phillips, who happily prepared breakfast for seven of the starving, foot-sore soldiers. "The thunder of their drums and cheers of the men had driven away all of my fears."[20]

Those fears had been raised considerably the previous evening when near sunset two men (both named Baker) arrived from Beverly with the startling news that the town

Brigadier General James A. Mulligan (Gil Barrett Collection, U.S. Army Military History Institute, Carlisle Barracks, Pennsylvania).

was in flames when they left it. But Mrs. Phillips and her fellow citizens took comfort in the knowledge that all of Roberts's available forces now were in Buckhannon. They expected the general to not only protect them, but also to take action against the Confederate invaders. It was an expectation held by many, including the administration in Washington.[21]

Roberts's united command now contained some 2500 infantry, consisting of the Second, Third, and Eighth West Virginia and the Twenty-eighth Ohio. His 200 cavalry included the companies of Captains Smith, Bowen, and Hagan, and Lt. Julius Jaehne. The 100 men of Chatham Ewing's battery made up his artillery.[22]

The Second West Virginia held the proud honor of being the new state's first three-year regiment. It also held the odd distinction of having fully five companies filled with Pennsylvanians who had been denied enlistment in their quota-filled home state. After months of outpost duty in western Virginia, the Second had been transferred east, where it marched hard and fought hard in both the Shenandoah Valley and Second Bull Run campaigns. After a brief time spent in the defenses of Washington, the regiment returned to western Virginia in the fall of 1862.[23]

The Third West Virginia, composed almost entirely of men from the trans–Allegheny, became the second "loyal" three-year regiment to organize, whereby it subsequently saw much the same hard service as its sister regiment, the Second.[24]

The Eighth West Virginia had been organized in the Kanawha Valley in the fall of 1861. It remained there until transferred east to share the same service as the Second and Third.[25]

The cavalry units, mostly from the Third West Virginia, had remained scattered on outpost duty throughout the state since the start of the war, given the thankless task of battling bushwhackers, guerillas, and partisans.[26]

The Twenty-eighth Ohio had served in western Virginia from the summer of '61 until it was sent to Washington in August of 1862, whereupon it subsequently fought on South Mountain and at Antietam in the Maryland Campaign. In November it returned to western Virginia.[27]

Chatham T. Ewing's battery had been organized in Pittsburgh, and saw much the same hard service as the Second, Third, and Eighth West Virginia.[28]

With all of these well-tested, veteran troops now united under his command, Roberts indeed had developed a sound, even bold plan to strike back at Imboden and retake Beverly. Back on the 25th, he had wired Mulligan at Grafton to push fifteen miles south to Philippi and secure the place for Latham, who had not yet arrived there. Assuming that Mulligan had done this, and now was unavailable by telegraph, Roberts the next day sent three couriers riding to Philippi to instruct the Irishman to make a diversion down the Philippi road toward Beverly on the 27th, while he, Roberts, moved against Imboden from Buckhannon. The plan, however, quickly fell apart before Roberts could begin to implement it. That same night (26th) one of the couriers came riding back into Buckhannon to report that Mulligan was not at Philippi, and that the other two couriers had been captured by the enemy.[29]

At Grafton Mulligan, proudly clad in Irish green and accompanied by his wife, indeed had received Roberts's initial order, and on the 25th he dutifully began marching down to Philippi. Near a large rock, a notable local landmark about a mile north of town, he ran into Major David Lang's detachment of two companies of the Sixty-second Virginia sent up by Imboden to scout from Beverly and make contact with Grumble Jones. After exchanging a few harmless shots, including artillery rounds clearly heard back in Beverly, both sides withdrew. This unexpected clash so close to Philippi startled Mulligan and when he subsequently learned that a large force of Confederate cavalry (Jones) was on the prowl somewhere in his rear to the northeast, he decided to abandon the place. At 1 a.m. the next morning he began the retreat fifteen miles back to Grafton.[30]

The next day, Monday the 27th, Roberts, too, learned about this new invasion force when seemingly incredible reports came in from forty-eight-year-old Colonel Nathan Wilkinson, commander at Clarksburg of the Sixth Brigade (consisting of only two widely-scattered West Virginia infantry regiments — the Sixth under Major John H. Showalter, and the Eleventh under Colonel Daniel Frost) of Kelley's First Division, that Grafton and Webster had fallen (they had not) and that Clarksburg was about to fall, Wilkinson preparing to evacuate in two hours. The colonel based his erroneous report, without verification, on the claims of a group of panicky civilians who in Grafton had commandeered a train and made their "escape" to Clarksburg.[31]

With Mulligan in retreat and Clarksburg about to fall to a new Confederate invasion force, Roberts quickly concluded that an attack on Imboden at Beverly was out of the question. The situation, as he perceived it, quickly had lapsed from a promising opportunity into a dangerous crisis. He told Wilkinson to hold on. He would try to reach him there by noon of the 28th, but if he could not hold till then, he was to destroy his excess supplies and head west for Parkersburg.[32]

Evacuation of Buckhannon

When the Third West Virginia came into Buckhannon near noon of the 27th, they brought with them Mrs. Phillips's husband, Sylvester, and her father, the two men trusting the Confederates not to harm the lady of the house they had left behind. "Poor Mother is left alone," Mrs. Phillips lamented. "I would give anything to have her here with us." Though elated to be reunited with the two men in her life, Maria Louise was devastated by the stunning news they told, with great despair in their faces, that Roberts had ordered an evacuation of Buckhannon and a retreat to Clarksburg.[33]

Panic and confusion took over. Wild rumors ran through the streets that as many as 20,000 Confederates were marching on the place. With unnecessary, demoralizing haste, Roberts's men moved out, the artillery causing much excitement when they thundered through town on the double quick. The cavalry companies rode out next. "They made the earth tremble as they swept along," wrote Mrs. Phillips. "Then the cheers and yells and sounding drums," she added, "announced that the dear old Third was on the move," the men barely having had time to remove their shoes and massage their swollen, blistered feet after their all night march. "I gazed upon its bloodstained flag through floods of tears that nearly blinded me," she went on, "till it was lost to view among the multitude in the streets."[34]

Leaving with the Third was Sylvester and his father-in-law, a heart-breaking separation for Mrs. Phillips. "It is hard that a man can not remain at home and protect his own family," said her father sadly, his face "pale as death." As she had done earlier with her husband, Maria Louise now begged her father "to go with the army, and to have no fear for our safety." For added emphasis, she sent a note on to her husband, "begging him not to think of returning until things were settled."[35]

Sylvester Phillips and his father-in-law were only two of scores, perhaps hundreds of other civilians who also decided to go with the army and avoid capture or harassment by the rebels. The horde even included many Southern sympathizers who feared being conscripted into the Confederate army. The streets for some time thus remained clogged with all manner of traffic, including foot, horse, wagon, and buggy.[36]

The Eighth West Virginia moved out next, followed by the Twenty-eighth Ohio after it sadly applied the torch "to the snug little city of tents on the hill" where it had lived for so long. "Alas," lamented Mrs. Phillips, "shall we ever again be delighted with the silvery bugle notes that have rung out so sweet and clear from that encampment every morning for so many months?"[37]

Being given the job of destroying the stores and ammunition that could not be carried, the Second West Virginia brought up the rear. This also gave the regiment a unique opportunity. While its men stood in the ranks directly in front of the Phillips house, the officers and quartermasters went through all the stores on the street, taking everything they needed or desired, offering in return the consolation that they were keeping these things out of the hands of the approaching rebels. "So it would appear," reflected one citizen, "that Buckhannon was about as bad off uncaptured as captured by the enemy."[38]

As time wore on, the men in the waiting ranks of the Second grew hungry and thirsty, until they finally reached the breaking point. "They came thronging into my backyard, to the well," wrote Mrs. Phillips, "and after drinking, sat down upon the grass to eat their dinner of raw bacon and crackers." She did not begrudge them anything, except the mess of empty cracker boxes left behind in her backyard. Moreover, "there was hardly a place as large as my hand," she observed, "which was not covered with bacon, as they ate the lean part and left the fat."[39]

While the soldiers were eating and drinking their fill in her backyard, Mrs. Phillips received a visit from two of their officers, Captain David D. Barclay of Company D and Lieutenant James Black of Company A (who would be dishonorably dismissed from the service on May 30, 1863), "both noble men, both looking weary and worn from their forced march and retreat from Beverly." During the course of their conversation, Barclay sadly told Mrs. Phillips that he had left his wife at Beverly, where they had boarded with Mrs. Laura (Jackson) Arnold, the sister of Stonewall Jackson, who, the captain now revealed, "mourned over the error her brother fell into when he espoused the cause of the South." Indeed, General Jackson, in turn, "regretted that his sister entertained Union sentiments," and no correspondence is known to have passed between brother and sister during the war.[40]

The conversation then came to a startled, abrupt halt when a great roar rose up from the east end of town, followed by the frantic sounds of people excitedly rushing down the street. "With a noise like thunder," the Star Mill Bridge had fallen into the Buckhannon River after being set on fire by the troops, an act that disgusted many citizens as being unnecessary since the spot easily could be forded and thus prove no hindrance to the enemy. The soldiers also burned the nearby Middle Fork Bridge, which Upshur County would not replace until 1893.[41]

The loss of the Star Mill Bridge proved most unfortunate for twenty-one-year-old Private Billy Day of Company K, Third West Virginia. A good soldier, Day had enlisted in Clarksburg nearly two years before and served for a time as a musician in the regimental band. The previous March, he had been appointed a clerk in the Provost Marshall's office. After his regiment left Buckhannon, he broke ranks and ran back through town, overcome with guilt and sorrow at not having been able to say goodbye to Jenny, his new wife (they had been married on New Year's Day). Jenny, however, lived across the now-bridgeless river. Undaunted, Billy swam the icy water and found his sweetheart. Tearfully resisting her sobbing pleas to remain, he kissed her goodbye and swam back across the river. When he saw Mrs. Phillips, he stopped in front of her yard and tearfully poured out his heart to her. "I tried to comfort him," she wrote, "and told him there were better days in store for them. He bade me good-bye and went up the street weeping bitterly."

Evidently, the pain of separation proved too much for young Day, for at Clarksburg on May 5, he would desert his regiment, never to return. Presumably, he went to his beloved Jenny, for a few days later at least one person, Olive Dix, who lived nearby on Buckhannon River at the mouth of Turkey Run, saw him, news of his desertion having spread through the community. "Today brings considerable excitement," she wrote in her diary, "on account of the traitor, Bill Day, passing through town." By way of disguise and protection, Day had shed his uniform and represented himself as a member of Jenkins's rebel cavalry, which he threateningly claimed was close at hand. Apparently, however, the attempted ruse fooled no one, nor did Day elicit much sympathy for the chronic lovesickness from which he suffered. (At the end of the war, Day would receive a dishonorable discharge.)[42]

By 4 p.m. (27th), meanwhile, all of Roberts's troops had gone. They rapidly marched twelve miles west to Weston, where they discovered the contagion of panic already had spread. The "Union men" had departed, leaving behind mostly women and children. Moreover, by order of Colonel Wilkinson, the supply stores had been destroyed. Roberts received the welcome news, however, that Clarksburg had not yet fallen, whereupon he sent assurances to Wilkinson that he would reach him by 2 p.m. the next day.[43]

The following morning (28th) Roberts took the Janelew road twenty miles north to Clarksburg, his cavalry arriving at 2 p.m. as promised, his infantry coming in that evening. The general then promptly reported to Schenck that three days of "forced marches" had exhausted his men and horses and rendered them useless for at least twenty-four hours. Nevertheless, the Iowan almost immediately put his "useless" men to work, to the point of exhaustion, "digging trenches and building earthworks around the town."[44]

On April 29, the day Hooker began his great turning movement by marching more than half of his magnificent army for an upstream crossing of the Rappahannock and Rapidan rivers, beyond Lee's left, Schenck dared to bother Halleck with a request for four or five thousand troops from Ohio. Though Old Brains did graciously take the time to ask General Ambrose Burnside at Cincinnati to send what help he could to Parkersburg and Wheeling without drawing on troops in Kentucky, he was in no better mood to deal with Schenck than he had been with Roberts five days before. "The enemy's raid is variously estimated at from 1,500 to 4,000," he growled in a wire sent to the department commander at 3:05 p.m. on the 29th. "You have 45,000 under your command. If you cannot concentrate enough to meet the enemy, it does not argue well for your military dispositions."[45]

Burnside agreed (9 p.m., 29th) to send two gunboats to the Ohio River, one from Cincinnati and one from Cairo, and he also promised to send an as yet undetermined force by boat down the Ohio from Wheeling to Parkersburg. All of this, of course, would be of little immediate help to Roberts at Clarksburg.[46]

Imboden Occupies Buckhannon

With all the soldiers and many of the civilians gone, Buckhannon now fell into an eerie quiet. Underlying that eeriness was the strange combination of fearing the Confederate soldiers on the one hand and trusting them enough on the other to not harm the ladies left behind by their men folk.

Not long after the last Union soldier left town, Mrs. Phillips received a visit from friend Kate Heavener, whose husband owned the hotel "Heavener House." The curiosity of the two ladies about the strange, new situation led them out into the street and over to the Janney house, "so lately resounding with the confusion of many tongues, and that trampling of many feet and brilliant with the rich uniforms of the splendidly attired officers, the Headquarters of the stately General Roberts." Mrs. Phillips added, "We wandered from room to room, admiring the rich furniture, and examined the

General's papers at our leisure and read with great curiosity the poetry scribbled on the walls. We wound up by practicing on the Piano a little." Going back out onto the street, the ladies made their way over to the smoldering, ruined bridge. "Everything in town looks so desolate, so desolate," wrote Mrs. Phillips. "It seems as if our ill-fated country was doomed. This night, as the gloomy cloud gathers thickly and dark over us, I feel like exclaiming, 'My God, my God, why hast thou forsaken us?' The morrow's sun may find us in the power of our enemies. Tomorrow will be Clara's 6th birthday, and my father's 51st birthday. They had been planning how they would spend it together, and how they would spank each other, but tomorrow will find grandpa far away from his little pet."[47]

After putting her children to bed that night, Mrs. Phillips stayed up, too anxious to sleep. "I have just left my chamber window and returned to the cozy fireside," she noted in her journal at 11 p.m. "I have been gazing upon this lonely, deserted, desolate town, as it lies bathed in the silvery moonbeams. What a contrast between now and last night. Then the streets were over flowing with our soldiers, happy, confident and triumphant, now so stilled, so gloomy. The merry revelers of that night are now retreating before our foes, the Confederates."

Finally, she drifted off to sleep. "When I opened my eyes this morning [Tuesday, April 28] the memory of yesterday seemed like some hideous nightmare," she wrote, "but when I went out and looked around, the desolate appearance of everything brought back the memory of our defenseless condition, and I burst into a flood of tears. The suspense we are living in is dreadful. It is exhausting soul and body. Everything seems so forsaken and still. The tavern bells and gong have not rung, for there are no boarders to call. Not more than a dozen men remain at home, the rest flying with our retreating army. Heavener's hotel looks so lonely, all gone but Mr. Heavener, Kate, and her two children. I never knew the meaning of loneliness before."[48]

Buckhannon was the seat of Upshur (population about 7300), the first county Imboden entered that had voted against secession. Under Union occupation, the town's Southern sympathizers had kept a low profile. Now the tables were turned. "The Secesh ladies have promenaded the streets in droves all day," Mrs. Phillips observed disgustedly, "and their insolent looks have shown plainly that something was on hand."

Finally, the awful suspense broke. "Just before dark," she wrote, "the dreaded invaders made their appearance."[49]

After his relatively easy triumph at Beverly, Imboden had considered following Latham north and finishing him off near Philippi. On the morning of the 25th, however, his cavalry reported that the road could not handle wagons or artillery, the mud "in places coming up to the saddle-skirts of the horses." This despite the fact that Latham successfully had made the journey to Philippi that day, making no mention in his report of bad road conditions. Moreover, having learned of the Federal concentration at Buckhannon, Imboden considered it unwise to move north on Philippi with Roberts on his left flank. He therefore decided to cross Rich Mountain and either move directly against Buckhannon or leave the pike on a country road four miles beyond Roaring Run and get between Philippi and Buckhannon and then decide which to strike first. After sending Major David B. Lang with two companies of the Sixty-second Virginia Mounted Infantry north to establish communications with the as yet unheard from

Jones and also to inadvertently run into Colonel Mulligan's command coming down from Grafton, Imboden pulled out of Beverly late in the afternoon of the 26th. He left behind not only part of the Thirty-first Virginia's Company F (French Harding's) under Lieutenant Perry Lewis to care for the wounded and the captured men and supplies, but also the boast that he would return to Beverly to celebrate the 4th of July. He crossed the Middle Fork and camped that night about twelve miles from Buckhannon. He then sent forward under his brother, Colonel George Imboden, all available cavalry to secure the bridge across the Buckhannon River, the same the locals believed had been destroyed unnecessarily by the retreating Union troops.[50]

While near the river, however, Colonel Imboden received startling news. It was his men who had captured two of the three couriers Roberts had sent to find Mulligan at Philippi. From them he learned of Mulligan's move to Philippi and Latham's march to Buckhannon, information promptly confirmed by two loyal citizens from Webster, who also claimed "that the cars had been running all the night previous, and other troops were in the vicinity." Now feeling dangerously exposed in this forward position, the younger Imboden asked his brother to send up two regiments of infantry and a section of artillery.

Around 11 p.m., the General called a meeting with his colonels to determine which of his fatigued units could handle the march that night. The gathering was attended by Colonel Hoffman of the Thirty-first Virginia, Colonel Smith of the Sixty-second Virginia, Colonel Higgenbotham of the Twenty-fifth Virginia, Colonel Patton of the Twenty-second Virginia, Colonel Jackson of the Nineteenth Virginia Cavalry, and Major Claiborne of the Thirty-seventh Virginia Cavalry Battalion. The agenda quickly changed, however, when Colonel Patton produced a dispatch captured in Beverly, which supposedly claimed that Schenck had assigned a division of six brigades to defend the B&O. This meant that if the Federals were able to send so many troops into western Virginia, with Mulligan apparently the advance guard, Jones had been unable to cut the B&O. Imboden and his colonels thus concluded that they were in a precarious situation, whereby the enemy in great numbers could descend upon them in a few hours and/or cut off their retreat across the mountains. Already, it seemed, the great expedition had been doomed to failure.

Imboden called in his cavalry from Buckhannon Bridge and at 5 a.m. on the 27th he began a countermarch to Beverly. The bad road, however, made the going agonizingly slow. They managed only two miles before his exhausted, muddy men went into camp at 2 p.m. near Roaring Run. Shortly after midnight, however, scouts brought in the rather startling report that the Federals had abandoned Buckhannon, burned the bridges over Middle Fork and Buckhannon River, and retreated westward, blockading the roads behind them.[51]

Delighted with this news, which meant that the Yankees would not be retreating if thousands of reinforcements were indeed pouring into western Virginia, Imboden now reversed course. On the 28th, he moved to within four miles of Buckhannon, from where he sent a detachment under Captain Poe to construct a crossing over the Buckhannon River at the site of the burned bridge, the same the locals vehemently believed had been destroyed unnecessarily by the retreating Union troops. And the locals proved correct, for Captain Poe had little trouble constructing pontoons from the wreckage.[52]

Just before dark on Tuesday, April 28, Poe cautiously led his men into town, slowly riding down Main Street, "looking on all sides, fearfully," observed Mrs. Phillips, "as if expecting to be fired upon, glancing furtively at every house, as if suspicious that every wall concealed a masked battery." To every citizen Poe met, he put the same question: "How long has it been since the last Yankee left here?"[53]

Satisfied that the town posed no immediate threat, Poe turned and rode back to report to Imboden. He left behind one trooper, who dismounted and stood guard on the parade ground opposite the Phillips house.

Mrs. Phillips and her children watched attentively from their upstairs window. When the lone Confederate soldier inevitably became bored and went for an exploratory stroll while his mount ate oats on the parade ground, it was all Maria could do to keep her son Leonard from running out, despite a bad cold that made him feel miserable, and stealing the rebel's saber off the horse.[54]

Extremely anxious over the imminent arrival of the Confederate horde, she determined to remain vigilant. "I did not dare to go to sleep till very late," she told her journal, "and did not undress at all. I put both of the children in my bed and then towards morning lay down by the fire, which I kept burning all night."[55]

The rebel guard, complete with unmolested saber, bravely remained at his post until the early morning hours of the following day (Wednesday the 29th), when Imboden's cavalry crossed the river on pontoons and came riding into town, followed shortly afterwards by the infantry. The ammunition wagons came over on rafts made with wood taken from torn up nearby government stables, all except one heavy vehicle that irretrievably sank in a deep part of the river, resulting in much loss of ammunition.[56]

The tramping of the soldiers in the street, meanwhile, startled Mrs. Phillips, abruptly waking her from a light snooze. "I now began to realize the horror of our situation," she later exclaimed in her journal. Added to the horror was great disgust at the sight of Southern sympathizers rushing out to offer a cheerful welcome to the invaders, the men in particular of the Twenty-fifth Virginia's Company B, the "Upshur Grays," enjoying the occasion as a festive homecoming. "Crowds of the hateful Secesh women are promenading the streets," she wrote, "arm in arm with the dirty scoundrels and taunting and sneering at every Union person that is visible."[57]

Maria warned her children not to go out of the house for any reason, stressing to her sick Leonard that if he died no one remained in town to bury him. "Mother," he whispered fervently, "I reckon I can go to Heaven just as well if I am not buried."

Leaving the children upstairs, Mrs. Phillips went out on the porch to watch the rebel procession. Presently, she saw one of the "hateful Secesh women" point to the house and loudly identify it as belonging to Captain Phillips. Only days before, this same woman had been arrested by Union troops as a Confederate spy. Maria and three other women (Kate Heavner, Ellen, and Mrs. Gibson) then had been asked to search the suspect and "give her a real talking to." They found nothing more incriminating than her attitude. "She was an ideal specimen of the female Southern Confederacy," Mrs. Phillips sarcastically told her journal. "She raved and fumed and said she expected to be shinning in glory while we were burning in hell. She ran over the usual formula 'Niggar War, Black Republicans, Lincoln Hirelings, etc.'" Now with Confederate troops in

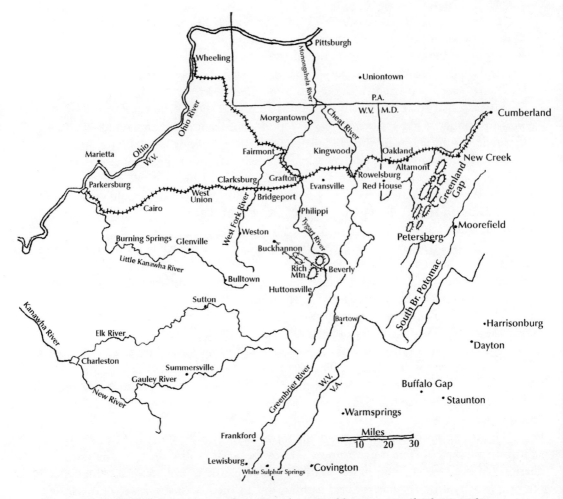

2. Imboden's movement from Beverly to Buckhannon, April 26–29, 1863.

Buckhannon, this "ideal specimen" took a special, grinning delight to see the favor returned.

Three rebels came through the gate and walked up to the porch. Mrs. Phillips braced herself, only to be somewhat taken aback by their "interrogation."

"Got any pies to sell?" one of them asked.

"No," she curtly replied.

"Got any bread to sell?" another inquired.

"No."

"Got anything to sell?"

"No."

Having dealt, however unsuccessfully, with what really mattered most, the rebels then turned to the subject that had brought them onto the porch in the first place.

"Ain't this where Capt. Phillips lives?" they demanded.

"Yes," Maria answered without hesitation.

"Where is his family?" they went on.

"I am his wife," she replied firmly. When one of the rebels then ventured into language that Mrs. Phillips considered abusive and disrespectful, she had had enough. "I looked him straight in the eye," she told her journal, "and with all the determination I could summon to my aid, and he said not another word, but left followed by his comrades. I mastered him and tamed him as other ferocious brutes have been tamed, by the power of a resolute will and a steady eye."

Maria barely had had enough time to savor the immense satisfaction she just derived from taming those "ferocious brutes," when another came through the gate and up to the porch. This one, however, properly introduced himself as Private Boggs of Webster County, adding that her husband's men had shot at him many times while scouting in that vicinity. Being thus more "respectful," this soldier received from Mrs. Phillips not only her pity but also a welcome plate of food.

But then having met enough rebels, she retreated inside and sat down to watch the street from her upstairs window. "There's a good many Secesh in this town, ain't there?" a soldier cheerfully called up to her, in the evident belief that she was a sympathizer. "Yes," she replied, "there are a great many," quickly adding, "but I am for the Union." The rebel's expression turned sour. "I never saw one's face fall as his did," she wrote.

Minutes later, she sat bolt upright at the sight of a squad, led by a Captain Crawford, coming up the walkway to the front door. Nervously, she hurried down to meet them. "Is there any government property in the house?" asked the captain while still standing outside the door. She told him about the crackers left in the back yard and of some old cartridge boxes upstairs. Assuming they wanted the boxes, she turned to get them, only to be unpleasantly startled by Crawford and his men coming into the house and proceeding, without her permission, to search the place. "All over the house they went," she wrote in horror, "peering into closets, under beds, &c, but little did they find to reward their search." Nonetheless, she had to concede that, despite this uninvited intrusion, the rebels behaved fairly well, even resisting temptation. "They ripped open a bag of tobacco," she wrote, "and looked very wistfully at it but I assured them it was private property, and it passed unmolested, except one small piece taken by a Rebel more hungry for the weed than his companions." The men then apologized for the intrusion, even going so far as to offer to put everything back in place that they had disturbed. "Capt. Crawford told me he did not like to trouble a lady in such manner, but that he had been ordered to make a search and he was bound to obey orders. After they left, I felt that I should die with fear."

Despite the relatively good behavior of the rebels who had entered her house, Mrs. Phillips worried that worse may lay in store for her. Such apprehension was more than she wanted to bear. When a soldier on the street pointed out to her General Imboden, who just then was riding up, she boldly inquired if she might speak to the general. After setting up his headquarters in the Janney house, which had been occupied for the same purpose only two days ago by General Roberts and his staff (several other officers took up residence in the Heavener house across the street), Imboden graciously consented to come over and see Mrs. Phillips.

He entered the house with Dr. William J. Bland of the Thirty-first Virginia, an elderly man with the rank of major who lived in nearby Weston. Mrs. Phillips received them politely, wasting no time in proclaiming herself "a Union woman," whose husband had been a captain in the Third West Virginia. Imboden assured her that since Mr. Phillips had resigned and no longer was in arms against the Confederacy, he would not have been harmed had he remained at home with her. Dr. Bland then expressed his regrets at her Union sympathies. "I wish to God that you were all for the Union," she shot back. "You have a perfect right to your opinion," said Imboden, who added the further assurance that she would not be disturbed because of her sympathies. "We do not come to make war upon women and children," he added, "or to destroy or burn. I have been sickened at the destruction your Federals have made in eastern Virginia. At one fine old mansion they have destroyed the rich furniture, some of it a hundred years old, and split it to pieces, even splendid pianos thrown out of doors and used as feed troughs for cavalry horses."

The story had little effect on Mrs. Phillips. "Did they not bring it upon themselves?" she wondered, while being careful not to say so, "for I was in their power, and did not want to incense them too much." She did, however, tell them of her love for the new state of West Virginia. "We will not yield one inch of Virginia soil," Imboden replied sternly. "We do not know yet, how it will terminate," said Mrs. Phillips. "Madam," Imboden quickly shot back, "I know how it will terminate. As sure as there is a sun in the heavens, we must, and will hold Western Virginia."

Having had enough of this contentious conversation, Imboden rose to leave. He assured Mrs. Phillips that there would be no further intrusions into her home; a sentinel would stand guard on her front porch and allow in no one unless invited.

Within moments, the guard duly arrived, nineteen-year-old Private Leonard Cutlep of Company C, Twenty-fifth Virginia Infantry. Born in Pocahontas County, Cutlep had enlisted at Sutton in May of 1861. He had been captured on Allegheny Mountain on December 13 of that year, and was a prisoner at Camp Chase until exchanged. At Spotsylvania in 1864, he again would be captured, but this time he preferred to take the oath of allegiance and serve in the Union forces, claiming in his post war pension application that he "never did render any service to the Confederate Army of his own free will," and that he had enlisted in the rebel forces "out of fear for his life."[58]

Despite these very questionable claims, Cutlep now was determined to fully perform his duty for the Confederacy. "My guard was a grim, surly looking rebel," observed Mrs. Phillips, "but he did his duty manfully, and not one of the many who tried coming in would he admit. When they made the attempt to enter, he would draw his gun up to a charge bayonet and sternly tell them, 'You can't come in here. The General ordered this house protected and I'm going to protect it.'"

Inevitably, some rebels came by to tease Cutlep. "What ye guardin'?" they invariably would ask. Eavesdropping from her parlor window, Mrs. Phillips enjoyed the playful exchanges. Cutlep gave different answers, telling some he was guarding the house, others that it was the porch, and still others a "Union lady." To this last answer one soldier asked, "Is she good-looking?" Mrs. Phillips quietly blushed at Cutlep's description of her as "a Union woman, and a very likely one, too."

Out of appreciation for her young protector, she took him around noon some food left over from yesterday's meal, "having no heart to cook and still less to eat anything."

She set before the grateful rebel a plate of mashed potatoes, cold bread and meat, stewed peaches and molasses, and a hot cup of coffee. The coffee "created as great an excitement among his fellow Rebels on the street," she observed, "as the entrance of Barnum's entire museum, dwarfs included."

As the day worn on, Mrs. Phillips's fears eased somewhat, overcome in part by her inquisitive nature, and she allowed herself, while holding the hand of little Leonard, to go out into the front yard and socialize a bit with the "brutes" who had occupied her town. Most wanted to know about the Yankees who had just left. "If we had had this place and been as fixed as they were," said one soldier, "we would not have left." It seemed to this rebel that all they had to do was point a gun at the Federals to make them run. "Maybe the Yankees think they are getting us into a trap here," he declared, "but they'll catch hell if they undertake to play that game."

Not all the rebels Mrs. Phillips met possessed such bravado. One told her that he was tired of the war, and wanted to go home. "It will never be ended by fighting," he said. "It is just like two brothers sitting down in the evening to play cards. Sometimes one of them beats and sometimes the other, and so it would be if they were to play on till all eternity. Just so with this war; the combatants are brothers, sometimes they gain a battle, sometimes we. We are so near alike it will never be ended by fighting."

Some graybacks took delight in a little good-natured teasing of Leonard. "Do you like us Rebels?" one asked.

"No," answered the boy.

"Do you like the Yankees?"

"Yes, I'm a real blue-bellied Yankee myself."

"Well," said the Rebel, "I guess we'll have to take you on to Richmond." When another Rebel joked that they would have to burn down his house because he was a Yankee, Leonard shot back that "some of their Secesh friend's houses would have to go too."

The boy's mother cleverly asked the rebels a few questions of her own, which they just as cleverly evaded. "I have quizzed a great many of them about their movements and intentions," she wrote, "but their stories are no two alike."

Around sundown, Private Cutlep received orders to return to his company. He thoughtfully reassured Mrs. Phillips that she need not worry, "that I might sleep safely and unmolested." Colonel William J. Wiley of the Thirty-first Virginia Militia then offered to provide one of his soldiers to stay the night on her porch, but she declined, "for I felt that they were not to be trusted, and that I should be just as much afraid of the guard as of the rest of them." She took the opportunity, however, to express her surprise at the different courses taken by the colonel and his brother, Senator Waitman T. Wiley. "He made the reply," she wrote, "that he did not think the word 'best' could apply to his brother's conduct."

Sure enough, soon after Cutlep left, Mrs. Phillips heard strange voices coming from her back porch. Finding three rebels there rummaging through her milk cupboard, she asked sharply what they wanted. "Oh, nothing," one casually replied, "just looking in here." She promptly informed them that her house already had been searched, and that General Imboden had forbidden any further intrusions. "I don't think it is right to search houses this way," one of them said in mock sympathy, adding, "It is too bad."

Nonetheless, one asked for and was allowed to keep a "U.S." belt buckle he had found in the cupboard, and another simply stole a sharp knife.

The bulk of Imboden's force then left town and set up camp across the river. "It was a relief to me to see them going out," wrote Maria Louise. "They marched out to the tune of 'Rio Grande' with their hateful flags flapping defiance and triumph at the despairing Union people in this God forsaken town. Oh! Lord, are we to endure this long? Can we endure it?" As if to deepen everyone's loneliness and gloom, a heavy rain and thunderstorm then came in.

All through the night, Mrs. Phillips nervously kept a vigil in her upstairs window, for "I dare not, dare not go to bed." While listening to her clock chime the passing hours, she derived comfort from writing in her journal or reading favorite Bible passages. Now and then, she heard soldiers passing by on the street below. "Is that a nigger up there?" she heard one say who spotted her vague image in the window. "Dogged if I know," said another soldier. "Apropos of dogs," she scornfully concluded, adding that the real dogs in town seemed especially restive tonight, howling and barking through the late hours. "They winded the grey-coated invader," she wrote contemptuously, "and did not like the smell thereof."

Mrs. Phillips and her children survived the night unmolested, only to discover the following morning, Thursday, April 30, that it was not the Union people who need be in fear. When a great commotion erupted in the street among the soldiers and their sympathizers, she went out to find out why. She was horrified to learn that during the night "a Secesh boy had been murdered, beaten to death with clubs by some Union men in the country."[59]

Exploitation of the Countryside

Beverly and now Buckhannon! At little cost, Imboden had taken two important towns that had been Federal outposts within the so-called new state of West Virginia. The humblest in the command could not help but appreciate the significance of these triumphs.

Imboden, however, now faced a serious problem. The bad roads had compelled him to leave at Greenbrier River about forty barrels of flour, and at Beverly several more. Moreover, the remaining seventy or so supply wagons could not come into town until the Buckhannon River bridge had been repaired. And the town itself had little to offer, the Yankees having burned all their abandoned stores and supplies (and destroyed two guns). His men and their animals were very hungry; many horses already having given out and died. He thus decided to hold at Buckhannon, both until he could supply his men and also hear something of what had become of General Jones.

To feed his men, Imboden sent out details to scour the countryside for corn, wheat and grain, all of which proved scarce, sometimes less than a bushel per house. What little did come in was ground at two nearby mills that ran "day and night."[60]

He also did not neglect the all-important task of gathering in cattle and horses to be sent to the rear for General Lee. On May 1, he posted in town a notice that received a somewhat less than enthusiastic response: "Having been sent by the Confederate Government to Northwestern Virginia for the purpose of making purchases for the use of the army, I hope patriotic citizens of Upshur and surrounding counties, will aid me in procuring cattle, sheep, hogs, &c. The highest marketable price will be paid. I can be found at any hour of the day in room No. 3, American Hotel. Signed J.W. Mitchell, Major and C[ommissary] of S[ubsistence]."

Though the take was disappointing, cattle and horses proved to be somewhat more abundant than grain. "I required everything to be paid for at fair prices," Imboden reported, "such as were the current rates before we arrived in the country." Then he added, almost disingenuously, "This gave general satisfaction in the country, and our currency was freely accepted."[62]

In his 1884 book "From Dawn to Dusk," the Reverend Loyal Young estimated that Imboden's men took from Upshur County about $30,000 worth of cattle, one neighbor living on French Creek having suffered the loss of more than $2,000 in stock. Being paid, if at all, with Confederate money or "horse bonds," the loss among Upshur citizens was total and complete.[63]

Then on Wednesday, April 29, nine days into the great expedition, Imboden finally received news of Grumble Jones.

CHAPTER FOUR

Greenland Gap

The Start

In early April, Grumble Jones began making almost daily personal inspections of the units in his command. Naturally, this aroused among the men suspicions and rumors that became increasingly focused as the days wore on. "The blue-birds had built [a nest] in [Colonel Turner] Ashby's favorite gun the 'Blakely' that at that time last year was never cool," the Eleventh Virginia Cavalry's Major Mottram Ball playfully wrote his wife concerning the inactivity leading up to the raid. A graduate of William & Mary and a cousin of Colonel Richard Dulany, twenty-seven-year-old Ball had been a lawyer and schoolmaster before the war. "But Old Jones was waking up," he continued. "He declared that the ladies of the Valley who had been 'talking' of him should yet weep for their husbands, and sweethearts in his command. Everybody knew he was going to 'make a break' two weeks before he started and most everybody knew the direction. How the Yankees happened to be so ignorant of it is a mystery to me."[1]

"Should nothing interfere now we will take up the line of march next Tuesday morning for somewhere," nineteen-year-old Sergeant William Lyne Wilson of Company B wrote in his diary on Sunday, April 19 in response to the many indications and rumors that his Twelfth Virginia Cavalry, camped near Harrisonburg, soon was going to move out. "The sound of the ringing anvil is heard all day long and an unusually large supply of horse shoes and nails are here." Born in Jefferson County, Wilson had graduated from Columbia College (now George Washington University) in Washington, D.C. before enlisting in the Twelfth on April 1, 1862. In a post war irony of this campaign, Wilson would become president of West Virginia University in Morgantown, and he would serve as a U.S. Congressman from the state of West Virginia.[2]

On Monday, April 20, the day Imboden set out from Camp Washington and President Lincoln signed the proclamation approving the admission of West Virginia to the union, Grumble Jones issued a circular to the various, scattered units of his command. From his headquarters at Lacey Springs, about nine miles northeast of Harrisonburg in the Shenandoah Valley's Rockingham County, he instructed them to rendezvous that evening at a place called Cootes' Store, some ten miles to the northwest.[3]

Already camped near there were the 400 men of the Eleventh Virginia Cavalry, commanded by twenty-eight year old Colonel Lundsford Lomax, an 1856 graduate of West Point who had been colonel of the Eleventh for little more than two months after having served as a staff officer for Ben McCulloch, Joe Johnston, and Earl Van Dorn.[4]

From two miles north of Harrisonburg came thirty-year old Lt. Colonel Elijah (Lige) White with 250 men of the Thirty-fifth Battalion of Virginia Cavalry, formerly a unit of partisan rangers known as the "Comanches," which had operated mainly along the Potomac between Harper's Ferry and Leesburg. A born scrapper, White fought in Kansas before the war, and in October 1861, he distinguished himself in a volunteer capacity at Ball's Bluff. He served in the Sixth and Seventh Virginia Cavalry before becoming captain in January 1862 of "White's Rebels," an independent Virginia cavalry company. In February 1863, he took command of the Thirty-fifth Battalion.[5]

Major Mottram D. Ball (Virginia Historical Society, Richmond, Virginia).

Forty-two year old Colonel Richard H. Dulany, a native of Loudon County who began the war as a captain in the Sixth Virginia Cavalry, came in five miles from Timberville with about 500 men of the Seventh Virginia Cavalry.[6]

From Harrisonburg came thirty-three year old Colonel Asher J. Harmon with 405 men of the Twelfth Virginia Cavalry. Born near Waynesboro, Harmon before the war

Sgt. William L. Wilson (Virginia Historical Society, Richmond, Virginia).

had operated a stage line in Staunton. After serving as a captain in the Fifth Virginia Infantry in 1861, he became a quartermaster of the station at Staunton. In June 1862, he became colonel of the Twelfth. This morning Harmon had tried to review the regiment but a heavy rain intervened to cancel the event.[7]

From Lacey Springs came twenty-nine year old Major Ridgely Brown with 230 men of the First Battalion of Maryland Cavalry. A native of Montgomery County, Maryland, Brown had been a lieutenant in the First Virginia Cavalry before assuming command of the First Battalion.[8]

Forty-five year old Lt. Colonel John Shackelford "Shac" Green, a farmer in Rockingham County before the war, brought in the Sixth Virginia Cavalry from a camp located between Harrisonburg and Lacey Springs. Entering the war as a captain in the Sixth, Green had been severely wounded in June 1862 at Harrisonburg during the Shenandoah Valley Campaign.[9]

Also from near Harrisonburg, came the Thirty-fourth Battalion of Virginia Cavalry commanded by twenty-six year old Major Vincent A. Witcher, a lawyer from Wayne County. Having formed in September 1861, many of the men coming from the western counties of Virginia, the battalion had operated mostly between Grundy and Piketon.[10]

And not to be left out of the expedition was its original author, Captain John McNeill, with fifty-five of his Partisan Rangers.[11]

All these units had proven themselves to be capable, tough fighters, the Sixth, Seventh, Eleventh, and Twelfth Virginia belonging to the famed Laurel Brigade that had formed in September 1862 after individually achieving great renown in the Shenandoah Valley Campaign. Many in the First Maryland had fought at First Manassas, and others had participated in the Shenandoah Valley Campaign.

Expecting to meet enemy resistance at Moorefield on the South Branch of the Potomac River, Jones also had secured the services of the First Maryland Infantry under Lt. Colonel James R. Herbert, Captain R. Preston Chew's Battery of four guns from the Stuart Horse Artillery, camped two miles below Harrisonburg, and Captain William H. Griffen's four guns of the Baltimore Light Artillery. Finally, but perhaps most important, came a long train of pack mules loaded with blasting powder to be used on the B&O bridges. The train was under the charge of twenty-three-year-old Second Lieutenant William Garnett Williamson of the First Regiment Engineers, a native of

LIEUT. CO<u>L</u> E.V. WHITE

Lt. Colonel Elijah V. White (Virginia Historical Society, Richmond, Virginia).

Norfolk and a graduate of Washington College whose blasting skills in destroying a bridge over the Monocacy River during the Maryland Campaign the previous September had sufficiently impressed General Lee to recommended him for this raid.[12]

All men and horses deemed unfit for the hard campaign ahead remained behind near Harrisonburg. Jones placed them under the command of Lieutenant Colonel Oliver R. Funsten of the Eleventh Virginia Cavalry, with orders to protect the Valley from "marauders." At Strasburg, Jones also left Major Samuel B. Myers of the Seventh Virginia Cavalry in command of a "picket" of three locally raised cavalry companies, one each from the Seventh Virginia, Eleventh Virginia (Capt. Joseph T. Hess) and Twelfth Virginia. If they got into trouble, Myers was to call on General Fitz Lee's cavalry brigade located at Sperryville.[13]

Captain Charles T. O'Ferrall (Virginia Historical Society, Richmond, Virginia).

Petersburg

During the pleasant evening hours of the 20th at Cootes's Store near the mouth of Brock's Gap, speculation raced through the ranks of Jones's gathering host. "Whither we were going or what object General Jones had in view," recalled twenty-two year old Captain Charles T. O'Ferrall of the Twelfth Virginia, "no officer below a colonel, and surely no private soldier, had the slightest conception." A future governor of Virginia (elected in 1894), O'Ferrall had attended Washington College before entering the war as a sergeant in the Eleventh Virginia Cavalry. Well liked and respected by his comrades, he made captain in the Twelfth the following year.[14]

Loaded with powder, the pack train, however, provided the biggest tip off. Many guessed that, with a major battle looming between Hooker and Lee, Jones was off to hit the B&O so as to prevent reinforcements from reaching the Army of the Potomac.[15]

At 9 a.m. the following morning, the beginning of a beautiful Tuesday, Jones broke camp, his men each carrying ten days' rations of "jerked beef" and forty rounds of ammunition. The command made fifteen miles on the Brock's Gap road, and camped that evening at the eastern base of Brock's Gap, a pass leading west over Little North Mountain. "Many speculations as to our destination," the Twelfth Virginia's Sergeant Wilson noted in his diary.[16]

With the Twelfth Virginia in the lead, the column pulled out on Wednesday the 22nd in a driving rainstorm, having already waited too long for the brigade quartermaster, who failed to deliver extra rations as ordered. "We crossed one of the main branches of the headwaters of the North Fork of the Shenandoah some six or eight times during the day," Corporal George Neese told his diary. A young, intelligent, witty recruit from New Market now in Chew's battery, Neese was a keen, appreciative observer of the wonders of nature spread out before him in these mountains and valleys. One of his stream crossings that day proved to be deeper than expected, and the water, much to the horror of the gunners who feared the loss of all their ammunition, rushed into the limber chests. A thorough inspection after the crossing, however, revealed only minor damage, the water having wet only the butt end of the shells. With great relief, the gunners moved on. "We followed one of the incipient headstreams of the Little Shenandoah until it dwindled down to a little mountain rill," Neese continued, "and then we crossed a little ridge and struck the headwaters of Lost River, which flows through a narrow mountain-hemmed valley along the southern edge of Hardy County."[17]

While Corporal Neese put the number of river and stream crossings at between six and eight, others in this increasingly wild and beautiful country considered them interminable. "At the highest point in [Brock's Gap]," Major Ball wrote his wife, "very near each other are the sources of two streams, one flowing east to the Shenandoah, the other west to the South Branch of the Potomac. The Gap is along the beds of these, and our road up one and down the other was very rough, crossing these streams fifty or sixty times, the fording deep and bad in some places."[18]

After climbing over Little North Mountain, the command proceeded north to an encampment just beyond the Mathias farm in the Lost River Valley, about twenty miles southeast of Moorefield.[19]

"At night," Major Ball wrote his wife, "my squadron was a little separated from the Regiment on account of the nature of the ground and bivouacked near a very fine Sulphur Spring which we enjoyed. There was a little cleared space in the edge of the woods covered with soft sod, enclosed like a stage, on all sides but one and here at night some of the boys gave an impromptu performance. The scene was romantic, our fires were the foot lights and the rugged precipice on one side the wild woods on the other, the busy little stream and the picketed houses and picturesque shabangs of the men made a beautiful scene, such as no stage artist ever got up."[20]

The "romantic scene," however, quickly ended when a steady, chilling rain came in. The unwelcome downpour lasted through the night and into the following morning (23rd), Corporal Neese being one of a fortunate few to have slept in a "little mountain barn."[21]

On roads "terribly cut up," the column on the 23rd looped back toward Mathias's so as to reach the gap over Branch Mountain, passing along the way a sulphur spring known locally as Howard's Lick. "It is a beautiful spring," observed Neese, "boxed with white marble slabs, and the water is as clear as the purest virgin crystal, and very sulphury. The surrounding mountain scenery is wild, grand, and magnificent; spurs of the Branch Mountain and long wooded ridges thickly clad with laurel and ferns rise around the spring and its neighborhood in every direction which bounds the view of the beholder. On one side not more than fifteen or twenty feet from the spring a steep bank rises almost perpendicularly, covered with mossy rocks and mountain fern, all darkly shaded by overhanging spruce and pine, foot-noted by the ever present shiny green of mountain laurel."[22]

Later that morning, the column started up the eastern side of Branch Mountain, and into a dark, heavy fog. Soon the men "could not see fifty yards," wrote Neese, "and the fog looked like wool packed among the trees and shrubbery." The pace slowed as the wet, miserable men struggled to reach the top of the pass. "After we had been some four or five hours in the damp, dense, cloud-like fog that hung around and hugged the rugged steeps," Neese continued, "the rain ceased and the clouds partially broke away. We suddenly descended below the fog line on the western slope of the mountain, and the beautiful Moorefield Valley lay before us in all its smiling splendor, with its wheat fields, pasture lands, and grass fields all arrayed in different hues of living green. Gentle spring had already trailed her bright emerald robe along the grassy hillside and scattered the fragrant children of the sunshine along its balmy track. The South Branch and South Fork meandered with sweeping bends through the rain-cleaned landscape like bands of silver woven in a divers green carpet. Moorefield, almost in the center of the picture, looked in the evening glow like a bright jewel with an emerald setting. All of which was a delicious feast for eyes that have been befogged for four or five hours in the gloom of a wet, dripping mountain."[23]

Corporal Neese was not alone in his appreciation of the splendor that lay before him. "[We] soon had a view, full and complete, of the famous Moorefield Valley," remembered twenty-two-year-old Captain Frank Myers of Company A, Thirty-fifth Battalion, "and great was the gratification and delight of all the men as they looked down from the mountain top upon the lovely scene, lying as it did like a picture of beauty at their feet, girt with its dark mountain frame, and fringed with its evergreen bordering of hemlock and cedar, white snow-caps all around, but everything fresh as springtime in the valley; where the South Branch was foaming and dashing over its rocky bed, sometimes winding along the base of one mountain, then crossing to the other, and sometimes rolling gloriously through the carpet of living green in the centre (sic) of the valley."[24]

"Here there opened on us," Major Ball wrote his wife, "the most beautiful valley I ever saw. There was spread 'the brightest of green' and in the bosom of the vale met two streams of surpassing beauty. It had been raining all day but the clouds parted for a moment as I looked on it and the sun peeped out and the placid vale 'lighted all over with his smile,' encircling the mountains assumed a pleased look as they threw off their somber robes which had been hanging around them and became clothed in their 'azure hue.' But I cannot describe it. I do hope we may gaze on it together some day."[25]

After coming down from Branch Mountain, the command that night camped near the "bright jewel" of Moorefield, the county seat of Hardy, whose population of nearly 10,000 was predominantly pro-Southern, its eligible voters having decidedly favored the ordinance of secession.[26]

To Old Grumble's great surprise, and relief, no Federal troops awaited him at Moorefield to contest the crossing of the South Branch. He soon discovered, however, that an even more formidable enemy stood in the way.

Jones had planned to cross the river at Goings Ford that evening, then rest his men and animals among the farms of a bountiful, friendly area called Old Fields, but the heavy rains had made the crossing impossible. He now faced the disappointing prospect of a costly delay in a detour that threatened to eliminate the chances of cutting the B&O before Federal troops used it to come into western Virginia from the east. Though it meant losing about 500 men, he decided to get rid of his slow moving infantry and the cumbersome artillery and supply wagons. Under Lt. Colonel Herbert of the First Maryland Infantry, they all immediately started back for the Shenandoah, going by way of Franklin in Pendleton County. It was a loss Old Grumble would come to regret.[27]

On Friday, April 24, Jones led his remaining 2500 men twenty-five miles southwest to a crossing of the South Branch at Petersburg. Still in fairly friendly country, the command enjoyed a warm reception. "On our arrival at the ford," Private John C. Donohue of the Sixth Virginia Cavalry told his diary, "the citizens and the ladies came to welcome [us]."[28]

The warm welcome, however, was offset by the disheartening discovery that the prospect of crossing there seemed nearly as daunting as at Moorefield. The river, reported Jones, was "wide, deep, rough, and, from the strength of the current, exceedingly dangerous."[29]

"The ford at that place," observed Captain Frank Myers, "is covered with rocks of almost every size and shape, making it a difficult passage at any time, but now the mountain stream was filled to overflowing and the waters foamed over the rock as some enormous mill flume."[30]

Leading the column, the Sixth Virginia went in first. The rushing water quickly swept downstream three men and their horses. "When a horse lost its footing," Lieutenant John Opie of the Sixth observed with horror, "he rolled over and over in the current, like a barrel, until finally, he disappeared in the raging torrent below." One of the three men, Private William Evans of Company F, lost his life. "The man who was drowned," concluded Opie, "caused his own death and that of his horse by swinging to his bridal rein."[31]

These tragedies occurred despite the help of local citizens who had positioned themselves on the banks to mark the best place to cross and from where they used long poles to tap the neck of any horse that tried to make the dangerous mistake of turning his head away from upstream. Another farmer, astride his strong, "seventeen hands tall" horse, bravely stood in midstream to mark the crossing (especially helpful, according to Jones's report, was a Mr. Cunningham and a Mr. Hutton, as well as Pvt. Aaron Welton, Co. F, 7 Va.). Likewise did the Sixth's regimental chaplain, Reverend Richard Terrell Davis, courageously remain in the water to offer fervent prayers for the safe passage of the entire command. Born in Charlottesville in 1830, and a graduate of the University of Virginia and the Virginia Theological Seminary, Davis had been appointed regimental chaplain the previous August. The men greatly respected and admired him. "He charged at the head of the regiment in every battle," wrote one.[32]

Despite all this courageous help, the crossing of the South Branch became for many a horrifying ordeal. "Amid the shouts of excited men & the shrieks of terrified and sympathizing women," the regiment's Private John Donohue told his diary, "the scene became truly distressing. One of the men clung to his horse's head with such tenacity that the poor brute was soon drowned. His rider continued his hold on the floating carcass now appearing above the surface now disappearing beneath the muddy waters until both approached near the bank. His rescue was now thought certain by many, but alas! striking the violent current both horse & rider sank to rise no more."[33]

After the Sixth Virginia came the turn of the First Maryland. "The raging stream was out of its banks," recalled nineteen-year-old Lieutenant George Wilson Booth,

Adjutant of the First, "with a swift current which buffeted the men as they essayed to make their way in the flood." Born and raised in Baltimore, Booth had witnessed the citizens' attack on the Sixth Massachusetts when that regiment tried to pass through the city on its way to Washington in early 1861. Though only sixteen years old at the time, Booth joined the First Maryland Infantry and fought at First Manassas. While serving as an aide to Bradley Johnson, he received a slight wound at Second Manassas. Though quite young, Booth possessed a talent for command, rising to lieutenant in the First Maryland Cavalry. "A number of men and horses were swept away," he recalled of the terrible crossing at Petersburg, "but the orders were imperative to move forward."[34]

The Twelfth Virginia then took its turn. "The water passed by as though it had wings," professed the regiment's Private Edward Green. "Men who would be quick to charge a battery," declared brigade historian Captain William N. McDonald, "were appalled at the rushing, angry water."[35]

The appalled included twenty-year-old Lieutenant George Baylor of Company B, Twelfth Virginia. "As the act of swimming was unknown to me," he later confessed, "I trusted in God alone to bear me safely over." After "making all necessary preparations for a struggle with the water," including raising cartridges, coats and weapons overhead, Baylor and his men went in. "The Israelites," he declared, "never moved through the Red Sea with more awe and solemnity."[36]

Born in Jefferson County, Baylor had graduated from Dickinson College and taught at Episcopal High School in Fauquier County until the war. On May 9, 1861, he enlisted in the Second Virginia Infantry. On March 1, 1862, he was appointed Third Lieutenant in the Twelfth Virginia Cavalry. He had been slightly wounded at Halltown on November 1, and on February 12, 1863 near Summit Point, the Fourteenth Pennsylvania Cavalry captured him. He was exchanged on April 6, just in time to participate in this expedition. (After the war, Baylor would practice law and become president of West Virginia University at Morgantown.)[37]

The "awe and solemnity" of the crossing at Petersburg produced "a depressing silence," judged Captain O'Ferrall, that ultimately proved a good setup for a touch of comic relief. "As we neared the opposite bank, beyond the danger line," Baylor later recalled, "this awful silence was broken by the stentorian voice of Sergeant Trussell, 'Close up, men; bear up the stream.'" Nineteen-year-old Charles William Trussell had been a merchant before the war, and he had served one year in the Second Virginia Infantry before joining the Twelfth Virginia Cavalry in April 1862. "This great display of courage, after the crisis was passed," continued Baylor, "caused much mirth among the boys at the Sergeant's expense, and the order was often repeated along our journey, never failing to provoke laughter and jollity."[38]

Though "wet as rats," Captain O'Ferrall observed of the crossing, "we had kept out powder dry." Not everyone in the Twelfth could say the same. While still out in midstream, beyond the reassuring sound of Sergeant Trussell's "stentorian voice," Sergeant Major James Henry Figgat of the Twelfth's Company F fell off his horse. Going under for what he believed was the beginning of a death agony, Figgat, a teacher and lawyer at Fincastle before the war, reflexively flailed about until he somehow managed to grab the tail of his panicked horse. To this wispy lifeline he desperately clung until they both safely washed ashore some 400 yards downstream. (Figgat would survive the war, continue practicing law, and serve in the Virginia Legislature.)[39]

Others could not lay claim to even that dubious success. Throughout Jones's command, many men with faint hearts or weak horses became stranded and had to be left behind. These included five from the First Maryland Battalion, two of whom had tried to cross "but were obliged to return with a thorough wetting," perhaps fifty from both the Seventh Virginia and the Thirty-fifth Virginia, and as many as 100 of the Eleventh Virginia. Thus despite not having faced the enemy at the South Branch, Jones had suffered fairly severe "losses," which included four precious hours consumed in the crossing. The stranded he sent back to the Valley (under Major Throckmorton), whereby his strength dwindled to no more than 2200 men. With these he marched down the north side of the river and camped (24th) four miles south of Moorefield.[40]

The whole unpleasant affair had brought down the spirits of many, particularly in the now greatly depleted ranks of the Eleventh Virginia, many of whom believed that they had been saved during the crossing by putting sticks in their mouths to help keep their heads afloat. Those low spirits then led to further, nearly disastrous consequences when the foul mood they produced in the Eleventh contributed to an argument with the First Maryland over what should have been a trivial issue concerning the possession of some hay. Tempers grew so hot that the two units verged on a brawl. "On going into camp for the night the first thing to be looked after was the care of our wearied horses," the First Maryland's George Booth later explained. "In the neighboring meadows were several large stacks of hay, and Colonel Brown directed the men to help themselves. On reaching one of these stacks it was found to be under the protection of a squad from one of the regiments of the brigade, who claimed they had orders from Colonel Lomax not to permit it to be disturbed save by their own people. A contention then ensued, which at one time bid fair to end in trouble, but our men came down in force and took possession, and in a little while the noble proportion of the stack were sensibly married to the immediate advantage of our hungry steeds."[41]

That morning the South Branch had forced a hundred or so of their fellow Virginians to back down, and now this evening the First Maryland had forced the remainder of them to do the same. Grumbling and unhappy, the men of the Eleventh went to bed, hoping for a better day tomorrow.

To Greenland Gap

Saturday, April 25, dawned promisingly bright and clear, but by the time the men finished boiling their morning coffee an icy rain cruelly swept in upon them. After waiting for the quartermasters to finish their fruitless efforts at foraging the local farms, the march resumed at 11 a.m., with the Seventh Virginia in the lead, followed by the First Maryland. Moving northwest on the Moorefield and Alleghany Pike (present state route 42), a road that in colonial days had been an important east-west link known as the McCulloch Trader Trail, the column crossed over Patterson Creek Mountain, marched through Williamsport, and then went over Knobly Mountain to Falls Gap.[42]

Despite the delays in getting around and over the South Branch, Jones felt quite

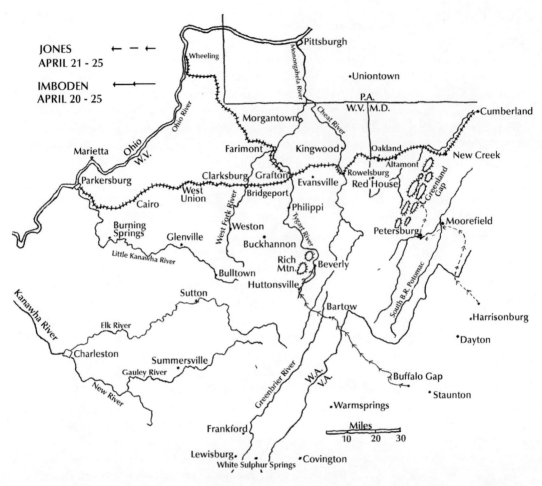

3. Imboden's movement from Buffalo Gap, Va., to Beverly, W. Va., April 20–25, 1863, and Jones's movement from near Harrisonburg, Va., to Greenland Gap, W. Va., April 21–25, 1863.

satisfied with the progress now being made by the column. His next objective was Greenland Gap, a pass over New Creek Mountain he expected to quickly cross, whereupon he meant to strike out for the Northwest Pike (present U.S. 50), a good road for cavalry. From there he would be only forty-four miles from his primary objective — the B&O at Rowelsburg, which he hoped to cut before Federal reinforcements arrived on the line from the east. If he accomplished nothing else, the destruction of the works at Rowelsburg would be sufficient to crown his mission a great success. And at the moment, all indications pointed in that direction.

While descending the road from Falls Gap, Jones met up with twenty-seven year old Lt. Colonel Thomas Marshall, grandson of Chief Justice John Marshall and a former aide to Stonewall Jackson. Marshall reported that while riding with the Seventh Virginia at the head of the column he had received word from locals that Yankees might be in Greenland Gap. After obtaining permission from Colonel Dulany to do a reconnaissance with Company A of the Seventh, he had ridden close enough to verify that indeed the gap held "one or two companies" of the enemy.[43]

Old Grumble's mood turned sour. He did not fear the inevitable consequences of dealing with so few Yankees. It was the loss of time that rankled him. Yet an even more time-consuming detour was out of the question. There was no choice but to bust his way through.

The Federals in the Gap

Narrow, steep Greenland Gap in Hardy County lay only twenty-five miles south of General Kelley's First Division headquarters at New Creek. When news reached him that an apparently significant force of Confederates had entered West Virginia, he immediately dispatched to the gap Captain Martin Wallace and Lieutenant Julius Fletcher with fifty-two men of Company G, Twenty-third Illinois Infantry. They were to serve as an advance picket against an enemy attempt to threaten this vital approach to New Creek.[44]

Using as a barracks Kane's brewery on West Polk Street near the river, the Twenty-third Illinois Infantry had formed in Chicago on June 15, 1861. The following month it went to Jefferson City, Missouri, from where it marched an agonizing 120 miles to the relief of Lexington. After a tough siege of nine days, it surrendered on September 20, 1861 with about 2800 other men to the overwhelming numbers commanded by General Sterling Price. After the men were exchanged in October, the regiment reformed and was sent east to New Creek, West Virginia, from where in January 1863 it marched forty miles in ten hours to save Moorefield from Grumble Jones's winter raid. In April, the regiment was assigned to the Fifth Brigade of the First Division, stationed at New Creek. Fiercely proud to be "Mulligan's Men" of the "Irish Brigade," the soldiers of Company G, originally called the "Mahoney Guards," almost all hailed from the tough streets of Chicago. Their thirty-one-year-old captain, Martin Wallace, had been with the company and the regiment since the beginning, having enlisted in Chicago as a private on April 20, 1861. With his men, he had been captured at Lexington and exchanged. Despite having been in effective command of the company since August, Wallace was not promoted to captain until April 9, 1862. Against overwhelming odds in Missouri, and again during the difficult march to Moorefield, he and his tough Irish Chicagoans clearly had demonstrated their stubborn mettle.[45]

On Wednesday, April 22, they reached Greenland Gap. In addition to stunning views offered by a magnificent gorge that had been cut over thousands of years by flowing water, with spectacular rock walls towering more than 800 feet, the place provided a good camp site, complete with a creek full of trout. The road through the gap had been part of the old McCulloch Trader Trail, named in the mid–1700s for John and Samuel McCulloch, early traders with the local tribes, and it later became an important westward migration route. In September 1784, George Washington passed through the gap on his return to Mount Vernon after inspecting his lands in western Virginia. For three days, the Illinoisans peacefully enjoyed these idyllic surroundings.[46]

About 4 p.m. on Saturday, April 25, thirty-five-year-old Captain Jacob Smith and thirty-four men of Company A, Fourteenth West Virginia Infantry, arrived from New Creek to relieve Wallace so that he and his men could rejoin their regiment, now at

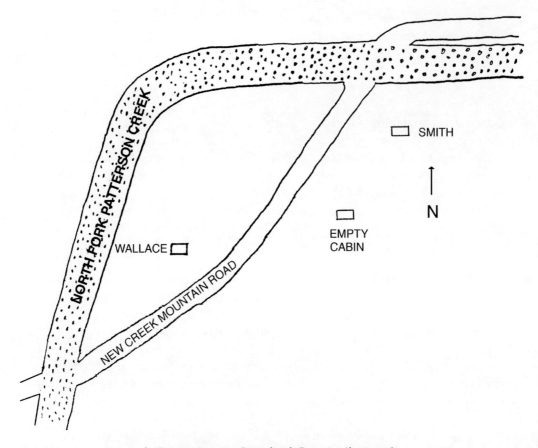

4. Engagement at Greenland Gap, April 25, 1863.

Grafton because of the fall of Beverly to Imboden. After forming in Wheeling the previous August, the Fourteenth West Virginia had been sent to New Creek for guard duty on the upper Potomac, being attached to the Fifth Brigade, First Division. Captain Smith now brought in his men to Greenland Gap on the double-quick, having learned along the way from a local farmer (who told a scout, Private James Richards) that "7,000 Confederates" were headed for the gap. This confirmed for Wallace the information locals had brought him around noon, and which his own scouts subsequently verified.[47]

Despite all this, some in Wallace's small command did not believe they were in any great danger. "When we reached Greenland Gap in the afternoon," recalled Private James Richards of the Fourteenth West Virginia, "we found five men of Co. G on picket duty and told them of the word we had received.... They did not appear to be much concerned, stating that it would be some time until they reached there, and that it was more probable that they would take some other route."[48]

Wallace, however, knew better. Under the circumstances, he probably did not intend to accept the relief of Smith and leave the gap, but he lost the choice anyway when scouts came riding in to report that the enemy was approaching. Despite having only eighty-nine men at his command, Wallace bravely determined to put up a fight.

It was a good place to make a Thermopylae-like stand, Greenland Gap being very narrow, wide enough only for the road and a mountain stream known as Patterson's Creek. About fifty yards south of the road, on a mound in a one acre clearing at the west end of the gap, stood a sturdy two story country log church. In this virtual fortress Wallace placed his own men, who promptly barricaded the windows and in the chinks cut holes from which to fire. He ordered Smith to put his West Virginians in an equally sturdy log schoolhouse, one of two such structures located some 100 yards across the road from the church. A curve in the North Fork of the ten-yard wide, two-foot deep Patterson Creek protected the defenders by way of a natural moat. Wallace then finished his preparations by putting out pickets.[49]

His decision to try to hold the gap unquestionably was brave, but also foolhardy, for he knew the Confederates vastly outnumbered him, and they no doubt possessed artillery that could easily blast to smithereens the two log structures. With no more than eighty-nine men, whom he encouraged "to be cool and deliberate," he nonetheless held a strong position that commanded for a mile the four-mile, steep approach to the gap. Bravely they awaited the rebel thousands.[50]

The Fight for the Gap

The reports of his scouts, supplemented by the view through his own field glasses, readily convinced Jones that the enemy, though few in number, held a surprisingly strong position. Now he sorely missed his departed artillery, which would have been perfect for the job of blasting the Yankees out of those sturdy-looking log structures. There was no choice, he concluded, but to throw at them a quick, powerful frontal assault.

By virtue of being at the head of the marching column, the Seventh Virginia received the task of leading the attack. The simple plan called for Lt. Colonel Marshall to lead with part of the regiment and for Colonel Dulany to follow up with the rest.[51]

"The men's teeth chattered together, and their knees rattled against the sides of their horses," nineteen-year-old Lieutenant John Opie of Company D, Sixth Virginia Cavalry remembered of his comrades in the Seventh as they formed for the charge. He then explained that this "was the effect of the cold, increased by nervous excitement." Born in Jefferson County, Opie had attended the Virginia Military Institute and enlisted in the Fifth Virginia Infantry before joining the Sixth Virginia in October 1862. (After the war, he would practice law, serve in the Virginia House of Delegates and become a state senator.)[52]

After instructing his men to remain closed up during the charge, Marshall gave the signal, and at 5 p.m. the Virginians took off for the two log structures. They quickly and easily overran the Federal pickets, capturing four, one of whom had been guarding a bridge over the creek about a half mile east of the church and who then promptly gave Marshall a much clearer idea of what he was up against. On toward the church they rode, though by now they no longer remained closed up, the great rush having broken their formation. "We had thus far ... effectively surprised the force in reserve," the lieutenant colonel later reported, "and could we have been closed in columns of fours I am satisfied that we could have overwhelmed the enemy with scarce any loss on our side. We were unfortunately a good deal strung out."[53]

Riding headlong singly and in clusters, the Virginians came up to the creek. "Although we were expecting them later," confessed Private Richards of the Fourteenth West Virginia, "we had no thought of their arriving so soon. I was seated on the banks of the stream when they came upon us, bathing my feet in Patterson's Creek. As I ran to join the other of our men in the log house I was shot at several times but not wounded."[54]

With remarkable patience and discipline, Wallace waited for the rebels to get within seventy-five yards before he gave the order to fire. The volley proved devastating, bringing down several horses and men.

Undaunted, the surviving rebels pressed on in the midst of an increasingly hot, random Yankee fire. The lead riders got to within twenty yards of the church before they could take no more. The entire regiment pulled back.

Marshall allowed no time for his men to feel dejected or the Yankees triumphant. He quickly reformed his command and came on again. This time most of the men, about 200, rode past the log structures to secure the opposite end of the gap and thereby effectively cut off and surround the Yankees.[55]

During this charge, nineteen-year-old (born in Warren County June 22, 1843) Private William Alexander "Sandie" Buck of Company E boldly sped right up to the church and, finding a crevice near a barricaded window, fired his pistol into the opening until his horse collapsed from under him with two fatal bullet wounds and a bayonet stab, whereupon young Buck managed to safely get away. "He is deemed every way worthy of a commission in our Regular Army," General Jones proudly reported. This had not been the first time the brash boy from Front Royal had lost a horse in combat, one having been shot from under him while serving as Colonel Ashby's courier at Buckton. (For the loss of his horse at Greenland Gap, Buck would receive from the government $225 compensation.)[56]

The two attacks had proved surprisingly costly to the Seventh Virginia. Three men had been killed and ten wounded. Moreover, several horses had gone down, including fourteen out of seventeen in Company E. Colonel Dulany's horse had been killed and the colonel severely wounded in the arm.[57]

Understandably, Jones became quite upset at this seemingly unnecessary and now costly delay. With a frontal assault having twice failed to take the position, he decided to surround it and squeeze the Federals into submission.

While sharpshooters of the Seventh Virginia secured the woods and hillsides on the left, Captain John L. Chapman's dismounted riflemen of Company B, Thirty-fourth Battalion did the same on the right. Companies D and E of the Maryland Battalion, commanded respectively by Lieutenant William Dorsey and Captain William I. Raisin, forded the creek some distance downstream and climbed up the southern side of the steep, rocky mountain to where they took cover behind large boulders and began shooting at the church and school house. Lieutenant Adolphus Cooke led the battalion's Company B along the north side of the mountain to the New Creek road, from where he could stop any Union relief force.

From all directions now, the Confederates poured a hot fire onto the two log fortresses, with, however, little effect. "We sorely missed our artillery," admitted George Baylor of the Twelfth Virginia.[58]

Desperate to settle the matter before dark, Jones tried a new tactic. He sent in a flag of truce with a demand for surrender backed by a declaration that the Federals were surrounded by thousands. Moreover, Jones warned Wallace that if he killed several Confederates while trying to hold a hopeless position, then, according to the accepted usages of war, the garrison would forfeit their lives.[59]

Despite the possibility of being executed by his captors, Wallace did not hesitate with his answer. "Go back with that rag," he defiantly replied, "I don't care if he has millions; I will not surrender until compelled."[60]

Firing then resumed for a fruitless ten minutes, whereupon Jones, unbearably frustrated and impatient, called a halt and sent in another flag. This time, however, he used as a bearer one of the captured Yankee pickets, a non commissioned officer to whom he had deliberately shown the strength of the Confederate force.[61]

But this had unintended consequences. Convinced, in the growing darkness, that a white flag held by a man in a blue uniform meant that the Yankees were surrendering, some of Captain Dorsey's and Captain Raisin's Marylanders came out and approached the church, thereby leading Wallace to conclude that they intended treachery. He called out for them to fall back. When they did not comply and came to within twenty yards of the place he ordered his own men to open fire. This tragic mistake mortally wounded Privates G. Frank Swamley of Company D in the hip, and John Spencer of Company E, while also severely wounding Private Charles Lambden of Company D.[62]

Spencer, a mere boy, had enlisted against the wishes of his father, a strong Union man, who subsequently cursed his son with, "May the first ball that strikes him bring death!" This terrible wish came true, for at Greenland Gap, young Spencer's first engagement, a bullet tore into his throat, he groaned once, and fell back dead into the stream.[63]

The flag of truce then came in. The written note, this time backed by the threat of artillery, stated that if the Federals did not surrender in fifteen minutes "he [Jones] would not be responsible for the consequences."

Wallace could not be fooled. If Jones had artillery he would have used it by now. "Tell him he has got none," he replied, "if he has, bring them on. We are Mulligan's men, and we will fight to the last crust and cartridge." Some accounts maintain that Wallace even threatened to shoot the next messenger sent in with a surrender demand (a surrender demand also had gone into the school house, but Smith sent this over to Wallace, who told him to hang on).

Apparently expecting Wallace's refusal, Jones authorized the flag bearer to ask for a truce to remove the wounded. Wallace gave them thirty minutes, during which time some of his own men slipped out and quietly gathered up a few Confederate carbines, pistols, and sabers. When the prescribed time elapsed, firing promptly resumed, with Wallace telling his men to carefully conserve their depleted ammunition.[64]

Jones then hit upon a new tactic. Though he did not have artillery, he had the next best thing — that black powder loaded on pack mules for the destruction of the B&O bridges. Using it, of course, reduced availability for its original purpose, but what good would it be anyway if he could not get at those Yankee bridges? Jones called for

Lieutenant Williamson and asked him to determine the feasibility of blowing up or setting fire to the log church.

Cautiously, Williamson went off to the right of the pike and crept up around the hillside behind the Yankee stronghold. A few moments of careful observation convinced him that it could be done, and he hurried back to tell Jones.[65]

That satisfied Old Grumble. He ordered the formation of a dismounted storming party, to be led by Captain Frank Bond's Company A and Captain Roger Smith's Company C, about 170 men, "all seeming anxious to engage in the fight," of Major Brown's First Maryland Battalion. They were to be followed by the pioneers carrying the powder, with Lige White's Thirty-fifth Virginia battalion bringing up the rear.[66]

The plan called for the Marylanders to rush up to the church and beat in the barricaded windows so that lit bundles of straw could be thrown in, followed by a keg of powder. Officers assured their men that "a signal would be given before the powder was touched off," thereby giving them time to run clear. At about 8:30 p.m., the storming party, which included men carrying axes and flammable material, quietly set out for the church.[67]

"The night was bright with the light of a brilliant moon," recalled George Booth, "which lit up the road and the rugged mountain sides with a weird brightness." Cautiously, stealthily the Marylanders approached, hoping to get as close as possible before the Yankees detected them. They forgot, however, to do one thing of seemingly minor importance. "If we had left our sabres," Captain Bond, a member the First Maryland only since the previous November, ruefully recalled, "we might have got much nearer before drawing their fire; but stumbling about in the dark over logs and rocks soon drew their attention and the house blazed up with the flash of a hundred muskets."[68]

Caution now aside, the Marylanders raised a yell and streaked for the log church. They splashed into knee deep, icy Patterson Creek. "The weather was bitterly cold," remembered George Booth, "and on emerging from the water their clothing soon stiffened in ice. But personal discomfort was not to be thought of in a time like this."[69]

The Yankees blazed away at them. "I remember distinctly noticing two lines of fire," Captain Bond later wrote, "one above the other cut by a perpendicular black object which I guess was a chimney."[70]

"One by one the men dropped," recalled George Booth, "victims to the well-directed fire; but onward pressed the column, and soon ranged itself around the house, where for a moment was a respite of safety, as under its walls the fire from the windows could not be depressed so as to be effective."[71]

Captain Bond believed he was the first to reach the church, where, ironically, he felt safe, "as the enemy, thrusting their guns out of the loopholes, could not reach us, and I was very soon closely pressed by a V-shaped body of men who could only in this way get out of range." Some of those cowering men, however, did get hurt. "Captain, I am wounded," Private Sprigg Cockey, shot in the shoulder, called out in panic from behind the chimney. "What shall I do?" Bond told him to head back for the rear. "If I leave this chimney," Cockey protested, "I will be killed sure." Bond then told him to keep calm and remain where he was. "If I stay here," pleaded Cockey, "I will bleed to death." Unable to comfort the distraught private, who had been with the First

Maryland since only the previous September, Bond "had to give it up," and said no more to him (Cockey survived the fight).[72]

Meanwhile, the Yankees on the second floor pulled in their rifles and frantically began throwing down on Bond and his men rocks and chunks of iron. Just as frantically, the Marylanders began smashing in the barricaded windows, knocking out chinks in the walls, and "firing in whenever they could find a crack large enough to admit the muzzle of a pistol."[73]

"No shots were fired by the assailing column," remembered George Booth, "except by those immediately at the doors and windows, as no enemy was to be seen, and the stout logs which protected them could not be penetrated. Soon the fire from the house was renewed, and the falling of our men at once disclosed that the chinking between the logs was being pushed out, and from the ground floor of the church its defenders were dealing death and destruction."[74]

Booth was standing with his back pressed up against the log wall when the muzzle of a musket suddenly and forcefully broke through the chinking behind him, painfully pushed aside his shoulder, and fired, just missing him. Barely did he breathe a sigh of relief at the narrow escape, however, when another bullet tore into his leg and he went down.[75]

"Where are the pioneers?!" men called out as the minutes at the church seemed to stretch into eternity. Presently, their question was answered when men came up with axes, and others arrived with tied up bundles of straw they bravely had rolled in front of them to the church. "Then came the ringing blows of the axe," said George Booth, "as door and window were assailed and battered." When the window nearest to Captain Bond gave way, the men quickly lit a large bundle and threw it in.[76]

Now came cries of "Where are the pioneers? Bring up the powder! Where is the powder?" But these demands unnervingly went unanswered.[77]

Meanwhile, Lt. Colonel White, having kept his men close to the mountainside until he saw the Marylanders begin their sprint for the Yankee stronghold, gave the order for his Virginians to charge. The transformation from partisan ranger to regular service had been difficult for White. He disliked discipline and paperwork, preferring the battlefield to the parade ground. This was the moment for which he lived. A wild dash, and he and his men reached the church. Their arrival on the scene, however, caused a most unfortunate confusion. In the frenzied darkness, the Marylanders and Virginians fired a few shots into each other, causing some casualties, before each realized their mistake.[78]

Now Colonel White, seeing the lit bundles of straw being thrown into the building, added his desperate calls for the powder, but for some as yet unexplained reason "it failed to come." The keg, it turned out, proved too heavy to transport all the way to the church, particularly when under fire from the enemy.[79]

This did not, however, prevent the rumor of its arrival. "Look out for the powder!" someone yelled. Many took this as the promised signal, which nearly resulted in a panicky stampede.[80]

The entire enterprise might then have failed but for the resourceful action of Private Thomas E. Tippett (who at Warrenton had enlisted in Company A of White's battalion on March 11, 1862). Apparently on his own initiative, he climbed the church chimney and set fire to the roof. So quickly and fiercely did the flames tear through the dry timber that at about 9 p.m., a half hour after the storming party had set off, the church roof caved in. The Yankees on the second floor scrambled down to the first, making it obvious to everyone that it was a matter of time before the ceiling collapsed upon them. Wallace finally put out a flag of truce, but in the darkness and confusion apparently no one saw it. He then assumed that the Confederates meant to show no mercy. He ordered his men to fix bayonets. "If they will not give us quarter," he shouted out to them, "we will die like men!"[81]

Unaware of the flag of truce, the Marylanders continued their forceful blows on the door until it slowly gave way, whereupon twenty-five year old Sergeant-Major Edward Johnson (Co. A, First Maryland) forced his way inside. Momentarily alone with the Yankees, Johnson nonetheless bravely demanded their surrender. Presently the door behind him collapsed and dozens of his comrades rushed in to back up his demand. "We surrender!" the Yankees loudly called out between smoke-choked coughs.[82]

Lying on the ground, the wounded George Booth took comfort in those desperate pleas before he lost consciousness. "[T]he last sight that I recall," he later wrote, "was in the very height of the scene, when cries of 'Surrender!' were ringing in my ears, and the light of the blazing fire, together with the brilliancy of the moon, made clear the ground surrounding the church, which was white with the forms of our brave boys who had fallen."[83]

At last, Wallace and his men gave up, but not before they performed one final act of defiance by throwing their weapons into the flames. Immediately upon their surrender, Lt. Colonel White took his battalion over to the schoolhouse, where they easily captured the men of the Fourteenth West Virginia. (Smith, however, claimed that he continued to resist until he, too, was burned out.)[84]

While the Federals, characterized by Captain Bond as "two companies of Chicago Irishmen well primed with whiskey," filed out of the church they received from their captors an angry wave of verbal abuse complete with curses and threats for not surrendering sooner. "Under the circumstances," recalled Bond, "our men were much incensed, and it was all I could do to protect the prisoners, and one I know was killed."[85]

Watching from a distance, nineteen-year-old Lieutenant John Monroe Blue of the Eleventh Virginia actually feared for the captured Yankees. Born near Romney, the oldest of six children, Blue grew up on a farm along the South Branch of the Potomac. "When they ... heard the revengeful threats of the Marylanders," he recalled in reference to the Chicagoans, "although they were no doubt brave men, yet many of them turned pale and quaked with fear, expecting, no doubt, to be massacred at any moment. It really looked for a few moments as though those Marylanders could not be restrained."[86]

At least one of Blue's angry comrades wanted to see the Marylanders' threats turned into action. "[I]f I could have had my way," Major Ball of the Eleventh wrote his wife, "they [the Yankees] should all have 'gave up.'"

Fortunately for Wallace and his men, General Jones quickly came up. "Boys," he called out to his angry soldiers, "these men have thrown down their arms and must be protected and treated as prisoners. It would be cowardly to do otherwise, these men have done their duty as brave men and what I hope you would do. These men must be cared for.'"[88]

Wallace then quietly surrendered his revolver to Captain Bond, who subsequently carried the weapon through till then end of the war. Lieutenant Blue maintains that the Chicagoan then offered something more. "The Yankee captain said he was sorry that they had fired on us and if they had known anything of our number would not have done so. They supposed that they were attacked by Capt. McNeill's company, as they had expected to be at any time."[89]

However diplomatic, if not dubious, may have been the apology offered by the man who only moments ago had declared of his enemy, "I don't care if he has millions," Wallace and his fellow Irishmen in this last attack had taken the lives of at least three Confederates, two from the First Maryland — Color Corporal Robert W. Carvil of Company B and Private Sam Dorsey of Company C, and from White's battalion, twenty-year-old Sergeant Kenneth (or Kennedy) Grogan, shot in the chest. Grogan had sneaked away from his own reserve Company F to fight by the side of his brother Robert of Company C, who also fell wounded. "I heard that General Jones had some Yankees up here in a box and you fellows were going to take the lid off," Kenneth had told some of his brother's inquiring comrades to explain why he had come over to their company, "and I thought I would go along."[90]

Moreover, the wounded included Major Brown, Adjutant George W. Booth, and Captain Roger C. Smith. Brown had been shot in the leg, the entrance and exit wound only two inches apart. He would remain on duty, however, supposedly not even examining the wound, until he reached Buckhannon, 168 miles later, whereupon he finally "started for home on the earnest solicitation of Dr. [R.P.] Johnson." (As a Lt. Col., Brown would be killed in action on the South Anna River, June 1, 1864.)[91]

Jones reported his total loss at Greenland Gap as seven killed and twenty-two wounded. The Compiled Service Records in the National Archives, however, show a loss of nine killed and thirty-eight wounded.

First Maryland Battalion
  Killed: Cpl. Robert Carvil, Co. B
      Pvt. Sam Dorsey, Co. C
      Pvt. John Spencer, Co. E
      Pvt. G. Frank Swamley, Co. D
  Wounded: Maj. Ridgley Brown, in the leg
      Capt. Roger C. Smith, in the arm
      Lt. George W. Booth, in the leg
      Lt. James A.V. Pue
      Lt. Edward Beatty
      9 pvts. (including Charles Lambden, Co. D)

Sixth Virginia Cavalry
  Wounded: Surgeon James S. Lewis

Seventh Virginia Cavalry
  Killed: Pvt. Clinton Fletcher, Co. A
      Pvt. Charles A. Holmes, Co. A
      Pvt. Lorenzo D. Elbon, Co. K
      13 horses

Wounded: Col. Richard H. Dulany, severe arm wound
                  2nd Lt. Phillip P. Kenon (or Kennedy), Co. B, slight leg wound
                  Pvt. Henry Mason, Co. B, slight leg wound
                  Sgt. Samuel E. Baily, Co. D, serious abdomen wound
                  Pvt. William L. Dulaney, Co. D
                  Pvt. James A. Rogers, Co. D
                  Pvt. Joseph Rogers, Co. D
                  Pvt. J.T. Dunlop, Co. G
                  Pvt. Isaac S. Pennypacker, Co. H, serious lung wound
                  Cpl. William Funkhouser, Co. K, right shoulder
                  3 other men and 9 horses

Twelfth Virginia Cavalry
Killed: Pvt. James A. Flynn, the regiment's only
                  fatality on the entire raid
Wounded: 4 pvts. in Co. G, including Albert Swindler, shot in the thigh

Thirty-fifth Virginia Battalion
Killed: Sgt. Kenneth Grogan, Co. F
Wounded: Pvt. F. Foley, Co. A
                  Pvt. Thomas Spates, Co. A
                  Pvt. F. Williams, Co. B
                  Pvt. S. Fouch, Co. C
                  Pvt. M. Foster, Co. C
                  Pvt. M. Rhodes, Co. E
                  Sgt. Thrift, Co. F
                  Pvt. Robert Grogan, Co. C[92]

Though Private Edward R. Rich of the First Maryland observed that "5 dead Federals were carried from the house and buried beside the fallen Confederates," Captain Wallace reported a loss of only two killed (including Private Michael Joyce) and six wounded. His remaining eighty men became prisoners, along with four wagons, an ambulance and their teams of horses. These men Jones sent on to Colonel Herbert, who would arrive at Harrisonburg the evening of the 30th after picking up 350 stragglers and forming them into a battalion while on his way back from Moorefield, "gathering up all the surplus bacon in his route." From Harrisonburg, Herbert took the prisoners to Staunton, from where he shipped them on by rail to the capital, all save one, "a noted bushwhacker," whom he kept heavily ironed in a Staunton jail. "The Jews," Herbert contemptuously reported, "I returned to Richmond."[93]

And despite Wallace's claim that his men threw their muskets into the flames before surrendering, Jones reported capturing ninety superb Enfield rifles. Since these weapons were not suitable for cavalry, however, and "Owing to a lack of transportation, the arms were destroyed."[94]

With the prisoners Jones sent his own lightly wounded men, all under the escort of Lieutenant James Parker and ten troopers of the Seventh Virginia. The more seriously wounded (including three from the Thirty-fifth Battalion) were taken to a nearby house, where they received treatment from the surgeon of the Maryland Battalion, Dr. Wilbur McNew.[95]

Some of the treated rebels, however, did not like this arrangement. "I was carried back to the point from which we had made the assault," recalled George Booth, who had been shot in the thigh, "and the house on the roadside was soon filled with wounded.... As our wounds were being dressed, the marching on the roadside indicated we were being left behind." Fearing capture, Booth and two other officers painfully took a wagon out of a shed, hitched up one of their thoroughbreds and started the long, bumpy ride back to Moorefield, gratefully receiving along the way help and shelter at the Van Meter farm. Another officer, Captain Roger C. Smith, wounded in the arm, followed on horseback. (Booth's fears proved correct, for the wounded left behind were captured the following day by Federals returning to Greenland Gap.)[96]

The mercy Jones had shown his prisoners at Greenland Gap he later reluctantly extended to a "Swamp Dragon," a Yankee named Shreve caught stealing in the countryside that evening and brought in by a rebel determined to have him executed. "You should never have taken him alive," Jones admonished, "but since you have brought him to me, he shall be treated as a prisoner of war."[97]

The "Swamp Dragons" originated as the Randolph County Home Guards, though they called themselves the Dry Fork Home Guards. They were led by Captain Sampson Snyder (b. 1840), son of John Snyder, whose family and kin were violently pro-Union. The Snyder's thus used the guards not only to protect homes and property, but also to harass and abuse Southern sympathizers, wrecking special vengeance on the Harpers, Huttons, and other families in Pendleton, Randolph and Tucker counties. Angry Confederates in the area resolved to "find old John Snyder and kill him," though they never did. Out of contempt, Job Parsons Sr. of Holly Meadows in Tucker, labeled Snyder's band "Swamp Dragons" because he believed they hid in the swamps like dragonflies. On April 26, a detachment of Jones's cavalry on patrol in Tucker County ran into the Swamp Dragons at Saint George. The two sides briefly exchanged shots before Snyder and his outnumbered men withdrew, no one getting hurt.[98]

Such was the nature of war in West Virginia.

CHAPTER FIVE

Rowelsburg

Aftermath of Greenland Gap

Captain Martin Wallace was sent to Libby Prison in Richmond. Fortunately, his captivity did not last long. He was paroled at City Point on May 14, and within a month he would return to duty as Inspector of the Third Brigade, First Division, Eighth Corps. (During the Overland Campaign in the summer of 1864, he would suffer a gunshot wound to the back of his right ear and neck.) His men captured at Greenland Gap also would be exchanged, and return to duty by October.[1]

Like Wallace, Captain Jacob Smith would be confined in Libby Prison and be exchanged at City Point in mid-May. (A year later he would face a tough fight with typhoid fever, but survive to be discharged from the service in June 1865.)[2]

On Tuesday, April 28, 1863, First Division commander Kelley visited Greenland Gap to view the site of the heroic stand, which, unknown to Kelley, had prevented Jones from reaching the Baltimore & Ohio in time to capture a train that carried to Grafton most of the officers of Wallace's Twenty-third Illinois. Kelley proclaimed the action at Greenland Gap "one of the most gallant since the opening of the war." He readily agreed with Wallace's overestimation of the enemy's loss at 104. "I counted to-day," he cited as evidence, "18 dead horses within musket-range." Convinced that Wallace and his men had saved New Creek, Kelley earnestly requested department commander Schenck, "to apply to the Secretary of War to have every officer, non-commissioned officer, and private engaged in the fight presented with a medal, in recognition of the gallantry displayed." Schenck endorsed the request and sent it on to general-in-chief Halleck. "Too much credit cannot be given the men of my company," Wallace later reported, "I strove to imitate Lexington."[3]

When it finally became clear that Jones had embarked on a full-scale expedition, the Federal high command at last began to stir. After warning Scammon at Charleston to be watchful toward Summersville, Schenck at noon on April 25 informed Halleck that Washington Elliott's First Brigade of the Second Division had left Winchester to reconnoiter toward Moorefield. "I must draw troops westward from Winchester and

Harper's Ferry," he told the general-in-chief, while at the same time suggesting that Julius Stahel's cavalry remain behind to watch the Blue Ridge and the Valley. At 4:25 p.m. that day, Halleck wired his approval.[4]

Schenck then came up with a sensible plan. Not only did the Ohioan hope to head off Jones, he also wanted to get in his rear and cut off the rebel's escape route. He told Kelley at New Creek to send Elliott's brigade to cross the South Branch. "If Jones goes toward New Creek, or anywhere against the railroad," Schenck admonished, "we must catch him."[5]

Convinced that Jones indeed was moving on New Creek, with between five and seven thousand men, Kelley on the 25th ordered Third Brigade commander Colonel Benjamin F. Smith at Martinsburg to send by rail to New Creek the 126th Ohio Infantry (Lt. Col. William H. Hallahan) and Thomas Maulsby's West Virginia Battery, "but I fear it will be too late," he told Schenck. The two units dutifully arrived on the 26th, from where they went the next day to Greenland Gap, and the day after to Camp Storm near the junction of the Moorefield and Northwestern pikes.[6]

Schenck, however, did not believe the Confederates meant to threaten New Creek. "The attempt may be to dash in on Rowelsburg and the Cheat River trestles," he wired Kelley on the 25th. Then he added, "Look out for that."[7]

To Rowelsburg

The unexpected five-hour delay at Greenland Gap made Jones desperate to make up the lost time. Despite the extreme fatigue of his command, he resumed the march northwestward at 11 p.m. that cold night (25th), now with only about 1900 men, many looking over their shoulders with mixed feelings at the conflagration left behind.

"[O]n we move again," Major Ball wrote his wife, "mounting a steep ascent from which the scene of the burning houses and the woods which had caught from them was truly grand, but the fires which made it so were the baleful fires of war."[9]

Those who were still wet to the waist from wading across icy Patterson Creek suffered terribly, as did many horses. After riding two miles the column began the four-mile climb over Alleghany Front Mountain. "We continue our long—and oh how dreary!—march," wrote Major Ball, "on over the slippery rocks of that weary, weary road, no house, no comfortable scene."[10]

They rode another six miles to arrive at Mount Storm at daybreak (26th), then crossed into Maryland to finally reach the Northwest pike at Red House.[11]

Jones allowed them only a short rest; the time had come to strike at the B&O, along which Federal reinforcements might arrive at any moment. To achieve maximum destruction of the line at this point, Grumble divided his forces. From Gorman, Maryland, nine miles east of Redhouse, he dispatched Colonel Asher W. Harmon with about 650 men of the Twelfth Virginia and the 200 men of Lt. Colonel Brown's First Maryland Battalion. McNeill and his Rangers were to act as guides, many of them having come from western Maryland. They were to ride about nine miles north to Oakland, Maryland, burn the railroad bridge there, and then proceed west via Kingwood toward Morgantown. From Gorman, Jones also sent Captains Edward H. McDonald and Foxhall Daingerfield with a squadron of the Eleventh Virginia, no more than perhaps fifty men, to burn the small bridges at Altamont, twelve miles east of Oakland, whereupon they were to catch up with Harmon heading west. With the rest of his command, Jones would head west for Rowlesburg.[12]

Having sent off Harmon and McDonald on April 26 to perform their assigned tasks, Jones and the remainder of his command, about 1200 men, rode west on the Northwest pike for Rowelsburg, the men scattering out, raiding farms along the way. After the long climb to the top of 3,360-foot Backbone Mountain, the highest point in Maryland, they came out on the broad plateau that stretched between it and Cheat Mountain. Soon afterwards, a number of rebels rode up to Red House Tavern, a favorite stop for drovers and others traveling on the pike. A hungry procession of raiders took turns enjoying the "griddle cakes" prepared by the owner's wife, Mrs. Swartzentruber, who cooked all morning till her flour ran out. Jones and his staff, meanwhile, had crossed into West Virginia and bought breakfast at White House Tavern near West Union (present Aurora) in Preston County. Mostly pro-Union, Preston voters among its 13,300 population had been decidedly against secession.[13]

Continuing west along the pike later that morning (26th), the rebels came upon three men, Daniel Beachy, C. Petersheim, and Peter Shrock, traveling in the opposite direction on their way from West Union to attend Amish services just across the Maryland line. "Dismount!" demanded a Confederate officer, "I must have these horses." Beachy protested that he could not spare his horse and have no team for farming. This had no effect on the unsympathetic officer, who then threatened to use force if the men did not comply. Petersheim then spoke up. "We people are on our way to church service and this man is our minister," he said, "how shall he get there?"

At this, the scowl left the officer's face. "Why didn't you tell us sooner?" he exclaimed. "We never molest such people." The Confederates allowed the men to go on their way, though while at the services Beachy's luck ran out anyway when other raiders stole three horses from his farm.[14]

The column, meanwhile, rode on to West Union, where a handful of rebels stole food and clothing from the store of David Ridenour. They also took a few hostages to question and serve as guides through the unfamiliar country. At about 10 a.m. (26th), the column began the difficult three-mile descent of Cheat Mountain, Rowelsburg now being less than 10 miles away.[15]

"It was a terrible march," Major Ball wrote his wife, "the ground was frozen hard and our column scattered for miles, yet on and on we go till we arrive near Rowelsburg, and then we stop to close up and rest. You may imagine how soon we dropped to sleep."[16]

The Fight for Rowelsburg

Named after James Rowels, a Division Chief Engineer of the B&O who had made his headquarters there in 1847, Rowelsburg was a small town, with perhaps twenty houses, a Catholic church, Methodist meeting house, school, tannery, hotel and tavern. Settlers first arrived in the area in 1756, but not until the railroad boom of the late

1840's and early 1850's did the town take on its name and begin to grow. The first steam locomotive arrived on Christmas day 1852 by crossing the new, costly and magnificent viaduct over Cheat River, whereupon Rowelsburg became a good market town. With the coming of the Civil War, the community took on a strategic importance that required the protection of troops, among whom were Captain Sampson Snyder's notorious Swamp Dragons, who in the past year had help thwart two of Imboden's attempts to destroy the bridge. Garrisoning the town itself was twenty-six-year-old Major John H. Showalter in command of 250 men of Companies F and K and parts of L and O of the Sixth West Virginia Infantry.[17]

Having enlisted in the Sixth (West) Virginia at Fairmont when the regiment formed in August 1861 for the specific purpose of providing protection for the B&O, Showalter became its major the following July. The regiment's companies, recruited from fifteen different counties, were strung out along the line from Harper's Ferry to Morgantown, and as such they generally lacked combat experience against regular Confederate troops.[18]

Jones, meanwhile, reached the bottom of Cheat Mountain at about 11 a.m., whereupon he, guide Bill Harper (brother of Zeke Harper), and the Sixth Virginia's Colonel "Shac" Green sat down on a log to discuss plans for attacking the town. Jones hoped to destroy not only the bridge and grand viaducts but also the railroad tunnel at nearby Tunneltown, the longest in the world at that time. He also wanted to gather forage there, having left camp with forage sacks empty, "trusting to fortune."[19]

Standing near Jones, Lieutenant John Opie of the Sixth Virginia heard the general order Green to charge across the Cheat River Covered Bridge, a fine 339-foot structure on the Northwestern pike, distant about one mile, and ride on to the town. Harper, however, spoke up to tell Jones that the town was five miles from the bridge. "Well, Colonel, your horses are in no condition to make a five-mile charge," Opie heard Jones say to Green. "Send out two men on fast horses and capture the picket at the bridge, without firing or creating any alarm. You will then proceed with great caution, until you get near the place, when you will charge, and I will support you with the rest of the brigade."[20]

Green duly sent two men on a fast ride to the bridge. They promptly surprised and captured the span's two guards before they could get off a warning shot, whereupon Green led the Sixth across and then on about a mile and a half to the intersection of the St. George-Rowelsburg Turnpike, where he halted, formed his men into a column of fours, and awaited Jones's final instructions.[21]

"My God, General Jones!" exclaimed a civilian named Morris, a prewar acquaintance of Grumble taken along as a guide from West Union. "I hope you don't think of attacking Rowelsburg; why, there are 1,600 troops there now, and more expected by every train; and them troops are not New England yankees (sic) either; they are West Virginia yankees (sic) at home, and will fight like wildcats." This rather dramatic admonition had little effect on Old Grumble, having learned from the captured bridge guards that no more than 300 men, albeit "wildcat" West Virginia Yankees, garrisoned the place.[22]

Jones and his staff then crossed the Cheat River Bridge, whereupon another local, Americus Jasper Wolfe, somehow dissuaded him from burning the structure. Jones settled for removing its flooring, which for two years made the bridge available to one-way traffic only. Jones then rode up to Green and his waiting men and presented the Colonel with a fairly simple plan. Two hundred men, including eighty sharpshooters, of the Eleventh Virginia and the Thirty-fourth Battalion, under Captain Octavius Weems of Company K of the Eleventh, were to cross Lantz Ridge and attack the railroad bridge, one mile away and "fire it at all hazards." While Weems distracted the Yankees, Green and the Sixth Virginia would rush down the St. George-Rowelsburg pike, pass the pickets in the pits on the ridges, leaving them to the Seventh Virginia coming up behind, ride into Rowelsburg and overrun the garrison. With the rest of his command Jones intended to remain at the turnpike bridge to act as a reserve for either Green or Weems, and to guard their rear by burning the pike bridge if the enemy came up from that direction.[23]

At about noon on the cool Sunday of April 26, local man John Wheeler, hatless and out of breath, came running across the railroad bridge shouting something about rebels having ascended Palmer's Knob, about one-and-a-half miles from town. Presently he burst into the Methodist meeting house with the stunning announcement, whereupon the service promptly broke up and the worshippers rushed out onto the street.[24]

Major Showalter hastily formed his West Virginians into a line that stretched from the west end of the railroad bridge to the River Hotel, his men, along with civilians armed with squirrel rifles and other assorted weapons, lying down behind the protection of the railroad embankment and some cross ties they earlier had stacked up at each end of the bridge. Some men also took cover in a nearby blockhouse, the first in a series built over the course of nearly a year by order of Edwin Stanton, whereby the Secretary of War decreed on March 31, 1863 that such mini-forts be erected to help secure the bridges of the Baltimore & Ohio. Showalter also sent one detachment to guard the Buckeye Run Viaduct and another of about twenty men, plus twenty civilian volunteers, under twenty-two-year-old Lieutenant William R. McDonald of Company L, about a mile out of town to man some rifle pits located high above the narrow approaches of the turnpike.[25]

Meanwhile, Captain Weems, with perhaps the most important assignment of the entire mission, crossed over Lantz Ridge (also called Quarry Mountain or Hogback) with his 200 men and began the slow descent to the bridge. From the high ground where he stood it appeared to the captain's grateful eyes that the Federals had abandoned Rowelsburg. Inexplicably leaving all but twenty-eight men on the other side of the ridge to guard his rear, despite Jones's assurances concerning that area, he moved on to a bench about half way down the mountain where he formed his small band and started forward, confident of having an easy job of destroying the great prize that for nearly two years had eluded all previous such attempts. Then suddenly, about 200 Yankees rose up along the seemingly deserted railway and unleashed a sheet of leaden flame. The stunned Confederates reflexively returned fire, but, despite the uphill advantage, with little effect. Under the incessantly heavy Yankee fire they began to scatter. Weems darted about rallying his men, whereupon he coaxed from them a sharp volley of return fire. That was all they were willing to give, however, and they rather quickly withdrew back over the ridge.[26]

Meanwhile, from out at the turnpike intersection Colonel Green led forward the rest of the Sixth Virginia. Upon reaching a narrow passage in the road they came under a sudden, intense fire from the Yankees under Lieutenant McDonald, Company L, with

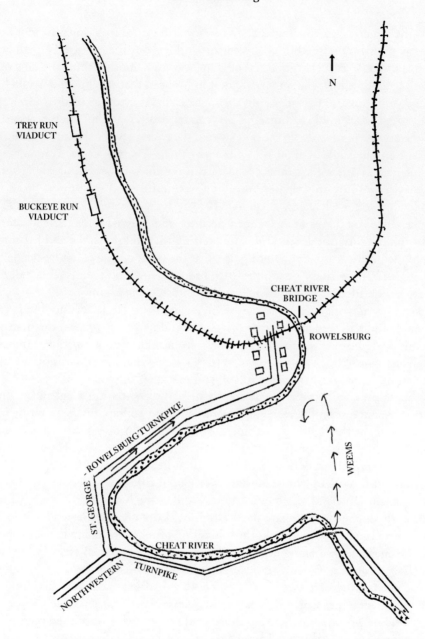

5. Engagement at Rowelsburg, April 26, 1863.

Sergeant (later 2nd Lt.) Valentine Gallion, Company F, and Lieutenant L.D. Hathaway, Company K posted on the heights above. Instead of rushing past this position as ordered by Jones, Green halted. "Charge! Let us charge!" some men cried out, but the colonel refused to listen. "Had we charged," he later rationalized, "we certainly could not have reached the men in the rifle-pits; but, on the other hand, would have been exposed to a heavy flank fire from them." Though having lost only one man wounded, a private in Company F shot through the lungs, Green withdrew.[27]

But he did not give up altogether. While awaiting word from Jones he sent forward a company of carbine-armed troops to engage and feel out the enemy. Though grateful Green had not ordered a charge, and though he was from another company now ordered to remain behind, John Opie somehow got it in his head that this mission would be fun. "Give me your gun and cartridges old man," he called out to one of the older veterans assigned to go, "and hold my horse." The veteran gladly made the exchange and Opie joined the others running down the pike toward the enemy. Before long they came under heavy fire from the Yankees in the rifle-pits above them. Many of Opie's comrades turned back, but he and at least six others made a run for the safety of a nearby farmhouse. There they found not only shelter but also a wonderful meal of "butter, bread, meat, vegetables, hot coffey (sic), etc.," abandoned by the panic-stricken family when the fighting broke out. First things first, the men decided, and they set aside their weapons and plunged into the inviting food. Only after getting their fill did Opie and his comrades return to the business at hand by firing uphill at the puffs of smoke left by the discharge of the unseen Yankee rifles. But this in turn brought down on them such a hail of bullets that they decided to pull in their carbines and stop provoking fate.[28]

Green, meanwhile, also sent another detachment to circle around and get above McDonald's hidden, well-placed men. "It was found necessary to send the sharpshooters around and above them to dislodge them from their strong position," the colonel subsequently reported. "This was done in part, driving them from positions nearest us, but they took others farther back and still commanding the road."[29]

When Jones finally came up, he angrily judged the situation a stalemate. Enraged at the performance of both Green and Weems, and also perhaps by the taunting of local man Morris about the fighting capabilities of the West Virginians, he ordered the Colonel to hold his position until dusk and then pull back to the pike. Here as at Greenland Gap, Jones sorely missed his artillery. With it he could have blasted those hillsides and driven out those Yankees from their well-placed rifle pits.[30]

Lieutenant Opie and his comrades, meanwhile, concluded that it might be unwise to remain any longer in the abandoned farmhouse, despite the hospitality it had provided. "We will go to the river bank," he told his new friends, "keeping the house between us and the enemy; crawl along under the bank until we get out of range, and then run for it." They all agreed. Quietly they slipped out of the house, made their way along the bank and then ran all the way back to where they had left the Sixth Virginia, only to find the regiment gone. Correctly determining where it went, they ran on another mile to the Sixth's new position, whereupon they readily and openly expressed their displeasure at having been left behind. Their anger cooled somewhat, however, by heartfelt displays of relief from their friends that they had not been killed or captured.[31]

Old Grumble, meanwhile, did not at all like what had happened this day, being furious with Green for allowing his charge "to be stopped by less than 20 men," and at Weems for "using only 28 men to attack while using the rest to guard his rear against no foe." For the good of the service and the sake of the present mission, however, he waited till after the raid to prefer charges against Green for disobeying orders (a court martial acquitted the colonel on September 17). Though perhaps justified in his criticism of both Green and Weems, Jones also deserved much of the blame for not playing a more direct role in taking so great a prize as the bridge near Rowelsburg. Even

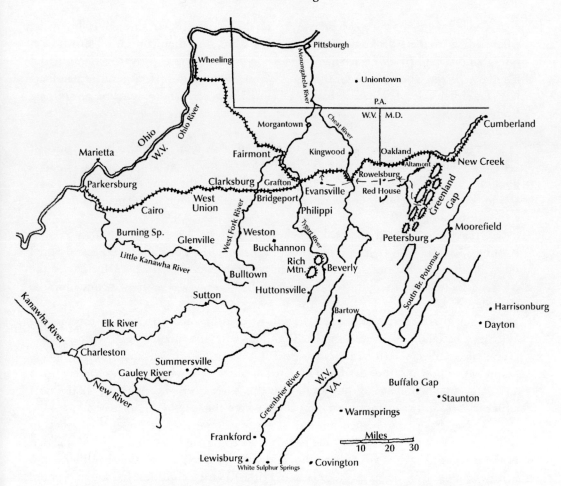

6. Jones's movement from Greenland Gap to near Evansville, April 25–28, 1863.

after the initial repulse, he still outnumbered the Yankees by nearly four to one, with no enemy reinforcements in sight. This was a primary objective of the raid, with months in the planning, and, after a brief struggle, he simply gave it up.[32]

To Independence

Failure to take the bridge forced Jones to make a decision. Having lost the element of surprise, he ruled out trying another charge on the town. He did not want to turn back and thereby abandon both Imboden and Harmon, but neither did wish to remain near Rowelsburg where there was no food for his desperate horses, which now had gone thirty-six hours without forage. He therefore decided to move on, look for forage, perhaps strike other targets, and meet up with Harmon at or near Morgantown. After marching a few miles west on the Northwest pike, he finally found some forage and camped at Red Oak Knob near the farm of William H. Brown, six miles east of Evansville.[33]

The following morning, Monday April 27, the column moved through Fellowsville, where a few troopers broke ranks to ransack a store, and then continued on through mountainous country to Evansville. "The scenery at this point," Private Donohue told his diary, "is the wildest seen on the entire scout. Lofty peaks rise almost perpendicularly on either side of the road, barren cliffs appearing in almost startling abruptness from some points whilst in others wild vines and trees were interwoven in fantastic wildness."[34]

A not so pleasant a sight, now increasingly frequent, was the bushwhackers. "[B]ands of armed men, in hunting shirts," wrote Captain Frank Myers, "could be seen on all the mountain crags, viewing from a safe distance the army of rebels, lying quietly in their country, but they seldom approached near enough to the main body to get a shot or be shot at."[35]

Others remembered the bushwhackers differently. "In passing through Preston [County]," wrote county historian Oren F. Morton, "the raiders were repeatedly fired upon by the citizens, but so far as known without effect. A citizen a little over the Monongalia line and thought to have been bushwhacking was severely wounded in the shoulder."[36]

When practicable, Jones gave the job of chasing bushwhackers to the men of Witcher's battalion, western Virginians familiar with mountain living. Mostly, however, situations were dealt with as they arose. One morning the advance of Brown's battalion came upon and shot dead two long red-bearded bushwhackers who had captured a private and a lieutenant of the battalion as they were eating breakfast at a house near a picket post, and contemptuously left them where they lay by the roadside.[37]

Bushwhackers represented but one of many reactions to the presence of rebels in this area. "Through this country the people were frightened half to death," Major Ball of the Eleventh Virginia wrote his wife, "and were hard to pacify." On the other hand, Private Donohue of the Sixth Virginia found time to visit a cousin, L.L. Hough, "whom I found to be a true Southerner."[38]

At Evansville, meanwhile, Jones became outraged when he discovered two of his men in possession of some odd, unauthorized plunder of absolutely no military value. One man had tied to his saddle a large bundle of hoop skirts and the other carried a feminine style umbrella. Determined to make an example of the two men, Jones "compelled the hoop skirt man to wear his plunder around his neck," remembered Frank Myers, "and the other to hold the umbrella over him during all the afternoon, in full view of the whole command."[39]

While the two men endured these embarrassing punishments in Evansville, Jones managed to secure some corn for his starving horses and meat for his men. He also tried to get information on both the unknown whereabouts of Imboden and also of the enemy, as "rumor put strong forces on all the roads, and the truth was nowhere to be had." To find Imboden, he sent south toward Newburg a scouting party under thirty-year-old Lieutenant Jacob G. Shoup of Company B, Seventh Virginia Cavalry, a railroad contractor in Rockingham County before the war, who the previous year had been credited with having "shot a Yankee officer."[40]

"A rumor reached us," read Jones's message for Imboden, "of your having driven the enemy out of Beverly." The note went undelivered. At Newburg, Shoup managed to capture the telegraph operator and his instruments, but he learned nothing regarding Imboden.[41]

To learn about the enemy, Jones sent to Independence, a small rail town a few miles to the northwest near the county line, a scouting party of eight men under Lieutenant Charles H. Vandiver of Company F, Seventh Virginia. They captured all of twenty local home guards by way of countering the rumor that an entire Federal regiment held the place.[42]

Unable to find the enemy, Jones did not doubt that the enemy was looking for him. Fearing news of his whereabouts might spread from the railroad at Independence, and now aware that the place was undefended, he sent back there Lt. Colonel Marshall and the entire Seventh Virginia to destroy the two span Raccoon Iron Bridge No. 2 over Raccoon Creek, located about a mile north of the town.

When about a half mile of the place, Marshall dispatched engineer Lieutenant Williamson with Lieutenant Jacob Mohler of Company C and five men to blow up the structure. The colonel then rode on to Newburg, where he destroyed a railroad machine shop, engine house, some rolling stock, and 300 feet of track. He camped that night a few miles west of Independence, where he sadly observed that the fight at Greenland Gap, the numerous horse breakdowns, and the seventy-five detachments now being used to guard prisoners, had combined to reduce his regiment to about 375 men.[43]

Jones, meanwhile, kept his men in the saddle till midnight, when he finally allowed them to go into camp a few miles north of Independence, many troopers literally falling to the ground exhausted. The men promptly went into a profound sleep, disturbed only by the 4 a.m. arrival (28th) of the detached force under Colonel Harmon.[44]

CHAPTER SIX

Morgantown

Oakland, Maryland

As General Jones prepared to head northwest for Rowelsburg and Captain McDonald got ready to ride northeast for Altamont, Colonel Harmon at 5 a.m. on Sunday morning of the 26th pulled out of Gorman, which lay just inside the Maryland border in Garrett County. Riding on a dirt road, he went north through Ryan's Glade and over Backbone Mountain at Kelso Gap. "The weather was bitter cold," recalled Private Edward R. Rich of the First Maryland, "and as we rode along the leather in our boots froze, and our clothes were a mass of ice ... all who were in the fight at the house [at Greenland Gap] being wet to the utmost, the suffering was intense. But we dared not quit, and on we pushed."[1]

In August 1862, Rich left his native Baltimore for Drainsville, Virginia, and attached himself to Hampton's Legion, though he never mustered in. After being captured near Poolesville and exchanged, he joined the First Maryland. (Rich's military career would take an interesting turn when he decided not to return to the First after recovering from a wound he received at Pollardsville in May 1864. He instead went to Washington, easily getting past the Federal pickets, and took a train home to Baltimore. Suspecting him of being a spy, Federal authorities in the city confiscated all his papers, including his diary, and brought charges against him, which eventually were dropped. He immediately and successfully sought the return of his precious diary, which survived to help tell this story.)[2]

Though few people lived along the route to Oakland, word of the rebels' approach spread quickly enough to allow most to hide their horses. Harmon's men stopped at every farm along the way, including that of John "Black Jack" Davis, a former slave who lived in the Glade near the White Church. After a fruitless search for the horses Davis had hidden, the rebels demanded food for themselves and their mounts. The frightened family quickly obeyed, Davis's daughters feeding the men and his sons tending to the horses. Then a rebel officer asked Davis for one son to act as a guide. "No, no. Take anything I have but not my children," Davis pleaded out of the justifiable fear that the rebels might keep the boy and sell him into slavery. "I will go with you and show you the road." Enjoying a good laugh from what they cruelly considered an amusing display of submission, the troopers rode off without the boy or his father.[3]

Other rebels took two horses from Samuel Specht's saw mill on Cherry Creek, and two each from the farms of Patrick Hamill and Abel Browning, though at the last place Abel's daughter, Maria Louise, managed in time to ride off on her beloved white-faced mare, "Baldy." She took the animal to a field on Roman Nose Mountain and hid there till she received word that the rebels had gone.[4]

At the Thompson farm on the Gorman road, Mrs. Katie Thompson had learned the night before that the rebels were coming. With her husband away on business, she acted quickly to save their valuable property. In a freshly plowed field she buried the family gold, valued at $3,000, intended for payment of the farm they recently had bought from the Bruce family, and by daybreak she hid all the best horses a quarter mile away in a wooded ravine surrounded by cliffs and overhanging rocks. When the rebels rode up later in the day, she went out to the ravine and threw a load of hay over the cliff to feed the horses and keep them quiet, thereby leaving for capture at the farm only the broken down and less valuable mounts. When Mr. Thompson returned after the rebels left, the couple at first had a difficult, nerve-racking time finding the gold, every square foot of ground looking like every other, but eventually they recovered the treasure and paid off their farm.

Also forewarned of the rebels' approach, Nathaniel B. Harvey took the best stock from his nearby farm and hid them in the woods, his two daughters, Rachel Olive and Huldah, wisely taking the added precaution of hiding their precious calico dresses in the forest as well.[5]

Further down the Gorman road at the Totten farm, near Oakland, stood a lone sentinel, twenty-two-year-old Private Cornelius Johnson, a farmer from Allegheny County, now, since December 1861, a member of Company O, Sixth West Virginia Infantry. Incredibly, word of the rebel approach somehow had eluded him.[6]

Most of the fifty-nine men of Johnson's company, including its captain, thirty-four-year-old Joseph M. Godwin of Kingwood, came from nearby Preston County, West Virginia. They had been stationed at Oakland in fulfillment of their part of the job held by the Sixth West Virginia to guard the B&O from there to Rowelsburg, during which time they earned from the locals the derisive nickname of Groundhog Company, both because of the perceived laziness of its members and also for the passion many in the company had for hunting the burrowing rodent.[7]

Upon spotting the lead rebel riders, Private Johnson, made aware at last of what every farmer in the area already knew, fired a shot into the air to warn his comrades garrisoned at Oakland. Then, with musket still in hand, he turned and made a scared run for it on foot through a field toward town, his boring job now providing a bit more excitement than he wanted. A rebel cavalryman put the spurs to his horse, jumped the roadside fence and gave chase. He fired at Johnson, knocking off the heel on one boot, but the Marylander kept running. "Drop that gun and stop you Yankee," the rebel called out. "Stop or I'll kill you!" Johnson wisely obeyed, satisfied that both his shot and the rebel's had served the purpose of warning Oakland. Disarmed, he climbed up on the rebel's horse and in angry silence rode behind him into captivity. (Upon Private

Johnson's quick parole and exchange, he did the sensible thing and went home. He stayed too long, however, and in July he forfeited fifteen days' pay for being AWOL, apparently an agreeable price to pay for an additional two-week vacation. He went on to honorably finish his enlistment, mostly in West Virginia, and mustered out of the service in December 1864.)[8]

To prevent the escape of the garrison, meanwhile, Harmon divided his command and approached Oakland, a village of about 300 residents, from several different directions. After capturing on the outskirts of town a small band of Yankees returning, appropriately enough, from a Sunday morning groundhog hunt, Harmon's men stormed into the place at 11 a.m. on the 26th, about the time Jones was planning his assault on Rowelsburg, some twenty-five miles to the southwest. Incredibly, no one in town had heard the shot fired by either Private Johnson or his captor, nor, unlike their rural neighbors, had they received any other advance warning. The rebels thus "scared the people out of their wits," recalled William L. Wilson of the Twelfth Virginia. "Had we dropped from the clouds they could not have been more perfectly astounded."[9]

Near the Little Youghiogheny River in town a trooper called out for a man he saw running by, the baker, Peter Helbig, to halt. Without giving much thought to the possible consequences of his action, not to mention its sheer lunacy, Helbig stopped, grabbed a handful of gravel, threw it in the face of the rebel, then ran into the bakeshop near his house and hid in the oven.[10]

That handful of gravel thrown by baker Helbig proved to be the extent of resistance in town. The Confederates quickly and rather effortlessly rounded up every man of Company O, except Captain Godwin and Lieutenant Jackson C. Saucer (both having enlisted in the regiment in late 1861), who were west of town inspecting a road over which they hoped to haul some timber for a blockhouse. "Many of the Federal soldiers were found (much to their credit) at [St. Mark's Lutheran] church with their sweethearts," recalled George Baylor of the Twelfth, "and it was with much regret that we were compelled to sunder these loving hearts for a short time." For some rebels, however, the most difficult part of that regretful task was dealing with those sweethearts. "We found the girls more pugnacious and less tractable than the men," concluded Baylor. "A very pious member of our company, ordered to arrest a Yankee who was walking with a girl, approached the couple with a courtly bow, tipping his hat and courteously informing the combatant he was a prisoner. The soldier recognized the situation and succumbed at once, but the girl broke out in a most awful tirade of abuse, which culminated in, 'You bald-headed son of a [bitch].' As our pious comrade returned with his prisoner, he exclaimed, 'Please, God, I never heard a woman talk that way before.'"[11]

In a different part of town a soldier named Wilson dealt with another "abusive" female by joking, "Don't you think the Rebels are better looking men than the Yankees?"

"You good looking!" she contemptuously replied. "You look like your moustache had been dyed three weeks in buttermilk!" Wilson just then was growing in a mustache that would become his most distinguishing physical feature as a successful post-war politician.[12]

The females were not the only civilians in Oakland to give the Confederates a hard time. Out on the eastern edge of the community lived Alexander B. McInnes, an artist who, since moving to Oakland from Great Britain in 1860, still proudly flew the Union Jack in front of his home every day. "Get off my property, Sir!" the Scotsman indignantly called out when a Confederate officer passed through the wicket gate between two tall pines and entered his yard. "I am a British subject and will appeal to her majesty the Queen!" Soldiers on the road stirred at the angry words, but the officer raised his hand to quiet them.

"I know who you are, sir," the Confederate officer replied while consulting a notebook he drew from his pocket. "You are Mr. McInnes. I have your name. You may rest assured that you and your property will not be disturbed." Still hoping someday for recognition from Great Britain, the Confederate government did not wish to harm British subjects, no matter where they might be situated.

McInnes then calmed down and, remembering his manners, politely invited the officer inside for refreshments. But with the very welcome tea and Scotch cakes came an unpleasant stern lecture from the Scotsman. "Sir, you appear to be a gentleman," he began. "I am amazed at you being engaged in guerilla warfare trying to destroy an established government." By democratic and peaceful measures, McInnes went on, the British government had abolished slavery half a century before. He did not understand why the people of one section of this country should want to resist the democratic majority, take up arms and "drench the nation with blood."[13]

If the "captured" Confederate officer debated McInnes on any of these points there is no known record of it. It may be safe to assume, however, that he felt glad to finally be free of his hospitality, wishing perhaps that he had not walked into the Scotsman's yard in the first place.

Many others in Oakland, meanwhile, gave the Confederates a surprisingly warm welcome. "We captured a few home-guards, who were more frightened than hurt," wrote Private Rich, "and were ourselves captured by the citizens. And a noble and delightful capture it was. Every house was thrown open — warm fires and bright smiles caused the ice to melt and hearts to glow, and the inner man, which had known but three crackers and a bit of bacon since early Thursday morning [April 23], was regaled and strengthened with that feast that made that Sunday a memorable one."[14]

Several officers enjoyed a fine meal prepared by Rebecca Baker, wife of Peter Baker, one of the first burgesses of the town of Oakland. When a sudden outside noise startled them, however, the men reflexively jumped up, one officer grabbing his unsheathed sword and accidentally drawing it across the varnished wood dinner table top, leaving a scratch about nine inches long. The saber-scarred table, a rare and beautiful Sheraton piece, thereafter became a treasured family heirloom, passed from generation to generation.[15]

About twenty yards from the Baker home, rebels entered the millinery shop owned by a Mrs. Davis. Missing the humiliating lesson General Jones would teach the next day to the men who had taken hoop skirts and umbrellas in Evansville, these rebels did not hesitate to help themselves to hat trimmings and other frivolous ornaments, offering to pay for them with Confederate money. They did draw the line, however, with a white ostrich plume, "declaring that they be damned if any blankety-blank Yankees would see them showing the white feather!"[16]

At the Rowan White Hotel on Second Street, Mrs. White was barely keeping up

with the demands of her hungry, uninvited guests when she happened to glance outside and notice her roan mare tied up among the rebel horses. It had been taken from
the Frazee farm, near Table Rock, where she kept it. She pleaded for the return of the
horse and an officer promised to leave it, but when the rebels finished eating they rode
off with the animal and Mrs. White never saw it again.[17]

Colonel Harmon, meanwhile, destroyed the surrendered muskets of Company O,
then paroled and released all fifty-nine of his captures, much to the delight of their
sweethearts.[18]

Private Solomon Sines, however, one of Company O's more colorful characters,
with a special talent for reinventing the truth, later disputed Confederate claims that
all fifty-nine men of the company had been captured. By "going fishing" that day when
they saw the rebels ride into town, declared Sines, he and a fellow comrade supposedly
avoided capture. His compiled service record in the National Archives, however, indi-
cates otherwise by way of providing solid evidence regarding the private's fondness for
telling whoppers. After the war Sines liked to relate the time a staff officer came to General Grant when the Army of the Potomac was in great danger. "What shall we do?"
asked the distraught officer. Grant thought for a moment. "Send for Solomon Sines!"
he ordered. Sines not only saved the army, he left the field strewn with enemy dead.
"See here, Sines," Grant protested, "you've carried things entirely too far. I only wanted
you to save the army. But you've gone and turned the field into a shambles."[19]

Harmon's men, meanwhile, destroyed both the turnpike bridge and the 180-foot
railroad bridge over the Little Youghiogheny River east of town. They burned a train
of cars and plenty of fixed stock. Because of the delay at Greenland Gap, however, the
colonel had arrived at Oakland too late to intercept the train carrying Mulligan's men
west to Grafton in response to the fall of Beverly.[20]

Cranberry Summit

Their job finished, the well-fed Confederates pulled out of Oakland in the early
Sunday afternoon of April 26 and headed west along the railroad line. Presently they
came upon and captured Captain Godwin and Lieutenant Saucer, thus completing the
total round up of Company O. Harmon paroled the two officers shortly afterward.
(Later that year Lieutenant Saucer would be killed by Private Asbury McCrobie while
the two men were hunting groundhogs. A "large, good natured soldier," McCrobie
allegedly had snapped under Saucer's persistent taunts and struck him on the head with
a mattock. He was acquitted on account of the perceived provocation.)[21]

While walking along the railroad track to his uncle's farm after helping his two
cousins collect spruce gum in the woods near the West Virginia line, nine-year-old
Parley DeBarry suddenly came upon two of Harmon's outriders scouring the area for
horses. When questioned, the boys tried to mislead the rebels, who listened attentively
if somewhat skeptically until they spotted a roan in a nearby field and went after it.
The boys then made a break for it, running all the way to the farm to warn Parley's
uncle. Together they hurriedly took four horses out into the woods and hid them under
some tall, thick pine trees. Barely had they returned to the road when they met more

rebels. The partially hidden animals were distant not more than 100 yards, but the troopers, sitting high in their saddles, did not see them and rode off. The whole affair gave much cause for excitement, which the young Debarry would relish for the remainder of his life.[22]

A DeBarry neighbor was not so fortunate. While enjoying his quiet Sunday at home, David Freeland suddenly heard a commotion outside. Looking out the window, he saw mounted men chasing his horses through a pasture. Quickly grabbing his gun, he ran out on the porch, only to hear the chilling, unmistakable sound of a gun being cocked. He turned to look up into the barrel of a carbine, held by a former neighbor, Jim Sprigg. "Uncle Dave, just let that rifle down there," said Sprigg. Freeland had no choice but to dejectedly stand there and watch the rebels take all of his animals.[23]

Harmon, meanwhile, now began for the first time to have trouble with bushwhackers. After crossing Cheat Mountain into West Virginia, his advance came under a sudden, intense fire, whereupon the 1st Squadron of the Twelfth charged into the woods from where the shots had come. "We caught nine men dressed in Yankee clothing," noted twenty-three-year-old Frederick County, Virginia, native Jacob Brumbock of Company C, "which were Yankees, I suppose [eight soldiers and one civilian]." Had these men not been in "Yankee clothing" their fate might have been far less fortunate than the parole extended to them by Harmon.[24]

The rebel column then rode onto Cranberry Summit (present Terra Alta), about eight miles west of Oakland. Having been forewarned, unlike at Oakland, of the raiders' approach, about twenty home guard citizens volunteered under a sergeant to help man a defensive line hastily set up at a sawmill just east of town.

From a distance, Harmon easily observed the makeshift line. He formed his men for attack and cautiously approached.

The sergeant on the line had instructed his nervous volunteers to wait for his signal to open fire. Two, however, Benjamin Shaw and Mathias Stuck, the Preston County Deputy Sheriff and a staunch Unionist, did not wait. They sent two bullets whizzing toward Harmon's men, one grazing the shoulder of Lieutenant Edmund P. Zane, a native of Wheeling. The Confederates paused for a brief moment, then charged. The volunteers promptly scattered and ran toward town after having fired only two unauthorized shots in defense of their community.[25]

The rebels rushed forward and rather easily swept up the town's would-be defenders. Four Confederates went after Stuck. They fired at him seven shots altogether, one bullet passing close by his right side, and another over his shoulder. "Throw down that gun," the pursuers called out. "I won't do it," the deputy sheriff shouted back, "you may take it, but I won't throw it down!"

The rebels did just that. They overtook Stuck, disarmed him, and tied his hands behind his back. "If my hands weren't tied and I had a gun," he defiantly cried out, impetuous with his mouth as he had been with his rifle, "I'd blow your heart out!"

The rebels took him back to Colonel Harmon, who ominously ordered the hot head to stand upon one of four nearby stumps. But with his hands tied, Stuck, who now was in no hurry anyway, was unable to step up without losing his balance. "Help him," Harmon ordered one of his men, and presently the prisoner stood alone above the ground.

"Do you hold any office under the restored government of Virginia?" Harmon sternly asked him.

"I am deputy sheriff of Preston County," replied Stuck, in full awareness of the hostile attitude Confederates held for his position.

"Have you any papers or any item else belonging to your office?" Harmon asked. Stuck said that he did not.

"What will you do with him?" asked Lieutenant Zane, the same whose shoulder had been grazed by a bullet, possibly if not probably fired by Stuck, in light of this information. "Shoot him," Harmon coldly replied.

Overhearing the Colonel's pronouncement, Stuck remained as defiant as ever. He loudly called Harmon and his men cowards for shooting down a man while his hands were tied. This last outburst produced a surprising effect on the colonel. He paused for a moment. "A man that has as much pluck as that," he suddenly told Lieutenant Zane, "I will take to Richmond and have him tried for treason for holding office under the government of West Virginia." Harmon told a little boy standing nearby, John Taylor, to untie the hands of the prisoner, whereupon Stuck's captors quietly acknowledged him as something of a hero, calling him by name and asking him how he was.[26]

Meanwhile, because its citizens had offered resistance, token as it may have been, the rebels felt justified in destroying not only the town's railroad property, including the depot, but also in ransacking its few retail businesses, especially the Nutter & Jones General Store. After severely damaging that place they threw into the street several bolts of fabric, over which they took much delight in pouring several gallons of molasses. Before destroying the telegraph office, Lieutenant Zane made a special point of having the telegraph operator send a defiant message to his hometown of Wheeling by way of announcing that it was he, Zane, who had burned the office. Then after paroling all the prisoners, except the hapless Stuck, Harmon moved out.[27]

Though the colonel obviously admired Stuck's "pluck," he had no intention of treating the deputy sheriff like a hero. He instead preferred to humiliate by placing the hot head on a saddleless horse, retying his hands and leaving him hatless while riding with the column in the hot sun.

Stuck remained undaunted. From a sympathetic rebel cavalryman he asked for and got a shade-providing hat, one of three taken from the store of Nutter & Jones. Then, when about 3/4 of a mile from town, he began demanding to see Colonel Harmon. Mindful of Stuck's luck thus far, the troopers advised him that the less said the better. The hot head so annoyed the soldiers with loud, persistent demands, however, that to shut him up they finally took him to see the colonel. "Stuck," chided Harmon, "you don't like to ride bareback do you?"

"Untie me, colonel," Stuck pleaded, "and treat me like a white man!" After the two rode on a bit further, Harmon's heart somehow finally softened, Stuck claimed by the exchange of secret Odd Fellow signals. When about three miles out from Cranberry Summit, he released the prisoner with the admonition that Confederates had better not catch him again. Stuck replied that he could give no assurances of not fighting them. "I don't blame you," said Harmon sympathetically.

Stuck turned to ride back to Cranberry, when a rebel reached out and swiped his hat. The West Virginian promptly complained to Harmon, who ordered the hat returned. As Stuck then rode back along the column the soldiers could not believe their eyes. "How did you get away from the Colonel?" they repeatedly asked. "That is between the Colonel and myself," he replied. Even more surprised to see the deputy sheriff were his friends and neighbors when he rode back into town.[28]

To Morgantown

Harmon, meanwhile on this busy day (26th), rode about nine miles on to Albrightsville on Cheat River, where he ordered his men to use axes to cut the cables of the turnpike suspension bridge in retaliation for being fired upon by citizens in the hills. He then allowed his stiff, sore, exhausted men to at last get some sleep for the first time in thirty hours.[29]

The following morning, Monday the 27th, they rode three miles on toward Kingwood, the seat of Preston County, arriving about the time Jones neared Fellowsville some fifteen miles to the southwest. To determine its attitude before entering, Harmon sent ahead Captain Frank Bond's company to scout Kingwood. The Marylanders found no enemy, and the town seemed to be deserted of men. Harmon entered at 9 a.m. "Here we found some 'secesh,'" recorded Sergeant O.P. Horn of Company H, Twelfth Virginia. Despite the fact that two or three shots had been fired upon them as they entered the town, Harmon enforced strict rules of behavior on his men. He placed a guard over the store of James C. McGrew. He protected the courthouse and stopped a soldier from chopping down its flagpole. "I did not come here to make war on flagpoles," he declared. He did, however, scour the area for horses, sending his men as far as the Pennsylvania line, some twenty miles, in search of suitable animals to "purchase."[30]

Also on the morning of the 27th, W.P. Willard, the supervisor of trains on the B&O in western Virginia, bravely rode an engine east from Grafton to determine how much of the line remained open. He went as far as Cranberry without trouble, but on the way back a squad of Harmon's rebel cavalry gave chase. Willard put on full throttle and escaped.[31]

After feeding his men and horses, meanwhile, Harmon moved on from Kingwood, heading for Morgantown, twenty-two miles to the northwest. Along the way, the column "took all the horses within its reach." In a grove near Reedsville, nine miles northwest of Kingwood, the men discovered and carried away a cache of goods owned by a Mr. Heidelberg, an unfortunate local storeowner who had done a poor job of hiding his merchandise.[32]

The Maryland battalion went first, with perhaps a two-hour lead on the rest of the column. On their approach to Morgantown, the decidedly pro-Union county seat of Monongalia, population about 13,000, the Marylanders received word that several hundred citizens of the town had armed themselves, apparently determined to offer resistance.[33]

That morning, several citizens of Kingwood had arrived in town to excitedly report that 5,000 rebels were headed this way, an estimate based on the 500 campfires they had counted the night before. "It was court day," reported the Morgantown *Monitor*, a new newspaper in town started only two months before by George C. Sturgiss and William P. Willey, mere boys in their early twenties, "and by 10 o'clock some 500 people were in town." The news gave cause for much excitement, and immediately many of the town's more prominent citizens prepared to leave. The fleeing included U.S. Senator Waitman Wiley, who was home in Morgantown for the opening of the circuit court's spring term. With a man named Price, he escaped across Collins Ferry, eventually going on to Washington D.C. The M&M Bank president, George Hagans, also left, as did the cashier, John Wagner, who carried with him the bank's funds.[34]

The remaining "prominent citizens" hurriedly called an emergency meeting at the courthouse, where they agreed to send out men to determine the number of rebels approaching. If the enemy numbered fewer than 100, they decided, the citizens would resist and defend the town. Colonel James Evans of the Seventh West Virginia Infantry, apparently home on leave, offered to lead a scouting party of ten men (including himself).[35]

Evans, however, found it difficult to get volunteers. After nearly an hour, he secured only six—J.J. Jenkins, Kinsey Fife, Evans D. Fogle, John Holland, Peter Hess, and Sylvanus Pierpont. They mounted up and rode out southeast on the Kingwood turnpike, Holland and Hess going up the Forge Road.

After a short ride, the four men came to the foot of a rising piece of ground. Not wishing to be unpleasantly surprised by what might be on the other side, they halted and sent Jenkins ahead to have a look. Moments after disappearing over the rise, he reappeared in the company of several men. By a prearranged signal, Jenkins raised his hat to indicate that he was among rebels.

"It was but the work of a second to 'bout face,'" reported the *Monitor*, "run, and down the hill they came like a thunder-gust." The rebels tore after them. On swifter horses, Fogle and Pierpont pulled away from the seemingly doomed Evans and Fife. Luckily, however, the two slower riders cleverly dismounted before the rebels came over the next rise, and led their horses into the woods from where they watched the troopers thunder past in pursuit of Fogle and Pierpont. Evans and Fife then made their way through the woods to Cheat River and safely followed it back into Morgantown. Likewise, soon after giving chase, the rebels forgot about Jenkins, who then slipped off into the woods and made his way back to Morgantown.

For two miles, meanwhile, the rebels pursued Fogle and Pierpont, but they got no closer than about seventy yards and finally gave up at the George Dorsey farm, some two miles from Morgantown.

Fogle, Pierpont, and then Jenkins came roaring into town to excitedly report that the rebels were "numberless" and only two miles away. Near panic engulfed the citizens. "The rebels are coming, Sally Ann!" one citizen called out to his wife. "The rebels are coming to town. Get out the Bible and let us have prayer!"[36]

Many others sought comfort not in the Bible but in hurriedly leaving by any means available. "Such skedaddling was hardly ever seen," resident Sarah Jane Lough wrote her sister Eliza. "The bridge [over Cheat river] was full from end to end as they passed. There were from 1500 to 5000." Hundreds of horses went with them. "There were strings of men went past here with horses," observed Sarah Lough, "sometimes sixteen to twenty at one time."[37]

Captain Frank Bond, meanwhile, obtained Major Brown's permission to ride into Morgantown under a flag of truce. With only one other trooper, the captain came in about 1 p.m. A delegation promptly met them and declared the town surrendered. Having heard of their wish to defend the place, Bond demanded that the citizens deposit their arms in the courthouse. The delegation readily agreed to comply, and the two rebels rode out of town.[38]

A half hour later, Major Brown rode in with about eighty men. He promptly ordered destroyed the weapons deposited at the courthouse, and, obviously still uneasy about what might be a volatile situation, he posted guards on the streets to prevent surprise attacks or rioting.[39]

"We surrendered to so few?" some in town indignantly grumbled. "Had we not agreed to defend the place if the enemy numbered less than 100?" The indignation, however, quickly turned into submission when Colonel Harmon around 5 p.m. (27th) rode in at the head of several hundred men.[40]

The Confederates received a chilly reception. "This was the meanest Union hole we have yet been in," observed William Wilson of the Twelfth Virginia. With great satisfaction the Virginians tore the Federal flag from the pole near the courthouse and replaced it with the stars and bars. "I was an accessory before, in, and after the fact," Baylor of the Twelfth Virginia proudly recorded.[41]

As promised by Captain Bond, the Confederate occupation of Morgantown was, for the most part, orderly. No great looting or destruction of private property occurred. The men of the Twelfth, however, did burn the personal library of "Governor" Pierpont. They did some drinking in the local bars, and two members of Company B "were with some difficulty prevented from fighting a duel in the street of the town over the charms of one of its fair ladies."[42]

While squads of soldiers scoured the town and surrounding country for horses, others went in search of food, going from house to house and visiting the taverns. "They went into peoples' houses," wrote Sarah Lough disgustedly, "and ate all they could & destroyed. They have about broken up Charles for they fed his grain up and stole all his clothes and destroyed everything in the house."[43]

They also tried the stores but all the shopkeepers had closed up. The determined rebels managed to find a few and forced them to open their doors and accept Confederate money for whatever they wanted. Other rebels were not so patient or considerate. They broke into at least three stores (owned respectively by Capt. William Lazier, Charles Watts, and Frank Demain), took many things they did not need, then sold much of it at reduced prices to unscrupulous citizens. The rebels kept all the men's boots, shoes and hats they could find. Lieutenant Ed Zane, a native of Wheeling now riding with the Eleventh Virginia Cavalry, the same who had been grazed in the shoulder outside Cranberry Summit, made a special point of selecting two pair of shoes "for Mrs. Charley Russell," the Wheeling *Intelligencer* reported on its native son, "who was reported to be entirely out of the article."[44]

"Our citizens, especially the ladies, talked freely with them," reported the *Monitor*, "and gave them to eat with as good a grace as possible." Some ladies proved to be uniquely defiant. To rebel requests for musical renditions they offered the "Star-Spangled Banner," or "Hooker is Our Leader," or the Union version of "Maryland, My

Maryland." Though probably somewhat bemused by this, the rebels also must have found it a bit annoying.[45]

The search for horses, meanwhile, turned up disappointingly few, the citizens having safely hid most. "They did not get any of our horses," wrote Sarah Lough. "We kept Jim hid in the woods and hollows." She went on to recount, however, that many of her neighbors, particularly those with Southern sympathies, had not been so fortunate. "All the Union men hid their horses," she wrote, "but the Secesh were so confident they said they were not going to hide their horses, but [the rebels] took all the horses that were not hid or all they could find. They took one from Mr. Stewart that he had paid $130 for the week before. They took the last horse that old Jimmy Brand had. They took two from Martin Fox, [including] that big bold face that he had. [Bank president George M.] Hagan wanted to buy him for the Government and Martin told him that old Abe and his abolition crew had not money enough to buy that horse, but the Rebels just went and took him. Martin followed them down the road and pleaded and cried but all did no good. They took one from Emily Arnett, one from Eddy and one from Yost and 3 from N. Stewart and I don't know how many from the Barkers but they got one back. One from Aunt Mary Arnett. They went to Fogles and Finnels but did not find any horses home. They took 2 from R. Finnels and one from Jim Snyder [and] 2 from Charles Brand." To the surprise of Sarah Lough and many others, the rebels even "took all the mares that had colts and left the colts in the field."[46]

Harmon was supposed to meet Jones in Morgantown, but having not heard from the general he decided about sundown to leave the unfriendly place. He stopped to rest seven miles south of there, then at 2 a.m. (28th) pushed on to Independence, where two hours later he came upon the camp of Old Grumble.[47]

Altamont

As Colonel Harmon set out from Gorman, Maryland, early on the 26th, thirty-year old Captain Edward H. McDonald, a merchant at New Creek before the war and a militia colonel, rode about ten miles northeast to Altamont with no more than fifty men. McDonald's second in command, twenty-four-year-old Captain Foxall Alexander Daingerfield of Company G, Eleventh Virginia, had been born at Westwood in Rockingham County. Daingerfield grew up in Warm Springs, studied law in San Francisco with his brother, initially opposed secession, but promptly joined the service when the war broke out. At Orange Court House in August 1862, he suffered a saber cut to the head and a gun shot wound, was captured and exchanged.[48]

While ascending a hill on the road to Altamont, Captain McDonald and his men heard a train approaching the town from the direction of New Creek to the east. The captain quickly concealed his men in the woods not far from the train station. The train, ten cars long, stopped at the depot, "and all hands," recalled Lieutenant John Blue of the Eleventh Virginia, "went to the grog shop near by." The Virginians then bolted out of the woods and easily captured the prize.

At first the capture seemed worthless as car after car was empty, but then came the happy discovery of two filled with sacks of oats. "We fed our horses all they would eat," recalled Lieutenant Blue. Each man then filled a two-bushel sack for later use.[49]

After the oats, the next order of business was destruction of the train. Captain McDonald set men to work tearing up the track behind it, whereby he meant to back it up, derail it, and let it tumble down a hillside. Doctor John Daily, the regimental surgeon, volunteered for the dangerous job of driving the engine, opening its valve at the right moment, then jumping off before it derailed.

The doctor, however, either had limited experience with such things or he misunderstood McDonald's instructions, for he set the train off in the wrong direction, going forward. He jerked open the valve and jumped off. In stunned if not somewhat bemused amazement, the men watched the locomotive take off "at a rate of speed," observed Lieutenant Blue, "I will venture to say never equaled before or since. We could see the train for a long distance, as it rushed toward Oakland, through a comparatively level grade. The farther it got the faster it seemed to run until at length it appeared to just sail through the air."[50]

With tales of Doctor Daily's train animating their conversations, McDonald's men set to work destroying the track and nearby bridge. Then they pulled out of town and headed west for Oakland.[51]

Along the way they stopped at the farm of Mrs. Elizabeth Friend, but found in her barn only one sore-backed horse not worth taking. They rode on to the Blackburn farm, where they took a mare (Mrs. Friend's) from a pasture, leaving behind her colt (owned by Mrs. Friend's son, Elijah Hoye).[52]

They rode into Oakland just before sunset. To their great surprise, they found the escaped train from Altamont stopped at the end of the bridge burned by Harmon's men, its front wheels hanging over the edge. Apparently the crewless train had begun to slow on its journey to Oakland because the pump style injector, which replenishes water in the boiler, had been left open, causing the boiler to overflow and force water into the cylinders, thereby reducing steam pressure. By the time the train reached Oakland it barely was moving. When the front wheels went off the end of the bridge, it strained the connecting rods enough to bring the engine to a halt. Surprisingly, Captain McDonald concluded that the engine had been so severely damaged he need do nothing more to it. (Within days, however, B&O wrecking crews would restore it to running order.)[53]

From Oakland, still abuzz over the recent visit of Harmon, McDonald quickly moved on, hoping to catch up with the colonel. Around 10 p.m., the small band reached Cranberry Summit, near where they stopped to get a few hours rest in a meadow by the road, which conveniently contained two or three haystacks for the horses.

They awoke before daylight the next morning (27th) to find the ground frozen and covered with a white frost. "We were a good deal chilled," wrote Lieutenant Blue, "but being in the enemy's country, [we] feared to make fires." The men fed their horses, ate some hard tack and a slice of raw bacon, then about daybreak set off toward Kingwood to find Harmon.

Following the same route as the colonel, but still several hours behind him, McDonald passed through "stirred up" areas, as readily evidenced by the seemingly numberless bushwhackers who took shots at them from the nearby wooded hilltops by way of turning the road into a dangerous gauntlet. Though none of the men got hit, at least three of their horses went down with severe wounds, all of which made for a very nerve-racking experience.[54]

Upon reaching the Cheat River just east of Kingwood, they stopped at the Fairfax farm, owned by the uncle by marriage of Private J. Don Parsons and Lieutenant Ike Parsons of the Eleventh Virginia. Having lost three horses to bushwhackers, including one belonging to J.D. Parsons, the men felt justified in taking that many from the Fairfax stable. Mr. Fairfax apparently was not at home, but "he was well represented by his wife," recalled Lieutenant Blue, "who began to show blood in her eye as she marched among the men with a good-sized hoop pole about ten feet long in her hand. The old lady expressed herself very emphatically, in a style peculiar to her family in which they generally said what they meant and meant what they said. The old lady came near demoralizing the whole troop."[55]

Meanwhile, Harmon the day before had burned the bridge across the river. Though fordable, the water was cold and deep. The men much preferred to cross in the small ferryboat, capable of carrying three or four horses per trip, they found on the Fairfax place. After about twelve men had crossed over, bushwhackers, perhaps as many as twenty, opened fire from a nearby knob. "The men, most of whom a few moments before had opposed fording the stream," wrote Lieutenant Blue, "suddenly changed their minds and took to water as freely as a flock of ducks." So quickly did the men dash into the river that they did not raise overhead their pistols and carbines, thus rendering them useless until the loads could be taken out and changed. The bushwhackers, meanwhile, kept up their unnerving fire during the entire crossing, but the range proved too great and no one got hurt.[56]

Just outside Kingwood the command met a man who claimed that an entire regiment of Yankee cavalry was in the town. To Lieutenant Blue, he "did not seem to be very bright," and probably had mistaken Harmon's men for Yankees. McDonald met with the other officers to discuss the situation. They all agreed they had no choice but to press on to Kingwood, "Yankees or no Yankees." Fearing the pro-Union citizens of the town nearly as much as the Yankee cavalry, having by now been stung so often by bushwhackers, McDonald ordered the column to proceed with caution and to keep well closed up. "We rode straight through the town without seeing more than a half dozen persons on the streets," wrote Lieutenant Blue. "All were old gray haired men who looked at us in a sullen way but said nothing. We felt relieved when we had left the town some distance in our rear."[57]

With tensions greatly reduced, McDonald about mid-day called a halt to allow for a short rest. After feeding their horses and eating a thin slice of raw bacon, the men set off again, heading for Morgantown. Anyone they met along the way received the same inquiry — had any soldiers passed by during the day, and if so, how far ahead were they? None of the answers proved reliable. One person reported rebel soldiers to be only a mile up the road, another said five miles, and yet another swore they were "just around the turn." Not until they reached Morgantown that night (27th) did they learn that Harmon recently had left the town and gone up the river. About 10 p.m., McDonald and his tired command finally reunited with their comrades. "We took our saddles from our horses' backs for the first time since they left Moorefield," wrote

Lieutenant Blue, "fed them, finished our rations of crackers and bacon, then lay down for a nap."[58]

Return to Morgantown

Jones's entire command now had been reunited. Old Grumble's next objective seemed clear: to move south and find Imboden. He chose, however, to do just the opposite.

Though risky, it was a clever choice, one the enemy least expected. It therefore promised the greatest results. Jones decided to go back north into Morgantown, destroy the suspension bridge left standing over the Monongahela River by Harmon, then perhaps go on as far as Uniontown, Pennsylvania. This surely would go far in making up for the failure at Rowelsburg.[59]

At dawn on Tuesday, the 28th, Jones's men broke camp and headed north, the First Maryland again in the lead, with Company E out front. Originally known as Raisin's Cavalry Company, Company E had been raised mostly by its current commander, Captain William Raisin.[60]

About seven miles outside the city, near the Howell house in Clinton District, Monongalia County, bushwhackers opened fire on the company, killing the horse of Captain Raisin. (Raisin later received $625 in compensation; $525 for the horse and $100 for equipment.) His men quickly dismounted and chased the culprits through the woods and down a steep slope. Presently, the gray-clad troopers emerged from the trees with three men, all of whom surprisingly proved to be highly respected local citizens — Lloyd Beall, Andrew Castle (or Johnson), and Albert Robey. Local tradition maintains that while squirrel hunting the three unwisely succumbed to the impulse to fire on the passing Confederates. A drum court speedily passed sentence and a firing squad led the three men to a nearby ravine within sight of the Howell house. After "giving them a short trial," reported Captain Frank Bond, "I had them shot on the spot where they were taken."[61]

Johnson immediately fell dead, but Beall had been grazed only in the forehead. Coolly, he remained standing, pulled out a handkerchief and wiped away the blood, whereupon a second volley promptly dispatched him with four bullets, one passing through the heart. Like Johnson, Robey immediately fell with the first volley, but he suffered only a flesh wound and wisely pretended to be dead. After the Confederates left, he crawled away to safety and survived to tell his incredible story. Locals later found his two slain comrades, whom they carefully wrapped in blankets, strapped onto saddles, and took back into town. (Beall first was buried on his father's farm before being removed to Oak Grove Cemetery in Morgantown. Johnson was buried in Fairview Church Cemetery.)[62]

Meanwhile, about 10 a.m., some sixty Marylanders, with pistols cocked and "yelling like devils," dashed into town at breakneck speed. Assuming they had seen the last of the rebels, the citizens, including many who had returned with their horses and other valuables from hiding in the country and were standing in small crowds on the streets discussing with relief the previous day's exciting events, were thunderstruck with shock.

They promptly scattered, reported the *Monitor*, "supposing that the rebels were intending to shoot, burn, conscript, etc."[63]

A few troopers excitedly fired pistols, probably in the air to increase the startling effect of their arrival, though some panicky citizens later maintained that the shots were directed at them. The rebels, however, knew what they wanted. "In a few minutes," the *Monitor* went on, "it was discovered that they were after horses." The men galloped down the streets, using swords to cut the halter-straps of hitched up horses, while other men followed to corral the animals and drive them off. "They canvassed every street," continued the *Monitor*, "searched every stable, and at the sound of the bugle, assembled in front of the bank, and left town within fifteen minutes after they had come in, with about thirty-five or forty horses." Moreover, the rebels conveniently had interrupted a hastily conducted trial of a southern sympathizer whom the townspeople accused of helping Harmon's men the day before.[64]

Fearing the worst, the town authorities again hastily assembled and agreed to send out a representative to once more offer the surrender of Morgantown. "This gentleman approached in great trepidation," remembered Frank Myers of the Thirty-fifth Virginia Battalion, "making all the Masonic signs he was master of, and on being brought to Gen. Jones, was

Captain William I. Raisin (Museum of the Confederacy, Richmond, Virginia).

informed that no damage was intended the town, provided the town did not attempt to damage the troops, which greatly pleased him, and he returned from his mission highly pleased with Jones and his men."[65]

Soon afterwards, Jones's whole command rode in, completely overawing the citizens. Unlike Colonel Harmon the day before, the general promptly took strict measures against plundering, placing guards at all the stores and bars. Determined, as he

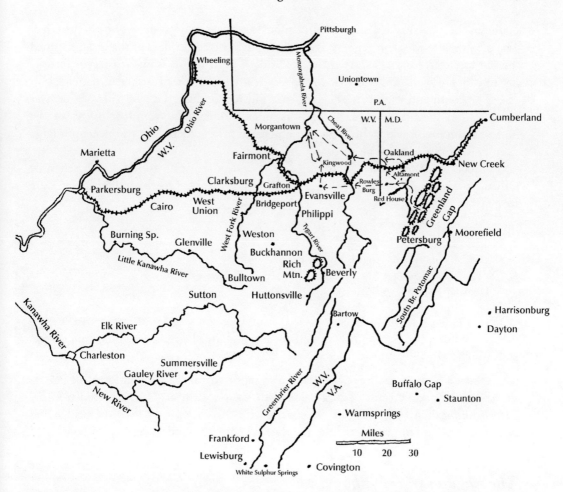

7. Movements of Jones, Harmon, and McDonald, from Greenland Gap to Morgantown, April 25–28, 1863.

had been at Evansville two days before, to keep his men from acquiring "rubbish" they did not need, Jones even compelled Adjutant Richard T. Watts to give up some calico he had paid for in U.S. money. This did not stop others, however, who secretly wrapped the precious material in their saddle blankets. Moreover, a few resourceful troopers even managed to get hold of some whiskey. "One soldier," reported the *Monitor*, "about half seas over, (a private in a Jefferson Co. company by the name of Bushrod Washington and a son of Lewis Washington, one of the witnesses against John Brown) apologized to the ladies for drinking so much, by stating that the whiskey they got here was so much better than what they got in the confederacy (sic), that they could not restrain themselves. Upon being interrogated as to the age of their whiskey down South, he replied, 'A week old, all to six days.'"[66]

Riding on through town, the command crossed the suspension bridge over the Monongahela River. For the Sixth Virginia, this turned into a very scary experience. When the regiment was about midway over, the bridge slipped off its supports on both banks and dangled by cables alone sixty feet above the river. Staggering like drunks to maintain their balance, the horses miraculously managed to get everyone safely across. The men then tried setting the bridge on fire, but the fervent pleas of the locals stopped them. Moreover, Jones, despite citing the bridge's destruction as one reason for return- ing to Morgantown, decided that the span already had suffered sufficient damage.[67]

The command then briefly rested in a hillside field on the west side of the river not far from the bridge. Quartermasters and commissaries provided forage for the horses, and meat, crackers, bread, coffee and sugar for the men. The troopers built large campfires, and soon were asleep.[68]

Altogether, the raiders, including search parties sent out by Jones on a ten-mile radius, had scooped up about 200 horses in the county. Other civilian losses were reported as follows:

Charles Watts: $500 for boots, etc.
Fitch & Scott: $300 for drugs.
Carr, Hanway, Nye & Co.: $1000 for drugs.
J.S. Hickman: $500 for hats.
F. Demain: $400 for groceries.
H.D. Murphy: $100 for various goods.
D.H. Chadwick: $100 for various goods.
Capt. William Lazier, $1000 for various goods, plus burned farmhouse 1 mile from town.
G.M. Hagans: $500 for various goods.[69]

(Private Rich of the First Maryland also reported that at Morgantown his battal- ion captured "a large train of cars laden with flour and meat for the Union troops." After stuffing their knapsacks and stomachs with the booty, they fired the bridge and ran the engine and nineteen cars into the river. No other source, however, verifies this.)[70]

The Saga of Major Showalter

The Confederate return to Morgantown generated the wildest rumors, fed by the rebels, to sweep through town: Wheeling had fallen, Fitzhugh Lee had taken Harper's Ferry and Winchester, and all now were under the command of mighty Stonewall Jack- son. "This time," wrote Sarah Lough, "no less than 70,000 Confederates reportedly were headed for Morgantown. Some of the men went so far as to dress themselves to go to Wheeling to join the Union army. If that report had been true there would not be any men left here."[71]

"This did not tend in the least to allay the painful apprehensions of our people," the Wheeling *Intelligencer* accurately reported, "and we were afflicted by vague and uncertain rumors all day, till late in the evening [29th] about 400 men under command of Maj. Showalter arrived. These forces were received with great demonstrations of joy, and were 'taken in and fed' rather more cheerfully than our people fed the rebs."[72]

After the Confederates left Rowelsburg on the 26th, Major Showalter that eve- ning received reinforcements by rail from Wheeling consisting of a company of volun- teers and a battery of four mountain howitzers under Captain Morris Downing. By rail from Fairmont, he also received Captain John Fisher and forty-eight men of Company A of the Sixth West Virginia Infantry. This brought his strength up to about 400 men.

The major knew, however, that the rebels still vastly outnumbered him, and he did not believe they so easily would give up a prize as valuable as Rowelsburg. Scouts he sent by locomotive on the 26th to Cranberry reported back the next morning that the B&O had been seriously damaged in both directions. This led the major to conclude that if the rebels returned to Rowelsburg to finish the job, as he fully expected, then his command would be cut off from help or supplies. Unable to decide what to do, he held a council with his officers. Most preferred to abandon the post and retreat toward Morgantown. Captain William Hall and the other officers of Company F, however, passionately tried to persuade Showalter to stay and defend their hometown. Their argument strengthened when word came in during the meeting that a local wealthy businessman, C.M. Bishop, personally would supply the soldiers with food if they remained. Regardless, Showalter decided to withdraw. Despite having successfully defended the place once against overwhelming odds, the major now was willing to simply hand it to the Confederates.[73]

After ordering thrown into the river any ammunition that could not be carried, he pulled out of Rowelsburg, much to the disgust of the citizens, on Monday afternoon of the 27th. (Jones at that time was near Evansville, only some thirteen miles to the west.)[74]

Though very anxious to get to Morgantown, Showalter moved cautiously slow. He did not reach Kingwood, only some eleven miles north of Rowelsburg, until 3 p.m. on the 28th. Despite having been mostly cleared out by Harmon's men the day before, many Kingwood citizens enthusiastically provided food for Showalter's command. They regaled the major with tales of Harmon's visit, and how he had destroyed the nearby wire bridge over Cheat River and taken from the area about sixty horses. Showalter did not know, of course, that Jones's united command now was in Morgantown.[75]

Showalter then led his men on about ten miles to camp for the night (28th) at Zinn's Mill, owned by ardent Union man Major George Zinn of the Eighty-fourth Pennsylvania Infantry. Major Zinn managed to feed the whole force, generously putting everything of his at their disposal.[76]

The next day, Wednesday the 29th, Showalter set out for Morgantown. "At the near approach to the town," the Wheeling *Intelligencer* reported in making the dubious claim that Showalter actually was looking for a fight (May 29), "the Major rode from the front to the rear, engaging the men, and telling them they would have to whip the rebels before they could get anything to eat. With this announcement the men pressed forward with quickened pace." He reached Morgantown around 8 p.m., nearly twenty-four hours after the departure of Jones. The relieved citizens welcomed them as saviors. "The demonstrations of joy were great," reported the *Intelligencer*. "Men, women, and children shed tears of joy, and threw open their houses and treated and toasted the tired soldiers in the most hospitable style."[77]

As he had done at Rowelsburg, however, Showalter wasted no time in disappointing the citizens. He briefly considered moving down to Fairmont, but when reports soon reached him that the town had fallen and the rebels, 4,000 strong, were returning to Morgantown, he decided to flee north for Uniontown, Pennsylvania. At sundown on April 30, he quickly pulled out.[78]

"Great consternation prevailed," the Morgantown *Monitor* (May 6) reported on the feeling of the citizens at the sudden, unexpected departure of their saviors. The courthouse bell rang and once again citizens assembled in an emergency meeting. In the midst of the wildest rumors that Philippi, Clarksburg, and Fairmont had fallen, that Colonel Mulligan was surrounded at Grafton, and that 15,000 rebels had reached Independence on their way back to Morgantown, the people were told to go home and keep cool. "You might have well as ordered Vesuvius 'to keep cool,'" said the *Monitor*, "or Niagara 'to dry up.'" Once again, many hundreds of people prepared to leave town.[79]

Around 9 p.m. the following day (May 1), however, about 100 men of the One Hundred Sixth New York Infantry, recently paroled at Fairmont, arrived in Morgantown. Evidently, these men had fooled Showalter's inept scouts, who apparently never got close enough to determine uniform color, into assuming that a large body of Confederates were heading for Morgantown. Though they welcomed the New Yorkers and happily fed and lodged them, the citizens remained uneasy. "Another restless night," reported the *Monitor*.[80]

Showalter, meanwhile, led a portion of his command up one road out of Morgantown while sending another under Captain Charles Harrison on a parallel road. Both contingents marched until 3 a.m. the following morning (Friday, May 1), when they reunited near Smithfield, sixteen miles from Morgantown. After a two-hour rest, they ate breakfast and hit the road, reaching Uniontown at 1 p.m., many men having given out on the tough eleven-mile march and being placed in wagons procured along the way to haul them.[81]

Despite receiving urgent orders from Governor Pierpont to hold his position at Uniontown, and getting ammunition sent from the deputy quartermaster at Pittsburgh, Showalter at 8 p.m. put his command on a train and left Uniontown for Pittsburgh, forty-five miles to the northwest, arriving there at 2 a.m. the following morning (Saturday, May 2). Though their arrival caused some alarm among citizens who feared the rebels might not be far behind, the men received a cordial welcome.

Department commander Schenck, meanwhile, was not at all happy with the major. "I have ordered Showalter back from Pittsburgh," he wired Halleck on May 2, "and will have him explain his eccentric movement."[82]

After getting breakfast, the men left Pittsburgh at 10 a.m. on the steamer Starlight. A ninety-mile trip down the Ohio River brought them to the wharf in Wheeling at 7 p.m. on Saturday, May 2. "The boys were much jaded and worn down," reported the *Intelligencer*, "and longed for nothing on Saturday evening so much as for some quiet rest."[83]

Around 11 a.m. the following morning, Showalter received orders from Schenck to return to Rowelsburg. "My object," the department commander angrily wired from Baltimore, "is to have you return as rapidly as possible to the Baltimore and Ohio Railroad at the point from which you left it." Showalter and his men promptly boarded a train and pulled out of Wheeling. "They went off in the most gala style in open cars," reported the *Intelligencer*, "with drums beating and colors flying."[84]

Meanwhile, when Showalter's "eccentric movement" came to the attention of Halleck, he sent Brigadier General William Barry, Inspector of Artillery, to Pittsburgh to investigate. "I think Showalter should be reported for dismissal," the general-in-chief wired Schenck on May 2.[85]

"There has been some alarm here," Barry wired May 4 from Pittsburgh to Halleck, "but I think without sufficient reason. All is quiet now. The rebel cavalry came no farther in this direction than Morgantown. They were not in Pennsylvania at all," adding, "the retreat of Major Showalter appears to be disgraceful."[86]

From Pittsburgh, Barry that night went on to Wheeling, trying unsuccessfully to catch up with Showalter. "Major Showalter," he wired from Wheeling to Halleck, "appears to have been impelled by a most discreditable panic."[87]

Barry, however, apparently never did get a chance to interview the major. Soon after completing his "eccentric movement" by arriving back at Rowelsburg, Showalter reported to Fort McHenry near Baltimore to serve as a witness in some judicial matter. There is no known record, either in the Official Records or elsewhere, of charges having been brought against him. And since he retained his command in West Virginia long after the raid it is safe to assume that the accusations against him either were dropped or he provided a satisfactory enough explanation to prevent an official inquiry. At any rate, the real reasons for Showalter's precipitate flight after a brave and successful defense remains a strange mystery.[88]

Meanwhile, his abrupt departure from Rowelsburg on April 27 had left this vital place undefended for three days, unbeknownst to General Jones, until the arrival of troops sent by Kelley from Harper's Ferry by order of department commander Schenck. With instructions "to watch, follow, intercept, and, if possible, capture the enemy," the Fourth and Seventh Maryland Infantries, 820 men of Kenly's brigade, left Harper's Ferry by rail for Oakland on the same day that Showalter began his retreat. After a 100 mile ride that brought them to Altamont on Tuesday, the 28th, the Seventh's Colonel Edwin H. Webster advanced the train cautiously over the hastily repaired track, using his soldiers to inspect the rails ahead of the locomotive. At Oakland they found the people still very "stirred up" by the recent visit of the rebels, most bemoaning the loss of their horses. Early on the 29th, Webster left Colonel Richard N. Bowerman and his Fourth Maryland to garrison Oakland while he marched the Seventh ten miles on to Cranberry Summit, which he reached that afternoon despite a difficult crossing of the Youghiogheny. Under a terrific thunderstorm, Webster marched out that evening and headed down the steep muddy mountain. After slogging thirteen miles, they spent the night around the shelter of a B&O water station. The next morning, Wednesday the 30th, they reached Rowelsburg, whose relieved citizens welcomed them with open arms and loud, bitter denunciations of Showalter as a coward for having abandoned them.[89]

Webster posted guards on the bridge and viaducts. With the ubiquitous Captain Sampson Snyder and some of his "Swamp Dragons" to act as guides through the difficult mountain paths, he sent Captain David Bennett with Company E south into Tucker County to search for signs of Jones's command. For the moment, it seemed, Oakland and Rowelsburg were secure.[90]

CHAPTER SEVEN

Fairmont

Union Response

The startling news that thousands of rebels had taken Morgantown, only twenty-seven miles to the southwest, gave cause for much excitement among the citizens of Uniontown, Pennsylvania. The courthouse bell rang out to summon an emergency meeting, whereby, among other things, the people decided to send the specie of the town bank to Pittsburgh.[1]

Likewise, in Wheeling, some seventy miles northwest of Morgantown, an anxious frenzy took over. Businesses shut down, citizens began forming a home guard, and much of the town's specie was sent off to Pittsburgh. "Post-office, banks, &c., all packing up to leave," A.R. Buffington, Captain of Ordnance, wired April 28 to Brigadier General J.W. Ripley, Chief of Ordnance at Washington. "Fifteen hundred Imboden's cavalry within 30 miles. I have no men or trains. Should I blow up the depot in case it is necessary?" (After consulting with Halleck, Ripley that afternoon told Buffington not to destroy the supplies until compelled.)[2]

That same day, Tuesday, April 28, Pennsylvania's Governor Andrew Curtin nervously wired Secretary of War Stanton that 4,000 rebels were near Morgantown, and that they were "coming into Pennsylvania. We are without arms, artillery, or ammunition here. What can you do for us?" adding, "We have no force in the State of any kind, as you are aware. Be pleased to telegraph me as soon as possible, as there is much alarm in this part of Pennsylvania."[3]

Stanton took the message to President Lincoln. "I do not think the people of Pennsylvania should be uneasy about an invasion," the president reassuringly wired Governor Curtin that afternoon. Lincoln, Stanton, and Halleck all mistakenly believed the raids to be nothing more than an attempted diversion from the main struggle then getting under way between the massive armies of Hooker and Lee around Fredericksburg to the east. The president, however, had learned his bitter lesson, taught him the year before by Stonewall Jackson, and refused to again fall into that trap. "Doubtless a small force of the enemy," Lincoln continued, "is flourishing about in the northern part of

Virginia on the 'screwhorn' principle, on purpose to divert us in another quarter. I believe it is nothing more. We think we have adequate forces close after them."[4]

Adequate forces indeed were available, but getting them "close after" the raiders proved increasingly difficult for the man who held that immediate responsibility, department commander Robert Schenck. From his headquarters in Baltimore, he desperately tried to implement and coordinate plans to secure vital areas in West Virginia while at the same time intercept the raiders and/or cut off their retreat. From Harper's Ferry on April 28, Mulligan's Fifth Brigade arrived at Grafton, followed two days later by the First (Colonel Nathan D. Dushane) and Eighth Maryland Infantries (Colonel Andrew W. Denison) and Milton L. Miner's Indiana battery of Kenly's First Brigade. Thus the forces under Mulligan at Grafton, some 2,000 men, and those at Clarksburg under Roberts and Wilkinson, another 3,500, not counting the hundreds of militiamen and home guards called out all across the area, posed the greatest threat to both Imboden and Jones. But none of these commanders could be induced to move, either in concert or independently. When prodded by Schenck on the 26th to get into Jones's rear at Rowelsburg, Roberts put out his usual excuse that his men were in no condition to march. Two days later Schenck tried to get Mulligan to move from Grafton and march into Jones's rear at Morgantown. The colonel protested that that should be done in concert with Roberts, but the burned bridge at Bridgeport prevented the two commands from uniting. Apparently not even considering the very realistic possibility of moving up to a junction with Roberts at Fairmont, Mulligan turned around the original proposal by asking Schenck if troops could be spared from Washington.[5]

An added irony to this situation was the fact that the bridge over the Monongahela River at Bridgeport, five miles east of Clarksburg and about seventeen miles west of Grafton, had been destroyed not by rebels but by Wilkinson. The colonel hastily made the decision after panic-stricken citizens came into Clarksburg on a train with two passenger cars they had hijacked in Grafton. Without verifying their report that Grafton had fallen to General Jones, he ordered the span at Bridgeport destroyed. "This was most unfortunate and needless," the Wheeling *Intelligencer* justifiably cried out, "for Jones did not even enter Grafton," adding, "The destruction of this bridge cuts off railroad communication for the present between this point [Wheeling] and Parkersburg, on the Ohio River, the direct line from Baltimore to Cincinnati."[6]

Schenck became outraged when he learned of it. "You are evidently in a causeless panic," he wired Wilkinson at 11:30 p.m. on the 27th. "Your burning of the bridge at Bridgeport is disgraceful."[7]

Wilkinson refused to openly admit he had made a mistake. "I have been going four days and nights without sleep," he offered by way of an excuse on the 28th, "and am somewhat wearied." Unimpressed, Schenck the following day (29th) told Halleck he wanted Wilkinson court-martialed for burning the bridge "when the enemy were not yet within 40 miles of him." No official charges, however, were ever brought against the colonel.[8]

Likewise, did Schenck face serious resistance when trying to coordinate efforts to cut off the inevitable rebel retreat into the Shenandoah Valley from whence they came. When he learned that Jones had sent back the rebel artillery, the department commander ordered Brigadier General Washington Elliott's First Brigade of Milroy's division at Winchester to march up the valley and get those guns. "Then I hope we may capture his [Jones's] entire force," he optimistically wired Halleck on the 26th. Elliott, however, had no luck at finding anything.[9]

The following day, Monday the 27th, Schenck got Halleck's approval to implement Milroy's "bold, yet practicable" idea of sending troops from Winchester to Woodstock and Harrisonburg in the Shenandoah to get in Jones's rear. If done with sufficient force, this surely would have posed a great problem for Old Grumble. For various reasons, however, mainly a lack of boldness, the plan never got off the ground.[10]

Halleck was losing his patience with Schenck and this whole irritating distraction in West Virginia. "Have you no troops in Pennsylvania and Maryland," he tersely wired at 1:30 p.m. on the 28th, "which can be promptly thrown into Wheeling by the Pennsylvania Railroad? The enemy seems to march more rapidly than we move by rail." Later that day he added: "You should concentrate forces on the rear of Jones' raid, so as to cut off his return. If Roberts and Kelley will act promptly, they can cut Jones completely off. It is believed that his entire force is not over 3,000. This raid," he erroneously concluded, "is unquestionably made to divert our attention from the Rappahannock and Suffolk."[11]

The hapless Schenck promptly replied that he had no extra troops in Pennsylvania or Maryland because all were either on the B&O line or south of it. "I have spared every man and gun from this vicinity," he explained. "With my troops on the railroad, and Kelley south of it on the Northwestern pike, and Roberts south of Grafton and Clarksburg, I hope to intercept the enemys' retreat. It is difficult, though," he added ominously, "to catch cavalry with infantry."[12]

While Schenck "spared every man and gun from this vicinity," others outside Washington worked to send him more. At Pittsburgh on the 28th, Quartermaster General O. Cross wired Halleck that he had sent to Uniontown a company of volunteers and seven companies of the Fifteenth Pennsylvania Militia. And from Clarksburg, Roberts wired the commander in Cincinnati of the district of Ohio, Brigadier General Jacob D. Cox, to ask that four to five thousand troops be sent to Parkersburg "without delay."[13]

Although Cox that same day told Governor David Tod that he did not believe the situation to be serious enough to comply with Roberts's request, the governor informed Stanton on the 28th that he had sent to Wheeling from Camp Chase three companies of Governor's Guards and two guns, 100 men from Camp Thomas, 100 men from provost guard duty at Columbus, and 300 men from Johnson's Island, 850 men in all. "This force, I doubt not," wired the governor, "will be sufficient to 'bag' the enemy if General Schenck sends sufficient force from the east to prevent their escape."[14]

Confederates Ride to Barracksville

Grumble Jones, meanwhile, briefly did entertain the exciting prospect of riding into Pennsylvania and going perhaps as far as Uniontown by way of dramatic compensation for the failure at Rowelsburg, but ultimately he decided the venture too risky. He cast his eyes to the southwest and a return to the Northwestern Virginia branch of the B&O and a junction with Imboden. He particularly wanted the magnificent cast iron, 615 foot, three span bridge over the Monongahela at Fairmont that had taken two years to build at a cost of half a million dollars. That great prize, second only to the one he did not get at Rowelsburg, lay only some seventeen miles from Morgantown.

Through the daylight hours of the 28th, Jones allowed his men to rest and feed their horses in camps west of the Monongahela just outside Morgantown. He moved out after dark, preferring that time of day to travel now so as to more readily conceal his route from the enemy.

From Morgantown, Jones took the most direct route to Fairmont, going southwest down the west side of the West Fork River on the Fairmont pike. After passing over Bunker Hill they entered Rivesville (on present U.S. 19), about three miles north of Fairmont, the county seat of Marion, whose 12,700 citizens were decidedly pro–Union.[15]

Riding through enemy territory in the dark, the men calmed their jittery nerves by quietly sticking close together. While passing up Main Street of the tiny village, they suddenly tensed up when a shot rang out from across the river. The bushwhacker's bullet found its mark. A trooper (possibly Thomas Vincent) in the column cried out, fell hard from his saddle, and died almost instantly.[16]

Soon afterwards, scouts brought Jones news that Federals had taken up the flooring of the bridge over Buffalo Creek, which flowed southeast into the West Fork, and were waiting in ambush on the south side of the stream. To avoid crossing the creek under fire, Jones detoured west, swung around the head of Buffalo Creek, and came back to the stream at Barracksville.[17]

Jones ordered Lieutenant Williamson to destroy the two nearby bridges, a thirty-foot span and a covered 148 footer built in 1854 by famed bridge builder Lemuel Chenowith. Within moments, the engineer had the shorter span in flames, but before attacking the longer one he received orders to spare it. For the second time on this expedition, the first being near Rowelsburg, locals had prevailed on Jones to not destroy their beloved bridge. This time Confederate sympathizers apparently had done the persuading, offering in return to provide the raiders "a coffee break and a place to leave a wounded comrade."[18]

Being now only about four miles northwest of Fairmont, Jones decided around 9 p.m. (Col. Marshall says 11 p.m.) to put his men into camp on the flat plain above Buffalo Creek, in and around the mostly pro-Southern village of Barracksville. After a short rest, he called a meeting with some of his regimental commanders. A few hours before daylight they gathered on the outskirts of town at the home of a local sympathizer. Over a pre-dawn breakfast of ham, eggs and hot coffee prepared and served by a male slave, the officers discussed the prospects of taking Fairmont. Scouts and local sympathizers had reported that the town was held by only a handful of regular troops, with a few militia and home guards, not more than two or three hundred men altogether. That meant light resistance, the officers concluded. Hopefully, the Yankees would skedaddle, as they had at Morgantown.[19]

Nevertheless, Jones decided, they would proceed with caution. "Jud," he allegedly called out to Colonel Harmon as the meeting broke up, "looks like we have a busy day comin' up."[20]

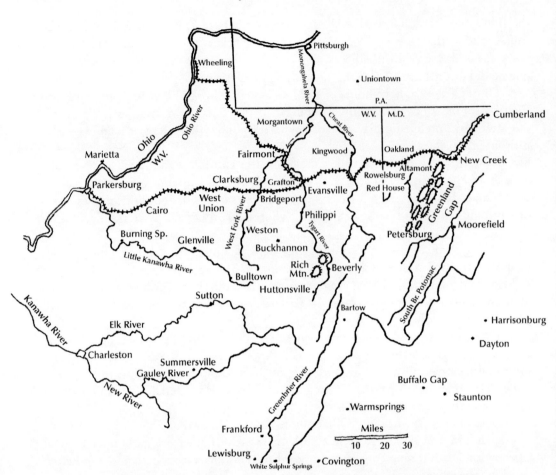

8. Jones's movement from Morgantown to Fairmont, April 28–29, 1863.

Fairmont Prepares

Despite his desire for surprise, Jones must have known by now that the Federals in Fairmont knew he was coming. Almost since leaving Morgantown, his path had been marked in advance by the signal fires and warning shots of fearful Marion County residents.[21]

Even before Jones had made his intentions clear by heading south from Morgantown in the late afternoon of the 28th, many of those citizens readily surmised that the strategic importance of the bridge at Fairmont soon would bring the rebels through their communities. Dozens, perhaps hundreds, packed up what belongings they could carry and fled, driving their livestock with them, some going to Wheeling while others went as far as Pennsylvania or Ohio. The refugees included a number of lads who only a few days before openly had boasted of the terrible things they would do to the rebels. They did not go far, hiding in a deserted mine near Barnesville, where they endured thirty-six hours without food.[22]

Many who chose to remain set about hiding their valuables and heirlooms, and concealing their horses and cattle in wooded, secluded areas, or deep inside nearby coal mines and caves. A. F. Ritchie of Katy sent his son and family horse to hide in the woods while he remained at home to bury the silverware in the garden. J.O. Watson, a buyer of horses and mules for the army, successfully hid several in coal mines in Coal Hollow Run near Fairmont.[23]

Not every effort at concealment met with success. Jonathon Pitcher rode his horse up to Hawkinberry Hollow, only to run into a squad of rebels, who promptly took the animal. Far worse, several neighbors together sealed fifty of their mounts deep inside a cave, only to later find them all dead for lack of oxygen. For many years afterward, horse bones littered the floor of the morbid cavern.[24]

Out by Helen's Run near Worthington, some eight miles southwest of Fairmont, nineteen-year-old Private Charles Primm of Company E, Twelfth West Virginia Infantry, a native of Shinnston home on furlough, was spending the night of April 28 with friends. To "avoid trouble with rebel sympathizers," he later wrote, he prudently spent his leave time in civilian clothes.

A late night pounding on the door woke up Primm and everyone else in the house. He listened from the bedroom as his friend opened the door and two men entered. "General Billy Rebel Jones is on his way from Morgantown," Primm heard one of them say, "with four or five thousand troops to attack Fairmont."

Still somewhat drowsy, Primm's friend at first thought this was a joke. Then he noticed the pistols in the belts of the two men and the rifles by their saddles. He called to Primm, who promptly arose from bed, got dressed and joined them in the front room.

Primm's friend was a member of the local militia. His commanding officer, twenty-three-year-old Major Festus Parrish, was one of the two men who had made this late night visit, the other being Charles Nutter (who after the coming battle served on burial detail).

"Is it the truth?" Primm asked Parrish in disbelief. "It is," the major replied quietly, "and a sorry truth, too."

"Will you fight with us?" Parrish asked of Primm. "I will," he promptly replied. The four men mounted up and made their way in the darkness to Fairmont, picking up en-route guardsmen and militia from Worthington, Shinnston and Farmington.[25]

Major Parrish commanded perhaps fifty local guardsmen and civilian volunteers. In Fairmont, he joined two companies, 117 men, of the One Hundred Seventy-sixth Virginia Militia. One company (C) belonged to Captain William Hall, the other, under Captain Jesse Shaw, had arrived earlier on the 28th by rail from Mannington, twelve miles to the west, in response to a delegation sent there from Fairmont. Fairmont also had a small company of home guards, perhaps twenty-five men under Captain Napoleon Altop, from the One Hundred Forty-seventh West Virginia Militia. Regular troops included two companies, 123 men, of the One Hundred Sixth New York Infantry. Company D belonged to twenty-six-year-old Captain Alvah W. Briggs, while thirty-four-year-old Captain Martin J. Chamberlain commanded Company F.[26]

The One Hundred Sixth New York, "the St. Lawrence County Regiment," had formed the previous August at Ogdensburg, located on the St. Lawrence River, and went immediately to western Virginia to help protect the B&O Railroad. Scattered along the line, the regiment as yet had seen no real combat (in July 1863, the regiment would be transferred to the III Corps, Army of the Potomac, and as part of the VI Corps the following year, it would see heavy combat throughout the Overland and Petersburg campaigns, losing more than 300 men).[27]

Also in town were fifteen men of the Sixth West Virginia's Company N, and thirty-eight men of Company A, which had been stationed at Rowelsburg until March 23 when it transferred eighty miles by rail to Fairmont. With Jones's attack on Rowelsburg, Captain John Fisher and forty-eight men of Company A went back to that place on April 26, leaving at Fairmont twenty-three-year-old Sergeant Charles Bayliss in command of the remaining thirty-seven men.[28]

Altogether, there were perhaps 325 men available to defend Fairmont. Most had seen little or no combat, and, although under the nominal command of Captain Chamberlain, many, especially among the militia, guardsmen and volunteers, were more apt to fight under the principle of "every man for himself." Vastly overwhelmed in numbers and experience, this motley group certainly was no match for Jones's tough veterans. But, their spirits lifted by the protective hillsides dominating the approaches to the town and by vague rumors of help coming from either General Roberts at Clarksburg or Colonel Mulligan at Grafton, they were determined to resist.[29]

The fifteen men of the Sixth West Virginia's Company N included twenty-three-year-old Corporal Henry Solomon White, a farmer from Monongalia County. From Clarksburg on April 22, White had been sent by Colonel Wilkinson with fourteen of his company (under Lt. Carico) to build a blockhouse for the protection of a railroad bridge at Bridgeport. Four days later they received an incredible dispatch from the colonel instructing them to destroy the span and fall back on Fairmont in order to meet the rebels coming in from Morgantown. This destruction was the incident that so enraged General Schenck.[30]

"We obeyed orders," White told his diary, "though rather reluctantly did we commence our first retreat, and that too without seeing a single Rebel. We left the citizens in a complete panic." They arrived in Fairmont about noon on the 28th to find "the town almost deserted of inhabitants and what were left were much frightened, thinking that Raiders would be in soon."

Not surprisingly, the town was filled with rumors. "Sometimes," wrote White, "the men were drawn up in line of battle — so many exaggerated reports reaching the commanding officer ... that he would think they were upon us every hour. We have orders to sleep on our arms tonight and be ready for any exigency or emergency."[31]

Around 5 a.m. on the cold, drizzly morning of Wednesday, April 29, Charles Primm and 250 or so men assembled in wooded Coal Run Hollow on the west side of town. The fifty-three men of the Sixth West Virginia formed up as a sort of reserve near the west end of the B&O bridge.[32]

In the narrow confines of the hollow, the assorted collection of men hoped to offer a Thermopylae-like defense against the overwhelming Persian horde, ominously, however, leaving undefended the two hills, Hamilton to the north and Watson to the south, that flanked the hollow and the Barracksville Road coming into town.

Huge, dense clouds of fog came in from the river and settled around them, almost deliberately it seemed by way of adding to the gloom and apprehension. "We collected in little bunches," remembered Primm, "and talked in whispers." The whispers passed along rumors that seemed to come in thick and fast as the fog, the most outrageous perhaps averring that the rebels intended to capture Governor Pierpont's wife and hold her for a high ransom.[33]

Above the whispers Primm and his comrades heard the strange sounds of mass exodus. "We lay in the dark," he wrote, "and listened to the people leaving town." Getting out while they still had time, civilians on foot, on horseback, in carriages and wagons, continued to go in droves. "We heard them talking," Primm wrote of the fleeing refugees, "and learned most of them were Rebel sympathizers, running away to keep from being drafted by Jones into the Confederate Army."[34]

Inevitably, the boys found various ways to break the tension and amuse themselves while waiting for the rebels. Primm took special delight in "quite a corker" named Johnny Bird, who possessed the enviable talent of being able to push a string up one nostril, "snuffle" one end out the other nostril and cough the other end out of his mouth, while at the same time wiggling his ears and bugging his eyes. "He was a solid Union man, though," Primm declared, as if to defend young Johnny, "and that's a fact." Bird might very well have been with the party that fired on Captain Raisin and his men near Morgantown, for this morning he told Primm that two days ago he had done some "bushwhacking" there, and that two of his comrades had been captured and executed.[35]

As the time passed, thoughtful citizens (Primm identifies Otis Watson and a man named Musgrave) circulated among the boys, asking if they could be of any help. The most appreciated offer came from an old man named Fleming and several young women, who appeared just before dawn pushing a cart loaded with three washtubs filled with hot coffee. In addition to the welcome brew, Phoebe Barnes offered prayers for the boys and for the Union, and she told them that General Roberts was on his way with thousands of troops. "What she said made us all feel good," Primm recalled, "but I don't think any of us believed it." Regardless, Miss Barnes went on, the boys would hear from her and her friends before the day was out, adding emphasis to the remark by revealing a pistol in the pocket of her cloak.[36]

About 7 a.m., the multi-talented Johnny Bird was selected with a few other men to go up the Barracksville Road to see how near the enemy might be to town. He returned in only half an hour to report that the rebels were on the road, less than two miles away. "We all knew we were overwhelmingly outnumbered," Primm recalled, "but I didn't hear anybody say anything much about it. An old man named Clayton said we weren't there to whip the Rebels, but to hurt them." Primm believed Clayton to be over seventy years old, as was another man with them named Morris. "Both of them carried their muskets like young bucks," Primm wrote admiringly, "and showed no trace of fear."[37]

Having overheard Bird's report, old man Fleming, the thoughtful coffee server, crossed over Coal Run Hollow and ran north up Jackson Street. "They're past Li'l Indian Creek and heading this way," he shouted while adding emphasis to the alarm by pounding an old horse-pistol on fences and doorposts. "Johnny Bird just got in with the news. They're somewhere 'twixt here and the Henry farm right now, riding four abreast and a mile long!"[38]

The alarm spread. Across the river near Palatine Knob, a church bell rang out.

Out near the Barnesville bridge, an old man with a long white beard came out on the roof of his house and blew loud blasts on his treasured War of 1812 bugle.[39]

Some in town, however, paid little heed to the warnings, being presently weighed down with more important concerns. These included the four dogs fighting and snarling on Quincy Street in front of Governor Pierpont's house, and the worried family living in a little house behind the livery stable above Jackson Street, whose suffering two-year-old boy would die this morning with the croup.[40]

Confederate Approach to Fairmont

After receiving their instructions during the pre-dawn meeting at the home of a sympathizer on the outskirts of Barracksville, General Jones's officers returned to their respective commands and gave orders to begin the march. "We were quickly awakened," recorded Lieutenant John Blue of the Eleventh Virginia, "and ordered to saddle up quietly as possible and take our place in ranks without further orders. We were in the saddle in a very short time not knowing what was going to happen." About 6 a.m., the column moved out.[41]

To an elderly couple living near the road at the head of Pharaoh's Run, the "whatty-whack" of hundreds of approaching hooves sounded like thunder rolling up out of the ground. The wife quickly lit a lantern and went out to the roadside, where she heartily cheered for the boys and for Jeff Davis and the Confederacy. The passing soldiers thoroughly enjoyed the support, adding their cheers and laughter. One pulled over to the roadside, bent over and kissed the old woman on the cheek. "I cried," she later confessed to her husband. "I couldn't help it. When he kissed me I felt no beard. His face was as smooth as a baby's. He was so young and so handsome, and we were both so much in love with the South — I cried. I had to."[42]

A much stranger sight greeted the boys when they came to a bend of the Arnettsville Hill. From a short distance to the side of the road they heard the eerie sound of maniacal, incoherent yelling and screaming. Four soldiers pulled out of the column to check the disturbing noise. To their utter amazement, they discovered a young man tied upside down to a tree, covered with tar and feathers. They judged by the man's ravings that he probably had been there for some time. They mercifully cut him down, only to see the poor wretch wander off mumbling to himself and wringing his hands.[43]

The Eleventh Virginia led the way on the Barracksville pike, with Lieutenant Blue and about twenty men of his company riding a short distance ahead as the advance guard. Following a local man familiar with the country, the lieutenant and his small command rode in silence till dawn when they received orders to halt.

That dense, wet fog still shrouded the morning light, making it difficult to see in the distance. Presently, General Jones rode up. He warned Lieutenant Blue to expect to run into an enemy picket within the next mile or so. When that happened, the general went on, he wanted Blue and his men to dash forward and capture the picket, so as to prevent the enemy from spreading the alarm.

"We moved forward slowly and cautiously," Blue later recalled, "peering through the fog to discover if possible the expected picket." After riding another half mile or so, shots rang out, and bullets came whizzing over the heads of Blue and his men. In accordance with the general's orders, the small command dashed forward. Presently, by the right side of the road they saw a number of men pour out of a log schoolhouse, clamor over a nearby rail fence, and disappear into the fog up on Watson Hill.

Blue and his men rode past the abandoned schoolhouse, going deeper into the hollow between the two hills. Suddenly, they came under heavy fire from Watson Hill on their right and from directly in front. Because the fog obscured everything at a distance, the Yankees did not see their targets and fired in the direction of the sound of approaching horses' feet. Most of their shots from in front thus fell short and those from Watson Hill either passed in front of the rebels or struck the fence by the roadside.

One bullet, however, found its mark. It passed through the saber-holding diagonal heavy leather strap, the overcoat, dress coat, waistcoat, and under clothes, of Lieutenant Blue to strike him in the shoulder. He dropped his saber and nearly fell from his horse. Maintaining his composure, he called for his men to turn around and go back.

In a short time, they came upon General Jones, who had sped forward at the sound of the firing and now wanted to know the situation. Blue stoically gave his report then slowly rode to the rear, convinced that he had suffered a severe injury.

"What's the matter, have you been wounded?" Lieutenant Ike Parsons asked with evident concern when he came upon his friend. "Yes," said Blue quietly, now feeling faint and queasy.

"Where are you struck?" asked Parsons.

"Shot through the shoulder," replied Blue as he pointed to the hole in his overcoat.

"Get down and let's examine it," said Parsons, adding by way of reassurance, "may not be as bad as you think."

Blue slowly dismounted. With his boot seemingly filling with blood, he began to fear bleeding to death as he sat down on a nearby stump. Parsons proceeded to carefully unbutton Blue's coat and vest. When he opened his shirt, an Enfield musket ball dropped out. "Ike roared with laughter," Blue recalled embarrassingly, "said I come near bleeding to death without having lost a drop of blood." The ball had scarcely broken the skin, but its impact created a painful massive purple bruise that for several days made it very difficult for Blue to raise his arm.[44]

Coal Run Hollow

Jones quickly deployed his forces. He set up a skirmish line with the dismounted sharpshooters of White's battalion to the left of the road and the long-range riflemen of Major Mottram D. Ball's company of the Eleventh Virginia to the right. The main line consisted of the Sixth and Eleventh Virginias on the left, under Colonel Green, and the Twelfth Virginia and the Maryland Battalion on the right (with McNeill's Rangers), under Colonel Harmon. Their assignment was simple enough — to sweep over the two hills framing the hollow, then push into the town and head for the river,

Harmon to make straight for the railroad bridge. (The Seventh Virginia was still on the road, bringing up the rear.)

Despite his strong disapproval of Colonel Green's behavior at Rowelsburg, Jones put him in charge of the left flank, and gave him the most important and complicated assignment. With the Sixth and Eleventh, he was to take Hamilton Hill, cross Jackson Street and make for the river on Madison and Jefferson streets. Then he was to cross the suspension bridge at the foot of Madison and sweep down along the east side of the Monongahela to the east end of the B&O bridge, thus completing a wide pincers movement that hopefully would trap the Yankees against the Twelfth Virginia and the Maryland Battalion, which were to come down Watson Hill on the right, cross the Beverly Pike (Fairmont Ave.), push the Yankees out of Coal Run Hollow and head for the west end of the B&O bridge. When the Seventh Virginia arrived, Jones planned to send it to the left, its dismounted sharpshooters under Colonel Marshall to reinforce the Eleventh sharpshooters, and the rest of the regiment to support the Sixth Virginia. Just before the attack began Jones told his officers that their men were not to burn any homes or mistreat old people, women, children, or men either if they behaved. At the signal, the massive line moved forward.[45]

"It was near 8 o'clock when we heard the Rebel yell from thousands of throats," Private Charles Primm, still dressed in civilian clothes, recalled in horror, "and saw thousands of enemy troops, all mounted, swarming down across the hills, no farther than a quarter of a mile above us."[46]

"I reckon we looked like about 50,000 men," Private Washington Smith of the Sixth Virginia recalled, "riding down Watson and Hamilton hills." A resident of nearby Pharaoh's Run, Smith before the raid came under a death warrant for his extensive recruiting efforts in the area. Because of his familiarity with the country, Jones the last two days had used him as a scout. "I rode beside Gen. Jones all the way from Morgantown," Smith proudly recalled.[47]

As the attack swept forward, the trooper remained on top of Hamilton Hill with Old Grumble, who clearly hoped the Yankees would offer little or no resistance and give him an easy victory. "I don't reckon anybody expected a fight," Smith recalled. "I know we were all surprised when the shooting started down at the lower end of Jackson Street between Harman's men and some Yanks."[48]

Private Primm and about sixty others bravely moved forward to the mouth of the hollow, where a sergeant of the One Hundred Sixth New York instructed them to mount up. They were going to ride out, he loudly and confidently declared, fire one volley at the advancing rebels then retreat back up the hollow.

About half of the sixty responded, the others deciding this the proper time to invoke the rule of "every man for himself." The mounted thirty closely followed the carbine-waving sergeant out to the Beverly Road. Before they got off a shot, however, something totally unexpected happened. Ahead of the rebels coming down off Watson Hill on the left were dozens of horses and cattle thought by some to be captured stock deliberately stampeded in front of them but more likely they were the neighbors' animals, panic-running free because all the nearby fences had been torn down. "We avoided the stock," Primm recalled in amazement, "which went bellowing, bawling, and nickering on down the hollow toward the river."[49]

Primm and his brave companions managed to get off that one volley, then beat a hasty retreat back down the hollow. It may have been one of their bullets that brought down Private D.M. Santmyers of the Twelfth Virginia's Company I, the first Confederate casualty in this fight. He died a few days later in the home of sympathizers who subsequently buried him near Barracksville.[50]

The rebels came on in close pursuit, and might have captured Primm and his comrades had it not been for another totally unexpected event. Several angry pro-Southern women, Primm guessed about fifty or sixty, suddenly appeared, seemingly out of nowhere, and began throwing rocks, curses and oaths at the retreating Yankees, one especially determined female even going so far as to thrust a pitchfork into the thigh of a passing soldier. "Those brave rebel women," Primm later professed admiringly, "I tell you if Lee had had them with him right along, I don't doubt one bit but what he would have won the war." This throng of "brave rebel women," however, got in the way of the pursuing Confederates, slowing them up, thereby giving Primm and his comrades just enough time to make it to the hollow, get through and escape.

"They cheered us as we rode by," a rebel trooper recalled of their female supporters, some of whom had small children with them, "and we were glad to know they were on our side."[51]

Swarming down Watson Hill, the Confederates poured through Coal Run Hollow, where, as a comrade of Primm predicted at the start of the fight, several "friends" waited in the woods on either side to give the rebels a warm reception. Surprisingly enough, the ambushers included a number of Union women, who were no less angry than their Southern sisters. Now it became the Confederates' turn to experience a gauntlet of female wrath. "The most vicious fighting I saw in the whole war," Private Primm declared, "was done there in Fairmont that day by the women, both Rebel and Yank."[52]

Private Washington Smith of the Sixth Virginia Cavalry confirmed Primm's incredible story. "Near the head of the hollow," he later recalled, "some women in the trees on our right opened fire on us." One shot hit a Private Leeds in the chest, dropping him hard from his horse. Smith and a few others carried the wounded cavalryman to safety and attended to him. As he lay on the ground bleeding profusely, Leeds told his concerned companions that he had seen the woman who shot him. "She was young and pretty and looked like my sister," he said. Leeds then became quiet. He looked around, said it was "an awful day," and died. "I found out nine of our boys were killed in the hollow," Private Smith later claimed. (The known casualties included, from the First Maryland, Private W. Miles, killed, and two others wounded.)[53]

Primm and his companions, meanwhile, sped on. "No less than 500 rebels chased us up the hollow" he recalled. While their comrades on foot scattered into the safety of the woods, Primm and his fellow riders pounded up the open flats, still following the sergeant from New York, who now called out to them to make for the railroad bridge. "We rode after him," Primm wrote, "all as fast as possible, not looking back." After suffering only a few minor wounds, the group made it through the hollow, passed through town, and rallied behind the handful of soldiers from the Sixth West Virginia on a slope protecting the west end of the bridge, where they found Lieutenant Jackson Moore and Sergeant William Hennen of the Sixth walking along the line telling their men "to be calm and cool."[54]

In town, meanwhile, many citizens, quite aside from being afraid, now seemed to be enjoying this thrilling spectacle playing out before them, almost as if they were attending a grand parade or some magnificent outdoor theatrical performance. Paying little heed to the bullets zipping by, they lined the streets, stood on porches and climbed trees to wave flags, handkerchiefs, and aprons in support of their heroes while shouting "Hurrah for Abe Lincoln," or "Hurrah for Jeff Davis," as first the Yankees and then the Rebels raced through town. "The more respectable citizens," concluded William Wilson of the Twelfth Virginia, with some degree of bias, "sympathized with us."[55]

After giving their best performances in this grand theatrical amphitheatre, the Confederates headed for the ridge protecting the west end of the B&O bridge, where they met unexpected resistance. "We ran into trouble on the slope above the river," Private Smith stated, simply enough. "We did a lot of shooting all the way from town to the railroad bridge, but we didn't do much good. We couldn't see anybody to shoot at, the fog was so thick."

In the face of heavy fire, the Confederates pulled up a few hundred yards from the bridge. One cavalryman, a Private Trueslow, however, did not stop. He rode on, aimlessly it seemed, loudly calling out for his mother until he fell from his horse, blood gushing from a bullet hole in his face. "I felt awful sorry for him," Smith sadly confessed after witnessing the horrifying scene.[56]

Meanwhile, not all the Yankees managed to reach the safety of the ridge, a lieutenant being felled by a pistol shot to the leg, fired by Captain O'Ferrall of the Twelfth Virginia. After bringing down his quarry, the captain cautiously approached, whereupon the stricken man, hoping for mercy, made himself known as a member of a "secret order" to which O'Ferrall fortunately belonged. Taking pity on a fellow "brother" he had grievously injured, O'Ferrall had the lieutenant carried to a house in town, "and made him as comfortable as possible." Under these somewhat unusual circumstances, the two men became acquainted, O'Ferrall discovering during the course of their increasingly friendly conversation that the lieutenant had been stationed near his home in Frederick County and knew his mother and sisters. "Captain, as soon as I can travel I will go and see your mother and sisters and if they need anything they shall have it," the lieutenant graciously declared in response to O'Ferrall's obvious concern for his family. The captain heartily thanked him, "expressed the hope that his wound would not trouble him much," and said goodbye. After the war, O'Ferrall gratefully recalled that the lieutenant "kept his word and promise."[57]

Outside of Fairmont, meanwhile, Private Edward Rich of the First Maryland ran down a mounted Yankee and took his large gray horse, new saber, and a revolver that Rich carried through the remainder of the war. And Lieutenant Benjamin F. Conrad with four men of Company A of White's battalion drove off an equal number of Yankees and captured their canon, an old twelve-pounder, which they later spiked and threw into the river.[58]

The Suspension Bridge

While Primm and perhaps a few dozen men made for the railroad bridge, most of the other New Yorkers, the militiamen and the home guards made a general dash for the suspension bridge at the foot of Madison Street. After quickly crossing over, Major Parrish and a few of his men bravely set about tearing up some forty feet of the flooring on the east end of the bridge and throwing the planking into the water below. They remained at this dangerous task until the Confederates nearly were upon them, two of Parrish's men getting shot, one falling into the river (both later recovered from their wounds).[59]

While the Twelfth Virginia, White's battalion, and the Maryland Battalion, this flank now under Colonel Harmon, headed through the streets for the west end of the B&O bridge, the Eleventh and Sixth Virginia, under Colonel Green, went over and around Hamilton Hill and made for the suspension bridge.

"I confess," Major Ball of the Eleventh wrote his wife, "I expected every moment to receive a bullet as I jumped out to lead the charge for they were whistling around us savagely and striking the trees behind which we were protecting ourselves with a thump that made me quiver almost, but I gave as loud a yell as possible under the circumstances and called on the 11th to 'pitch in.' The boys leaped out with a rousing cheer and on we rushed. The miserable cowards fired two or three shots and broke. On we sped and reaching the crest of the hill, there lay Fairmont below us. The enemy were now seen flying in all directions. Our charge had broken their entire line. Down the steep hills we rush after them into the town."[60]

Behind them, trying to catch up, rode Lieutenant Blue, with his new lease on life. "After discovering that musket ball," he recalled in relief regarding what he mistakenly thought might have been a mortal wound, "I felt better at once." While still enduring the good-natured ribbing of his friend Ike, he mounted up with the lieutenant and the two rode down the Barracksville pike in pursuit of the Eleventh Virginia as it entered Fairmont.

Only then, when his horse refused to break into a run, did Blue discover that his mount had received a serious wound during that early morning confrontation with the Yankee pickets. A quick examination revealed that a ball had passed through the poor animal's neck and shoulder blade.

Keeping on the lookout for another horse as he tried to catch up with his regiment, Blue slowly rode the injured beast into Fairmont, now cleared of Yankees down to the river. He soon came upon a hotel, whose large stable miraculously contained several horses. After choosing one he liked, Blue generously offered the hostler to trade his injured mount for it. Not surprisingly, the old man refused, with the argument that the horse Blue wanted belonged to another man and was not his to trade. "Oh well," Blue retorted in reference to the absent citizen, "if he is not satisfied with the trade, tell him to bring my horse over to Harrisonburg and I will trade back to pay him the difference."

Unable to lift his painful right arm, Blue directed a private (Isaac Wolf) to put his saddle on the new steed, which he named "Mulligan." "I was soon mounted again," he recalled with satisfaction, "well pleased with my trade."[61]

Perhaps it was from this same hotel that a guest, a former drummer boy in the Revolution, now a somewhat demented old man, rushed out into the street when from his window that morning he saw the soldiers swarming through town. Local tradition maintains that while still in knee-length nightgown and with his wig on backwards, he furiously brandished an umbrella while repeatedly shouting, "Hurrah for George Washington. Down with the king!" Another tradition maintains that the hotel guest

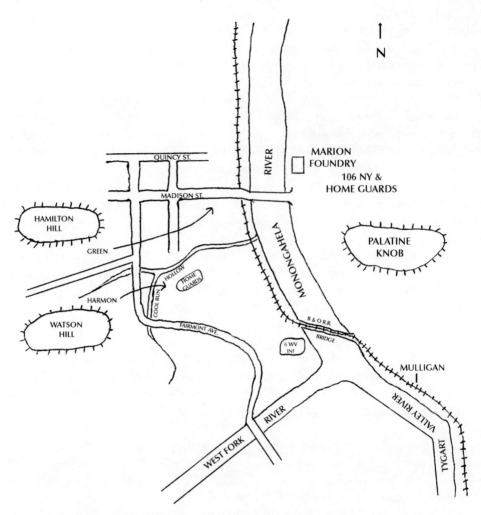

9. Engagement at Fairmont, April 29, 1863.

was a traveling salesman, who became so frightened by the invasion that he went into the street in his nightgown, with wig on backwards, ranting that his great-grandfather was an American patriot who had fought at the battle of Lundy's Lane, and that he was no Tory nor did he favor paper money.[62]

After riding over and around Hamilton Hill, meanwhile, Blue's companions in the Eleventh Virginia thundered down Quincy and Madison streets, and converged at the foot of the latter only to encounter an unexpected bottleneck.

With its floor planks missing, the suspension bridge, built in 1852 by the Chenowith Brothers, could not be crossed. Moreover, from the windows of the thick walled Marion Foundry and Machine Shop across the river, several Yankees had taken refuge and they put up a hot fire each time the Confederates rushed forward in an attempt to replace the planking. The stubborn Yankees hit at least one rebel, who fell into the river and floated downstream.[63]

With each rush of a repair crew, the Confederates, sheltered in vacant buildings, stables, behind trees, "and whatever else would conceal their cowardly carcasses from our unerring aim," showered the foundry with a hail of bullets, one of which struck and killed Lon Coffman (or Kaufman) as he and Major Parrish fired from the same window. The owner of a sawmill in town, Coffman was the only death this day in Parrish's command. His body later would be sent to his former home (Bingamon) in Harrison County.[64]

With their ammunition running low after a brave, exhausting fight of more than an hour, and with the Confederates having nearly finished replacing the planking, the out-numbered Yankees slowly melted away, each man looking out for his own safety, but generally making a run for it up the east bank of the river toward the B&O bridge.

When firing from the foundry finally seemed to have petered out, the Confederates cautiously approached. After making the surprising but welcome discovery that the building was empty, they swarmed over the repaired bridge and resumed the chase south up the east side of the river. General Jones crossed shortly afterward and set up a command post on Palatine Knob, the high ground east of the river that provided a panoramic view of the town to the west and the final struggle for the great prize, the B&O bridge to the south.[65]

Surrender

The bulk of the Federals on the east side of the river ran up to the B&O bridge and crossed back over to the west side, where they joined those forces that now were hemmed in by the Virginians and Marylanders under Colonel Harmon. "About 80 blue-jackets came across the bridge and joined us," Private Primm recalled. "More than a thousand Rebels soon appeared in their wake, and crossed the bridge under our fire. I saw eight of them get hit and fall off, into the river. I think one swam to shore, the others must have drowned."[66]

Many Federals on the east side of the river, however, did not make it to the bridge. Some hid in the woods on the high ground near the river and took shots at the passing Confederates, thereby creating a deadly seventy-five yard long gauntlet. Amidst a hail of bullets, the rebels rushed through, the men lying low and hugging their horses as they rode.

When it came the turn of Lieutenant Blue, he gave his horse "a severe dig with the spurs." Obviously possessing a sharper intelligence than his new master, however, "Mulligan" reared up, turned around and sped off in the other direction. After Blue gained control of the wise animal, he fashioned "a good sized cane" from a tree branch and rode back to the opening of the gauntlet. With the "cane" in his left hand, his right arm in a sling, and the reins in his teeth, Blue again gave Mulligan a dig with the spurs. "I fired him pretty freely with the cane," the lieutenant recalled, "and he went through all right." About half way into the gauntlet, Blue saw a comrade who hadn't made it, his dead horse lying nearby and the trooper (David Ream of Romney) still defiantly firing his carbine while flat on the ground. To stop and help him would be suicide, Blue concluded, so he rode on. "He was a very cool and brave man," he sadly recalled of the comrade he did not save.[67]

The Sixth, Eleventh, and a portion of the Seventh Virginia, meanwhile, came up and closed off the eastern end of the bridge, thereby effectively surrounding the trapped Federals. Finding the enemy positions guarding the bridge too strong, however, Colonel Green dismounted his sharpshooters of the Sixth and, with those of the Seventh Virginia, which had been unable for a while to find the Sixth, the men opened fire from behind rocks, trees, or whatever cover they could find.[68]

Old Grumble was not happy with Green's decision to dismount and shoot it out with the Yankees. "Colonel Green again failed to execute the part assigned him," he later wrote condemningly in his report. Jones wanted an immediate all out assault on the Yankee position and he promptly sent up orders to that effect. The Seventh Virginia then formed in column of eights and moved to flank the enemy. "Why the hell don't you surrender?" someone heard Jones call out in frustration as he watched from the top of Palatine Knob. Then, to the general's great relief, the Yankees put out the white flag.[69]

After a stubborn three-hour fight against overwhelming odds, and with the rebels obviously preparing to charge down upon them, the Yankees at last realized the hopelessness of their situation. Just before 11 a.m., they prudently put out a white flag, some say a woman's petticoat, while others more plausibly believed it to be a white pillow slip attached to a broom. Whatever the original purpose of the material, the sight of it now brought a cheer from many Confederates throats.[70]

"We fought them two hours and 50 minutes manfully," the Sixth West Virginia's Corporal Henry White proudly told his diary, "but surrendered just in time to save ourselves from a grand charge, which they were making." Alongside Private John S. Barnes and Fontaine Smith, an "outraged" civilian with a muzzle-loading squirrel rifle, White had been firing from a ravine near the river when he suffered a painful wound, a bullet having passed through and shattered the bones above and below the elbow joint. Worse yet, Barnes took a shot in the forehead and fell back hard, apparently dead.[71]

The Confederates, meanwhile, called off the attack. "We went to the house where the white flag was hanging from a shot-out window," the Sixth Virginia's Private Washington Smith recalled. "There wasn't anybody in the house but an old man by the name of Wilson, and he was drunk. He said he was [General] Bob Lee's uncle and asked me for a chew. I gave him some homemade I had, and we went out of there, and on down the river."[72]

Mulligan's Counterattack

Full of a relief and satisfaction that must at last have brought a smile to his face, Jones came down from Palatine Knob and gave instructions for Colonel Marshall and his Seventh Virginia to round up the prisoners and take them off the field. Not all the Yankees, however, had surrendered. Some managed to slip away, including privates Primm and the Sixth West Virginia's Joe Baxter (Co. N), who together, without explaining how they accomplished the rather remarkable feat, rode up to Shinnston, "taking 11 rebel horses, all with fine saddles and other gear, with us as a big prize." (Primm served through the end of the war, spending the last few months with the ambulance corps.)[73]

Primm went on to recall that when Major Parrish and about forty of his men arrived at the railroad bridge after their flight from the suspension bridge, the major said that Colonel Mulligan was expected at any moment to arrive by train with reinforcements from Grafton. "We were very glad to hear about this," the West Virginia private remembered. By the time of the surrender, however, many men concluded that the major's expectation had been based on just another rumor.[74]

But then while the jubilant Confederates "crowded in a rather confused mass around the prisoners," who had just stacked arms, the rumor turned into fact when an artillery shell suddenly screamed overhead from the east side of the river. The shot came from a brass gun, one of two mounted on a flatcar and commanded by Lieutenant John McAffee, Battery L, First Illinois Light Artillery.[75]

"We heard a train come thundering down the road," Lieutenant Opie of the Sixth Virginia Cavalry recalled, "which pulled up in full view, and began to disgorge, like the Trojan horse, a great number of men." By rail from Grafton ten miles to the southeast, Colonel Mulligan indeed had sent reinforcements.[76]

Just south of the B&O bridge, the train came to an abrupt halt and "disgorged" Company B, Captain Andrew M. McDonald of the One Hundred Sixth New York Infantry, and Company K, Captain Daniel Quirk, of the Twenty-third Illinois Infantry, all under Major Moore. While the brass cannon fired shots that "caused the mountains to reverberate with thunder," the two infantry companies ascended the hill opposite the bridge and began to deploy.[77]

Colonel Marshall quickly moved his men under cover of a nearby hill. He then ordered them to dismount and pick up the enemy's just surrendered long-range muskets and open fire. Several men went after the Yankees.[78]

"I and some others ran up and armed ourselves with guns and ammunition," continued Lieutenant Opie, "and we, then, under the command of Lieut. George Shumate, double-quicked down to the cliff, above the train, which moved back into a deep cut."

Opie and his comrades soon found themselves in a hot fight. For several stressful minutes the lieutenant traded shots with a Yankee sheltered behind a rock, whose bullets came "too close to me to be agreeable." The tension and strain mounted until the Yankee finally made the mistake of exposing part of his body while reloading. Opie took careful aim, pulled the trigger, and the blue-clad soldier "fell upon his face."[79]

While this deadly duel was going on, several men of the Twelfth Virginia circled around the ridge to come up behind the Yankees and rush them with drawn pistols. Though outnumbering their assailants, the Yankees panicked in the face of this unexpected attack and made a run for it back to the train.[80]

Harmon sent word to Jones that with a slight reinforcement he could capture the whole lot. Jones, however, preferred not to bother with "troops who could do me no more harm to escape." Incredibly, he let pass another opportunity to inflict severe physical and psychological damage on the enemy.[81]

"We, seeing the state of things," Opie went on, "made a dash for the cut in which the train had halted, reaching which, we poured volley after volley into them. The enemy, at last, having succeeded in getting on board, hurriedly moved off, leaving us a double, but fruitless victory."[82]

The rebels then tried to cut off the train by getting around behind it and tearing up the tracks, but the company of New Yorkers held them off long enough for the train to get away. "Major Moore," reported the Wheeling *Intelligencer* on May 13, "finding such a sharp fire in his rear, as well as in front, turned his whole attention to the railroad obstructionists, and, at the point of the bayonet, soon succeeded in clearing them away sufficiently to allow the engine and car to return towards Grafton." Moore had lost in killed and wounded two officers and eleven privates.[83]

Destroying the Great Bridge

Jones now turned his full attention to the great bridge his men had just captured. The job of destroying it, of course, went to Lieutenant Williamson, the work details to be under the supervision of Captain John Henderson, "a civil engineer of considerable experience," formerly of Ashby's cavalry.[84]

With the pioneers not yet up, Williamson decided to work fast in case enemy reinforcements from Grafton returned. The bridge superstructure lay upon tubular columns of cast iron that rested on stone piers, which alone had taken six months to erect. Williamson ignited three kegs of powder placed under the iron piers in three different locations. Despite the great noise, the tremendous explosion "did not do the slightest damage" to the strong bridge. Fortunately, the disappearance of the threat from Grafton allowed Williamson to give more careful consideration to his now obviously daunting task. He decided to weaken the span by using the Sixth Virginia, given him by Jones, to load it with timbers and rails, set the whole thing ablaze and then detonate another massive charge underneath. But again, the mighty bridge failed to show the slightest inclination to fall. With the span now burning from one end to the other, Williamson considered the situation too dangerous for any further effort.

Captain Henderson, however, did not give up. Despite Williamson's alleged destructive talents, it was the captain who hit upon the idea of pouring powder directly into the support tubes. Soon after dark the charges went off with a great, muffled roar, giving Old Grumble "the satisfaction of seeing this magnificent structure tumble into the river."[85]

The Prisoners

With the threat from Grafton over, the process continued of rounding up the prisoners. Several of the scattered militiamen made it easy for the Confederates by simply walking down the railroad into town and giving themselves up. At the courthouse, the victors eventually counted 222 prisoners, 119 from the One Hundred-Sixth New York, and 103 altogether from the Sixth West Virginia, the militia units and the home guards.[86]

Not wanting to be burdened with these men, General Jones directed that they all be paroled. By 9 p.m. the job was finished. "Most of them were old men and home guards," Washington Smith commented on the captured locals, "and gladly promised they wouldn't ever cause us any more trouble. I was acquainted with nearly all of them, and knew most of them wouldn't keep their promise. But they had been friends of mine before the war, and I didn't say anything."[87]

For the New Yorkers, the militia and home guards, the paroles went fairly smoothly. The men of the Sixth West Virginia's Company A and Company N, however, "were subject to many imprecations by the rebels." The Confederates considered these men especially vile for betraying their home state and serving in a so-called "West Virginia" regiment. The "imprecations," however, apparently went no further than insults and other forms of verbal abuse, and some rebels even complimented the West Virginians for fighting "like damned tigers."[88]

The Saga of John Barnes

While the Confederates still were gathering prisoners down by the bridge, they received around noon a somewhat startling if not pleasant surprise. Coming toward them up Locust Street or Beverly (Fairmont Ave.), they saw two young ladies pulling a buggy. To the pleased and curious soldiers who readily gathered around, the girls identified themselves as Phoebe Barnes and Drusilla Hamilton, and they asked if anyone might know the whereabouts of the body of Phoebe's brother, John Barnes, the same who had been fighting in a ravine (near the present sight of 9th and 10th streets) near the bridge with Corporal Henry Solomon White and the civilian Fontaine Smith.

This may have been the same Miss Barnes who early that morning had helped serve coffee to the grateful Federals waiting near Coal Run Hollow, and who showed some of them a pistol hidden in her cloak while declaring that they would hear from her before the day was over. The compassion and bravery of the two incidents, immediately before and immediately after the battle, certainly matched.

Having been a delegate to the Second Wheeling Convention, John Barnes, a prominent businessman, devoted churchman, and ardent supporter of the Union and the new state of West Virginia, became recognized and condemned by the rebels as a traitor to Virginia and the Confederacy. Like his fellow convention delegate, Fontaine Smith, however, he bravely chose to remain with the home guards and fight the raiders coming into Fairmont.

During the battle, Phoebe somehow received news at her home in nearby Barnesville that her brother had been hit and was laying on the field. With incredible bravery and determination, she resolved to find his body and bring it home.

With the horses having been either taken by the Confederates or sent away into hiding, she and her visiting friend Drusilla set out on foot, pulling the family buggy. After the long, tiring trek into Fairmont, the two young ladies received rather surprising consideration from the rebels, who readily led them to where lay John Barnes.

To her great surprise and relief, Phoebe discovered that her brother, though unconscious, still breathed. The bullet that struck him in the forehead had not penetrated the skull. The missile probably came from a wide muzzle single shot Maynard carbine fired at long range. If so, the thumb-sized projectile would have lost most of its velocity before reaching Barnes, though when it did he undoubtedly felt as though a mule had kicked him in the head.

Rebel soldiers, probably from the Seventh Virginia, kindly helped place Barnes in the buggy, which they pulled uphill to level ground before turning it over to the girls with the concerned admonition that, with Mulligan's recent attack in mind, it yet was too unsafe to be in this area. The girls thanked the kind soldiers and pulled the buggy down the street to the doctor's office, located in a basement beneath a shoe and boot store owned by kinsman Newton Barnes that rebels soon would deprive of nearly its entire stock, despite being locked the previous day by "the young and dapper" clerk Frank E. Nichols before he fled to Wheeling.

After the doctor cleaned and treated the wound, he advised against putting John through the jostling ride to Barnesville. He and the girls made arrangements to carefully move him down the street to near the bridge to stay at the home of a family friend, Mrs. Rowann "Ran" Walklate. After three days, John felt strong enough to endure the ride home. Thanks to the bravery and determination of his sister and her friend, as well as the kind consideration of a few rebel soldiers, John Barnes recovered from his wound and lived to a ripe old age.[89]

Being near the center of the action that day, the Walklate home had been the scene of considerable excitement (years later, Mrs. Allie Haymond contended that the Federal flag of surrender at Fairmont was a woman's petticoat taken from the Walklate house). William Walklate earlier had gone off to hide the family horse (up in Reuben Fleming's hollow above the Peacedale farm), leaving at home "Aunt Ran," her visiting niece, and ten-year-old Emory Hill, apparently an adopted orphan, all of whom had been up that morning on a nearby hill feeding the new calves when they heard the cry, "The rebels are coming!" They ran over to the safety of the Kelley home, only later to be scared out of their wits when one of the shots fired from Lieutenant McAffee's gun that had come down from Grafton struck the chimney, knocked it down, and shattered the windows. Once again, "Aunt Ran," her niece and Emory made a run for it, this time with the Kelley family. "I could not run so fast as the others," the niece later recalled, "so the Kelley girls and myself ran and hid in a coal bank just below Clem Shaver's home."

When the firing finally stopped, seemingly for good, everyone cautiously returned to the Walklate home. Then in addition to taking in John Barnes, "Aunt Ran," with the help of young Emory, pulled in a dead Union soldier to keep him from the hogs who were running wild now that most of the fences in the area had been torn down. "All that night," remembered the niece, "my aunt cared for Mr. Barns and tried to clean up the dead soldier."[90]

Occupation of Fairmont

While the Confederates who had helped John Barnes probably did not recognize him for the "traitor" he was, there would be no such mistake regarding Francis H. Pierpont. Several days before, the governor and his wife had fled to Wheeling, leaving their fine home to the mercy of the rebels, many of whom wanted to burn down the place. Restrained by General Jones, however, the men contented themselves with the destruction of Pierpont's fine library, which contained dozens of law books for the new state

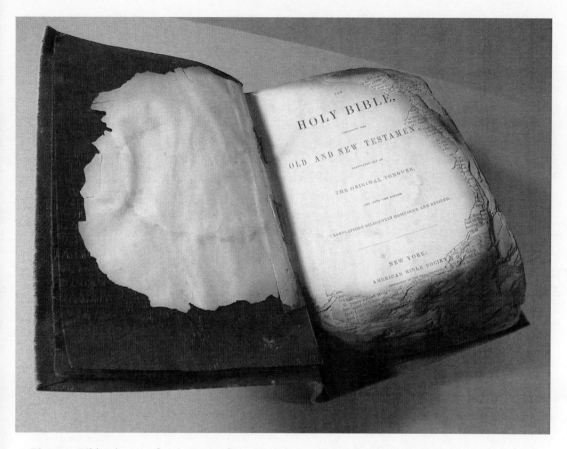

Pierpont Bible, showing fire damage inflicted by rebels at Fairmont (West Virginia State Archives).

of West Virginia. "The library of Pierpont was burned," Jones later proudly admitted, "in retaliation for a like act on the part of the ambitious little man."[91]

According to Corporal Henry White, who observed the burning from across the street while being treated for his painful arm wound at the home of Mrs. W.D. Wilson, "who I will never forget for her kindness," the savage rebels even went so far as to desecrate the Pierpont family Bible. (White would return to duty by the following July and serve through the end of the war.) Other witnesses claim they saw the Bible being dragged through the street, tied to the tail of an officer's horse, then burned, incensing the citizens "more than any other single act," reported the Fairmont *Times*, "and it was said afterwards that it was mere luck that the officer was not shot down by the outraged Fairmonters."[92]

The Pierpont library aside, Jones did give orders against looting and destruction, and he seemed satisfied with the compliance. "One or two stores were plundered," he reported, "but as far as practicable the goods were restored."[93]

Many townspeople and Union soldiers saw things quite differently. "After we were dismissed," Corporal White told his diary, "the Rebels commenced plundering and stealing from every citizen in town at a rate which beggars description. They stole all of the horses in the town and country around to the disgust of even the sympathizers."[94]

Even some of Jones's officers admitted to seeing things a bit differently. "I broke open the Express Office," Major Ball wrote his wife, "and distributed about twenty boxes of oranges, lemons, and raisins with cigars and preserves in plenty, among my gallant S[harp] S[hooters]. I went in several stores where the frightened proprietors were selling at old prices for Confederate money and bought some things for you all."[95]

And of course, the rebels showed no mercy when it came to taking horses. Many years after the war Mrs. Mary Ice Smith recalled that when she was a little girl playing in the yard with her sister (Ella Augustus) and cousin (William Bice) the rebels suddenly appeared. She ran to tell her father but the sad look on his face told that he already knew, the raiders having taken his finest animals. "I remember my grandmother crying," recalled Mrs. Smith, "because they took her best riding horse."[96]

As they had done throughout the expedition thus far, Jones's men made no distinction between Yankee and Rebel horses. Many local unionists derived from this much consolation, even gratification. Their newspapers seemed to take special delight in recounting instances of Southern sympathizers being inconvenienced by the raiders. "We are told that the rebels around Fairmont curse their friends, the raiders, with all their might," the Wheeling *Intelligencer* reported with obvious satisfaction, "and say if they had known they were such a scaly set of robbers they never would have hoped to see them. As it is, they never want to see them again. The raiders made no discrimination between them and white people, but took their horses and plunder also. They took eight horses from Ed. Straight, which although the number rhymes very well with his name, was dreadfully harassing to his feelings. He begged and implored them not to be so hard on friends, but they simply damned him for a stingy Southern man and moved off with his horses.

"They also took two horses from his brother John Straight," the paper went on, "a worse rebel even than Ed., and although he joined them and went off with them they wouldn't give him one of his own horses to ride, but mounted him on an old raw boned skeleton that bid fair to cut old Straight through to the collar bone.

"One old secesh, who rode into town on a very fine horse, was telling Gen. Jones how much he was doing to help their cause, when the General suddenly interrupted him by a requisition for his horse. And they took it in spite of all the old fellow's protestations that he was one of them. The General told him he ought very cheerfully give his horse to aid them in fighting for the cause he loved so well. The old gent went away without his horse, but he couldn't 'see it.' A prominent secessionist at Barracksville lost four horses, all he had. He put in the same plea and got the same answer. The last heard of him, he was following them begging for his horses back."[97]

In sympathy with many local Unionists, the *Intelligencer* obviously was glad to see this happening, for hopefully it strengthened resentment against the rebels and their cause. "We rather like this way of doing business on the part of the raiders," the paper happily confessed. "We hope they will do it more everywhere they go. Their friends in West Virginia are a shabby set of citizens, and we don't wonder they, in common with other people, have little respect for them. Naturally enough, people who invite their friends to come and see them, ought to be willing to entertain them, but the shabby sympathizers wanted the enemies of their friends, the Union men, to bear the expenses of the entertainment. The raiders couldn't appreciate such hospitalities, and therefore, just to give their friends a little touch of Southern rule, turned in and stole their horses, along with those of their Union neighbors.

"This sort of 'rights' is not what the patriots among us, who are praying for the success of the rebellion, covet. Their idea of success involves no personal sacrifices on their part at all. Secession, with them, is a grand Utopia free of expense, sacrifice, trouble, or suffering. In the meantime, and until it is all ready, prepared, carpeted and furnished to their hand, they want to go on making as many greenbacks as possible, and get clear of the taxes to the 'Lincoln despotism' during the process."[98]

The *Intelligencer* thus did not tire of relating supposed atrocities committed by the rebels in and around Fairmont. "At the east end of the iron bridge," the paper went on in another edition, "lived a German generally called 'Dutch Charlie,' who had been watchman on the bridge ever since it was built. He had accumulated in the years he had been serving the company about $700 in gold, and also had about $200 in greenbacks. Some scoundrel knew this, and he knew he kept it in the house, apprized the rebels of it, and they went to the house and robbed him of every cent. A similar instance happened at Barracksville. An old man, who had accumulated a few hundred dollars in the service of the railroad company, had put it into a little stock of groceries, confectionary, &c. The rebels broke into it and swept it of every farthing's worth and left the old man almost a beggar. Such is chivalry!"

The same paper went on to report that General Jones supposedly had been so impressed with the defense put up by so few, that he complimented Captain Chamberlain, remarking that he had never seen "such a set of devils to fight, anywhere." There was more to cheer the Unionist's heart. "The citizens further assert," the newspaper went on, "that when the rebels were crowding the streets after the fight, the stench was perfectly intolerable, so filthy were they in their persons—a dirty, greasy, unkempt, unshorn, ragged and Lazarus-like crew. Gen. Jones," the paper graciously added, "is represented as being a very fine looking officer."[99]

The following day, May 6, the paper picked up where it left off. "Every store in town was robbed of everything the thieves fancied," it declared. "The home rebels pointed out the private property they wanted destroyed and it was done. A valuable steam sawmill, belonging to J.N. Cromwell & Co., was burned. The National printing office was destroyed because it has been uncompromisingly Union, while the butternut concern in Morgantown was uninjured, because, as the traitors said, it was on their side and devoted to the cause.... At least five hundred horses were taken out of Marion County alone."[100]

For two more days, through May 8, the paper continued to rant. "After the fight the rebels returned to town, paroled their prisoners and then inaugurated a system of brigandage, theft, plunder and vandalism scarcely known to the vandals of ancient Europe. They ransacked every store and shop in town—stole all the horses that were within six miles of town."[101]

The Toll

Fontaine Smith, the "angry citizen" with the muzzle loading squirrel musket who had been fighting beside his fellow convention delegate, John Barnes, and Corporal

Henry Solomon White when those two received their wounds, had been captured, paroled at the courthouse, and before dark had gone home. Now he seethed at the personal indignities he believed he had suffered at the hands of the raiders. He found especially galling the attitude of the young, perhaps eighteen-year-old rebel, who at the courthouse had shoved at him a parole paper. "Here," the boy snapped, "sign your name. I ain't got all day to fool with you Yankees, especially you damned milish!"[102]

Riley Fleming also seethed. From his new home in Barnesville, he earlier had taken the precaution of safely hiding his horses and cattle in the woods on nearby Fort Hill. When the Confederates arrived at the home later that afternoon, they began a thorough but fruitless search of the place. While Fleming's twelve-year-old daughter tauntingly played "Yankee Doodle" and other Union tunes on the piano, the frustrated rebels in the front yard demanded to know the whereabouts of his livestock, driving home their point by jabbing long pistols in his face and stomach.

His honor and midsection both bruised, Fleming brooded all day, until that evening when he chanced to look out the window and see a lone dismounted Confederate soldier walking north up the river road toward Rivesville. Almost without thinking, the offended West Virginian grabbed his squirrel rifle, rushed out the kitchen door, crossed the back yard and found a good place near a big sugar maple to wait in ambush for the unsuspecting rebel. Presently, when the lad came into view Fleming drew a bead on his head and gently wrapped his finger around the trigger. Conscience suddenly intervened, however, and he did not shoot. For the remaining forty-nine years of his life, Fleming daily gave thanks "that the blood of that Rebel soldier was not upon my head."[103]

How many other Confederate soldiers who were not so fortunate as the boy walking by the Fleming place is difficult to determine. Accounts vary widely. Jones reported his losses at Fairmont as only one killed and two wounded in the First Maryland, three wounded from the Sixth Virginia, one wounded in the Twelfth Virginia, who was left in Fairmont, and five from the Twelfth being "taken prisoner from straggling." Surely, this is inaccurate. But so are other accounts that place the Confederate loss at well over a hundred men.[104]

In his *History of the Upper Monongahela Valley* published in 1923, James Morton Callaghan, a professor of history for many years at West Virginia University, gave the Confederate loss at Fairmont as sixty killed and sixty wounded. Local historian Glen Lough, however, came up with a different figure, based largely on interviews with several battle participants and eyewitnesses. "Eleven old soldiers," he wrote in *Fort Prickett and Marion County*, "six who wore the gray, and five who wore the blue, told this writer that thirty-nine Confederates died here," adding, "three of them helped bury their dead companions, in a common grave, dug in the shape of a crescent, on the little flat a few hundred feet up-river."[105]

One of the three who supposedly helped bury the thirty-nine dead Confederates was Captain Billy Branson, a member of McNeill's Rangers. Branson later became especially noted for his participation in a daring exploit with thirty other partisans, who on February 21, 1865, dashed into Cumberland and captured generals George Crook and Benjamin Kelley from under the noses of some 7,000 Federal troops. About 1890, Branson came to live near Fairmont, settling on land bordering on "old Virgin Alley, between Merchant Street and the river," that included the mass grave of the thirty-nine men he had helped bury some twenty-seven years before. After dark every year on Jefferson Davis's birthday, Branson knelt for several minutes in silent prayer beside his fallen comrades, whose names and hometowns he knew by heart. He vowed to some-day erect a monument to their memory, a promise he unfortunately never was able to keep.

Feeling no bitterness toward his former enemies, Branson nobly became friends with the former home guard major, Festus Parrish, whom he openly admired for the stout defense he and his comrades put up at the foundry near the east end of the suspension bridge, a defense that both men believed brought down no less than thirteen Confederates.[106]

Other participants calculated things differently. "We lost five men killed at Rowelsburg and eleven others killed by bushwhackers between there and Morgantown," a Confederate soldier (Richard Showers of Richmond) wrote after the war (to Adam O. Heck, a local resident). "One was shot dead from across the river at Rivesville, and one died from loss of blood at Pitcher's Church. We buried these men in Palatine with the twenty-one killed there and at Fairmont. The way I count we lost 39 men between the time we entered Rowelsburg and the time (10 o'clock at night) we left Fairmont. We lost seven more in Harrison County, two killed outright at Maulsby's Bridge, and five of those wounded there dying later. That amounts to 47 of us dead before we met Imboden."[107]

Private Charles Primm declared that "Nine Confederates were shot and killed in Coal Run Hollow," adding, "The Union men were hidden in the brush on both sides of the hollow, and when about 400 rebels rode up through there, they let them have it. The Leeds boy was killed at this time. It was said a young woman shot him. I shot into that bunch a couple of times.... Four wounded rebels I know of, were left with friends near Boothsville until they got well. Two of them died. One got well and followed after his company. One got well and stayed where he was (and married a Boothsville girl)."[108]

Civilians also held strong opinions on the matter. While the Reverend Moses Tichnell professed to know that indeed thirty-nine Confederates had been buried in a common grave, Mrs. Anna Mathoit believed that the rebels lost only seven men. "There was but one man seen in the river," she wrote the Fairmont *Times* after the war, "and he fell from the bridge. At that time," she went on, "flour was $50 a barrel; grown men were working from sunrise to sunset for 50 cents a day; Calico was 50 cents a yard, and everyone was scorching wheat and chestnuts and grinding them together to use as a substitute for coffee."[109]

With regard to all these accounts, local historian Glen Lough wisely remained objective. "Is it a true story?" he wrote in reference to the thirty-nine Confederates supposedly killed at Fairmont. "Who can say"? adding, "there were three persons, two men and a woman, all eye-witnesses to certain phases of the battle, who told this writer that no one was killed here."[110]

Union losses were not as subject to speculation. The One Hundred Sixth New York lost one man killed, Private C. Brown of Company D, who was buried where he fell but afterwards was removed to his home in New York state. The regiment also lost one man wounded, Private Trough shot through the knee, perhaps by Lieutenant Opie during their skirmish duel, and 119 men taken prisoner. The Sixth West Virginia lost one man wounded, Corporal Henry White, shot through the arm. The Twenty-third Illinois lost one man wounded. Mulligan's Battery lost three men wounded. The militia lost one man killed, Lon Coffman. And the home guards lost one man wounded, John Barnes, shot in the head. The Sixth West Virginia, the militia and the home guards lost between them 103 men captured (30 of Company A's 38 men were captured). Total Union losses thus came to 231 men.[111]

Back on April 28, meanwhile, General Joseph A.J. Lightburn, commander of the District of the Kanawha, Department of the Ohio, had been on leave in Wheeling when General Schenck placed him in command of all troops in the area and ordered him to make for Fairmont. With a contingent of militia from Ohio and West Virginia, Lightburn left Wheeling the same day and headed down the railroad, repairing the burned bridges at Burton and Mannington as he went. He reached Fairmont on May 2, and promptly reported to Governor Pierpont the damages done there by the rebels.[112]

"Your public and private library was destroyed," he wired the governor; "eleven horses taken from Mr. Watson, John S. Barnes was wounded; young Coffman was killed; no property burned except your library and Coffman's saw mills. Money taken from N.S. Barnes, $500; Fleming, $400; A. Fleming $300 in boots and shoes; Mrs. Sterling $100, Jackson in flour and feed, loss great; Major Parrish lost all of his goods; every one who had good horses lost them; National newspaper office destroyed and type all in 'pi'; United States property destroyed, $500; Monongahela river railroad bridge of the Baltimore and Ohio road, destroyed, piers only left standing, bridge in river. Coal Run, Buffalo and Barracksville bridges all destroyed. It was Lieutenant Zane of Wheeling [the same whose shoulder had been grazed by a bullet outside Cranberry Summit] who destroyed your library by burning it in front of your office."[113]

CHAPTER EIGHT

Weston

Jones Approaches Clarksburg

The triumph at Fairmont lifted to new heights the confidence of the men in their commander. "Gen. Jones had been in command of the brigade for more than a year," a soldier later wrote, "and the men knew his mettle. He was brave, without being fool-hardy; was alert, cautious, and a good strategist. Aside from Stonewall Jackson, I do not believe there was another general officer in the Confederate army whom the men immediately under his command would have been more ready to follow blindfolded than William E. Jones. He was a fine disciplinarian, yet without the least manifesta-tion of harshness." The soldier considered the general "a little crusty at times but very democratic." The men especially appreciated the occasions he mingled with them socially when off duty.[1]

Old Grumble did not linger to savor his very gratifying accomplishments. "After a few hours rest at Fairmont, enjoying a social visit with our prisoners and taking lunch with them in their camp," a soldier later recalled, "we moved on."[2]

"Leaving our wounded in the hands of kind friends," Jones reported, he moved out around 10 p.m. (29th), thereby maintaining his preference to march primarily at night. Hoping to find Imboden, he headed southwest toward Clarksburg. A few hours' ride took them through Worthington to a camp north of Shinnston, where Old Grum-ble, tired and worn-out, slept through the remaining night in his cloak.[3]

Along the way, about forty-five rebels stopped at the home of Union sympathizer Ruhama Miller, where they enjoyed a free chicken dinner while several Yankees, refugees no doubt from Fairmont, nervously kept quiet while hiding in the attic.[4]

Near Thoburn (Monongah), above Shinnston, several other weary Confederates stopped at the fine large farm owned by John Anderson. Though a Southern sympa-thizer, Anderson, unlike many other naïve local citizens with similar views, was no fool. For at least two days he had been preparing for a visit from his "friends."

To protect "Scat," his cherished, valuable Arabian horse, he cleverly drove a nail deep into one hoof so as to provoke a limp and thereby make her unappealing to the raiders, a successful tactic from which the horse easily recovered later. Anderson also selected from his large herd ten of the best cattle and hid them in a nearby coal mine, which he then covered with brush. A favorite rifle he hid under a board in the attic.

While their gaunt horses that evening enjoyed a feast at Anderson's corncrib, the hungry raiders sumptuously ate at his table, devouring plenty of beef, pork and chicken. After his guests left, Anderson carefully retrieved the grains of corn spit out by the rebel horses and saved them to plant that year's badly needed crop.[5]

In ironic contrast to that day's many confiscations, Lieutenant John Opie of the Sixth Virginia gave up his horse while in camp that night. He had acquired the animal only the night before, when during the ride to Barracksville he convinced his friend, George Calmes, to go with him ahead of the advance guard "and look for an adventure." When the two subsequently heard horsemen approaching, they pulled to the side of the road and drew their pistols. Presently, two men rode up. Opie and Calmes moved out and stopped them.

"Who are you?" asked Opie.

"We are citizens," the stranger replied. "The Rebels are coming and we want to save our horses."

"How far off are the Rebels?" Opie playfully asked in the realization that the evening darkness concealed his true identity.

"Five or ten miles off," replied one of the strangers.

"Are they pretty good horses?" Opie continued. When both men declared that they had fine animals, the lieutenant dropped the ruse. "We are Rebels and want your horses," he suddenly announced. "Dismount and flee for your lives." With lightening speed, the two men got down and disappeared into the darkness. Opie and Calmes each took a horse.

During the fight at Fairmont the next day, Opie sent back for his captured, extra horse and gave it to Private Robert Pendleton of his regiment, whose own mount had been killed by a bullet to the face, about two inches below the eyes. That night in camp Pendleton somehow lost the animal to another soldier whose horse also had been killed that day and reclaimed him only by the use of physical threats. Feeling sorry for the soldier who relented to Pendleton, Opie gave him his own mount. "Though the laugh was on Pendleton, who was the subject of much merriment," Opie concluded, "I was the only loser by the transaction."[6]

Resuming the march around 9 a.m. on Thursday morning, April 30, the command three hours later passed through Shinnston in Harrison County, most of whose 13,800 citizens were decidedly pro-union, having voted against secession and for the new state ordinance. Along the way, the men relentlessly continued collecting livestock, which in turn slowed the column considerably, making for a dangerous situation this deep in enemy territory.[7]

In desperate need of a new horse, his own showing critical signs of extreme fatigue, William Hammond this morning called on his friend John Opie, who, after giving up his own mount the night before to trooper Robert Pendleton, possessed still another, to leave the column and help him find a fresh mount. Always eager to "look for an adventure," Opie readily agreed to go along. The two men visited several farmhouses before they found a suitable horse, only to then discover that they were lost. A kind citizen graciously gave them directions on how to get back to the main road, but after a fruitless ride of eight or ten miles the two men realized that they had been duped. Finally reaching the pike by a series of lucky turns, Opie and Hammond learned that the command had passed by about two hours before. They broke into a trot and set off to catch up.

Rounding a bend, they suddenly came upon about twenty-five armed men gathered in front of a house by the roadside. "Bushwhackers!" the two rebels immediately concluded, though the armed men more probably were home guards.

Like most of his comrades, Opie held the bushwhackers in extreme contempt. "These people," he wrote, "who generally operated in bands or companies, went about murdering the unarmed men in their community who entertained Rebel sentiments, and shooting from the bushes at Rebel soldiers as they passed along the road. I, myself, came very near falling victim to them while passing through Upshur County.

"We lost several of our people during the raid by these murderers, who shot them down in cold blood, from the bushes, as they passed along the road. White's Battalion captured several of them in the very act, and shot them on the spot."

At any rate, having been spotted by the determined looking men, Opie and Hammond now realized that they were in a tough spot. Thinking fast, the lieutenant decided that a run for it would be hopeless. "Here they are!" he called out as he drew a revolver and turned in his saddle as if to give the charge command to troopers concealed around the bend. He and Hammond then rode fast into the midst of the "bushwhackers," firing rapidly as they went.

The daring ruse worked. To a man, the "bushwhackers" fell for it, scattered, and ran into a nearby thicket, whereupon Opie and Hammond fled down the road, "never drawing rein until we overtook the command." The two men nearly swooned with a relief that henceforward served to greatly curtail Opie's appetite for "adventure" away from the column. "This narrow escape," he later declared, "taught me to remain in the ranks during the rest of the raid."[8]

Meanwhile, on the way to Shinnston, the column met up with Marinda Martin Fortney (wife of Rev. Williams Perry Fortney), one of those naïve Southern sympathizers who put too much trust in the visiting raiders. Upon learning that Confederates had approached to near Shinnston (at Bingamon Junction), she borrowed a fine riding horse from her father-in-law, Dr. Jacob Holmes Fortney, a man of strong Union sympathies who amiably regretted her political views. She galloped down the river road from Shinnston, eager to greet her heroes, only to receive in turn a most disheartening welcome. "What a handsome horse you have there," one soldier remarked, quickly adding, "We'll be taking it for the Cause."

"But I'm a Southern sympathizer," she protested in stunned disbelief. "You can't have the horse." In disillusioned anger, Marinda walked back home and tearfully explained to her father-in-law how she had lost his fine animal. "Well, Marinda," the understanding doctor calmly chided, "if you have learned all the wrong is not on one side, I'll not mind losing my horse."[9]

After passing through Shinnston around noon, the column continued in the direction of Clarksburg, the seat of Harrison County, about twelve miles to the south. Out in Prospect Valley, Dr. Jesse Flowers, who practiced medicine near Lumberport, three miles southwest of Shinnston, proved equally naïve as Marinda Fortney when he happily rode out to welcome approaching Confederates. "That's a mighty fine horse you're riding," a rebel immediately observed. "I guess we can use it."

"Oh, but I'm your friend," the doctor explained.

"Well then," replied the rebel, "you should be the more willing to help us. Get off, please."[10]

Dr. Flowers' neighbors, the Chalfont family, had been wiser. Upon learning of the raiders' approach, John and his thirteen-year-old daughter Minerva made several trips leading the family's many horses into the concealment of nearby wooded hills. They lost not a single animal.[11]

Other nearby residents proved equally resourceful. When the wife of Dr. James Denison heard that rebels were nearing their home near Gypsy, three miles south of Shinnston, she cleverly sent out her daughter to hang linen on a line in the yard. When a rebel foraging party rode up, the girl explained that she was airing out the bedding of a small pox patient. The soldiers immediately rode off.[12]

The Denisons' neighbor, Mrs. Aaron Vincent, was not so fortunate. "Please leave me at least one ham," she pleaded with a party of foraging raiders, "I can't eat fat." The rebels were unmoved. "Ma'am," one explained, "we don't like fat either," and they took all the meat and left the fat.[13]

This would not be the only or by any means the worst misfortune to befall the Vincent family, which served as a tragic epitomizing example of this war of brother against brother. Three of its sons ardently favored the Union while three others just as fervently supported the Confederacy. Thomas, one of the "secesh" boys, recently had married a Miss Jane Holbert. When home alone one night she raised a window to investigate a strange noise outside. A shot rang out, presumably from a bushwhacker. A bullet tore into the young bride's lung, she collapsed and died. To complete the disaster, her new husband Thomas would be killed in ambush while riding with Jones's column outside Fairmont (possibly at Rivesville).[14]

Meanwhile, when at home in Pine Bluff near Shinnston, Solomon and Jeremiah Shinn heard the raiders were coming, they quickly hid their aged parents, Isaiah and Nancy, in a nearby coal bank, then stood guard in the woods over the family's seven fine horses. The rebels, however, easily discovered and flushed out the two brothers, forcing them at sword point to give up the animals.

"I reached home late in the evening," Solomon recalled in relief at being allowed by the rebels to go free, "met the wife at the gate with tears of joy in her eyes that I was permitted to return." The harrowing experience burned into his memory things that before may have gone unnoticed or had little lasting impression. "The moon shone dimly that night," he went on, "dogs in the distance were barking, and we heard human voices down the valley. Many restless days and sleepless nights came to our home those days, not to be forgotten by those who were there."[15]

Another life-long memory was created not far from the Shinn place, when sixteen-year-old Union boy George Hulderman drew a bead on a passing rebel soldier and put a finger on the trigger. Just then, the boy's father quickly grabbed the rifle and pulled it away, thereby saving the life not only of the Confederate but probably also that of his son. George Hulderman lived to be an old man, dying in 1928 at the age of eighty-one.[16]

The Fight at Simpson's Creek

Old Grumble's pulse no doubt quickened at the prospect of getting his hands on Clarksburg, the largest Union supply base in western Virginia. Its capture not only would be a prize greater than Fairmont, it might even rival the lost opportunity at Rowelsburg. When about four or five miles from the place, however, he learned from captured Federals on furlough that it held as many as 5,000 enemy troops. Taking the Yankees at their word, he decided for the moment to avoid the town. Still hoping to link up with Imboden, he accordingly detoured to the left, crossed to the east side of the Monongahela and headed up Simpson's Creek toward Bridgeport in Harrison County, five miles east of Clarksburg. When taking the Shinnston Road across Simpson's Creek (30th), seven miles from Clarksburg, however, his rear suddenly and unexpectedly came under severe attack from Company E of the Third West Virginia Cavalry.[17]

Though nominally part of a regiment, the various companies of the Third West Virginia Cavalry had been mustered in at different times for the purpose of scouting particular counties or areas in the new state, and they would not serve together as a unit until the early summer of 1864. Company E had been raised in 1862 at Clarksburg by Captain Lot Bowen.[18]

Born in Greene County, Pennsylvania, in 1824, Bowen settled in the Sycamore section of Harrison County (West) Virginia in 1850, whereupon he became the region's most prominent and successful cattleman. Despite initial mixed feelings about secession, during the first months of the war he supplied great quantities of beef to the Federal Army at Clarksburg, and as a delegate to the First Wheeling Convention he gave eloquent speeches in support of the Union. His additional valuable talent as a superb horseman led General McClellan to request that he raise a company of cavalry.[19]

Bowen more than fulfilled Little Mac's expectations, Company E being generally recognized as one of the best-trained cavalry units in western Virginia. When it lunged out from Clarksburg on the morning of April 30, however, the captain was too ill to lead and command fell to Lieutenant Timothy Roane. By order of General Roberts, Roane that morning rode out with sixty-five men and twenty civilian volunteers to scout the Shinnston road.[20]

After riding seven miles down the West Fork River towards Shinnston, the advance guard caught sight of a considerable enemy force 300 yards off making for a ford at the mouth of Simpson's Creek and Lambert's Run. Roane came up and promptly ordered a charge. His whooping men rushed forward and at short range poured a volley into the rebels, throwing them into some confusion. About 100 made it across the river before another forty or so broke off and headed up the Federal side of the stream. Roane came up and without hesitation split his small command, leaving about half to guard the ford while taking the other half in hot pursuit of the forty rebels still on his side of the river. The chase went on for three miles before the lieutenant gave up and broke off. The men back at the ford, meanwhile, had dismounted and repelled several attempts by the rebels to recross the river. The whole affair lasted barely an hour, during which time Roane had lost one man killed (Pvt. J.W. Custer) and two wounded (Sgt. W.H. Jones and J.C. Swentzel), two horses killed and three wounded. He claimed to have captured nine rebels and eight of their horses. The Confederates admitted the loss of one man killed in the Eleventh Virginia (Pvt. Peter Armstrong, Co. G), four privates and three officers (Capt. A.C. Swindler, Lt. J.W. Kratzer, Lt. William F. Anderson) wounded in the Twelfth Virginia, and from the same regiment eight privates lost by capture (five from Co. G, two from Co. H, one from Co. F). Private Washington W. Smith of the Sixth Virginia Cavalry, however, claimed that the Confederates lost seven men killed, "two killed on the spot, and five dying in the next few days from wounds." (The Eleventh Virginia later was compensated somewhat by the addition here of two new recruits.)[21]

In the fight at Simpson's Creek, Captain A.C. Swindler of the Twelfth had taken a bullet in the lower leg. Though not severe, the wound was quite painful, causing Swindler at times during the rest of the day to "bellow like a bull-calf without its mother." This "unmanly" behavior in turn brought on the captain some bemused derision from his comrades. John Opie, for one, shook his fist and challenged Swindler to come out of his carriage, halted by the roadside, his wounded leg resting on pillows, whereupon the lieutenant promised to "give him the devil." To the delight of those watching nearby, Swindler merely groaned in reply.[22]

Bridgeport

To protect his rear against any further such annoyances as had happened at Simpson's Creek, Jones at 3:30 p.m. on the 30th detached Company B of the First Maryland to picket the Clarksburg road. He then ordered the rest of the battalion to seize Bridgeport, distant some four miles to the southeast.

As it rushed into town, the battalion came under heavy fire from troops hiding among the posts and rail fences along the railroad, losing one man killed (Pvt. Clinton Myers, Co C), Major Brown being slightly wounded (again). Nonetheless, Brown and his Marylanders captured an entire Federal company (probably militia or home guards), about forty men (and sixteen railroad workers) with their arms and horses.[23]

Out on the Clarksburg road, meanwhile, Company B came under attack from about 200 mounted infantry firing long-range rifles. Having only pistols, the Marylanders fell back to a ford where they took up a good position that enabled them to hold off the enemy, neither side apparently suffering any casualties.[24]

Jones then set about destroying Bridgeport's B&O connection. To guard his command while it worked, having learned of the attack on the Maryland battalion's Company B, he put White's battalion two miles out on the Clarksburg road, where the "Comanches" happily used the opportunity to tear up the nearby track. Jones sent a detachment of the Eleventh Virginia under Captain Weems to burn a bridge below town, while at the same time dispatching Captain William T. Mitchell's company of the Sixth Virginia to help the engineer Lieutenant Williamson burn some tall trestles about a half-mile above town. Other troopers threw into a stream a large freight engine and car, and they destroyed "a full set of Government carpenter tools." Satisfied with another day's fine work, Jones moved on in the direction of Philippi, camping near there after dark.[25]

Philippi

That night in Philippi, seat of Barbour County, population about 9,000, town resident Spencer Dayton conscientiously set about trying to save the county records. He hurriedly placed the most valuable in a coffee sack, which he took for safe keeping to the home of Joshua Glascock, in Pleasant District.[26]

Other Barbour County citizens were decidedly of a different attitude, the most notable being twenty-year-old Margaret Reed, arrested for allegedly providing Imboden with information regarding Union troop strength. Confined to a room in the local hotel, the spirited and defiant Reed relentlessly tormented her captors, hurling at them both insults and spit until they had had enough and rushed her off to Wheeling. There she continued the abusive behavior, including a physical assault upon her jailor. All this in turn brought her such notoriety as to gain the attention of a newspaper reporter, who presently arrived at the jail to interview the "Secessionist Amazon." Somewhat surprisingly, he admitted, the newsman found her to be "a very intelligent young woman [who] is rather prepossessing," adding, "She looks as if she could take care of herself."[27]

Meanwhile, as the great battle between Lee and Hooker finally began to play out some 150 crow-flight miles to the southeast, Jones entered Philippi around noon on Friday, May 1. As they had done in every community they entered thus far, the men set about gathering supplies and livestock. And once again, sympathizers seemed to get hit the hardest. "Jones' men behaved very badly," Isabella Woods complained (May 17) to her husband, "treating Secessionists worse than Union men."[28]

Depending on a number of factors, including circumstance and just plain whim, some victims received payment, most did not. While a man named D. Bryer begrudgingly accepted Confederate money for his leather, Thomas Hite, despite having two sons serving in the Confederate army, received only curses when he sought payment for his sixty head of cattle and four horses. Likewise, John R. Williamson, who had worked to help resolve the hostage crisis resulting from Sheriff Trayhern's kidnapping the previous November, lost thousands of dollars worth of livestock and other property. (The Barbour hostages taken for Trayhern had been transferred to Camp Chase out of fear Jones might liberate them should he attack Wheeling. The hostages then successfully petitioned Governor Pierpont to be returned to West Virginia, but not before one, Samuel Elliot, died of disease amidst the horrendous conditions of Camp Chase.) And although William McClaskey had resigned as deputy sheriff rather than serve in the "Pierpont government," the rebels helped themselves to the goods in his store, paying with Confederate money at pre-war prices. On occasion, however, some rebel hearts did soften. When James Corder, whose brother Edward was with Imboden's command, pleaded for the return of his cattle he at first received angry threats. He bravely persisted, however, until the exasperated rebels finally allowed him to return home with one yoke of oxen.[29]

At Philippi, Jones decided to finally rid himself of the growing and increasingly cumbersome herds of livestock he had accumulated on the expedition thus far. After Lieutenant Williamson repaired the bridge across the Tygarts Valley River that the enemy had damaged by ripping up the flooring and cutting some flooring joists, Jones sent across it the Sixth Virginia to escort to Beverly the 500 or so captured horses and cattle. The great herd, the largest ever seen by many awestruck residents along the way,

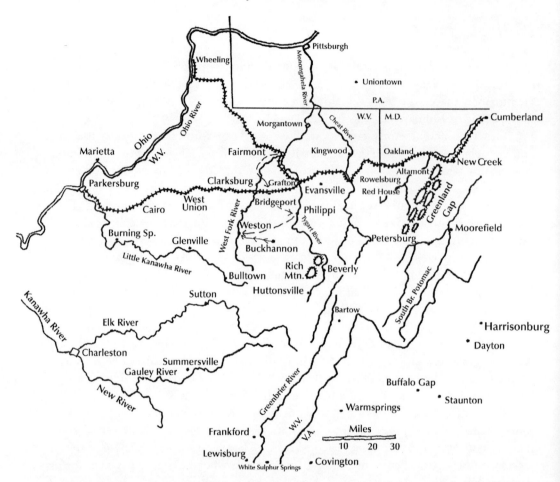

10. Jones's movement from Fairmont to Weston, and Imboden's movement from Buckhannon to Weston, April 29–May 2, 1863.

eventually was put out to pasture in the relatively friendly areas of Pocahontas and Greenbrier counties.[30]

Jones also sent off the sick and wounded, including the First Maryland's Major Brown, who finally conceded the need for treatment of that leg wound he had received at Greenland Gap five days before. He turned over command of the battalion, now only 120 men, to Captain Frank Bond.[31]

Jones also let go all men deemed unfit to continue on the expedition, "giving all who desired it permission to go home," Colonel Marshall reported disapprovingly, "and the strength of the command was again materially weakened." Why Jones allowed this is unclear, unless he considered the raid to be near an end. More than one remaining soldier disapproved of the action. That night William Wilson of the Twelfth told his diary that he was "much dissatisfied" with the decision to detach the Sixth Virginia and so many other men. Nor did he approve of sending off all the cattle while he and his comrades went hungry. "Horses fed but no rations," he complained. "Three water crackers and veal issued tonight."[32]

After the Sixth Virginia set off for Beverly, Jones intended to destroy the just-repaired bridge over the Tygarts Valley River, his soldiers having piled straw on it for firing. Before the rebels lit the bundles, however, Joshua S. Corder, church Elder and brother of James, whom the rebels just recently had deprived of all his livestock save a pair of oxen, went out on the span, knelt down and began to pray, refusing to budge. Evidently fearing God's wrath more than that of General Jones, the confounded soldiers mounted up and rode off, leaving the bridge intact.[33]

"Rid of this encumbrance," Jones reported of the departed horses and cattle, "the remainder of my force marched on the road to Buckhannon," where he hoped to finally find Imboden. "Being less apprehensive of danger," he added, "the march became more moderate." They camped May 1 somewhere between the two towns. When a few miles from Buckhannon next day (2nd), Jones received from one of Imboden's men on furlough the first information regarding the former Staunton lawyer's position. Twelve incredible days had passed without either general knowing the whereabouts or fate of the other.[34]

Union Panic

From Parkersburg on the Ohio River in the west to as far as Philadelphia on the Delaware River in the east, the Confederate invasion of western Virginia gave cause for much excitement and alarm. Excitement and alarm inevitably led to rumor, which only heightened the tension if wildly inaccurate, as often it was. The citizens craved reliable information. "Since Friday last [April 24]," the Wheeling *Intelligencer* reported on April 27, "the city has been filled with rumors of a rebel advance on Beverly and this side of there." Later that same day reports confirmed that the enemy indeed had not only captured Beverly and attacked Oakland and Rowelsburg, but they also had taken Morgantown. This led to the rumor, later refuted, that the rebels had advanced on Waynesburg, Pennsylvania, only about thirty miles southeast of Wheeling. Moreover, communication having been lost with both Grafton and Fairmont (their telegraph operators had panicked, packed up and left), the gravest speculations rose as to the fate of those two communities.[35]

On Monday the 27th, the citizens of Wheeling, seat of Ohio County's decidedly pro-union population of about 24,500, held a town meeting, whereby they resolved to form a Committee of Public Safety, whose main duty would be the all important job of ringing a bell to summon the people together for a decision on how to deal with the emergency. Officers of the Twenty-fourth Battalion of Militia, meanwhile, promptly met at the county courthouse and agreed to call out their two regiments. "We are assured," the *Intelligencer* stated, "that ample and reasonable provision has been made to check any further advance of the rebels."[36]

The following afternoon, Tuesday the 28th, some 700 militiamen assembled at the courthouse and received new weapons. The two regiments General Schenck placed under the command of Brigadier General A.J. Lightburn, commander of the District of the Kanawha, Department of the Ohio, who happened to be on leave in Wheeling. Four men under a Major Trimble then took a forty-mile train ride up to Waynesburg in Greene County, Pennsylvania, to check on rumors that rebels had seized the place. They arrived near midnight to discover that although the enemy had not yet been to Waynesburg, its citizens "were excited," the bank having taken the drastic steps of destroying $60,000 of its paper money and shipping its specie to Pittsburgh.[37]

Wheeling, meanwhile, began to swell from refugees fleeing towns in the path of the rebels, and the city took in dozens of train engines and cars from Newburg, Grafton and other threatened stations. The refugees included Reverend R.V. Dodge of Wheeling, who happened to be in Oakland when Harmon's men rode into the town. "Mr. Dodge says he was courteously treated by the rebels," reported the *Intelligencer*, "though subjected to an examination and pretty closely questioned."[38]

All this, combined with the confirmed reports about Beverly, Oakland, Rowelsburg and Morgantown, "threw the whole population" the *Intelligencer* reported on the 28th, "into a great state of excitement."[39]

The excitement bred, among other things, suspicions of collaboration with the enemy. Back on the 24th, remembered the *Intelligencer*, Mr. Daily, the owner of the Glades Hotel in Oakland, arrived in Wheeling by train to stock up on provisions for his business, something he did on a regular basis. "This time, however," the paper recalled, "he purchased such a large quantity of 'grub' as to arouse suspicions that Daily, an avowed secessionist, was preparing for the arrival of the rebs in Oakland, anticipating a visit from his friends in the Southern Confederacy." The paper then voiced a complaint destined to gain ominous strength in the days ahead. "This is but one more instance of the perfect understanding existing between our home rebels and those in the Confederate army."[40]

On May 2, the *Intelligencer* printed an accusation it had picked up from the Pittsburgh *Dispatch*, whereby five men of Kingwood (C.J.P. Cresap, attorney at law, Benjamin Gilbert, proprietor of the Brandon House, E.T. Brandon, Gustavus Cresap, and Jonathon Huddelson) "were reported as actively operating with the rebels." This in turn brought in a vehement protest from one of the accused. "C.J. Cresap is not a citizen of Kingwood," Gustavus Cresap wrote to the newspaper, "and had not been here for more than two years. Huddelson lives two miles from Kingwood, and was not there on the day of the raid; and the rest of us instead of acting with the raiders were actively engaged in protecting both public and private property, and had it not been for our efforts, Kingwood might have fared far worse than she did. There was no property wantonly destroyed, no stores broken open, nor any person molested, except myself, who was threatened to be shot for trying to recover a horse that was taken from me."[41]

This in turn brought in another heated response a few days later from someone signing his name on the letter to the editor as "Union Man." He professed outrage at Cresap's claim to have saved property at Kingwood. "Now, I do say that this is as basest a lie as ever was sent to an editor," he fumed. "He forgot to say that when those thieving devils came into Kingwood, he pointed out the farmers who had good horses and plenty of oats. He is as grand a traitor as Preston County can afford. He refused to vote for the new State, and to cap the climax, his daughter went out into the streets and held the rebels' horses, and urged them to break open the door of J.C. McGrew's store, and destroy his goods, saying it was a Yankee store, tear it up." Thus regardless of the defense offered, in the eyes of Union men Cresap and his friends were forever branded as traitorous collaborators with the enemy.[42]

On Thursday, April 30, National Fast Day, as proclaimed by President Lincoln on the eve of the great and perhaps final Armageddon between the Army of the Potomac and the Army of Northern Virginia, the *Intelligencer* tried to make light of the wilder rumors then circulating. "A great many persons around town amused themselves yesterday," the paper began, "by giving currency to various little rumors concerning the enemy. In some parts of the city it was reported and very currently believed that they had taken Washington, Pa. Some were so anxious to believe it that passengers from there by the Hempfield, had difficulty in convincing them of the contrary. We even heard of one chap who asserted in a remote part of the city that Imboden had burned the bridge over Wheeling creek. If it had not been for the fact of its being stone, we have no doubt he would have had plenty of people ready to believe it.

"Mr. Imboden is a wonderful man," the paper declared rather sarcastically. "We don't believe there is any man in the country who has been in as many different places, as widely distant from each other, within the last four days as he has. One hour he is at Beverly, the next at Morgantown, then at Fairmont, and within a few minutes at Uniontown, Pennsylvania. There is one place he hasn't been yet, so far as known, and that is Wheeling. His friends have about quit looking for him. The little 'stars and bars' that were to have decorated the windows will have to be laid away for some other time."[43]

Reports of rebels at Uniontown spread the excitement to Pittsburgh, where anxious citizens, hoping to learn more, jammed the post and newspaper offices. At 2 p.m. on the 27th, they held a mass meeting presided over by ex-governor William F. Johnson, whereupon they resolved to raise 500 men for the militia. Notwithstanding all these precautions, the president of the Fayette County Bank took no chances and fled to Wheeling with all the bank's funds. The citizens then became even more alarmed when Major Showalter's command came in from Morgantown during the early mourning hours of May 2.[44]

"Great excitement existed here today in consequence of reports from Morgantown," the Pittsburgh *Dispatch* reported on May 2. "A meeting was held at General Howe's office, of which Governor Pierpont, of Virginia, Senator Willey, Colonel Cross, commander of the Post here, and several of the most influential citizens were present. After an earnest discussion, it was decided that nothing could be done for want of proper authority."[45]

Not surprisingly, encouraging rumors could be just as wild and exaggerated as the more ominous ones. When word reached Wheeling of the rebel repulse near Simpson's Creek, the *Intelligencer* labeled the fight a great victory that had rendered Jones's whole force vulnerable to capture.[46]

At least one clever person in Wheeling, however, kept his head during the crisis, and counseled others to do the same. "ATTENTION MILITIA!" shouted his week-long advertisement in the *Intelligencer*. "THE REBELS AT GRAFTON—OUR CITY IN DANGER—Keep cool by calling at the Odd Fellow Hall Drug Store and trying a glass of COLD AND SPARKLING MINERAL WATER, drawn from Porcelain fountains. The largest assortment of Syrups always on hand."[47]

Jones and Imboden Unite

At Hightown back on April 21, Imboden's command had reached its peak strength of 3,365 men. To this number the new brigadier fervently had hoped to add hundreds, even thousands, by way of recruitment among the many southern sympathizers in western Virginia waiting for just such an opportunity as he presently meant to afford them. Setting out on this raid to help the former Staunton lawyer realize those high hopes was thirty-year-old Captain Edward Corder of Philippi, a veteran of the Fourteenth Virginia Cavalry and the Sixty-second Virginia Infantry who had been commissioned to organize a company for Colonel William Jackson's command, and whose brother James recently had lost to the rebels all his livestock save a pair of oxen, and whose other brother Joshua's fervent prayers had saved the bridge over the Tygarts. When the Federals pulled out of Barbour County and fell back to Clarksburg, Corder, who began the raid at the head of forty local volunteers from Barbour, successfully filled out his command, the future Company D of the Twentieth Virginia Cavalry. Unfortunately for Imboden's high hopes, this proved to be the only noteworthy recruiting effort thus far. Moreover, Corder's success did not compensate the general for the losses sustained, so that by the end of the month his command at Buckhannon actually contained far fewer men than when he set out from Hightown ten days ago.[48]

The drain was caused mostly by desertion, whereby Imboden had to face the ironic fact that instead of drawing men to his command, his veterans were disappearing into the very countryside from which he had hoped to reap a rich harvest of recruits. About 200 men from the Thirty-seventh Battalion alone had gone, as had a substantial number from the Twenty-fifth Virginia Infantry, many being disgruntled with Imboden's orders forbidding the seizure of horses and property for private use. Lieutenant Edwin D. Camden of the Twenty-fifth, for example, angrily reported that the cause of desertion in his Company C was the result of his complaint lodged "against a certain element stealing horses from the citizens without authority, need or pay." Moreover, Imboden's seemingly clever insistence on including in the expedition the trans–Allegheny men of the Twenty-fifth and Thirty-first Infantries now appeared to be backfiring somewhat, as many of these men could not resist, even for a short time, seeking out the comforts of their nearby homes.[49]

From Buckhannon on Friday, May 1, meanwhile, General Imboden sent his brother with the Eighteenth Virginia Cavalry to approach Weston, ten miles to the west, in order to make contact with Jones, having heard nothing further from Old Grumble since the day before. To his great surprise, Colonel Imboden discovered that Jones was not at Weston. Instead, the enemy just recently had destroyed their own stores there and retreated a few miles north to Janelew. This led the General to sadly conclude that Jones had been cut off in his attempt to join him and he consequently issued orders to pull back early the following morning to Philippi, the raid seemingly having been brought to an inglorious end. "I think we will then go back to the valley," Doctor Abram S. Miller of the Twenty-fifth Virginia happily told his diary that night.[50]

A raft had been prepared and on Saturday morning the command was ready to cross the Buckhannon River when a courier arrived with the surprising news that Jones was within six miles of the place after having destroyed the iron bridge at Fairmont.

(About the same time, Imboden learned that a party he had sent out under Lieutenant Sturms of the Nineteenth Virginia Cavalry had burned all bridges for thirty miles west of Fairmont, and a bridge six miles east of Clarksburg at Bridgeport on the Northwest Virginia Railroad.) Emboldened by this good news, his spirits dramatically lifted by the possibility of yet achieving further great results, Imboden decided to hold at Buckhannon, unite with Jones and convince Old Grumble to move in concert against the Federals at either Janelew or Clarksburg.[51]

On Saturday, May 2, Jones rode into Buckhannon and met with Imboden, the two generals heartily shaking hands while exchanging broad smiles and happy greetings of relief at having finally united after twelve tumultuous days in western Virginia. They then quickly got down to business. After giving careful consideration to the over-all situation, the two Confederate commanders now readily agreed that their combined strength, despite Imboden's severe losses by desertion, offered a good chance to overwhelm the Federals at Clarksburg, an accomplishment that undoubtedly would serve as the glorious crowning achievement of the entire expedition. Wasting no time, they moved out that afternoon for Weston, the seat of Lewis County, whose population of about 8,000 was mostly pro-Union. Colonel Imboden and the Eighteenth Virginia Cavalry reached the town that evening, but the bad roads delayed the remaining troops of the two commands. They camped two or three miles from Weston and marched into town the following morning.[52]

Jones established headquarters on the grounds of a hospital for the insane, and Imboden took over the Bland House. Their men set up camps along the Glenville road and in the streets, with pickets placed on all the roads leading into town. The two generals stationed sentinels at all the stores, and they issued a proclamation that all goods taken must be paid for at regular prices. "I have purchased fifty dollars worth here," forty-eight year old Mortimer Johnson of Company H, Thirty-first Virginia Infantry wrote his wife (May 5) from Weston, "but do not know what to do with them — having no transportation. There are plenty of goods but the difficulty is what to do with them."[53]

This had not been the first time on the expedition that Johnson encountered the problem of "transportation." "At Buckhannon," he wrote his wife in the same letter, "I purchased about two hundred dollars worth of goods, mostly plain dry goods — put them in a box with some purchased by the Qr Master of the 31st Virginia Regt. I believe he has the goods with him, do not know whether he will ever have an opportunity to send them out."

At Weston, Johnson learned that the 1200 or so captured horses brought in by Jones included some that belonged to his own family. "Father lost about 30," he told his wife, adding hopefully, "he will be paid some day." The middle-aged private, however, was not bitter. "Gen. Jones has consented that [brother?] Dick may take one of the horses taken from Father," he explained, adding, "I am glad our troops got the horses pay or no pay." (Following the expedition, Johnson would be discharged after typhoid fever caused him to go deaf, only to be killed in ambush near his home.)[54]

Occupation of Weston

As they had done throughout the raid thus far, both Jones and Imboden used this "pay or no pay" policy to confiscate many horses and cattle in the Weston area. And since their men used Confederate money to pay for the other goods, the community in general suffered great financial loss. Otherwise, little disturbance marked the occupation of the town, and except for the government commissary on West Second Street, the Confederates destroyed no property.[55]

A special prize was a splendid white horse effortlessly captured outside Weston on the Parkersburg Pike. The magnificent stallion belonged either to John Rau or George Ross, operators of a military telegraph station located on the pike above an army storage room. With the news of Roberts's retreat to Clarksburg and Imboden's approach to Weston, the two men cut the wires, buried the instruments, and took refuge with friends at Burcher's Settlement, regretfully forgetting in their haste the magnificent white horse.[56]

The departure of the Federals soldiers, meanwhile, created a dilemma for Weston's many Union sympathizers who genuinely feared that the Confederates might arrest or otherwise harass them. At a hastily convened meeting, Mayor Mintor Baily, Postmaster George W. Strickler (1834–1878, a native of Fayette Co., Pa.), and two other prominent citizens, Allen Simpson and Elias Fisher, decided that the best course of action was to leave town. "Old Ad," a trusted slave, prepared the Baily family buggy, the four men got in and rode out on the Polk Creek road, the horses struggling to pull the weight of its well-fed, heavy-set passengers.[57]

The fleeing men left behind their wives, trusting in the Confederates not to arrest them or bother their homes. Some of these wives subsequently displayed more fortitude than their wavering husbands, a case in point being Mrs. Louisa Strickler, wife of the town postmaster. After quickly taking down the U.S. flag flying in front of the post office, located on Main Street in a two-story brick dwelling that adjoined the office of the *West Independent* newspaper, she hid the banner inside the decorative cornice of a clothes closet that she then covered with a shawl. When she bravely refused to produce the flag on demand, angry Confederate troops began a rather disruptive search of her house. She ran outside, saw a Mr. E. Ralston passing by and frantically appealed to him for help. Ralston went at once to the Bland House down the street and explained the situation to Imboden, who sent four men to guard the Strickler house, two in front and two in back, to thereby prevent further intrusions.[58]

Among the many West Virginia communities that embraced sharply divided opinions on the current national crisis, Weston was no exception. With most of the prominent Union sympathizers having fled, and with Confederate troops now in town, the Southern sympathizers, formerly in the minority, became more outspoken and emboldened. Many businessmen, having heretofore carefully disguised their Southern feelings, now openly offered to the visiting Confederates whatever comfort and aid they might be able to provide. The most appreciated assistance, however, came from the ladies, who, seeing the tattered condition of the uniforms and clothing worn by their heroes, set about mending, repairing, and making new shirts, socks, and other items. "When Jones' brigade reached Weston on this raid," Captain O'Ferrall gratefully recalled, "the men were in wretched condition generally in the way of clothing and in other respects which an old soldier can readily conjecture. However, we were able to secure plenty of soap, and a river was at hand. We were also fortunate in obtaining a large quantity of calico of all shades and figures, and the fingers of many a fair hand were soon busy making the calico up into undergarments. How many they made I could not form the slightest idea, but enough to supply those who needed them the most and to send us away feeling far better and more respectable than when we reached the town." Other soldiers derived simple satisfaction from just being around such sympathetic members of the opposite sex. "I am tonight at the Baily Hotel, visiting with the ladies," Captain Frank Imboden of the Eighteenth Virginia Cavalry happily told his diary on the night of May 3.[59]

While their commanders considered plans for the move on Clarksburg, the butternuts at Weston enjoyed a much-needed two-day rest. Some men relaxed by playing ball on the grounds of the hospital for the insane. "Weston is a pretty place and its better inhabitants are loyal," observed a member of the Twelfth. "Lewis Co. has some good people in it. No wheat is raised here but we get corn bread and fare very well. Fuel is inexhaustible in Western Va. In nearly every Co. the hills are full of coal."[60]

In addition to planning ahead, Jones used the break to recapitulate the past. After sending Colonel Harmon to retrieve the Sixth Virginia from Beverly (where the regiment was to leave one company as a picket) so that the regiment could share in the attack on Clarksburg, he made out a report detailing the success of the raid thus far. He claimed to have destroyed nine railroad bridges, two trains and one artillery piece, captured 500 prisoners, 1200 to 1500 horses and about 1000 cattle, the bridge and trestle works at Rowelsburg being conspicuously absent from this list of otherwise impressive numbers.[61]

The following day, May 4, Harmon came in from Beverly with the Sixth Virginia after a tough journey that aroused among the men mixed feelings about their new orders. "Crossed Birch Mountain to accomplish which we had to march single file about 18 miles," Private Donohue complained to his diary, "leading our horses most of the way. Suffered much from hunger not having had anything to eat today."[62]

Clarksburg

Having captured Weston, Jones and Imboden now were eager to take the next dramatic step and move against Clarksburg, one of the most important military depots on the B&O and the largest base of supply in West Virginia (with smaller commissaries located at Bulltown, Buckhannon, and Weston). "It was not an unusual sight," observed Walter M. Morris of Company E, Third West Virginia, "to see fifty or more wagons, loaded with provisions and munitions of war, leave these ware houses in a single train to be hauled to the several detachments of the army then occupying different positions in the mountains of West Virginia." Moreover, a huge corral there held hundreds of army horses and mules, as well as tons of hay and grain.[63]

To capture or destroy all this, and, perhaps more important, to capture or destroy the troops defending it, would give the two Confederate generals a glorious success that might have unlimited consequences. "We can whip them on equal ground," Imboden wired General Albert Jenkins down at Princeton on May 3, "but I understand they are fortifying at Clarksburg. We shall make a reconnaissance in force there to-morrow or next day and see what they intend to do." So confident now was the former lawyer that he looked beyond Clarksburg to a union with Jenkins and a grand sweep of the Kanawha Valley. "If you were within co-operating distance of us," he continued in his wire to the cavalry commander, "we could utterly demolish the railroad from Clarksburg to Parkersburg, and then force the enemy to fight on our own terms, and, turning upon the Kanawha, clear the valley.... Rumor [false] reaches us that you are at work toward Parkersburg. I trust such is the case, and that we may get together this week. If we do, I believe the northwest is saved." Clearly, Imboden had not yet given up on his grand vision, a "wild expectation" so convincingly presented to General Lee some two months before, of liberating western Virginia from Yankee oppression.[64]

To "see what they intend to do," Imboden on Monday, May 4, sent a detachment of the Nineteenth Virginia Cavalry (including, perhaps, Private Nicholas Stulting) under Captain John Sprigg to reconnoiter toward Clarksburg, some twenty-four miles to the north. The mission failed. Near Fisher's Hill, just beyond Janelew, Sprigg and his command ran into an ambush by "three German companies of Federals." Bullets flew everywhere, several finding their mark among the Confederates, though none fatally. Sprigg and his men beat a hasty retreat back to Weston, riding hard all the way to and through town, galloping furiously up Main Street. This dramatic entrance, made shocking by the sight of blood flowing from wounded men and horses, caused such a commotion among both the soldiers in town and its citizens that "for a time pandemonium reigned." The alarm sounded, people frantically ran about the streets, horses thundered down along the river pulling two batteries, and troops hastily formed to rush out and meet the pursuing enemy, believed to be near the Smithe farm, all of which, one citizen later declared, made for "the most exciting occurrence during the war." With the rousing sounds of fife and drum added to further stir the emotions, many mothers had great difficulty restraining their children from following the soldiers. "Who in the hell wouldn't fight?" one of the eager boys reflected later in life. Then came the disappointing let-down; the Federals had not followed Captain Sprigg.[65]

Another, more serious alarm, however, occurred the following day, Tuesday, May 5, when a large Federal force jumped the picket Imboden had posted up at Janelew, only five miles to the north. This proved to be one of the few aggressive moves made by General Roberts during the entire raid. The force he sent out from Clarksburg, to see what the Confederates "intend to do," consisted of a portion of the Twelfth Pennsylvania Cavalry, Captain Hagan's company of the First West Virginia Cavalry, two companies of the Twenty-eighth Ohio Infantry, and Lieutenant Thomas F. Roane in command of a portion of Captain Bowen's Company E Third West Virginia Cavalry. (Roberts reported that the expedition consisted of the Third West Virginia Infantry under Col. Thompson, a section of artillery and about sixty cavalry.) They nearly captured the entire lot of surprised, outnumbered Confederates. "This expedition," Lieutenant Roane proudly reported, "brought in 4 prisoners, 1 two-horse wagon, 4 mules, 4 barrels of flour, and killed a number of the enemy near Janelew." (Roberts reported that they executed a vigorous attack without loss, while killing at least two, wounding five and capturing seven.)[66]

The hasty return of the Confederates to Weston, "their speed augmented by the screeching shells from a couple of guns in Bassel's meadow," prompted the two surprised rebel generals to quickly prepare for battle. "We expected a fight," Imboden later reported. But Roberts had no intention of following up this promising success with a general move on Weston. He quickly returned to his preferred strategy of cowering in Clarksburg, awaiting reinforcements, and digging-in.[67]

Spies, meanwhile, accomplished for Imboden what Captain Sprigg's patrol did not, and indeed could not. The general "received from a confidential and perfectly reliable source an accurate statement of the enemys' forces at Clarksburg, giving regiments, their size, and their batteries." Some 5,000 Federals (under generals Roberts and Kenly) with twelve guns, he learned, now held the town, and they were busy fortifying the place as well as the pass at the mouth of Lost Creek, eight miles to the east. Moreover, this incredible source told Imboden that by tomorrow Clarksburg would receive 3,000 reinforcements, including militia sent from Wheeling.[68]

Jones and Imboden Split Up

This rather startling intelligence understandably put out the aggressive fire stoked up by both gray commanders for the conquest of Clarksburg. Imboden estimated Jones's effective force at no more than 1200 men, and his own at between 2200 and 2300. This meant that since the expedition began each command had lost at least a thousand men (not including the infantry and artillery Jones sent back from Petersburg). Many had deserted. Still others Imboden had left behind at Beverly and Buckhannon, too sick or worn out to go on. And numerous guards had been sent east driving captured cattle and horses. In the face of all these discouraging facts, the two generals took stock and pondered their next move. Realizing "defeat so far in the interior would have been destruction," they wisely decided to avoid Clarksburg. That left two options: to either beat a hasty retreat back to the Shenandoah Valley, or look for other opportunities in western Virginia. Not surprisingly, especially when comparing their own naturally aggressive natures with the lack of initiative shown thus far by the Yankees, who after all were digging in at Clarksburg, the two Confederate commanders chose the second option.

They still, however, eventually would have to return to the Shenandoah. Assuming the Federals by now had blocked the passes over Cheat Mountain (they had not), giving them credit (falsely) for that at least, the generals concluded that it would be too risky to go back by way of Beverly and the Staunton-Parkersburg pike. Thus they decided that while Jones continued west to again strike the Northwestern Virginia railroad at various points, Imboden would head south in order to clear an escape route between Sutton and Summersville in Nicholas County, and wait at the latter place until the cavalrymen completed their destructive sweep and rejoined him. From there the Confederates would go on through Lewisburg and White Sulphur Springs to the Shenandoah.[69]

The safest course of action would be for both commands to now head back together for the Shenandoah via Lewisburg. Relying, however, on the continued inertia of the enemy, the two Confederate generals daringly hoped to yet fulfill the raid's vastly unrealized expectations, at least to the degree that it might be labeled a success, even without being able to point to the smoldering ruins of Rowelsburg, the original inspiration of the entire undertaking, or present to General Lee thousands of new recruits marching under the Southern cross.

On Wednesday morning, May 6, Imboden prepared his command to leave Weston. For many it was a moving occasion. From the town's southern sympathizing ladies the Eighteenth Virginia Cavalry received a hand-sewn Confederate flag, whereupon the regiment's Lt. Colonel David Beall delivered a stirring address to the appreciative crowd. The soldiers then formed up and paraded through town.[70]

Sadly joining the departing column were George and Isabella Imboden, the parents of John, George Jr., and Frank. Having lived near Weston since selling their Shenandoah property in Augusta County in 1855, the elderly couple now reluctantly complied with the wishes of their three sons, who were determined not leave them to the mercy of the hated Yankees. "They have suffered martyrdom from the accursed abolitionist," Frank Imboden fumed in his diary. The brothers fitted up a five-horse team, loaded the wagon with clothes, some bedding, and a few other personal items from the house, leaving behind all the furniture. They carried their sick father to the wagon and tearfully sent it off through the mud.[71]

After sending orders, meanwhile, for all sick men and captured stores at Beverly and Buckhannon to start east for Monterey in the Shenandoah, Imboden pulled out of Weston on Wednesday morning, May 6, and headed south on the Kanawha and Fairmont pike. A few stragglers from his command, however, remained behind to do their worst. At nearby Jacksonville, they partially destroyed a covered bridge and looted the utensils and fine china from the homes of John Arnold and Captain John Cook, a recent arrival from Highland County. At the nearby village of Bennetts Mills post office, locally called Walkersville, several homeowners, regardless of allegiance, lost nearly everything that could be carried away, and the rebels cleaned out the hat shop, including the blocks, of Abram Blagg. But even the stragglers eventually moved on, leaving the area once again to the "tender mercies of the Yankees."[72]

Roberts Makes Great Plans

The war that had been brought to West Virginia now was being fought to a great extent by West Virginians. When Sergeant J.C. Kildow and six men of Company E, Third West Virginia Infantry, assumed their picket post on the road leading to Milford, one mile from their camp at Lost Creek near Clarksburg, they all were more than just familiar with the area. One hundred yards away stood the home of Kildow's mother. Nearby was an old log schoolhouse where the sergeant had been a teacher, two members of this picket being former students — Private Walter M. Morris, whose father's house stood half a mile to the south, and Private E.W. Sullivan, whose home was a half-mile to the north.[73]

On May 1, West Virginia's Governor Pierpont pleaded by wire with Lincoln to order Burnside to send four or five regiments to Parkersburg and for Washington to send a similar number to Oakland. "If not stopped," Pierpont warned the president, "they [rebs] will carry 6,000 horses out of Western Virginia and Pennsylvania."[74]

After passing on reports to Secretary of War Stanton that the rebels in West Virginia numbered 20,000 men under none other than Stonewall Jackson, Pennsylvania's Governor Curtin that same day sent the beleaguered president two telegrams, one pleading for troops from the east and the other asking if the state should call out the local militia. "The whole disposable force at Baltimore and elsewhere have already been sent after the enemy which alarms you," Lincoln patiently replied the same day. "The worst thing the enemy could do for himself would be to weaken himself before Hooker, and therefore it is safe to believe he is not doing it, and the best thing he could do for himself would be to get us so scared as to bring part of Hooker's force away, and that is just what he is trying to do." The next day the president advised Curtin not to call out the militia. "Our forces are exactly between the enemy and Pennsylvania," he reassured the governor.[75]

On May 1, Curtin also received reassurances from Schenck, who told the governor that the only serious loss inflicted thus far by the rebels was at Fairmont. The Yougiogheny bridge at Oakland, he said, already had been repaired and was in operation. "The wild panic at Wheeling and at Pittsburgh," he told the governor, "has been to me all along unaccountable."[76]

But the panic understandably persisted. For relief from their anxieties, citizens throughout West Virginia naturally looked to General Roberts. So did the military. "After a fight of three hours," Colonel Mulligan at Grafton anxiously wired Roberts at Clarksburg in the afternoon of April 29, "our forces have been drawn back from Fairmont to Grafton. I will be attacked here to-night." Then, quite as if to bolster the confidence of Roberts, if not himself, Mulligan the next day told him, "I defy all the rebels in Western Virginia," fervently adding, "God and the right."[77]

During twelve days of the great raid thus far, however, Roberts had done nothing more aggressive than to send out Lieutenant Roane's company on the Shinnston Road, and the reconnaissance in force to Janelew, but they clashed with the enemy only by chance, not design. Yet the Iowa general apparently assumed he was accomplishing a great deal. When, after taking Fairmont, General Jones detoured around Clarksburg in search of Imboden, Roberts tried to take credit for the movement, bragging that "as rapid a retreat as the condition of the roads permitted was effected by the rebels." But instead of lunging out at and finishing off the "retreating" Confederates passing around him, Roberts continued to cower in Clarksburg and await reinforcements from outside his jurisdiction. According to one of his officers, the general even wanted to abandon Clarksburg and make for Parkersburg, some seventy miles to the west on the Ohio River, but he relented to the vehement entreaties of his colonels to remain.[78]

Reinforcements, meanwhile, did indeed continue to arrive. From Milroy's division in Harpers Ferry, Kenly's Maryland brigade came in around midnight of May 1–2 after pushing on from Grafton and Bridgeport to "raise the siege" of Clarksburg. Various militia units, including the contingent from Ohio and West Virginia led by Brigadier General A.J. Lightburn, also arrived. All this raised the strength of the command at Clarksburg to nearly 5,000 men with ten guns, more than double that of Jones, only twenty-four miles to the south in Weston. Still, Roberts did nothing.[79]

"Gen. Roberts has prepared himself for a successful defense in anticipation of an attack," the Wheeling *Intelligencer* wrote (May 11) while still believing in the Iowa general, "and he feels confident of being able to whip the rebels should they attempt to take this place [Clarksburg]. It is feared by the citizens here that the rebels design making an attempt to treat this place as they did Fairmont, and great excitement prevails among the people in consequence. The Harrison county militia is coming in by squads from all directions and the town is already filled with soldiers and citizens." Still, Roberts did nothing.[80]

He did, however, appear to keep busy. By the 2nd he had repaired the bridge destroyed in a panic by Wilkinson near Bridgeport, thus opening the line to Grafton. He urged Schenck that day to have Milroy move on Moorefield with artillery and cavalry and for Scammon with three to four thousand men to take Summersville. "This would effectually cut off a retreat," he correctly concluded.[81]

Schenck, in turn, continued his own increasingly desperate efforts to motivate and coordinate the various officers under his command in and around West Virginia. On the 2nd, he asked Burnside at Cincinnati if his troops had reached Parkersburg and if so to push them on by rail for Clarksburg, clearing the line of guerillas as they go. These with Kenly, Roberts and Wilkinson, Schenck concluded, should be enough to bag Jones and Imboden. The same day he told Milroy that Roberts believed Jones was retreating on Philippi (though on May 3, Schenck told Kelley that he suspected Jones might be making another try at Rowelsburg), and that Milroy therefore should move up the Valley to catch Jones on his probable return. He wanted Roberts to pursue Jones and for Scammon to send what he could to Summersville.[82]

At Clarksburg on the 3rd, Roberts received the Twelfth Pennsylvania cavalry, sent from Martinsburg by order of Schenck, though the Iowa general complained that all 320 horses of the regiment were broken down. Nevertheless, he at last came up with another grand scheme to move against and crush the invading rebels, whose strength he estimated at 6,000 under Jackson and Jenkins, whom he believed intended to remain at Buckhannon in order to "keep up a perpetual guerilla war." With the two regiments of militia from Wheeling provided by Pierpont available with others from Grafton to guard the rail line from there to Parkersburg, Roberts decided to use his own troops in a three pronged attack on Buckhannon. Having tasted a partial victory in the rear guard attack on Jones on May 1, whereby he boasted to Schenck on the 3rd of having done great damage, killing thirty and wounding even more, Roberts's blood was up. While Wilkinson remained at Clarksburg, Mulligan would move on Buckhannon via Philippi, Kenly by the direct road, and Augustus Moor with part of the Fourth Separate Brigade would go via Janelew and Weston. Roberts told Schenck, however, that he would implement this grand scheme, "The moment I get rations, forage, and transportation together." Then he added, "No means of transportation here yet. It will be several days before I can do anything but protect the railroad." In other words, the Confederates had little to fear.[83]

The confusing inaction created growing resentment among the soldiers, officers and enlisted men alike. Some complained about Roberts from the very beginning of the rebel invasion. For Lt. Colonel Polsley of the Eighth West Virginia Infantry, the feeling gradually went from suspicion to a firm conviction that Roberts was woefully incompetent. "My Darling Nellie," Polsley wrote his wife from Philippi on April 25, "from Beverly we fell back to this place and are now on the way to Buckhannon to assist Gen. Roberts who could not or would not assist us." Four days later, Polsley wrote to express his disapproval of Roberts's retreat to Clarksburg. "Leaving Buckhannon was not so well," he told her, "for there we had the whole Brigade together. All Northwestern Va. is now open to invasion."[84]

In a letter to the Wheeling *Intelligencer*, a soldier identifying himself as "Upshur," considered the retreat from Buckhannon to be nothing less than a disgrace. "The present writer is informed," he wrote, "that some officers and men shed tears over the strange and unaccountable movement, while all with the deepest sorrow, regretted it. The boys wanted to fight the enemy, but were not permitted." At Clarksburg, he added, "we are now sickened and disgusted. Our whole country, east and south of here, is thrown open to the enemy, and roving bands of rebel cavalry are plundering and destroying the country. Is there no help for us? Yes, there is. Give us our own army we have so freely sent into the field and a Brigadier General, with more brains and less regulations, and the new State of West Virginia will take care of itself."[85]

Though Roberts rightfully took credit for saving Clarksburg by concentrating great strength there, this did not satisfy the many critics who believed he could have done much more. Even those in the ranks realized the lost opportunity. "There was from ten to twelve thousand men here at Clarksburg," Perry H. Buzzard of Upshur County, a member of the Third West Virginia (Lt. G.A. Sexton's company), wrote from Clarksburg to a friend, "enough to run them every last one across the mountains if it hadn't been for General Roberts. If we had old Milroy here they would a went faster than they did."[86]

Roberts contented himself with the "recapture" of Weston after the Confederates left, whereupon he promptly implemented those harsh policies for which he had become so well known and hated. He took swift revenge against those who had offered even the slightest show of support for the enemy. He forced sixty-three people, the wives, children, mothers, and sisters of Confederate soldiers, to leave their homes and pass through the lines into Southern held territory, and an equal number of prominent citizens he sent as prisoners to Camp Chase in Ohio. Thus did General Roberts make war.[87]

CHAPTER NINE

Burning Springs

Harmon's Mission

"Gen. Jones," William Wilson of the Twelfth Virginia Cavalry told his diary on the night of May 5, "after very foolishly coming this far with his small force, seemed panicked this evening and wanted to commence a precipitate retreat because his pickets were attacked."[1]

Having gone so deep into enemy territory with such a small force, Jones had begun to lose the confidence of Wilson, and no doubt other increasingly apprehensive troopers. But Old Grumble had not panicked, nor did he have any intention of retreating just yet. He meant to go even deeper into Yankeedom.

The two-day rest at Weston had worked wonders on his men. "[We went] away feeling far better and more respectable than when we reached the town," recorded Captain O'Ferrall, the future governor of Virginia. "Soap and water and clean clothes had a most wonderful effect, and all of us felt that John Wesley was right when he declared that 'cleanliness is, indeed, next to godliness.'"[2]

Nevertheless, the anticipated continuing hardships, emphasized by the day's cold rain, intensified in many the wish to go home. "The vision of house & wife & children, dressing gown & slippers, a couch and a warm fire, with a hot supper to boot," the Sixth Virginia's Chaplain Richard Davis wistfully wrote his wife, "rose before me with a distinctness that was tantalizing." As if to strengthen those visions, Davis carried with him some precious calico recently purchased for his wife.[3]

Jones now intended to hit more targets on the Northwestern Virginia Railroad, which broke off from the B&O at Grafton and ran eighty miles west to Parkersburg. To once again achieve maximum damage, he split his force, sending Harmon with the Twelfth Virginia, Eleventh Virginia, and the Thirty-fourth Battalion to hit the rail line at West Union in Doddridge County, twenty-six miles to the northwest. Moreover, he wanted to know if rumors were true that a sizeable force of Yankees had arrived at West Union to thereby threaten his rear. With the rest of his command, Jones headed west on the Parkersburg pike.[4]

A five mile ride west on the Weston road brought Harmon to Camden, where he turned northwest and rode through Churchville, then he entered Doddridge County (population about 5,200, mostly pro-Union) and passed through Avon and Blandville. When about a mile from West Union at 6 p.m. (May 6), his advance under the Eleventh Virginia's Lieutenant Edmund Pendleton captured fifteen pickets and three scouts, who readily revealed that the town was heavily defended by units of the Second West Virginia Infantry and Wood County's two brass militia cannon.[5]

By order of General Roberts, who somehow had anticipated the raiders' next move, Colonel Latham had left three companies of the Second West Virginia at Salem, fifteen miles west of Clarksburg, and proceeded eleven miles by rail to West Union with the regiment's remaining six companies, about 400 men, arriving at 3 a.m. on the 5th. Later that morning a train came in from Parkersburg with one company of the Eleventh West Virginia Infantry, the rest of that regiment having been dispersed at various points along the rail line. When news reached him next morning that the Confederates were approaching, Latham quickly set up a strong defensive line that stretched from one end of town to the other.[6]

Late that afternoon (May 6), Harmon approached the position through a narrow gorge framed by rocks and hills on the right and a swamp on the left. Latham's long-range muskets determined that the Confederate advance should stop about 600 yards off. "[I]n consideration of our weakened forces and the utter exhaustion of men and horses," William Wilson correctly surmised, "Col. Harmon prudently declined attacking." This proved to be one of the few times during the raid the Federals acted promptly to successfully head off the Confederates.[7]

Harmon did not allow this unusual situation to give cause for discouragement. If he could not have the town, he determined to do damage, however minor, elsewhere. While remaining threateningly in line "amusing" the enemy, he sent a squadron of the Eleventh under Captain Daingerfield two miles east to Smithton (Smithburg) to burn two small railroad bridges, after which Harmon drew off around dusk, taking with him a herd of cattle daringly captured while it grazed between the lines. "The Yankees may learn from this," scoffed O.P. Horn of the Twelfth Virginia. "[T]hey cannot starve us out as long as they have anything to eat, for we can take it from under their noses, with loaded guns in their hands." (Latham would remain at West Union until the 11th, and go on to Weston two days later.)[8]

The daring acquisition of the cattle herd notwithstanding, Harmon is known to have lost at West Union at least one trooper, who possessed the unusual distinction of being a recently deserted Yankee sergeant now serving voluntarily in Captain O'Ferrall's company of the Twelfth Virginia. While trudging along on foot near West Union after abandoning his broken down horse, the former sergeant and two others in the same situation spied some good horses in a nearby field, perhaps a quarter mile from the road, and set off to get them. Just before reaching the animals, however, they suddenly came under fire from hidden citizens. Two men went down, including the ex–Yankee, while the third escaped and ran back to the road. O'Ferrall never saw the sergeant again. "Always at his post," the captain fondly recalled of him, "faithful to every duty, ever ready to perform any service and encounter any danger. He was a deserter," he wistfully added, "and no doubt opposite his name on the muster rolls at Washington is written the word 'deserted,' and if he had ever been captured alive his fate would have been that of a deserter, yet I shall always believe he deserted because he was fighting in what he regarded as an unjust cause against what he believed to be a righteous cause."[9]

The following day, Thursday, May 7, Harmon rode sixteen miles northwest on the Northwestern Pike to Ellenboro in Ritchie County (population about 6,900), then turned south and headed five miles for the county seat of Harrisville. Just outside the town he came upon what at first appeared to be an ominous sight when he spied in the distance a solid line of defenders. A few shots from his own troopers, however, quickly scattered what he later learned had been a home guard of about seventy-five old men and boys, some of whom walked up and quietly surrendered. The rebels then rode undisturbed into town. "They were astounded to see us," the Twelfth's William Wilson observed of the local citizens, "as I doubt not the loyal farmers were who loaned them their horses for the 'scout.'" Then he added by way of expressing his contempt for "disloyal" communities, "H[arrisville] is a strong Union place. The 'Ritchie Press' was knocked into 'pie' as also Pierpont & Co's store." As was the U.S. Post Office, a symbol of Federal authority Wilson's comrades took such pleasure in destroying that they did not stop until they had trampled all its stamps in the mud.[10]

After paroling his prisoners and destroying their weapons, Harmon rode four or five miles on the Parkersburg road before finally going into camp that night (7th) near Cairo, where he linked up with Jones. "This was a very disagreeable day and disagreeable night," William Wilson complained to his diary, despite the apparent success of Harmon's mission, "and our company was on picket. Rainy and cold." Then in reflection of his home-sick mood he added, "Jones' stock lower than ever this evening."[11]

Jones's Mission

After beginning the march at 9 a.m., Jones camped the night of May 6 in a meadow on the Parkersburg pike several miles west of Weston. It rained hard during the afternoon. "My oil cloth coat kept me from getting wet," Reverend Davis wrote his wife, "but my clothing was damp, & I was chilly, and I remember that the vision of home & wife & children, dressing gown & slippers, a couch and a warm fire, with a hot supper to boot, rose before me with a distinctness that was tantalizing as the gloom of the evening increased." Once in camp, they "received orders to be up by 12 and to march at 1. We kindled some rail fires, after much delay, & tho' I had no couch of down or roses to rest upon, I found that mother earth would suffice for a resting place to a weary & sleepy man. With my rubber coat wrapped about me, & a rail for a pillow, I soon fell asleep."[12]

The next day, Jones went on to Smithville, some forty miles west of Weston, where he left the pike and proceeded some twelve miles northwest to Cairo on the Parkersburg Branch of the B&O, his trying two-day journey having covered "upward of 80 miles without unsaddling."[13]

To take the town, which appeared to have few defenders, Jones sent the Thirty-fifth Battalion sharpshooters to the right of the road, from where they dismounted and seized the high bluff to the south. The rest of the battalion formed into squadrons for the purpose of charging the town. The First Maryland, meanwhile, went around to the rear of the place, where Captain Bond deployed the battalion into a single rank in order "to magnify our numbers," he reported, adding, "I advanced in full view." Surrounded and outnumbered, the Federals, all of twenty men and one lieutenant, put out the white flag without firing a shot.[14]

Jones then set Lieutenant Williamson to work. With the help of part of the Thirty-fifth battalion under Company A's Captain Frank M. Myers, the engineer destroyed three sixty-foot spans over the North Fork of Hughes River above Cairo. They then turned their attention to a series of short railroad tunnels bored through solid rock. In the space between the wood support frame and the side of the tunnels, Williamson and his helpers packed a considerable amount of dry cordwood, which they soaked with coal oil and set on fire, "causing the top to fall in from the heat," Lt. Colonel White reported with great satisfaction, "and thus damaging the road to a considerable extent."[15]

These efforts, much to the relief of his exhausted and sore-backed mules, used the last of Williamson's powder, which meant that from now on Jones no longer held the option to do large explosive demolition. Then to further lighten his load, the lieutenant, by order of Jones, threw away all his iron tools, "it being almost impossible to carry them."[16]

After paroling his prisoners and destroying their weapons, as well as a nearby sawmill to prevent it from being used to repair the bridges, Jones moved three or four miles back out on the road and camped the night of May 7, where Colonel Harmon rejoined him.[17]

Union Reaction

General Roberts, meanwhile, remained baffled, confused, and idle. On the 4th he alarmingly informed Schenck that Jones, Imboden, and (W.L.) Jackson had united at Weston with perhaps 10,000 men. He also claimed to know that a General Wilder (no such person) with 4,000 infantry had left New River to join Jenkins's 2500 troopers to operate in the Kanawha. Thus did the Iowa general become convinced that Confederate forces were carrying out not simply a raid but a full-scale invasion. "You will see the necessity of throwing large forces into West Virginia," he alarmingly told Schenck, "to prevent its being overrun." The department commander at first was inclined to agree. "This notice and call from Roberts is, perhaps, not without reason," he told Kelley the next day (5th), while urging him to send Roberts the Fourteenth Pennsylvania Cavalry and "whatever else is possible."[18]

Unlike Roberts, however, Kelley refused to become unduly alarmed. The 1st Division commander saw things quite differently, even going so far as to conclude that not only had Roberts vastly overestimated Confederate strength in West Virginia, but that also since Jones had been sending captured stores to Beverly, the rebel leader must be retreating that way, thereby bringing the raid to an end. Therefore, instead of sending more troops to Roberts, Kelley wanted returned those already sent to Clarksburg from the 1st Division. Rightly suspecting the 4th Separate Brigade commander of using wild estimates of Confederate strength as an excuse for inaction, Kelley believed only one course of action remained. "I most respectfully suggest to the commanding general," he wired Schenck, "to send General Roberts positive orders to move on the enemy at once. I fear the rebels will get out of West Virginia before General Roberts gets ready to leave Clarksburg."[19]

Schenck now swung back the other way. "Unless you have some certain evidence that the enemy is massed in greatly superior force in front of you," his adjutant wired Roberts on May 5, "the commanding general is of the opinion that you ought at once to move against and pursue him."[20]

Not surprisingly, this did not have the desired effect upon Roberts. Despite having twice the strength of Jones and Imboden, he remained convinced that the reverse was true. Moreover, he rightly complained that while the enemy possessed abundant cavalry, he had but 450 mounts, "most of which are broken down." "[Y]ou have underrated this raid," he scolded Schenck, adding, "I think it had just commenced.... I expect to be cut off from Parkersburg."[21]

When news came in that the Confederates had hit West Union, Schenck again reversed his thinking, being forced, somewhat embarrassingly, to agree with the seemingly immovable Roberts. "The rebel movement against West Virginia is by no means over," the department commander wired Cox at Cincinnati on the morning of May 7, adding that Jackson, Imboden, and Jones had between them as many as ten thousand men. Despite the current scarcity of rail cars because of the need to transport "prisoners taken by Hooker," Schenck ordered Milroy to at once send the Fourteenth Pennsylvania Cavalry and the Ninth and Tenth Virginia Infantry (Hays's brigade) from Winchester to Martinsburg and thence by rail to Grafton, and he ordered Kelley to proceed there as well and take command.[22]

(Schenck also took the time on May 7 to ask Col. J.C. Kelton for the dismissal of Col. J.C. Paxton of the Second Virginia Cavalry for getting drunk and failing to carry out a diversionary attack on Lewisburg, as ordered by General Scammon at Charleston. Paxton was dismissed May 8.)[23]

"I have sent and am sending all troops I possibly can westward from Harper's Ferry and Winchester," Schenck informed General Barry at Wheeling on the morning of May 8. Moreover, when Kelley reached Grafton (which he did the following day), Schenck wanted him to send the Ninth and Tenth regiments on to Wheeling and thence downriver to the perceived threatened point of Parkersburg.[24]

With Jones once again heading west and the raid obviously still not over, Governor Pierpont urgently wired President Lincoln on the 7th to ask for help, while also pleading for governors Curtin and Tod to provide 4,000 militia each. "With that force and with what I can bring into the field," the West Virginian confidently told the president, "I think we can drive the rebels to the Allegheny Mountains."[25]

General Roberts, meanwhile, again developed a grand plan, his third in two weeks. On the 8th he told Schenck that he was reestablishing depots at Weston and Webster, and with the Fourth Separate Brigade, Ewing's battery, and three skeleton companies of cavalry, some 2500 men under Colonel Augustus Moor, "I shall push forward to reoccupy Sutton and Birch as soon as it can be accomplished." Kenly with his three regiments of infantry, the Twelfth Pennsylvania Cavalry and a battery, some 1800–1900 men, would retake Buckhannon, while the Ninth, Tenth and Fourteenth West Virginia Infantries, the Fourteenth Pennsylvania Cavalry, just arrived from Martinsburg, and a battery would retake Beverly.

It did not take long, however, for this plan, like the others, to be scrapped. On the 10th, Roberts told Kelley that it would be unwise to send from Clarksburg either Moor or Kenly while Jones's whereabouts remained unknown.[26]

Burning Springs

On Saturday morning, May 9, Jones left the Cairo area and rode a short distance west on the Parkersburg pike. He then diverged left and headed southwest toward Burning Springs in Wirt County. About three miles from town, near Cherry Ford, he left his plunder of stolen livestock under a guard. He arrived at Burning Springs about 2 p.m., behind Captain McDonald's company of the Eleventh Virginia, which had captured several wagons and teams, farmers' hay and grain, before riding into town around 10 a.m.[27]

Burning Springs surely had not been on Jones's original agenda when the raid began. After Rowelsburg, he seemed to select his targets on the basis of circumstance and opportunity. Nine days before at Philippi on May 1, he obviously had given serious consideration to bringing the raid to a close and returning to the Shenandoah. After uniting with Imboden and taking Weston, however, he had wanted to strike at Clarksburg. When that proved unfeasible he decided to make a lunge toward Parkersburg and then return to the Valley by way of Summersville to the southeast. Exactly when the idea occurred to him of hitting Burning Springs is unclear, but considering the fact that he overlooked other nearby important oilfields at California in Wirt County and Horseneck in Pleasants County, it seems probable that here Jones acted more on impulse than careful planning.

A mere four years after the world's first oil well began operating near Titusville, Pennsylvania, in 1859, Burning Springs, located on the north bank of the Little Kanawha River atop one of the largest shallow pools of oil ever discovered, some forty-two miles upstream from Parkersburg, had become the largest oil producing region in the world. In that four-year time span, the town grew from 100 people to more than 6,000, with 1,000 men employed in the oil fields.[28]

At depths ranging from twenty-eight to 200 feet, some eighty to 100 noisy steam operated wells produced about 250 barrels a day of high quality oil. The barrels were loaded onto flatboats and sent some forty-two miles down the Little Kanawha for processing in Parkersburg, where the rich ooze was made into kerosene for lamps, both civilian and military, and lubricants for machinery, the B&O buying 200 barrels a month for the latter purpose.[29]

News of the rebels' approach, brought to Burning Springs about 7 a.m. by a lone rider galloping hard into town, set off a mad frenzy among citizens desperate to hide their horses, their property, and themselves. Several people got in the small flatboats tied up at the wharf and fled down the Little Kanawha towards Parkersburg. Some rode

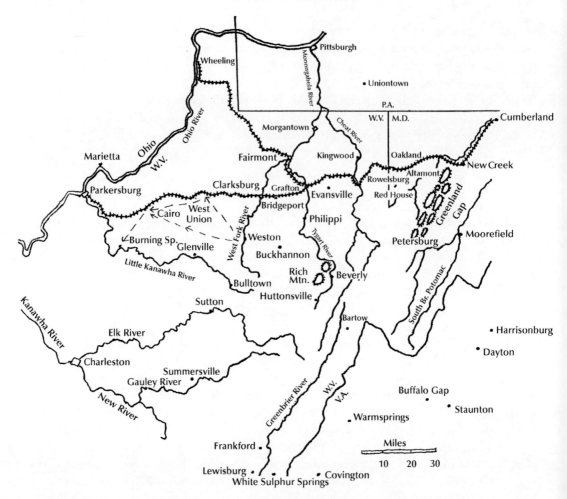

11. Jones's movement from Weston to Burning Springs, May 6–9, 1863.

off on their horses, forgetting in their panic to take their wagons. Others simply ran into the woods.[30]

Still others maintained cooler heads. Saloonkeepers quickly made deals with teamsters to send their precious whiskey out of town, their great stocks of beer they sadly poured into the street. The whiskey-loaded wagons headed up the Little Kanawha for Burning Springs Run, the teamsters occasionally stopping along the way to hide a barrel in the woods.[31]

"On the morning of the invasion," recalled George Conley, who operated two teams of horses in the oilfield, "we loaded three barrels of whiskey into each wagon and took off up the run at 8:30 o'clock, two hours ahead of the Rebels.

"When we were across the divide, we attempted to hide our loads, but the first barrel slipped through our nervous hands and went crashing down the hillside, struck a tree near the foot of the hill, and whiskey and barrel staves flew in every direction. The odor of whiskey filled the air, and would have been a dead give-away to pursuers. Therefore, we drove a mile farther and hid our remaining barrels in a large clump of

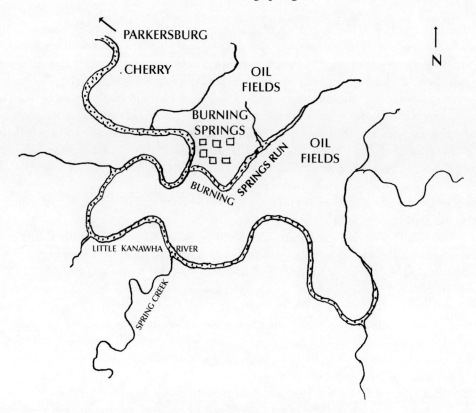

12. Burning Springs, W. Va., May 9, 1863.

blackberry briers." His sacred mission successfully finished, Conley tied his hoses in the woods and calmly walked back to town.[32]

Ed Ball now also put his two oilfield teams to use in the same good cause. While a saloonkeeper and his assistant loaded one wagon, Ball rushed over to his nearby home to get the other team. After harnessing them, he put his twelve-year-old daughter on one horse, gave her the halter strap of the other, and told her to follow him. "As I neared the head of the run," Ball later recalled, "another teamster, with three barrels of whiskey on his wagon, passed by at a rapid pace. Apparently, he was too scared to stop and hide his load. He never returned to Burning Springs, and the saloon keeper lost his whiskey."[33]

Soon after all this commotion ended, the rebels entered an eerily quiet town. "The whole village seemed to be deserted," recalled John Blue of the Eleventh Virginia Cavalry. They did, however, see Alf Greathouse calmly sitting on his porch near the abandoned Wheaton's Store. When questioned by the graybacks Alf pretended to be deaf and dumb. "Now there is a typical Goddamned Yankee for you," one rebel scornfully remarked as they rode away. "They can see a little, but they are all as dumb as hell."[34]

"Our company was the advance of the command," Lieutenant Blue went on, "and not finding any one at home proceeded to unlock the store and having been a little short of rations for several days proceeded to help ourselves to whatever we saw of which we were in need, such as sugar-cured hams of which we found a nice lot on board [a flatboat, one half filled with barrels of oil, the other half a warehouse], almost every man had something for his mess; one a ham, another a bushel or so of crackers, another a half bushel or more of sugar, another coffee or tea, hats, boots, in short our company supplied ourself [sic] with many needed articles before the brigade arrived."[35]

Meanwhile, out in the noisy oilfields, many workmen did not hear or get word of the emergency, but continued working until they saw dozens of the gray-clad strangers moving among them. "After a while," recalled a rebel in White's battalion, "they learned the character of their visitors, and surmising their object, the workmen turned away from the wells, and shutting off steam, remarked, with doleful faces, 'I guess oiling is played out now.'" The derrick-covered fields and surrounding hillsides, and the hundreds of barrels of oil stacked up everywhere by the river and on flatboats, presented a view like nothing the Southerners had ever seen.[36]

But Jones's men did not forget that they were after horses too. While riding that morning toward a branch of his law practice he had established in Burning Springs some two years before, Josiah Lee of nearby Elizabeth came upon a man galloping fast in the other direction. "Hide your horse quick," the man cried. "The Rebels have taken over the town and are stealing all the horses they can find. I am riding out to warn the farmers!" Lee promptly took his horse into the woods and tied it to a tree. He then calmly walked into town, now swarming with rebels, and went to the home of his friend Val Rathbone, a relative of the colonel formerly in command of the Eleventh West Virginia Infantry and one of the oil fields' major owners in partnership with J.N. Camden of Parkersburg. (Another person who had held substantial interest in the oilfield was Colonel William L. Jackson of Parkersburg, now with Imboden as commander of the Nineteenth Virginia Cavalry.) Lee had arrived in time to witness Rathbone offer Jones a large sum of cash to spare the oil works. No fool, Rathbone took the precaution of adding that that kind of money was not readily available but would have to come from Parkersburg. Not surprisingly, Jones refused to wait.[37]

Knowing, or at least assuming, that the Federal government owned these wells, as well as did Northern businessmen who had confiscated much of the property from Southerners, Jones determined to destroy it all. "In a word," he reported, "everything used for raising, holding, or sending it off was burned." This included the derricks, tanks, barrels, pumping engines, engine houses, wagons, and flatboats.[38]

From a hill near the junction of the run and the river, Josiah Lee watched the conflagration. "The fires were an awesome sight," he later recounted to his grandson. "The surface of the run storage basins was a sheet of flame that rose a hundred feet into the air, and hundreds of smaller fires from burning tanks, derricks, engine houses, and homes dotted the valley from the mouth of the run to its source — a distance of two miles. Billows of jet black smoke rose a mile high, creating myriads of fantastic silhouettes against the sky.

"The wooden storage dams across the run soon burned away and turned thousands of additional barrels of flaming oil into the river. An hour later the volume of burning oil was further increased by the torrents of burning oil that came down the run from exploded tanks along its banks; and eventually the river became a sheet of flame as far as the town of Elizabeth —13 miles below. So intense was the heat from the river that most of the trees and vegetation along the banks for 25 or 30 yards from the water were killed."[39]

Everett Schoolcraft, a worker in the oilfields, had been one of about fifty people who earlier had rowed across the river to hide in the woods. While now watching the awful holocaust, a man turned to him and said quietly, "You know, I think hell must look like that."[40]

The scene left an indelible life-long mark on all who saw it. "These boats, after being set on fire, were cut loose from the shore and allowed to float away," recalled Frank Myers of White's battalion, "and as they burst, letting the blazing oil spread over the water from shore to shore, the truly wonderful spectacle of a river on fire was presented, while to heighten the grandeur of the scene, explosion after explosion boomed out upon the night air, and columns of dense black smoke twined with the red flame from the wrecks of the boats, loomed skyward a hundred feet from the blazing sea; and on shore the oil barrels were burning and bursting, their contents flowing in streams of liquid flame all over the ground, and from the wells themselves great fiery pillars rose up, and added to this, the many buildings contributed their quota of flame to the great conflagration; in fact no better illustration, on a small scale, could be presented of the popular idea of the burning brimstone lake, where 'The devil sits in his easy chair, Sipping his sulphur tea, And Gazing out, with a pensive air, On the broad bitumen sea.'"[41]

O.P Horn had much the same reaction to the ghastly scene. "It was a grand and imposing sight to see thousands upon thousands of barrels, which were on the boats to be sent away, all on fire," he wrote, "and as it progressed the barrels would burst, making a noise like distant thunder." The burning oil spilled into the water to create "the novel spectacle of a river on fire." Great black clouds rose "like mighty mountains." "These pillars, or pyramids, of flame," he went on "after ascending separately some distance in the air, seemed to unite in one great sheet of fire, and it looked as though the firmament was one vast conflagration. This appalling and supernatural spectacle was beyond conception or description. It was, in appearance, the flames of an expiring world, and I believe that the men would have so considered it, but for the fact that it was of their own creation.

"The fire also extended to the river, which was soon enveloped in flames, containing many colored lights. The current carried the flames over the water-falls, producing the most fantastic shapes and figures, resembling fiery demons, dancing upon the surface of the river, ever and anon disappearing in the darkness and again appearing, when on a line with one's vision. The men were greatly relieved when we left this scene of desolation, and many a man that night dreamed of hell and of a personal devil."[42]

John Opie also likened his experience to a scene resembling Hades. "The current carried the flames over waterfalls," he remembered, "producing the most fantastic shapes and figures, resembling fiery demons dancing upon the surface of the river."[43]

The flames even spread to the treetops in the nearby woods where many terrified townspeople were hiding. The green spring foliage, however, kept the fire from spreading too rapidly, thereby allowing the panicked citizens to move on to safety.[44]

So great was the conflagration that people in Parkersburg, forty-two miles distant, gathered in the streets and on rooftops to watch the amazing red glow in the southeastern sky. When they learned the cause of the blaze, the fear arose that the fire might spread down the river to Parkersburg, but the flames never got past Elizabeth, some eight miles downriver from Burning Springs.[45]

The temperature in the surrounding area became unbearably intense. "We had secured feed for our horses and gone back several hundred yards on the side of the mountain and halted for the purpose of feeding our horses and making a cup of coffee," remembered John Blue, "but the heat became so oppressive from the burning oil, that we were compelled to move farther away."[46]

There is at least one known tragic incident. Apparently unaware of the explosive capability of oil, a trooper climbed a ladder to the top of a one-third full storage tank and dropped into it a burning torch, blowing himself and four others to smithereens. Comrades buried their mutilated bodies in a common grave on the run bank.[47]

"Night came," recalled Josiah Lee of his observations from the nearby hilltop, "and the scene was even more terrifying. No words can describe it — everywhere a raging inferno of fire and smoke. It looked like hell had been brought to earth. People, fearing for their safety, fled from the lowland to the hills. Around me were a hundred or more men, women, and children — the men, stolid, silent, impassive, sat or stood staring at the fires; the women, some hysterical, some silent, all frightened; the children, uncertain, scared, crying."[48]

In contrast to the horror most felt at the sight, even by those who had caused it, Grumble Jones took great satisfaction and pride in what he saw. "A burning river," he reported, "carrying destruction to our merciless enemy, was a scene of magnificence that might well carry joy to every patriotic heart."[49]

Though Jones's men did not deliberately try to burn the town, numerous places inevitably caught fire. These included business establishments, both the Methodist and Baptist churches, several homes, and the Chicago House, the area's notorious twenty-room hotel, gambling house and prostitution establishment built by a group of clever speculators. (After the raid, smaller establishments of six to ten girls each then sprang up, whereby Burning Springs "became the Sodom of Sin, anointed with oil." They lasted until a new, more luxurious forty-room Chicago House was rebuilt in 1865, but it, too, eventually burned down.)[50]

Having witnessed, and indeed created, hell on earth, many of Jones's men felt great relief when the order finally came to leave. Enthralled by the spectacle before them, Edward Rich and some of his comrades in the First Maryland did not realize their tied up horses stood on a burning bridge. "The bugle summoned us to mount," recalled Rich, "and hastily we sought our well-nigh maddened horses and the march resumed."[51]

The destruction was complete. "When we arrived at this place, we found much oil and whiskey," John Opie declared, despite the best efforts of the town's saloonkeepers to save their liquor, "and when we left, there was neither oil nor whiskey there. The two most combustible fluids known to science are coal oil and corn whiskey. The men were ordered to destroy both of these useful fluids, as they were considered contraband goods. This they did in the usual way — they drank the whiskey and fired the oil."[52]

Effects

"As the night of horror passed," Josiah Lee later related, "the fires began to die down, and by noon the next day they had gone out. The smoke cleared, and there before us lay a valley of desolation and ruin."[53]

A few days later, J.N. Camden and the Rathbones met to decide what to do next. They sadly concluded that the threat posed both by local Southern sympathizers as well as rebel raiders who might return at any time, made it too dangerous and risky to reopen the oil fields until after the war, "and Burning Spring," recalled Josiah Lee, "died in a night." Workers, businessmen, and their families left, "and the city soon reverted to a country village in population." All the whiskey that had been saved in the woods eventually was shipped by flatboat to better markets in Parkersburg.[54]

After the war the town quickly revived. Camden leased land from the Federal government to build locks on the Little Kanawha to facilitate shipment of oil to a refinery in Parkersburg. Businesses sprang back to life, people returned and rebuilt homes, and, with the reopening of the Chicago House in 1865, the city became bawdier than ever. In 1885, however, oil production began to decline as the fields played out, and five years later it ended altogether. Burning Springs died once again.[55]

Jones claimed that at Burning Springs he destroyed 150,000 barrels of oil. Some have since concluded that the Southern general underestimated the damage by half, that he actually had burned around 300,000. Both figures, however, are far too high. Production for all of 1862 amounted to 87,000 barrels, and for 1863 it came to no more than 70,000. It is known that Jones's men destroyed five-and-one-half barges loaded with oil. Each barge held 2,000 barrels, meaning 11,000 had gone up in flames. Perhaps as many had been destroyed on the ground, making for a total loss of about 20,000 to 22,000 barrels.[56]

Though such direct losses were quite severe, even more devastating was the loss of potential production, which may have been in the hundreds of thousands of barrels. Thus Burning Springs ultimately proved to be the greatest destruction of an industrial complex ever committed by the Confederates during the entire war.[57]

Few at the time, however, seemed to realize or appreciate the magnitude of the loss. The national and local press gave it little attention. "A Pittsburgh telegram of the 11th," reported the Wheeling *Intelligencer* on May 13, "says the rebels made a raid to the Burning Spring oil well, and destroyed the well. They burned the boats and destroyed large quantities of oil." Nothing more. On the same day, the Marietta *Intelligencer* gave the story just a few more words. "On the 7th inst.," it reported, "a party of rebel cavalry appeared at the Burning Springs, Wirt Co., W. Va., and burned all the oil wells and tanks that would take fire and most of the boats at that point. They took the goods from the store boats — not destroying those boats — the goods on one of them belonged to Justus Moore of this city."[58]

Other than General Jones's report, the Official Records contain no account of the dramatic events that occurred at Burning Springs. Moreover, no Federal officer was ever held accountable for the terrible loss, in part because the government, despite receiving one dollar per barrel in taxes, had made no effective provisions for protecting the valuable oilfields. At least one historian (Louis Reed) suggests that Federal authorities covered-up the story in order to suppress the disheartening effects it may have had on public morale. It seems more likely, however, that few people at the time fully appreciated the true extent and effect of the great damage done by the Confederates at Burning Springs.[59]

CHAPTER TEN

Summersville

Imboden Marches to Summersville

In anticipation of a move south toward Summersville, Imboden some days previous had sent fifteen men from Weston with a dispatch to go via Braxton to General Sam Jones at Lewisburg in Greenbrier County, some 100 miles to the south, "with instructions to get it through by any means in their power." Imboden wanted Jones to create a diversion toward Fayetteville and in the Kanawha, but he never heard back from him on the subject. As far as Imboden knew, he would be on his own during the march to Summersville.[1]

The poor condition, as a result of the weather, of the Gauley Bridge and Weston Turnpike, which generally ran southwest out of Weston, permitted him to make only five miles on May 6. Since the raid began on April 20, the men had seen only six days that did not have rain, a situation that made all the roads nearly impassable while providing the horses with little to eat except the young grass found along the way. "The roads are in the worst order of any I have ever seen," James Hall of the Thirty-first Virginia told his diary. The terrible conditions led to a number of desertions, the highest rates occurring among men who could not resist the temptation to seek out from relations living in the community a comfortable, dry bed and a warm home cooked meal.[2]

"We have no idea of our destination or whereabouts," Private Hall wrote the next day. Putting twelve horses to pull each cannon, and throwing away the spare wheels of the artillery and fifty solid shot from each caisson, the command, "with extraordinary labor," reported Imboden, made two-and-a-half miles on the 7th and six miles on the 8th, making for only fourteen in three days. "Very rainy & disagreeable," Sergeant Joseph Snyder of Company C, Thirty-first Virginia noted in his diary on the night of the 8th. About dark the following day, they dragged themselves into Bulltown, where, by way of reducing desertion rates, three companies of the Twenty-fifth Virginia received brief furloughs to visit their nearby homes.[3]

The harsh conditions, however, did not stop Imboden from searching for animals. "Many and pitiable were the scenes of women, girls and old men, pleading for their horses and cattle," remembered Paul McNeil, "but the Confederate soldiers who had been sent there to execute the orders of their government, did it faithfully," regardless of their victim's political sympathy. "We are making more enemies than friends," Dr. Miller growled in his diary on May 8. "I think this expedition was more for the purpose of getting cattle than fighting Yankees."[4]

Moreover, at Bulltown Imboden managed to collect a few recruits, mostly from Harrison County, enough perhaps to fill out two companies in the Thirty-first Virginia. Welcome as these additions may have been, however, they only added to an ongoing problem, that of finding enough food for everyone. "We drew no rashions (sic) except beef last night," the Thirty-first's Sergeant Snyder complained to his diary on the night of May 10.[5]

After burning the enemy's stores, the Yankees having already destroyed all the salt works and stopped up the wells, Imboden pulled out of Bulltown on Sunday, the 10th, and marched fifteen miles in welcome dry weather before going into camp at 3 p.m., nine miles north of Sutton. There the Thirty-first, at least, received a "treat," wrote Lieutenant James Potts, without naming the source, of "Peachbutter, Applebutter, Preserved fruits, Molasses, Bacon, Flour, Potatoes, &c &c."[6]

The Twenty-second Virginia had not been so fortunate. The men broke camp back on April 20 with only seven days' rations, which they consumed long ago, and they now resorted to such measures as smoking cigars and sucking on candy to distract their growling stomachs. Some men became so desperate that "it was said that the trail of the Twenty-second could be traced by the birch bark pulled off the trees for the men to eat."[7]

Starting out early, the command about noon the next day, Monday the 11th, passed through Sutton, the seat of Braxton, where Imboden and his men at last felt relieved to be in friendlier country, the county's 5,000 residents being decidedly pro-southern. Clearing the way for Jones, who was about one day's march out, Imboden set his men to work destroying more enemy stores and entrenchments, then he crossed big and little Birch Mountains before going into camp for the night.[8]

"The Regt. undergoes the fatigue of marching splendidly," Private Hall proudly wrote in his diary that night. "Today I was much pleased by getting into a canoe to ride across the river-though the other boys had to wade-but about the middle of the river the canoe upset, and as a matter of course I got very wet."[9]

On the 12th, the command made it to Birch River in sparsely populated (about 4600 people, mostly pro-southern), semi-wild Nicholas County, fifteen miles north of Summersville, the county seat. That night Imboden sent his brother ahead with about 200 men of the Eighteenth Virginia Cavalry to scout toward Summersville. When about three miles from the town, Colonel Imboden sent word to the general that the Yankees were preparing to evacuate the place. The young Imboden wanted to attack but he needed help.[10]

Realizing the Yankees might get away before that help arrived, however, Colonel Imboden drew up his men and stormed into Summersville, sabers drawn. He quickly made the disappointing discovery that the enemy, the Ninety-first Ohio (Colonel John A. Turley, 2nd Brigade, Col. Carr B. White, Scammon's 3rd Div.) and two companies of cavalry, indeed had gotten away, having left about an hour before, heading west for

Gauley Bridge. Riding hard after them on the Gauley Bridge Road, Imboden caught up with the rear guard in the dark about four miles from Summersville. A wild melee ensued, with shouting men running and riding in all directions. When it was over, Imboden counted twenty-three captured Yankees. The greatest prize, however, was the wagon train of thirty vehicles, each pulled by six mules, making for 180 altogether, and loaded with thousands of pounds of corn and great quantities of molasses, bacon, and hard bread.[11]

When General Imboden received word of this at 2 a.m. (13th) he immediately ordered reveille. By a forced march his men reached Summersville about 3 p.m. "Marched early," Sergeant Snyder told his diary, "and got to Summersville ... in eager anticipation of commissary captured by Imboden's cav." Despite their extreme fatigue, the famished soldiers dove into the food on the Yankee train, each man having since Beverly subsisted mostly on half a pound of meal per day. The captured mules they used to replace their own worn out artillery and wagon horses.[12]

That same evening, the two rebel commands reunited once again when Grumble Jones came riding into Summersville.[13]

Reaction in Parkersburg

When news came in that Confederate forces had reached the Clarksburg area, some seventy-five miles to the east, forty-one-year-old Colonel Daniel Frost of the Eleventh West Virginia Infantry, commander of the post at Parkersburg, declared on April 30 martial law throughout Wood County. Even though Wood County's 11,000 citizens were decidedly pro-union, Frost, in command since February, threatened that if the enemy occupied Parkersburg and destroyed the property of Union citizens, he would take retribution on the local secessionists.[14]

Among exasperated Unionist throughout the new state, this seemingly harsh course of action received increasingly strong support. "Let it once be well understood in West Virginia," declared the Wheeling *Intelligencer* (May 3) in voicing its strong approval of the action taken by Colonel Frost, "that when loyal men suffer from an invasion secessionists shall be held responsible for their sufferings, and there will be little wishing and hoping for Jenkins and Imboden and Jackson to come on. The trouble had been that sympathizers among us could hope and wish and write for the rebels to invade us, and all the time feel secure themselves, whatever might happen. Whether the invaders came or not these sympathizers were well off. They were protected just as usual. Their business and their property went on. Their condition was really enviable. They were exempt from almost every hardship of the war.... It is about time that this condition of things was stopped.... We hope to see it become a perfect and unmistakable understanding that the dangers of an invasion shall fall upon the heads of all alike; that a strict responsibility for the raids shall be imposed upon the disloyal.... If their property is exempted by the invaders and that of Union men pillaged and destroyed, recompense the loss out of their property."[15]

By means of handbills distributed throughout the county, Colonel Frost called out the 113th Virginia Militia, commanded by Major Rathbone Van Winkle. Between 500 and 1,000 men responded (including Captain J.H. Henderson's company from Claysville, Captain John D. Roberts's company from Limestone, and Captain L.A. Beckwith's company from Lubeck). Moreover, Frost obtained Governor Pierpont's permission to keep the gunboat Belleson on the Ohio River to help protect Parkersburg.[16]

Through the last days of April and the first week of May, nervous Wood County residents scanned the newspapers and passed along the latest rumors in an anxious attempt to follow the progress of the Confederate march through West Virginia. Their concern increased dramatically when Colonel Frost bitterly complied with General Roberts's order to distribute the Eleventh West Virginia along the line of the B&O, leaving in Parkersburg the mostly unarmed militia (and Dr. William P. Marr, a civilian surgeon working under contract for the army whom Roberts could not force to leave with the Eleventh. Marr continued his work at the general hospital, which was filled to capacity with soldiers on sick leave).

Colonel Daniel Frost (Roger Hunt Collection, U.S. Army Military History Institute, Carlisle Barracks, Pennsylvania).

When on May 3 the Confederates reached Weston, a two–day, seventy mile ride to the east, anxiety in Parkersburg reached a fever pitch, especially when it became known (incorrectly) that with Jones rode Colonel William L. Jackson, the Parkersburg district judge who two years before had summarily tried to dismiss charges brought against three Confederate sympathizers who had tried to burn a railroad bridge east of Parkersburg to prevent the passage of Union troops. When the Wood County Prosecuting Attorney (M. Jackson) protested, Judge Jackson cited him for contempt, whereupon tempers flared, pistols were drawn, and the citation was dropped. In retaliation for the humiliation he had suffered at the trial, Colonel Jackson, went the rumor, now was bent on plundering and burning the city.[17]

Imagining the Confederates to number some 8,000 men, the Parkersburg Safety Committee, under J.E. Wharton, editor of the Parkersburg *Gazette*, met in emergency session to plan the town's defense. There was little the committee could do, except try to stiffen resolve and morale by authorizing the Belleson to fire a thirty-five gun salute that evening (May 4) "in honor of the new State of West Virginia," the thirty-fifth to join the union.[18]

Anxiety then turned to near panic when word came in that Confederates under Colonel Harmon had reached Harrisville. "Col. Frost at Parkersburg," General Roberts wired Governor Pierpont, "reports by telegraph the advance of Rebel cavalry twenty miles from Parkersburg. Frost wants to know what is being done by General Cox or Burnside for the safety of Parkersburg." Apparently neither Frost nor Roberts received an answer.[19]

Desperate for accurate information, Colonel Frost on May 7 sent out toward Cairo a mounted patrol of five men, under his son, nineteen-year-old Sergeant Major B. Taylor Frost. The sergeant and his men promptly discovered, by way of being captured by Harmon's troopers, that Confederates indeed were in the vicinity.

Harmon took the captives on to Cairo, where they came under intense questioning regarding troop strength at Parkersburg. Frost fooled no one when he said that the city had been reinforced by troops from Ohio and by gunboats on the river. "You're a damned liar!" a lieutenant angrily shouted at the boy-sergeant. "You're a damned liar!" Frost shot back with the only defense he could think of at the time, whereupon General Jones intervened to call off the heated interview.[20]

Though he did not know it at the time, Sergeant Frost had been at least partially truthful with the rebels. On May 7, the day the young sergeant left on his patrol, the gunboat *Naumkeag* arrived at Parkersburg under forced draft from the Ohio River Naval Command to assist the Bellson. And in response to Governor Pierpont's plea for help on May 6, Ohio's Governor Tod ordered R.W. Putnam in Marietta to send all available troops and Ohio Militia to Parkersburg. But Putnam provided only 400 militiamen, and these Roberts quickly took away to guard the railroad.[21]

Seemingly reassuring news then came that General Kelley had sent the Fourteenth Pennsylvania Cavalry, and the Ninth and Tenth West Virginia Infantries, but Colonel Frost knew these regiments could not arrive in time to save Parkersburg. Feeling helpless and abandoned, he prepared to evacuate the seemingly doomed city.

Citizens easily read the portends of doom, and quickly acted accordingly. Banks and other businesses took their valuables across the river into Ohio, the post office moved to Marietta, and hundreds of people fled, leaving the town almost deserted. Frost now could do nothing more than place at the intersection of the Northwestern and Staunton Turnpikes a mounted patrol to give advance warning of the Confederate approach.[22]

The town's hastily departed included delegates who had met on Wednesday, May 6 to nominate officials for the new state, the election for governor and state officials being scheduled for May 28. After completing their nominations on Friday the 8th, "encouraged no doubt," the Wheeling *Intelligencer* reported (May 13) rather scornfully, "by two gunboats on the Ohio River," they departed. "Steamboats going upstream to Wheeling suddenly were filled with delegates," the *Intelligencer* went on, "who struck a bee line for the nearest haven of safety."[23]

Not everyone, however, was upset about the current situation. The departure of the Eleventh West Virginia and news of the approach of the raiders, put the local secessionists "in a holiday mood," and they openly disregarded Frost's martial law edict.

Everywhere, it seemed, the Stars and Bars suddenly appeared. Singing "The Red, White, and Red," punctuated with yells of "Hurrah for Jeff Davis," Southern sympathizers came out into the streets to celebrate the anticipated arrival of the Confederate cavalry. A thirteen-year-old girl at the time later recalled in her old age that this was the only happy day she could remember during the entire war.[24]

But the Confederate cavalry did not come. Instead, Union troops, including one complete regiment, began pouring into the town in the afternoon of May 9, sent there on boats and trains from Marietta by Ohio's Adjutant General Hill. News of their arrival quickly spread, and almost as quickly, citizens began pouring back into town. Then word soon came in that the Confederates had turned south, away from Parkersburg.[25]

To celebrate their safe deliverance, the elite of Parkersburg society went to dine with commissioned officers at the elegant Swann House. The evening (May 9), however, was abruptly cut short when word spread of a strange red glow in the sky to the southeast over Burning Springs. Scampering up to the hotel roof, the diners readily understood what they saw. With mixed feelings, they silently watched the eerie spectacle. Grateful that Parkersburg had been spared, many of the city's elite now standing on that roof (especially the Rathbone family) had invested heavily in those distant oil fields.[26]

Jones Marches to Summersville

When Jones left Burning Springs (but not before some in the Sixth Virginia had ridden to within eight miles of the Ohio border in search of horses) he took the Valley road southeast down the valley of the Little Kanawha and camped a few hours on Saturday night of May 9 at Pine Bottom, three miles below Grantsville in Calhoun County. Early the next morning, he again split his command, this time, among other reasons, in order to better secure forage. He sent Colonel Lomax with the Eleventh Virginia and White's battalion across the river at a point about twenty-one miles southwest of Glenville in Gilmer County, so that they could proceed through a wooded, thinly populated safe area and provide protection to Jones's right flank.[27]

That night Lomax camped at Arnoldsville (Arnoldsburg) in Calhoun County. Jones went northeast up the valley on the other side of the river, going via Stumptown to stop on the 11th at Glenville, gathering horses and cattle along the way while at the same time losing several mounts. "The day being warm & the horses not having had anything to eat since yesterday morning," Private Donohue told his diary, "several fine horses were left on the road, mine being one so much exhausted I had to lead him. Not a mouthful for our horses tonight."[28]

"Reached Glenville early this morning," William Wilson of the Twelfth Virginia told his diary. "A good many of the 25th reg't," he observed, "are here on furlough — at home for the first time since the war.... The Union men had run off," he added disdainfully, "the Southern men had been forced to take the oath several times."[29]

At Glenville, "the Gen. had compassion on the horses," Reverend Davis wrote his wife, "which, now, for many days past, have been failing, falling lame, and giving out, one after another, day by day, and allowed us to halt at noon, & go no further. I got my boots half soled in the village of Glenville, and then toiled across the mountain to the camp, which I found pitched in a green meadow, through which a fine little stream was running.... After unsaddling & turning Bill loose to graze, I lay down on a grassy bank, and slept a while; then, rousing up, I addressed myself to the task of washing my drawers, socks, under flannel & linen shirt, which stood in bad need of a renovation." Three weeks had passed since the Reverend had last washed his clothing. "Capt. Owen & Dr. Galt, impressed like myself, with the absolute necessity of abluting our under-garments, joined with me. We had soap, a kettle used by a family for washing, stood near, by the branch side, a trough of lye was at hand, and we set to work in fine spirit. Owen, who seemed to be very knowing, directed the process, the soaking & the rubbing & the soaping, and the boiling and the rinsing; and all would have been done very well, had not Owen made his mixture in the kettle too strong, by putting about ½ as much lye as water," thereby ruining the flannels.[30]

The following day (12th), despite the increasingly dangerous fatigue among the horses of his command, Jones pushed on about twenty-six miles southeast, crossed Elk Creek and entered Sutton in Braxton County, reuniting there with Lomax, and camped five or six miles beyond the town. "Very kindly entertained," Private Wilson told his diary about his stay near Sutton. "This country has suffered considerably," he added. "Coal & produce all sent down the Little Kanawha to Parkersburg on rafts."[31]

"This is certainly the most barren country yet seen in our scout," Private Dono-hue noted his diary, "the entire country seeming to consist of barren mountains & rocky ravines. On our scout today for the first time since our entrance into Western Virginia we had from the top of a high mountain an extended view of the surrounding country which presented nothing but a continuation of mountains to the blue Allegheny of the East." The magnificent scenery was not the only thing that impressed Donohue. "Igno-rance & poverty," he observed, "prevailed to a greater extent then it has ever been my pain to witness. An illustration of the prevailing ignorance was afforded in the fact that several persons, both male & female, on being asked in what country they lived expressed entire ignorance on the subject."[32]

Moving about in this vast, intimidating wilderness, some men actually came to appreciate the ubiquitous bushwhacker, if only as a means of breaking the boredom. "At every turn," recorded Frank Myers of the Comanches, "the bushwhackers enlivened the route by popping away with their old rifles, but they would not venture in range of the Sharpe's carbines and Colt's revolvers carried by the brigade, and consequently did no damage, but on the contrary did much good, acting as provost guard, to keep up the stragglers; and their sprightly style of warfare kept Jones' men in a good humor all the time, in fact the most pleasant part of the whole raid was through the bush-whackers' special territory, for without anything to vary the monotony of the march, this continual roaming through that interminable sea of mountains was a very tiresome business."[33]

On the 13th, word reached the command of Lee's great victory over Hooker at Chancellorsville, though they would not know for two more days of the tragic loss of Stonewall Jackson. The men perhaps were cheered even more when they learned that at Summersville Imboden had captured a great wagon train of provisions. "This is a god-send to his army," Wilson told his diary, "and he writes that he can provision us."[34]

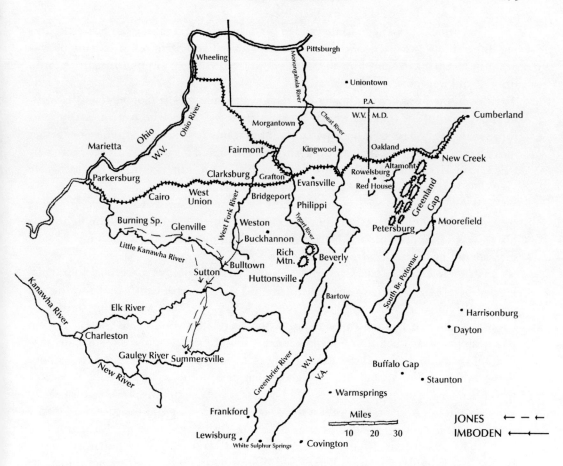

13. Jones's movement from Burning Springs to Summersville, May 9–14, and Imboden's movement from Weston to Summersville, May 6–14, 1863.

The command marched over Powell Mountain and camped that night "in a good field" eight miles from Summersville in Nicholas County. "Marched on slowly to Summersville," Wilson recorded on Friday, the 14th, adding bitterly "where all of Imboden's promises vanish into thin air." To the great dismay of Jones's troopers, the captured Yankee provisions already had disappeared among Imboden's own famished men. "Crossed the Gauley river by a miserably rough ford," Wilson went on, "and after an hour or two's march went into camp hungry, worn out & desponding."[35]

General Roberts

On Monday, May 11, Roberts told Schenck of the wild rumor, eventually proved false, that General John B. Floyd, former Virginia governor and a major participant in the 1861 campaign in western Virginia, was marching into West Virginia with 10,000 rebel reinforcements. Schenck immediately responded with sensible advice — to at once attack Jones and Imboden before Floyd arrived. Roberts chose to ignore the advice.[36]

That same day, General Kelley added his desperate pleas to those of Schenck, urging Roberts to waste no more time and strike with "all you have," even offering by way of an inducement to send him the Tenth and Twelfth West Virginia Infantries. Still, Roberts did not move.[37]

When the Iowa general finally did retake Weston after the Confederates had left, he spent most of his time, as we have seen, arresting citizens who had shown support for the enemy. "I have sent back parts of all my trains to bring up supplies for further movements," he wired Kelley on the 13th. Then he added his usual excuses. "Have neither transportation, subsistence, nor forage to go on, until they return. Movements are very slow because of the bad condition of the roads."[38]

Like Schenck and Kelley, many others had lost patience with the Iowan. "Gen. Roberts had 1,000 in Clarksburg but had not the Stamena (sic) to give them fight," the Sixth West Virginia's Corporal Henry White told his diary on May 2, adding, "all such men should be dismissed [from] the service."[39]

For several days in Clarksburg, the Eighth West Virginia's Lt. Colonel John Polsley had been eagerly anticipating a visit from his wife. "I have had two or three letters written for you, darling, lately," he wrote her on May 7, "but the trains having all stopped because of the Rebels, I destroyed them. When I wrote for you to come here," he went on, "I supposed that before you could get here Gen. Roberts would make some demonstration that would compel the Rebel Army to fall back. But he remains here without doing a thing. It is shameful and outrageous that such a thing as he is should have command here or anywhere. He is perfectly helpless — consult nothing but his own safety and ease and is nothing more nor less than a curse to the cause and the country. Oh, my own dear Nellie, you cannot know how sick I am of this thing — how utterly disgusted."[40]

When Roberts finally moved and reoccupied Weston, Polsley remained unimpressed. "It is intolerable, humiliating and disgusting to serve under such a thing," he wrote Nellie from Weston on May 14. "And Western Va. suffers. The army and the Cause suffers."[41]

"There is nothing to say, however," he wrote with bitter sarcasm the next day to a friend, "save that we retreated safely from Buckhannon to Clarksburg and that Gen. R. is safe. With two Brigades and a reserve of militia anyone ought to be safe. We kept together as much as possible and gave the enemy free scope-did not even annoy him by an armed reconnaissance. It never before had been my fortune to serve with a man so humane so considerate. He wants no lives lost-no town exposed to shells. And singularly enough he has been the first one to discover that there are no tenable positions in this country. Buckhannon not being tenable, he fell back to Clarksburg. Arriving there he discovered that it was no better and came very near making a strategic move to Fairmont and Wheeling, and would have done so had we not all remonstrated. He continually imagined that we were surrounded and that the enemy would dash right through us. It is a great thing to have the right man in the right place. We now hold Weston and will in a few days commence a rapid and vigorous pursuit of the enemy. We have allowed him to savage the country all around us and have given him time to collect and carry off an immense amount of Booty. He is not now more than one hundred miles distant (having crossed Elk at Sutton last Monday) and when he gets a good start we will follow him up closely-regular army style.

"Cannot something be done? Why is it that such men are sent here? [Roberts is an] old, childish, fearful imbecile. The most fitting place that could be found for him is a room in the new building that is going up here on state account. Let him remain in command and another raid will make this portion of W. Va. not worth the holding— and it will be depopulated."[42]

Newspapers that previously had been very supportive of the commander of the Fourth Separate Brigade, even to the point of adulation, now began having second thoughts about him. "We hope that Gen. Roberts will be able to show that he has been of some earthly account thus far," the Wheeling *Intelligencer* fretted on May 9. "There is a feeling of indignation that our military have been utterly powerless in the hands of this raid, and have actually been as much despised as so many men in buckram by the raiders."[43]

That feeling of indignation spread rapidly among the local civilians. In early May, Maria Phillips, the same who had endured the rebel occupation of her home town, Buckhannon, wrote the Wheeling *Intelligencer*, "giving the coward, Roberts, such a tongue lashing, as only a woman can give." At her home, she read the letter to two of her friends. "Kate [Heavener] clapped her hands with delight," she proudly told her journal, "and Mrs. Cooper said, 'My dear Mrs. Phillips, I want a copy of that, that I may lay it in my desk and read it every day of my life.'"

Maria's father, however, had reservations about the letter. "Father looked very serious," she observed, "and said he was afraid I had been too hasty, that it was rather a serious matter to attack a high officer in such manner, although he richly deserved it."

Searching for approval, Mrs. Phillips then asked for the opinion of her father's friend, a Mr. Taft, an attorney. "He sprang from his chair," she wrote with great satisfaction, "his teeth clenched, his eyes flashing and his whole frame quivering with excitement. Said he, 'It is God's eternal truth! You did right. We are a free people. The freedom of speech and liberty of the press are ours, and must we be silenced? No! by the Almighty! Never!'"

The published letter turned Maria into something of a local celebrity. "Kate [Heavener] said she had a good joke to tell me," she told her journal, with some degree of pride, on May 15. "She said Lieut. Stuart of the 12th Pa. [Cav.] came to her and asked her if [I] was single. She told him that I was Capt. Phillip's wife. He then made inquiries about Capt. Phillip's health, wondering if he was not predisposed to consumption, and likely to go off in a decline &c."[44]

Despite the outspoken offensives taken by Maria Phillips and others, General Roberts still had his admirers, some of whom promptly came to his defense. He who criticizes to the newspapers, read an anonymous letter printed in the Wheeling *Intelligencer* on May 8, "does gross injustice to Gen. Roberts and injures our cause," delusionally adding, almost as if written by Roberts or a member of his staff, that by cleverly concentrating at Clarksburg, thereby saving the valuable stores there, and his command, "that officer has defeated every plan of the rebels."[45]

CHAPTER ELEVEN

Home

Imboden

At Summersville on Wednesday, May 14, Imboden finally heard from department commander Sam Jones at Lewisburg. Obviously not aware of the worn down condition of Imboden's command, Jones considered it to be on the verge of even greater accomplishments in western Virginia. Moreover, coveting what he believed was substantial booty in Imboden's possession, he finally decided to get more involved in the campaign. He offered to send up from Lewisburg John Echols with a regiment and two battalions of infantry, and a supply of flour, to relieve Imboden of his surplus cattle and thereby free him for no less a spectacular achievement than a march in concert with Old Grumble on Charleston. Moreover, by way of diversion, Jones proposed to send McCausland up from Princeton to Fayetteville with 1200 men. Enemy strength in the Kanawha Valley, Jones wrote Imboden, probably did not exceed 3000 men, whereupon "you ought to be able to clear it out easily."[1]

Imboden and Grumble Jones, however, were in no mood for such grand schemes. For the moment, they had had enough of western Virginia and thought only of getting their tired, hungry, depleted commands back to the welcome confines of the Shenandoah Valley. After an uncomfortably rainy night, the march began at 8 a.m. on the 15th, the men by order of Imboden each carrying a ration of cooked beef issued to them the day before. The Twenty-second Virginia and the Thirty-seventh battalion went down to Hughes Ferry, where they raised a sunken boat and crossed Gauley River. The rest of the command Imboden put on a little known country road upon which it marched about twenty miles up the Gauley to a ford at the mouth of Cranberry Creek. "We had to wade across," Sergeant Snyder of the Thirty-first Virginia told his diary, adding, "had great difficulty in getting our wagons across on account of the big rocks & deep water."[2]

The next day they went on the Cherry Tree River road and crossed into Greenbrier County, covering about ten miles. Like Pocahontas and Pendleton, Greenbrier County had been brought rather unwillingly into the new state of West Virginia, its

178

12,200 inhabitants being sufficiently pro-southern for Jones and Imboden to trust them until General Lee should send for the captured cattle left grazing in their midst.[3]

Rising at 4 a.m. on the 17th, the command trudged over Cold Knob on a road by the same name, "over which it was said but two wagons had ever passed before." In this seemingly endless expanse of wilderness forest, many of Imboden's men began to wonder if Greenbrier County might be uninhabited. For thirteen miles, the Twenty-fifth's Doctor Miller carefully noted in his diary that night (May 17), they saw not one sign of a house or other human presence. "The front of our Reg. saw 5 deer in one drove not far from the road" wrote the doctor. "Some of them fired at them but hardly scared them. All that country is fit for is deer and other wild beasts." Finally reaching a sparsely populated area on Sinking Creek known as the McClung settlement, the command went into camp about 3 p.m.[4]

Starting at 7 a.m. the next day, the men made only eight miles before going into camp around 2 p.m. at Falling Springs near Frankfort, where Imboden gave them a welcome one-day rest after a tough march of some fifty miles in four days. Here at last the entire command might relax and feel more at ease for the first time in nearly a month. "Reaching Greenbrier," Imboden reported, "our troubles ended."[5]

The men thoroughly enjoyed the welcome respite. "This is a most beautiful country," Private James Hall of the Thirty-first Virginia told his diary on May 19. "The sun smiles blandly upon the green hills, the cattle are standing in the cool shade of the different groves, and the far off mountains are clothed in a smokey purple hue. What a still, quiet day! Scarcely a sound can be heard to break upon the deep quietude. After so many long and weary marches, one day of rest is very gratefully received, and I have been asleep nearly all day under a low spreading cedar."[6]

Early on Tuesday, the 20th, exactly one month since setting out from Camp Washington ten miles northwest of Staunton, Imboden's command resumed the march and in hot, sticky weather made it that afternoon to Lewisburg, the county seat. The following day they made nine miles on the James River and Kanawha Turnpike to White Sulphur Springs, and on the 22nd they covered sixteen more miles on hot, dusty roads to cross over into Virginia proper and reach Callaghan's in Bath County of the Shenandoah Valley.[7]

On Friday, the 23rd, Colonel William L. Jackson broke off with the Nineteenth Virginia Cavalry and the companies that would become the Twentieth Virginia Cavalry and returned to Camp Northwest on Knapp's Creek in Pocahontas County, where he resumed his outpost position on the "Huntersville Line." That same day, Imboden went on with the rest of the command about twenty miles to Hot Springs in Bath County.[8]

On the 24th, they marched five miles up to Warm Springs, then went on another eight miles to the northeast before going into camp. "Shoes have entirely worn out," Private Hall noted in his diary that night. When a heavy rain inconsiderately came in, Hall "with 3 other 'poor soldiers' put up at a barn."[9]

The next day, a Sabbath, May 25, the command made an incredible march of perhaps as many as twenty-five miles, to reach Buffalo Gap at the eastern base of Buffalo Mountain, nine miles west Staunton. Imboden and his weary men had completed the circle.[10]

Colonel Lomax

"Our exhausted condition and exhausted supplies," Jones wrote after meeting Imboden in Summersville, "rendered homeward movement necessary." That said it simply enough. There would be no clearing of the Kanawha Valley, or for that matter, any other adventure in "West Virginia." Save for the one final challenge of getting home to the Shenandoah Valley.[11]

While still back at Sutton on Tuesday, the 13th, some twenty-five miles north of Summersville, Jones decided for reasons of celerity and security to split the command. With instructions to reach Warm Springs in the Shenandoah by the most direct route, some sixty-five crow-flight miles to the southeast, he sent Colonel Lomax with the Eleventh Virginia Cavalry.

Starting out that morning, Lomax rode ten or twelve miles up the Elk River into Webster County, then struck out across the densely oak and pine forested Yew Mountains into Pocahontas County. A guide on foot led them single file up a narrow path, an old Indian trail the locals called it, which became so narrow in places as to require the men to dismount, while in other stretches the laurel and the thickets were so dense, tall and overgrown as to block out the sun and make it seem like nightfall. The frequent screams of a panther or mountain lion caused a chill to run up many a man's back while he reached for his carbine and quickened his pace to catch up with the man in front of him. Upon reaching the top, those at the head of the winding column looked back with delight to see the tail, about one mile down the mountain.[12]

They camped that night near some unknown small wilderness stream. The horses went hungry, but the stream being alive with mountain trout, two or three men from each mess went in search of crickets and other insects to use as bait. Soon the entire regiment was enjoying ample quantities of trout broiled on coals, supplemented by cornmeal baked on smooth stones found nearby.[13]

The following day, the 14th, the regiment pressed on in much the same manner, finally stopping to camp that night in a large clearing on top of a mountain. A sturdy log structure, the first house seen in some time, stood on the open land, but the men's interest quickly shifted from that to a lamb they saw frolicking in a nearby pen. A knock on the door brought out two elderly women, a Mrs. Hinkle and her white-haired slave. Mr. Hinkle was away, the wife explained, the boys figuring he was hiding in the brush. They did not care about that. They wanted that lamb and offered to pay as much as fifty Confederate dollars for it. Mrs. Hinkle adamantly refused. That was her pet, she said loudly, and would not give it up for any price. Taking the wise precaution of not trusting the uninvited guests on her land, she quickly brought the lamb into the house and locked him in the kitchen.

Resigned, the boys went to bed. Several, however, could not sleep, visions of roasted lamb, complete with hallucinatory smells and tastes, keeping them awake. Finally, they rose and held a "council of war," whereupon they resolved that military necessity required the acquisition of that lamb. They quietly lowered into Mrs. Hinkle's wide, rock-lined chimney a Private Dailey, who by means of a halter secured the lamb, taking for good measure a washtub to be used as a cooking pot.

"Get up," Lieutenant John Blue heard someone say. "We have something to eat."

Not having succumbed to the culinary hallucinations that tormented his comrades, Blue quickly had fallen asleep, rolled up in a blanket, whereby he missed the "council of war" and the action it had authorized. "In a case of this kind I very seldom asked questions," he subsequently explained, "but wondered how or where the eating came from."

Not waiting for a second invitation, Blue quickly rose and followed over to a large, bright fire his friend Ike Parsons, the same who outside Fairmont more than two weeks before had roared with laughter upon discovering that the "mortally wounded" Blue had suffered no more than a bruised shoulder. A metal washtub sat on the fire, round which stood a number of men, all savoring the delicious aroma rising from it. The man in charge of the kettle kept probing into it with a sharp stick until satisfied that its contents were done. The men then carefully removed the kettle from the fire and pitched in. "I thought it the best and sweetest meat I've ever tasted," proclaimed Blue, correctly adding, "I knew the old woman would never see her lamb again."

Never suspecting that her uninvited guests had contrived to descend her chimney, Santa Claus like, not to give but to steal, Mrs. Hinkle the next morning searched everywhere for her precious pet lamb. Whether from naiveté or an unwillingness to face the truth, she finally concluded that its fate was "a great mystery" that never could be solved.[14]

From the Hinkle farm on Thursday morning of the 15th, the command descended "into that fertile and lovely valley known as the Little Levels of Pocahontas," a trooper later recalled, "which seemed to us a veritable Canaan. At any season of the year the Little Levels of Pocahontas County is one of the fairest spots on earth, and, looking down upon this valley from the top of the mountain presents a landscape picture unequaled on this continent. But at this time, in the month of May, the famous little valley wore its loveliest garb, and its hospitable people welcomed us with open arms. After weeks of toilsome march and adventure, we were at last back in God's country." The warm welcome, the beautiful surroundings, and the comforting feeling of being back "in God's country," however, were more than offset by the terrible news told to them by the locals: Stonewall Jackson had died five days before from wounds received at Chancellorsville.[15]

After three days of severe marching, mostly through tough, wilderness areas, Lomax reached Back Creek in Highland County in the late afternoon of the 15th. Two days later he made Warm Springs, where at least fifteen of his men staggered into town on foot, their horses having broken down or died.[16]

Jones

While Colonel Lomax and the Eleventh Virginia headed generally southeast from Sutton, Jones on the 13th led the rest of the command south. That day they made about fifteen miles to camp on the Hill farm near Birch River. Before bedding down for the night, Jones ordered Marshall and the Seventh Virginia to destroy a nearby Yankee stockade, an assignment described by the colonel as "a pretty hard job."[17]

On the 14th, the command took the Wilderness Road seventeen miles south to

Summersville, where Jones sent on ahead Colonel Harmon and a small detachment from the Twelfth Virginia. They were to make speed for Staunton and arrange there for supplies and provisions to be sent to Warm Springs. From Summersville, the rest of the command made another fifteen miles to stop for the night on the Dorsey farm. The order to "Unsaddle your horses & go into camp," Reverend Richard Davis wrote his wife Louisa, was "an annunciation which the poor weary fellows have answered with a cheer." After not writing Louisa in a while because of a lack of writing material, this letter was courtesy of a storekeeper in Glenville from whom the Reverend had "begged" a bottle of ink, and of a woman by the roadside who gave him a quill.[18]

The next day, the 15th, while Imboden started out from Summersville, Lomax rode through Pocahontas County, and General Roberts "reoccupied" Weston and Buckhannon, Jones crossed over the mountains into Greenbrier County and camped for the night on the McFarland farm near Meadow Bluff. "In these mountain gorges," Private O.P Horn recorded, "we saw poverty in the most affecting shape-families cooped up in hovels and cabins no better than rail pens, with no visible means of support." And he added ruefully, "it was amusing to see these simple and deluded people trembling ... and when we passed along they would inquire where all these people came from, and my that this must be the whole Southern army." These isolated mountain folk "didn't think there were so many people in the world."[19]

Several of Horn's comrades drew similar conclusions about the rough-hewn people they saw along the way. "I don't think I ever saw as many children before," Lieutenant Jonathon Mann (killed at Brandy Station June 9, 1863) of the Sixth Virginia Cavalry wrote his wife, "nearly every woman I saw over fourteen had a child in her arms."[20]

On May 16 the command moved to near Lewisburg, the seat of Greenbrier County, camping one mile from the town. Here for the first time they heard of the momentous events of the Chancellorsville campaign, including the tragic loss of Stonewall Jackson. "Jackson's death," Captain O'Ferrall remembered, "cast the deepest gloom over the brigade. All hoped and prayed it was a false report, and yet the information seemed to be authentic as to leave no doubt of its truth."[21]

At Lewisburg, O'Ferrall's fine, dark bay horse finally gave out. Having paid $800 (undoubtedly in Confederate money, to a man named Abe Bright) for it only a few weeks before, he became quite attached to the animal, highly prizing the stallion for his coolness in battle.[22]

O'Ferrall was not alone in his predicament. "Scores and scores of horses have played out," Reverend Davis observed in a letter to his wife, "and have been left along the road," adding in reference to his own mount, "but old Bill has scuffed along." Davis had kept Bill going, he believed, by dismounting and walking him up or down steep slopes, which in this country meant frequently. Still, he worried that time was running out for his beloved friend. "Old Bill is still on his legs and standing up to his work," he told his wife, "but is getting very thin & very weary & slow."[23]

After giving most of the day to rest, Jones at 3 p.m. on Saturday, the 17th, pulled out of Lewisburg and led the command nine miles east to White Sulphur Springs, perhaps the most renowned of the many natural spas straddling the Virginia-West Vir-

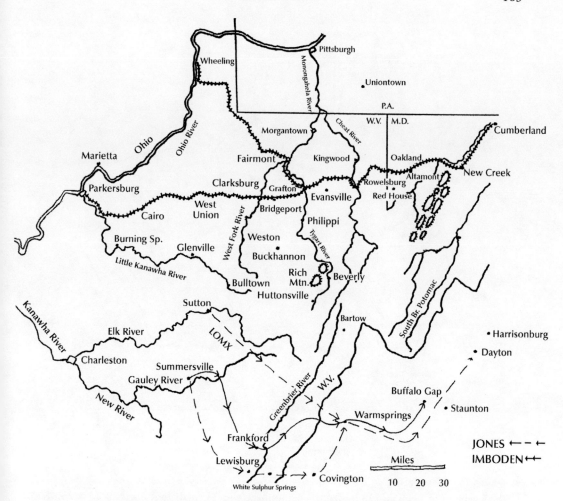

14. Jones's movements from Sutton and Summersville, W. Va., to Dayton, Va., and Imboden's movements from Summersville, W. Va., to Buffalo Gap, Va., May 14–25, 1863.

ginia border. Now in friendlier country, Jones allowed the men to ease up and "take the water," which they gratefully enjoyed. "This fashionable watering place," William Wilson of the Twelfth Virginia told his diary, "exceeds in the extent and beauty of its grounds and buildings all my previous conclusions."[24]

"The place is really beautiful," Reverend Davis wrote his wife. "After seeing it, we were not able to appreciate the other watering places, the Hot, the Warm, and lastly, a little one horse concern in Augusta, the Stribling Springs."[25]

The following day, May 18, they marched sixteen miles, crossing back over the Alleghenies, to camp near Callahan's in Alleghany County, Virginia. On the 19th, they covered about twenty-five miles, crossed Jackson River and camped at Warm Springs, where presumably they obtained supplies sent up from Staunton. "Enjoyed springs," Wilson noted in his diary.[26]

On Wednesday, May 20, the command marched twenty-seven miles, crossing Warm Springs Mountain and Cow Pasture River. On May 22, they camped at Hogshead

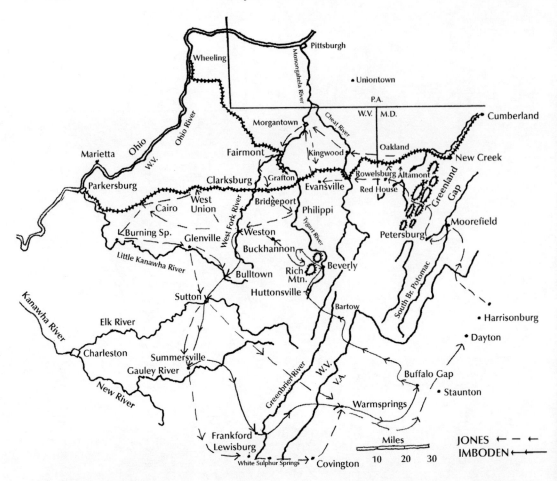

15. Movement of Jones and Imboden throughout the entire expedition, April 20–May 25, 1863.

near Mt. Crawford, and the next day they made it to Dayton, about five miles south-west of Harrisonburg.[27]

Jones and his men now had completed their circle.

Roberts

While Imboden and Jones were returning to the Shenandoah Valley from the Sum-mersville area, the Federals did virtually nothing, other than send a flurry of telegrams. Despite having an abundance of troops in and around West Virginia, they sent none into the Shenandoah to cut off the retreat of the rebels, nor did they make any aggres-sive moves to actually confront them.

"I have re-occupied Buckhannon with cavalry," Roberts informed Schenck on May 15, "and am here with the infantry of the Fourth [Separate Brigade] and General Kenly's brigades, waiting rations and transportation to re-occupy Sutton, Birch, and Bulltown."[28]

Roberts, too, now had completed his circle.

CHAPTER TWELVE

The Breakdown

Confederate Disappointments

"Soldiers!" began General Imboden's general order issued Napoleonic fashion to his men at Sinking Creek in Greenbrier County on May 17. "You have nobly performed your duty. Within 28 days you have marched through rain & mud, climbed mountains and waded rivers for a distance of nearly 300 miles without one murmur of complaint that has ever reached my ears.

"You formed part of an expedition that has successfully accomplished a most important work. Damage to the amount of millions of dollars had been done [to] the enemy in the form of the destruction of the Baltimore & Ohio and N.W. Va. Railroads. The destruction of these roads was one of the primary objects of your expedition. The actual damage was mainly done by the Cavalry Brigade of Gen. W.E. Jones, but is no less on that account a part of your work, because you supported and protected his operations by drawing the enemy to concentrate his largely superior forces at one point in your front, thus compelling him to abandon the whole line of the Railroad to Gen. Jones' rapid attacks.

"You have enabled the agents of the Confederate Government to purchase and drive to a place of safety about 3000 head of cattle of inestimable value at this time to our great army in Virginia. You compelled the enemy to destroy large amounts of army stores at Beverly, Buchanan (sic), Weston, Bulltown, and Sutton, and captured a fine train of wagons and teams at Summerville (sic).

"But rising above these mere property considerations, you have accomplished a work of the highest political importance to the Confederate States, and especially to Virginia, in certain national contingencies, that will probably exist in the next few weeks or months. You have proven that the pretended State of Virginia is not under the exclusive control of the Washington and Wheeling despotisms, but that we can, whenever we chose, go into and occupy almost any portion of it. In the event of foreign intervention, this fact may be of immense importance.

"You had an opportunity of meeting the enemy but once — at Beverly — and there two companies of skirmishers under Maj. Land [Lang] whipped him 1500 strong, with the aid of a few rounds from one gun of McClanahan's Battery, before you could reach a position of attack yourselves. The perfect coolness with which the entire command pressed forward under a somewhat annoying cannonade would have elicited praise of an older soldier than I am.

"It will be a pleasing duty in my report to our Government to bear more ample testimony to the high soldierly qualities of the officers and men, who have so faithfully followed me on this long and trying expedition. Many of us met as strangers — we part as friends and brothers....

"It has been my aim to act justly with the people where we have been. Many of you have your homes in N.W. Va., and your families have been victims to the atrocities of our brutal enemies and their sympathizers, the Union traitors, and you naturally felt resentment, which is a part of human nature, but I am proud to testify that no one of this command disgraced himself and comrades by imitating the infernal practices of our enemies.

"We have left N.W. Va. not from fear of the enemy, but from the destitution of army supplies. This destitution will not always exist; and I promise you, whenever we can live there, no one will be more willing to return with you than I, and then, if our forbearance on this occasion has not been reciprocated, we will go as avengers, and teach the cowardly oppressors of women that brave men can inflict punishment, as well as they can bear injury with patience."[1]

Imboden had ample reason to be proud of his men. By the time the expedition truly ended, at Buffalo Gap near Staunton on May 25, they had marched some 400 miles in thirty-six days, subsisting most of the time on half rations.

Though he did not issue congratulatory orders, Jones in his official report was no less praiseworthy of his own men. "In thirty days we marched nearly 700 miles through a rough and sterile country," he wrote, "gathering subsistence for man and horse by the way." And like Imboden, he downplayed the discontent in his command. "Throughout this arduous march," he declared, "the men and officers evinced a cheerful endurance worthy of tried veterans. They have shown a skill in gleaning a precarious subsistence from a country desolated by two years of oppressive tyranny and brutal war that would have won the admiration of the most approved Cossack. With such troops the country of the enemy can be reached at almost any point."[2]

Both commands indeed had endured much suffering with little open complaint. But was it worth it? How successful were Imboden and Jones in realizing the major objectives they set out to achieve on April 20?

Imboden stated that he captured some 3,100 head of cattle, whereby he proudly declared that he had saved the government about $300,000 in purchasing costs. Grumble Jones brought in about 1,200 more head. Jones's and Imboden's men consumed some of these animals, others Sam Jones confiscated for his own department, but the overwhelming majority was put out to pasture in the friendly counties of Pocahontas, Greenbrier, Monroe, and Augusta.[3]

General Lee wasted no time, writing June 1 to Sam Jones and Secretary of War James Seddon in an effort to secure the beeves for the hungry men of his Army of Northern Virginia. Reluctant to give up provisions, as he had been his own troops, Jones put off Lee by recommending that if the cattle were allowed to graze undisturbed until mid-October they might fatten up to perhaps double their weight. About to set off on his invasion of Pennsylvania, Lee apparently agreed, for later on October 15 the Confederate commissary reported owning some 10,000 head of cattle in the Shenandoah area. Lee probably used the West Virginia beeves to feed his men over the winter, thus rendering at least this aspect of the raid a moderate success.[4]

Horses were another matter. Jones reaped the greatest harvest, taking some 1200 to 1500. Imboden gave no figure on the number he took, instead placing an estimate of $100,000 on their value. He probably gathered in a few hundred, including the 180 mules captured at Summersville. But all these barely offset the terrible losses sustained by both commands. Hundreds of horses gave out along the way (seventy-two, for example, in the Eleventh Virginia Cavalry) and many of those that made it back to the Shenandoah Valley were unfit for further duty for some time, if not indefinitely. The expenditure thus proved hardly worth the gain, making for a very small net profit.[5]

Almost the same might be said of the effort to gather in new recruits. The number fell far short of Imboden's prediction in March of "several thousand." Overestimating Southern support in West Virginia while underestimating the discouraging impact of the raid even among sympathizers, he took in not more than 500 new enlistments. Jones received perhaps a few dozen more.[6]

About thirty men joined the Thirty-first Virginia Infantry, perhaps seventy-five went into Imboden's brigade, while the rest, thanks in large measure to the efforts of Captain Edward Corder in Barbour County, filled out the ranks of the newly forming Twentieth Virginia Cavalry, with some going into the Nineteenth Virginia Cavalry. "In this respect we were all disappointed," Imboden wrote bitterly in his report. "The people now remaining in the northwest are, to all intents and purposes, a conquered people. Their spirit is broken by tyranny where they are true to our cause, and those who are against us are the blackest hearted, most despicable villains upon the continent."[7]

And as with the horses, these meager gains were largely if not wholly offset by the losses sustained along the way, mostly by desertion. By the time Imboden left Weston on May 6, he had lost several hundred men to desertion, some 200 alone from the Thirty-seventh Virginia Battalion. Reasons varied, from bitter disappointment with the restrictions on plunder, to simple, sheer exhaustion. Imboden's seemingly clever wish to include in the expedition the trans–Allegheny men of the Twenty-fifth and Thirty-first Virginia Infantries backfired somewhat when many of those men, particularly in the Twenty-fifth, could not resist the temptation to give up their current harsh life in exchange, even for a moment, for the hot meals and the comfortable beds of their nearby homes. And, many men simply gave out or were too sick to go on, some sixty-seven in the Twenty-second Virginia, for example, being left at different homes along the way. By comparison, Jones's losses in this regard appear to have been slight, but so were his gains (Colonel Harmon of the Twelfth Virginia Cavalry, for example, reported having left Harrisonburg with 405 men and returned with 415. "Only 3 men of my command left improperly.") The objective then of augmenting the commands of both Imboden and Lee with several thousand men obviously fell far short of realization.[8]

What about the destruction of B&O property, particularly its bridges, and the subsequent disruption of traffic along the line? Jones claimed to have destroyed sixteen bridges, Imboden eight more, and the Federals brought down two, one at Bridgeport and another at Buckhannon, making for twenty-six altogether.[9]

Having learned from past experience, the officers of the Baltimore & Ohio, not the Federal government, had taken remarkable precautions to protect the property of their company, even going so far as to have wooden duplicates made ready for the quick replacement of bridges along the line in western Virginia. With supreme organization and foresight, they had gathered and stockpiled all the necessary material to deal with such an emergency. Sometimes within only hours, therefore, after the rebels had left the scene, workers swarmed in like bees to begin repairing the damage. "We have strong work forces at all points," B&O president J.W. Garrett accurately assured the Wheeling *Intelligencer* on April 28.[10]

With the help of Daniel E. Offutt's nearby sawmill, by May 1, five days after Colonel Harmon's visit to Oakland, the 180 foot long wooden bridge over the Yougiogheny River had been repaired, the surrounding torn up track had been replaced, and the Altamont-to-Oakland runaway train had been put back in service. At 6 p.m. on Sunday, May 3, the two-span bridge over Buffalo Creek, about a mile east of Barracksville, reopened (the train carrying Major Showalter's men immediately passed over and went on to Fairmont). By the following day, other gangs working east from Grafton had used a wooden trestle to replace Raccoon Iron Bridge No. 2, and still other crews had finished repairing the small bridge over Coal Run just above Fairmont, as well as the bridges at Altamont, Cranberry Summit, Newburg, Independence, and Bridgeport, plus all five bridges burned by Imboden west of Fairmont. Thus a mere ten days after the rebels began their work of destruction, the entire B&O main line in West Virginia had reopened, save for the gap at Fairmont. For ten days more at that point, passengers and freight, whose travels in western Virginia until then had been "suspended any further of course," reported the Wheeling *Intelligencer* (May 1), "until the excitement subsides," crossed the West Fork of the Monongahela on ferries or pontoons. On May 14, a special, large work force completed a temporary wood trestle to replace the fallen 615-foot iron bridge over the Monongahela.[11]

"The Company displays great energy in the replacing of these bridges," the *Intelligencer* marveled on May 5. "All the force that can work at them is put on; timber is provided beforehand for the repair of any bridge on the line, so that it is at once shipped to the point needed, and the bridges are put up on the shortest possible notice. It is wonderful too, how well it is done. These wooden structures appear to be fully as solid and safe for the passage of trains as the original iron ones."[12]

With great satisfaction, then, did the Directors of the B&O meet on Wednesday, May 13 to receive President Garrett's reassuring report that "the trains leaving Baltimore today would pass over the entire line of the road with all its structures restored, and without detention." On May 17, through traffic resumed on the Northwestern Virginia branch of the B&O to Parkersburg.[13]

Measured against George Stoneman's recent cavalry raid on the Virginia railroads in Lee's rear, the Confederates had done much more damage to the B&O, but with much less effect. Thus the destruction wrought by Jones and Imboden on the rail line proved to be little more than an annoying inconvenience, prompting the Wheeling *Intelligencer* to speculate (May 19) that the rebels came to West Virginia mainly to plunder and demoralize. "That they did not come with any special design on the Baltimore road," the paper scornfully declared, "is shown from the very little damage which they did to it. They could have destroyed the road very badly if they had given themselves up to the work."[14]

A more determined effort undoubtedly would have included the destruction of the great bridge and trestle works at Rowelsburg, the original inspiration for the entire expedition that now, much to the great displeasure of General Lee, President Davis, and Secretary Seddon, was its major unfulfilled goal. Perhaps now these three regretted having succumbed to the temptation that led them astray of the original, much simpler plan proposed by Captain "Hanse" McNeill. Ironically, the most severe and lasting damage done by the rebels had been at a place not originally on the target list: the oil fields at Burning Springs, whose loss ruined many investors while depriving the Federal government of much needed tax revenue.

How successful was the expedition in destroying and capturing the Union forces scattered throughout western Virginia? Grumble Jones reported that his command had killed twenty-five to thirty of the enemy, wounded perhaps three times that many, and captured with their arms nearly 700 soldiers, militiamen and home guards. Adding the few casualties inflicted by Imboden's command, Union losses amounted to around 800 men, probably a fairly accurate figure. Jones reported his own losses as ten killed, forty-two wounded, and fifteen missing. Imboden reported losing only two killed (Lt. Vincent of the 19 Va. Cav. and one man in the 18 Va. Cav.), three men wounded and left behind, eight men sick and left behind, and three captured, for a total loss of sixteen. These reported losses, only eighty-three altogether, undoubtedly are far too low, Imboden, for example, not bothering to mention the desertions in his command, but the overall score still greatly favored the Confederates.[15]

What makes that truly remarkable is the fact that it occurred in the face of incredible odds. Jones and Imboden commanded no more than 6,000 men between them. When the Confederates entered West Virginia, Benjamin Kelley's division of 10,000 men were positioned at various points along the B&O from Harper's Ferry to the Ohio River, Benjamin Roberts's 2,500 men of the Fourth Separate Brigade held positions at Beverly, Buckhannon, and elsewhere, and perhaps 3,000 more Yankees were in the Kanawha Valley area under Eliakim Scammon. Moreover, as the raid progressed those odds increased dramatically. From Winchester Robert Milroy sent several detachments to Clarksburg; from the Department of the Ohio Ambrose Burnside sent what troops he could spare to Marietta and Bellaire, and he arranged for two gunboats to speed up the Ohio for Parkersburg; thousands of militiamen and home guards reported for duty in eastern Ohio, western Pennsylvania, and throughout West Virginia, with many being sent on to Clarksburg, Fairmont, and Grafton. Thus by the end of the first week in May, perhaps as many as 25,000 of the enemy had been aroused against Jones and Imboden.[16]

The four-to-one odds, however, were evened considerably by those fortuitous circumstances that so often appear during war, in this case the most influential being the right combination of skilful daring and resourcefulness on the one side, as displayed by Grumble Jones, with timidity and incompetence on the other, as exhibited by but not limited to Benjamin Roberts. The swift moving Confederate forces that seemed to be everywhere in such great numbers, striking several targets simultaneously, baffled and confused the Union commanders to the point of paralyzing impotence. This kept the initiative in Confederate hands throughout the raid, whereby Imboden drove the Federals, with great loss of supplies, out of Beverly, Philippi, and Buckhannon, while Jones conducted a bold counter-clockwise sweep across the new state, both Confederate leaders along the way easily frustrating the Federal defensive strategy of anticipated interception.

But such bold audacity, so successfully executed, had its negative effect, at least as far as the Confederates were concerned. It created a reaction that made sure such success never happened again in West Virginia. Despite his inabilities, General Roberts had been right when he repeatedly bemoaned the lack of a sufficient cavalry force that could pursue, harass, and keep an eye on the enemy. But being right also made him expendable, for the administration in Washington, their eyes now finally opened by the exploits of Jones and Imboden, quickly replaced Roberts on May 18 with Brigadier General William Averell, an experienced cavalryman who promptly proceeded to convert the infantry regiments of the Fourth Separate Brigade into a tough, capable force of cavalry. Never again did the Confederates dare enter West Virginia as they had in the spring of 1863.[17]

The raid's greatest failure, as measured against its initial lofty expectations, was the attempt, or at least hope, to bring down the Wheeling government and thereby open the way for nothing less than the "liberation" of the oppressed people of northwestern Virginia. Other than the temporary, brief disruption of political conventions at Parkersburg and Wheeling, the Confederates achieved nothing in that regard. Ironically, the raid for the most part produced quite the opposite effect, whereby its destructions and confiscations crystallized and hardened opinion against the Southern cause, even among sympathizers. "Jones' company of cavalry has done our cause great harm in the N.W.," Isabella Woods regretfully wrote her husband Samuel on May 14. "Great outrages have been committed upon Union and 'secesh' alike, so I hear," adding three days later, "Jones' men behaved badly while there [Philippi], treating Secessionists worse than Union men."[18]

Moreover, the raid created a severe backlash, with loud, angry and effective calls for increased repressive measures against Southern sympathizers. Imboden had come to avenge and bring relief from such oppression, only to see it intensified in his wake.

"All persons are sick of such visits," the Wheeling *Intelligencer* howled on May 4. "The general observation around this town is that the sympathizers are about as sick of the invasion as other people. They see some things which they have very imperfectly seen before. They find that there is an unconquerable and vengeful hatred in the hearts of our people towards their friends. They find also that since the raid this feeling had become doubly intensified, and more than that, that this feeling is transferring itself to a very perceptible extent to local secessionists themselves. The feeling of our people towards the disloyal in our midst was never so bitter and so malignant, so to speak, as they are now. This city is dead set against the slightest manifestation of disloyalty. Woe would betide the man who should now provoke the public feeling. The rebels realize this. They see their situation. They begin to feel that their future is implicated in the result of this raid. There is no alternative for them but to ardently hope for its defeat.

Their day of trial will come if the invasion results in permanent mischief. The loyal people are simply holding themselves in abeyance to ascertain that fact. They have made up their minds as to what shall be the future of the secessionists among us if serious trouble results from our present danger."[19]

Two days later, the paper seemed to find special comfort in the contemplation of future agonies for local Southern sympathizers. "Aside from the loss of property," it began, "we have no doubt the raid will have a good effect. It will open the eyes of the people and of the Government to the necessity of adopting far more rigid measures with home rebels, who act as spies, furnishing the information which enable these raids to successfully enter and escape from our lines. We used to hear a great deal about confiscating their property and leaving them poor as a church mouse.... Let us for the future take prompt and effective measures for the removal of every disloyal person, male and female, old and young, south of our State and military lines. What else can be done with the women who fired from houses on our soldiers as they were retreating through town the other day, who waved handkerchiefs and cheered the thieves and robbers as they came into town, and jeered and laughed at our gallant boys as they were marched prisoners of war into town from a hard fought battlefield? What should be done with rebel men and boys who spent the day in riding about the street with the rebels, pointing out private property which they wished destroyed? They are not as poor as church mice, for they can store up carloads of sweet cakes and pies several days before the rebels came in ... yet the rebels here have the unblushing impudence to boast of having saved the whole town from being burned to the ground. If something is not soon done with these home rebels, companies will be organized who will undertake to dispose of them in a way that may be deemed rather more hempish then red tapish."[20]

In a frenzied atmosphere, fed by the press, people began informing on one another, and raising accusations, often false, of having collaborated with the rebels during the recent raid. Those who came under suspicion justifiably feared that their personal correspondence was being searched, and their property and persons were subject at any moment to seizure. The long list of unfortunates so accused included Nathaniel Barnes and his son Thomas James, prosperous farmers living near Shinnston whom Union soldiers arrested and sent off to prison at Camp Chase near Columbus, Ohio, where they both later died of disease.[21]

For the raid's lost potential, which he bitterly regretted, Imboden laid the blame at the feet of bad luck. Jones was not so kind. He professed to be aghast to find Imboden still bogged down at Weston with some seventy supply wagons, which thereby prevented the two commands from carrying out swift movements together. This is unfair, since Jones up to that time seems to have been considering ending the raid and returning to the Shenandoah. "Had our original plan been carried out," Grumble complained in his report, "I feel confident Northwestern Virginia could have been cleared to the Ohio."[22]

Though justifiably impressed with the skilful conduct of Imboden, Jones, and their respective commands, General Lee was disappointed with the overall results of the campaign. "Although the expedition under General Imboden failed to accomplish all the results intended," he wrote, just shy of being critical, in response to Imboden's report, "it nevertheless rendered valuable service in the collection of stores and in making the enemy uneasy for his communications with the west."[23]

In response to Jones's report, the commanding general was somewhat kinder. "The expedition under General Jones," he wrote, "appears to have been conducted with commendable skill and vigor, and was productive of beneficial results. The injury inflicted on the enemy was serious, and he will doubtless be induced to keep troops to guard the railroad who might be otherwise employed against us. General Jones displayed sagacity and boldness in his plans, and was well supported by the courage and fortitude of his officers and men."[24]

After the great raid into West Virginia, Imboden went on to perform valuable service for General Lee, screening his retreat from Pennsylvania in July and at Williamsport preventing the loss of wagons carrying baggage and wounded. The following October, he again forayed into West Virginia, receiving from Lee a commendation for capturing a Union garrison at Charles Town. At Port Royal on May 11, 1864, the former lawyer surprised and captured some 500 Union cavalry, and four days later he helped General John Breckinridge defeat Franz Sigel at New Market in the Shenandoah. Imboden provided good service in the 1864 Valley Campaign, fighting in the June battles of Piedmont and Lynchburg, and marching with Valley commander Jubal Early as far as Washington. Typhoid fever later that year took him out of service, leaving him unfit for field command. Upon recovery, he received an administrative post as commander of Confederate prisons in Georgia, Alabama, and Mississippi. The infamous Andersonville falling within his jurisdiction, he took pity on its prisoners and tried to have many released. After the war, Imboden strove to help Virginia recover by way of industrialization. Having discovered in southwest Virginia's Washington County a large vein of bituminous coal that came to be known as the "Imboden seam," the former general founded there the city of Damascus, which he hoped to make into a new iron and steel center. He also wrote several articles for Battles and Leaders of the Civil War (4 volumes; 1887–1888), but modern historians generally consider him an unreliable source. He died at Damascus on August 15, 1895.[25]

On October 9, 1863, Grumble Jones and his command rejoined the Army of Northern Virginia. After cooperating with Longstreet in the disastrous campaign in east Tennessee, he took over the defense of southwest Virginia against Federal raiders. The following spring, he moved into the Shenandoah Valley to help resist the invasion by David Hunter. While rallying his troops at the battle of Piedmont on June 5, Jones was shot in the head and killed.[26]

John "Hanse" McNeill, the original author of the expedition, returned to his specialty: raiding Union supply trains, camps, and railroads. To scare off the troublesome raider, Union authorities arrested his wife, daughter and four-year-old son when they tried to return to West Virginia from Ohio, where they had been living as refugees, and sent them to Camp Chase. This made Hanse only more determined in his efforts, which may help explain why he then alienated his superior officers, who ostensibly held command over him. In the Moorefield area in late 1863, Brigadier General Thomas Rosser openly criticized McNeill's performance and methods, and Imboden later had the raider court-martialed for refusing to turn over Confederate deserters he had accepted into his command. Cleared of the charges, McNeill continued his raids with renewed vigor, until October 3, 1864, when with sixty Rangers he attacked about 100 Union troops at Mount Jackson in the Shenandoah. Felled by a severe wound, he ordered his men to leave him at a nearby home, where Sheridan's men captured him a few days later. Under their care, and interrogation, he died on November 9, 1864.[27]

Union Disappointments

"Their visit into West Va. was not appreciated at all," the Sixth West Virginia's Corporal Henry Solomon White wrote in his diary on April 30 in reference to the rebel raid. In addition to the great loss of property sustained by so many, hardship now loomed for those people left with no animals to tend their farms, many having had their crops ruined by the thousands of rebel horses who trampled through or grazed upon the wheat and corn fields, "completely destroying the labor of months." Many West Virginians simply were stunned. Demanding to know how this tragedy could have befallen them, they looked for someone to blame. They found an easy target.[28]

"The people have been amazed, demoralized and paralyzed," howled a letter to the editor appearing in the May 15 issue of the Wheeling *Intelligencer*, "as they looked on at the doings of the raiders from day to day, and waited for something to be done by our forces to counteract, capture or destroy the villains. We need not say what everybody knows, that public expectation was bitterly disappointed. Nor need we say that the people have now not a single iota of belief or confidence with Gen. Roberts' ability with any amount of infantry to protect the country."[29]

Among the bitterest, suspicions inevitably arose concerning Roberts's loyalty. Though now very critical of the general, the *Intelligencer* dismissed such notions as belonging only to the most ignorant. "Yet it does seem a little strange," the May 22 issue reflected, "that Gen. Roberts should have let Jones with twenty-five hundred men escape for the night within five miles of him, and pursue his course again in the morning without molestation."[30]

Roberts produced a long list of excuses. "I regret to report that my forces and my means made it impossible for me to adopt offensive operations against the enemy," he wrote. "I had no effective cavalry, no means of transportation, and, in fact, barely supplies to feed the men at Clarksburg until the rapid retreat of the enemy put it out of my power to follow him. The roads were literally impassable to loaded wagons. I have never seen anything in the nature of roads so bad.... My 200 cavalry were broken down when I reached Clarksburg. The enemy had about 5000, and they left in all directions their jaded horses, seizing all the best and fresh horses in the country as they passed through it."[31]

After being relieved of command of the Fourth Separate Brigade on May 18, Roberts was reassigned to a series of relatively quiet posts, first as a Nineteenth Corps division commander in Louisiana, then as chief of cavalry in the Gulf Department, then, in early 1865, as commander of a cavalry division in western Tennessee. He finished the war as a major general of volunteers, with the brevet rank of brigadier general in the regular army, both ranks granted in acknowledgment of his services at Cedar Mountain and Second Bull Run. After the war, he became Lt. Colonel of the Third Cavalry, serving on frontier and recruiting service until 1868, when he became a professor of military science at Yale, while at the same time directing the manufacture and sale of his invention, the Roberts breech-loading rifle. He died in Washington D.C. on January 29, 1875.[32]

Jones and Imboden had departed West Virginia, leaving in their wake death, destruction, and bitterness. "The rebels have now left for Dixie," the Wheeling *Intelligencer* scornfully remarked on May 8, "with the just execrations of all loyal Virginians and most of their former sympathizers. Also, their father the devil left with them. May West Virginia never be again disgraced with such greasy Southern 'chivalry.'"[33]

Chapter Notes

Introduction

1. Edward Longacre, *Mounted Raids of the Civil War* (Lincoln, NE: University of Nebraska Press, 1972), pp. 123–124.

2. Virgil C. Jones, *Gray Ghosts and Rebel Raiders* (McClean, VA: EPM Publications, 1989), p. 160.

3. John W. Shaffer, *Clash of Loyalties: A Border County in the Civil War* (Morgantown, WV: University of West Virginia Press, 2003), pp. 90–91.

4. United States War Department, *The War of the Rebellion: A Compilation of the Official Records of the Union and Confederate Armies*, 70 volumes in 128 parts (Washington, DC: Government Printing Office, 1880–1901), series 1, vol. 25, pt. 2, pp. 656, 658.

Chapter One

1. "The Baltimore & Ohio Railroad," *Encyclopedia Americana*, 1943 edition, vol. 3, pp.121–122.

2. Stephen French, "The Jones-Imboden Raid." *The Blue and Gray Education Society*, 10 (March 2001), pp. 5, 41 (hereafter cited as French, "The Jones-Imboden Raid."); Rowelsburg Historical Society.

3. Edward Longacre, *Mounted Raids of the Civil War* (Lincoln, NE: University of Nebraska Press, 1972), pp. 123–124 (hereafter cited as Longacre, *Mounted Raids*); Dennis E. Frye, *12th Virginia Cavalry* (Lynchburg, VA: H.E. Howard, Inc., 1988), pp. 21–22 (hereafter cited as Frye, *12th Virginia Cavalry*).

4. Longacre, *Mounted Raids*, p. 123; Patricia Faust, ed., *Historical Times Illustrated Encyclopedia of the Civil War* (New York: Harper & Row, 1987), p. 37 (hereafter cited as Faust, *Historical Times Illustrated Encyclopedia*).

5. Virgil C. Jones, *Gray Ghosts and Rebel Raiders* (McClean, VA: EPM Publications, 1984), p. 160 (hereafter cited as Jones, *Gray Ghosts*).

6. Spencer C. Tucker, *Brigadier General John D. Imboden: Confederate Commander in the Shenandoah* (Lexington, KY: University of Kentucky Press, 2003), pp. 1–110 (hereafter cited as Tucker, *Brigadier General John D. Imboden*).

7. Tucker, *Brigadier General John D. Imboden*, pp. 110–112; Harold R. Woodward, Jr., *Defender of the Valley: Brigadier General John Daniel Imboden* (Berryville, VA: Rockbridge Publishing, 1996), p. 114 (hereafter cited as Woodward, *Defender of the Valley*).

8. Tucker, *Brigadier General John D. Imboden*, p. 112; Faust, *Historical Times Illustrated Encyclopedia*, p. 465.

9. Boyd Blynn Stutler, *West Virginia in the Civil War* (Charleston, WV: Education Foundation, 1966), pp. 124–128 (hereafter cited as Stutler, *West Virginia in the Civil War*).

10. *Ibid.*

11. *Ibid.*; John Taylor, "The Civil War in and About Pendleton County, West Virginia." Master's Thesis, Penn. State, 1975, p. 122 (hereafter cited as Taylor thesis).

12. Taylor thesis, p. 123.

13. United States War Department, *The War of the Rebellion: A Compilation of the Official Records of the Union and Confederate Armies*, 70 volumes in 128 parts (Washington, D.C.: Government Printing Office, 1880–1901), series 1, vol. 25, pt. 2, pp. 656, 658 (hereafter cited as *OR*, all subsequent references are to series 1).

14. *Ibid.*

15. William C. Davis, ed., *The Confederate General*, 6 vols. (The National Historical Society, 1991), vol. 3, pp. 209–212 (hereafter cited as Davis, *The Confederate General*).

16. Faust, *Historical Times Illustrated Encyclopedia*, pp. 707–708.

17. Faust, *Historical Times Illustrated Encyclopedia*, pp. 788–789.

18. *OR*, vol. 25, pt. 2, p. 846; First Brigade: 22 Va. Inf., Col. George S. Patton; 45 Va. Inf., Col. William H. Browne; 23 Va. Inf. Bn., Lt. Col. Clarence Derrick; 26 Va. Inf. Bn., Lt. Col. George M. Edgar; George B. Chapman's Va. Btty. Second Brigade: 63 Va. Inf., Col. John J. McMahon; 45 Va. Inf. Bn., Lt. Col. Henry M. Beckley; 21 Va. Cav., Col. William E. Peters; Va. Partisan Rangers, Capt. D.B. Baldwin; William M. Lowry's Va. Btty. Third Brigade: 50 Va. Inf., Col. Alexander S. Vandeventer; 51 Va. Inf., Lt. Col. Augustus Forsberg; 30 Va. Bn. Sharpshooters, Lt. Col. J. Lyle Clarke; Timothy Stamps' Va. Btty. Fourth Brigade: 36 Va. Inf., Maj. Thomas Smith; 60 Va. Inf., Col. Buehring H. Jones; Thomas A. Bryan's Va. Btty. Albert Jenkins's Cavalry Brigade: 8 Va. Cav., Col. James M. Corns; 14 Va. Cav., Col. James Cochran; 16 Va. Cav., Col. Milton J. Ferguson; 17 Va. Cav., Col. William H. French; 19 Va. Cav., Col. William L. Jackson; 34 Va. Cav. Bn., Lt. Col. Vincent A. Witcher; 36 Va. Cav. Bn., Maj. James W. Sweeney; 37 Va. Cav. Bn., Lt. Col. Ambrose C. Dunn. Unattached commands: 54 Va. Inf., Col. Robert C. Trigg; Va. Partisans, one company, Capt. Philip J. Thurmond; Va. Partisans, one company, Capt. William D. Thurmond; William Otey's Virginia btty.

19. Tucker, *Brigadier General John D. Imboden*, p. 116.

20. *OR*, vol. 25, pt. 2, p. 656.

21. *OR*, vol. 25, pt. 2, pp. 658–659.

22. Davis, *The Confederate General*, vol. 3, pp. 217–218; Virginia Civil War Biographies Page, online.

23. *Ibid.*

24. *Ibid.*

25. *Ibid.*

26. *OR*, vol. 25, pt. 2, pp. 660–661.

27. *OR*, vol. 25, pt. 2, pp. 652–653.

28. *Ibid.*

29. *Ibid.*

30. *Ibid.*

31. *Ibid.*

32. Davis, *The Confederate General*, vol. 3, pp. 137–138.

33. John W. Shaffer, *Clash of Loyalties: A Border County in the Civil War* (Morgantown, WV: University of West Virginia Press, 2003), pp. 90–91 (hereafter cited as Shaffer, *Clash of Loyalties*).

34. *OR*, vol. 25, pt. 2, p. 661.

35. see Richard Armstrong, *25th Virginia Infantry and 9th Battalion Virginia Infantry* (Lynchburg, VA: H.E. Howard, Inc, 1990), (hereafter cited as Armstrong, *25th Virginia Infantry*); and John Ashcraft, *31st Virginia Infantry* (Lynchburg, VA: H.E. Howard, Inc., 1988), (hereafter cited as Ashcraft, *31st Virginia Infantry*).

36. *OR*, vol. 25, pt. 2, pp. 661, 670, 674–675.

37. *OR*, vol. 25, pt. 2, p. 679.

38. *OR*, vol. 25, pt. 2, pp. 684–685.

39. *OR*, vol. 25, pt. 2, pp. 685–686.

40. *OR*, vol. 25, pt. 2, pp. 689–692; Jones, *Gray Ghosts*, p. 162.

41. *OR*, vol. 25, pt. 2, pp. 710–711.

42. *Ibid.*

43. *Ibid.*

44. *OR*, vol. 25, pt. 2, pp. 711–712.

45. *OR*, vol. 25, pt. 2, pp. 712–714.

46. Armstrong, *25th Virginia Infantry*, p. 56; Ashcraft, *31st Virginia Infantry*, p. 47.

47. *OR*, vol. 25, pt. 2, pp. 716–717.

48. *OR*, vol. 25, pt. 2, p. 717; Terry Lowry, *22nd Virginia Infantry* (Lynchburg, VA: 1991), p. 39 (hereafter cited as Lowry, *22nd Virginia Infantry*).

49. *OR*, vol. 25, pt. 2, pp. 716–717.

50. *OR*, vol. 25, pt. 2, pp. 704–705.

51. Davis, *The Confederate General*, vol. 3, pp. 158–159; Paul McNeil, "The Imboden Raid and Its Effects," *Southern Historical Society Papers*, vol. 34, p. 295 (hereafter cited as McNeil, "The Imboden Raid and Its Effects.").

52. *OR*, vol. 25, pt. 2, pp. 721–722, 728; Angus James Johnston II, *Virginia Railroads in the Civil War* (Chapel Hill, NC: University of North Carolina Press, 1961), p. 151 (hereafter cited as Johnston, *Virginia Railroads in the Civil War*).

53. *OR*, vol. 25, pt. 2, pp. 652, 684.

54. 1860 Census Virginia; George Ellis Moore, *A Banner in the Hills: West Virginia's Statehood* (New York: Appleton-Century Crafts, 1963), pp. 79, 101–105 (hereafter cited as Moore, *A Banner in the Hills*); Richard Orr Curry, *A House Divided* (Pittsburgh: University of Pittsburgh Press, 1964), pp. 147–149 (hereafter cited as Curry, *A House Divided*); Charles H. Ambler, *Francis H. Pierpont: Union War Governor of Virginia and Father of West Virginia* (Chapel Hill, NC: University of North Carolina Press, 1937), pp. 1–160 (hereafter cited as Ambler, *Francis H. Pierpont*).

55. Moore, *A Banner in the Hills*, pp. 100–158.

56. see Jack Dickinson, *Tattered Uniforms and Bright Bayonets: West Virginia's Confederate Soldiers* (Huntington, WV: Marshall University Library Association, 1995).

57. Faust, *Historical Times Illustrated Encyclopedia*, p. 491.

58. Faust, *Historical Times Illustrated Encyclopedia*, pp. 660–661; *OR*, vol. 25, pt. 2, p. 588.

59. *OR*, vol. 25, pt. 2, pp. 589–590. Milroy's Second Division: 1st Brig., Brig. Gen. Washington L. Elliott; 2nd Brig., Col. William G. Ely; 3rd Brig., Col. A.T. McReynolds. Scammon's Third Division: 1st Brig., Col. Rutherford B. Hayes; 2nd Brig., Col. Carr B. White. Kelley's First Division: 1st Brig., Brig. Gen. John R. Kenly; 2nd Brig., Brig. Gen. William H. Morris; 3rd Brig., Col. Benjamin F. Smith; 4th Brig., Col. Jacob M. Campbell; 5th Brig., Col. James A. Mulligan.

60. Faust, *Historical Times Illustrated Encyclopedia*, p. 410.

61. *OR*, vol. 25, pt. 2, pp. 589–590. Kenly's Maryland Brigade: 1 Md. Inf., Col. Nathan T.

Dushane; 4 Md. Inf., Col. R.N. Bowerman; 7 Md. Inf., Col. Edwin H. Webster; 8 Md. Inf., Col. Andrew W. Denison; 14 Pa. Cav., Col. James N. Schoonmaker; 17 Indiana Btty., Capt. Milton L. Minor. The 1st Separate Brigade was scattered throughout Delaware and eastern Pa.; 2nd Sep. Brig., throughout eastern Pa.; 3rd Sep. Brig., at Baltimore and other points in eastern Maryland.

62. Faust, *Historical Times Illustrated Encyclopedia*, pp. 636–637.

63. *OR*, vol. 25, pt. 2, pp. 192–193.

64. *OR*, vol. 25, pt. 2, pp. 193–194.

65. Theodore F. Lang, *Loyal West Virginia From 1861 to 1865* (Baltimore: Deutch Publishing Co., 1895), p. 106 (hereafter cited as Lang, *Loyal West Virginia*).

66. *OR*, vol. 25, pt. 2, p. 198.

67. Ruth Woods Dayton, *Samuel Woods and His Family* (Charleston, WV: privately published, 1939), pp. 83, 101 (hereafter cited as Dayton, *Samuel Woods*).

68. *OR*, vol. 25, pt. 2, p. 225; Wheeling *Intelligencer*, April 22, 1863; Compiled Service Records for "Kelley's Lancers," National Archives, Washington, D.C. (such records hereafter shall be cited as CSR, NA).

69. Wheeling *Intelligencer*, April 22, 1863.

70. *Ibid.*

71. *Ibid.*

72. *Ibid.*; Nimrod Hoffman CSR, NA.

73. *OR*, vol. 25, pt. 2, p. 225.

74. *Ibid.*

75. *OR*, vol. 25, pt. 2, p. 230.

76. Roy Bird Cook, *Lewis County in the Civil War* (Charleston, WV, 1924), p. 63 (hereafter cited as Cook, *Lewis County*).

77. *Ibid.*

Chapter Two

1. McNeil, "The Imboden Raid and Its Effects," p. 305; French, "The Jones-Imboden Raid," pp. 12–13.

2. McNeil, "The Imboden Raid and Its Effects," p. 303; 1860 Census Pocahontas County, Va.

3. McNeil, "The Imboden Raid and Its Effects," p. 305.

4. McNeil, "The Imboden Raid and Its Effects," p. 305; Robert K. Krick, *Lee's Colonels: A Biographical Register of the Field Officers of the Army of Northern Virginia* (Dayton, OH: Morningside House, Inc., 1992), p. 351 (hereafter cited as Krick, *Lee's Colonels*); Roger U. Delauter, *62nd Virginia Infantry* (Lynchburg, VA: H.E. Howard, Inc., 1988), pp. 1–45 (hereafter cited as Delauter, *62nd Virginia Infantry*).

5. McNeil, "The Imboden Raid and Its Effects," p. 305; Krick, *Lee's Colonels*, p. 192.

6. McNeil, "The Imboden Raid and Its Effects," p. 305; Krick, *Lee's Colonels*, pp. 194–195.

7. McNeil, "The Imboden Raid and Its Effects," pp. 305–306.

8. Tucker, *Brigadier General John D. Imboden*, pp. 2–3, 16, 25–26, 30.

9. Tucker, *Brigadier General John D. Imboden*, pp. 25–26, 71; Frank Imboden's CSR, NA.

10. French, "The Jones-Imboden Raid," p. 12; *OR*, vol. 25, pt. 1, pp. 98–99; Tucker, *Brigadier General John D. Imboden*, pp. 120–121; Robert B. Boehm, "The Jones-Imboden Raid Through West Virginia." *Civil War Times Illustrated*, 3 (May 1964), p. 16 (hereafter cited as Boehm, "The Jones-Imboden Raid Through West Virginia").

11. McNeil, "The Imboden Raid and Its Effects," p. 306.

12. Roger U. Delauter, *18th Virginia Cavalry* (Lynchburg, VA: H.E. Howard, Inc., 1985), p. 5 (hereafter cited as Delauter, *18th Virginia Cavalry*); Delauter, *62nd Virginia Infantry*, p. 13; French, "The Jones-Imboden Raid," p. 13.

13. Curry, *A House Divided*, pp. 49, 148; Elizabeth Cometti, and Festus P. Summers, eds., *The Thirty-Fifth State: A Documentary History of West Virginia* (Morgantown, WV: West Virginia University Library, 1966), pp. 286–290.

14. *OR*, vol. 25, pt. 1, p. 99; Elizabeth Teter Phillips, ed., *James E. Hall: Diary of a Confederate Soldier* (privately published, 1961), p. 75 (hereafter cited as Hall diary).

15. *OR*, vol. 25, pt. 1, p. 99; French, "The Jones-Imboden Raid," p. 13.

16. *OR*, vol. 25, pt. 1, p. 99.

17. Lowry, *22nd Virginia Infantry*, p. 39; *OR*, vol. 25, pt. 1, p. 99; McNeil, "The Imboden Raid and Its Effects," p. 306.

18. *OR*, vol. 25, pt. 1, p. 99; Curry, *A House Divided*, pp. 49, 148.

19. Lt. James Potts diary, Marshall University, Huntington, WV (hereafter cited as Potts diary).

20. *OR*, vol. 25, pt. 1, p. 99.

21. Victor L. Thacker, ed., *French Harding: Civil War Memoirs* (Parsons, WV: McClain Printing Co., 2000), p. 88 (hereafter cited as Harding memoir); Ashcraft, *31st Virginia Infantry*, pp. 114, 136. In 1872, Harding was a delegate to the West Virginia state constitutional convention, and he later twice (1887 and 1895) represented Randolph County in the state House of Delegates.

22. *OR*, vol. 25, pt. 1, p. 99; McNeil, "The Imboden Raid and Its Effects," pp. 306–307.

23. *OR*, vol. 25, pt. 1, pp. 93–94; George Latham CSR, NA.

24. Harding memoir, pp. 88–89.

25. *OR*, vol. 25, pt. 1, p. 99.

26. McNeil, "The Imboden Raid and Its Effects," p. 307.

27. *OR*, vol. 25, pt. 1, p. 93.

28. *Ibid.*

29. *Ibid.*

30. *OR*, vol. 25, pt. 1, pp. 93, 99–100; Lowry, *22nd Virginia Infantry*, p. 40; Delauter, *62nd Virginia Infantry*, p. 13.

31. Harding memoir, pp. 89–90.

32. *OR*, vol. 25, pt. 1, pp. 91, 94.

33. Lowry, *22nd Virginia Infantry*, p. 40; *OR*, vol. 25, pt. 1, p. 100.

34. *OR*, vol. 25, pt. 1, p. 94; William Gardner CSR, NA.

35. Richard L. Armstrong, *19th and 20th Virginia Cavalry* (Lynchburg, VA: H.E. Howard, Inc., 1994), pp. 7–8 (hereafter cited as Armstrong, *19th and 20th Virginia Cavalry*).

36. Armstrong, *19th and 20th Virginia Cavalry*, p. 8.

37. *OR*, vol. 25, pt. 1, pp. 91, 94.

38. *OR*, vol. 25, pt. 1, p. 94; Armstrong, *19th and 20th Virginia Cavalry*, p. 8.

39. *OR*, vol. 25, pt. 1, p. 94; Frank S. Reader, *History of the Fifth West Virginia Cavalry, Formerly the Second Virginia Infantry, and of Battery G, First West Va. Light Artillery* (New Brighton, PA: F.S. Reader, 1890), p. 193 (hereafter cited as Reader, *Fifth West Virginia Cavalry*).

40. *Ibid.*

41. *OR*, vol. 25, pt. 1 p. 94.

42. *Ibid.*

43. *OR*, vol. 25, pt. 1, p. 95.

44. Reader, *Fifth West Virginia Cavalry*, pp. 194–195.

45. Potts diary.

46. *OR*, vol. 25, pt. 1, p. 100; Lowry, *22nd Virginia Infantry*, p. 40; Delauter, *18th Virginia Cavalry*, p. 5.

47. McNeil, "The Imboden Raid and Its Effects," p. 308.

48. *OR*, vol. 25, vol. 25, pt. 1, p. 100; Lowry, *22nd Virginia Infantry*, pp. 40, 42.

49. Richmond *Whig*, May 2, 1863.

50. *OR*, vol. 25, pt. 1, pp. 94–96.

51. *OR*, vol. 25, pt. 1, p. 100.

52. Harding memoir, p. 90.

53. *Ibid.*; David Armstrong, "South Elkins Was Its Own Town At Turn of Century," website.

54. Shaffer, *Clash of Loyalties*, pp. 90–93; Dayton, *Samuel Woods*, pp. 78–79; Hu Maxwell, *The History of Barbour County, West Virginia* (Morgantown, WV: Acme Publishing Co., 1899), p. 270 (hereafter cited as Maxwell, *The History of Barbour County*).

55. Ambler, *Francis H. Pierpont*, pp. 194–195.

56. Ambler, *Francis H. Pierpont*, p. 187.

57. Joseph C. Snider, Journal of the Civil War (unp.). West Virginia and Regional History Collection, West Virginia University Library, Morgantown (hereafter cited as Snider journal); Tucker, *Brigadier General John D. Imboden*, p. 123.

58. Tucker, *Brigadier General John D. Imboden*, pp. 123–124.

Chapter Three

1. *OR*, vol., 25, pt. 2, p. 246.

2. *Ibid.*

3. *Ibid.*

4. *OR*, vol. 25, pt. 3, pp. 231, 247.

5. *OR*, vol.25, pt. 2, pp. 248, 259.

6. *OR*, vol. 25, pt. 2, p. 253.

7. *OR*, vol. 25, pt. 2, p. 248, pt. 1, p. 91.

8. Wheeling *Intelligencer*, May 5, 1863.

9. *OR*, vol. 25, pt. 2, p. 253.

10. Maria Louise Sumner Phillips journal, West Virginia University Library, Morgantown (hereafter cited as Phillips journal); 1860 U.S. Census, Upshur County, VA; Sylvester Phillips CSR, NA.

11. Phillips journal.

12. Phillips journal; Betty Hornbeck, *Upshur Brothers of the Blue and Gray* (Parsons, WV: McClain Printing Co., 1967), p. 120 (hereafter cited as Hornbeck, *Upshur Brothers*).

13. Phillips journal.

14. *Ibid.*; Hornbeck, *Upshur Brothers*, p. 118.

15. *OR*, vol. 25, pt. 1, p. 94.

16. Lt. Colonel John Polsley to "My Dear Nellie," April 25, 1863, John Polsley letters, West Virginia University Library, Morgantown (letters hereafter cited as Polsley letters).

17. Phillips journal.

18. *Ibid.*

19. *Ibid.*

20. *Ibid.*

21. *Ibid.*

22. *OR*, vol. 25, pt. 1, p. 94.

23. Terry Lowry, *Last Sleep: The Battle of Droop Mountain* (Charleston, WV: Pictorial Histories, 1996), pp. 12–13 (hereafter cited as Lowry, *Last Sleep*).

24. Lowry, *Last Sleep*, p. 13.

25. Lowry, *Last Sleep*, pp. 15–16.

26. Third West Virginia Cavalry Record of Events and CSRs, NA.

27. Twenty-eighth Ohio Infantry Record of Events and CSRs, NA.

28. First West Virginia Artillery Record of Events and CSRs, NA.

29. *OR*, vol. 25, pt. 1, p. 91.

30. Maxwell, *The History of Barbour County*, pp. 269–270.

31. Nathaniel Wilkinson CSR, NA; *Wheeling Intelligencer*, May 13, 1863.

32. *OR*, vol. 25, pt. 1, pp. 91–92.

33. Phillips journal.

34. *Ibid.*

35. *Ibid.*

36. Hornbeck, *Upshur Brothers*, p. 121.

37. Phillips journal; Hornbeck, *Upshur Brothers*, p. 121.

38. Phillips journal; Hornbeck, *Upshur Brothers*, pp. 121–122.

39. Phillips journal.

40. Phillips journal; James I. Robertson, Jr., *Stonewall Jackson: The Man, The Soldier, The Legend* (New York: Macmillan Publishing, 1997), pp. 690–691; Lt. James Black CSR, NA.

41. Phillips journal; Hornbeck, *Upshur Brothers*, p. 120.

42. Phillips journal; William Day CSR, NA; Hornbeck, *Upshur Brothers*, p. 114.

43. Phillips journal; Edward C. Smith, *History of Lewis County, West Virginia* (Weston, WV: pub. by author, 1920), p. 311 (hereafter cited as Smith, *History of Lewis County*); *OR*, vol. 25, pt. 1,p. 92.

44. *OR*, vol. 25, pt. 1, p. 92; H.E. Matheny, *Major General Thomas Maley Harris* (Parsons, WV: McClain Printing Co., 1963), p. 55.

45. *OR*, vol. 25, pt. 2, pp. 285, 295.

46. *OR*, vol. 25, pt. 2, pp. 299–300.

47. Phillips journal.

48. *Ibid.*

49. Curry, *A House Divided*, pp. 49, 148; Phillips journal.

50. *OR*, vol. 25, pt. 1, pp. 100–101; Armstrong, *19th and 20th Virginia Cavalry*, p. 8.

51. *OR*, vol. 25, pt. 1, pp. 100–101.

52. *Ibid.*; Hornbeck, *Upshur Brothers*, p. 122.

53. Phillips journal.

54. *Ibid.*

55. *Ibid.*

56. *Ibid.*

57. *Ibid.*; Armstrong, *25th Virginia Infantry*, p. 58.

58. Phillips journal; Ashcraft, *31st Virginia Infantry*, p. 117; Armstrong, *25th Virginia Infantry*, p. 149; Leonard Cutlep CSR, NA.

59. Phillips journal; Krick, *Lee's Colonels*, p. 492.

60. *OR*, vol. 25, pt. 1, p. 101.

61. Wheeling *Intelligencer*, May 16, 1863.

62. *OR*, vol. 25, pt. 1, p. 101.

63. Hornbeck, *Upshur Brothers*, p. 126.

64. *OR*, vol. 25, pt. 1, p. 102.

Chapter Four

1. Mottram Dulany Ball (1835–1887) to Rebecca French Ball, May 25, 1863, Mss 5:1B2106:1, Virginia Historical Society, Richmond (hereafter cited as Ball letter); W.W. Goldsborough, *The Maryland Line in the Confederate Army, 1861–1865* (Gaithersburg, MD: Olde Soldiers Books, 1987), p. 169 (hereafter cited as Goldsborough, *The Maryland Line*); Krick, *Lee's Colonels*, p. 44.

2. Festus P. Summers, ed., *A Borderland Confederate: The Civil War Letters and Diaries of William L. Wilson* (Pittsburgh: University of Pittsburgh Press, 1962), p. 56 (hereafter cited as Summers, *Borderland Confederate*); William L. Wilson CSR, NA.

3. William N. McDonald, *A History of the Laurel Brigade, Originally the Ashby Cavalry of the Army of Northern Virginia* (Baltimore, 1907), p. 118 (hereafter cited as McDonald, *Laurel Brigade*).

4. *OR*, vol. 25, pt. 1, p. 132; Davis, *Confederate General*, vol. 4, p. 85.

5. *OR*, vol. 25, pt. 1, p. 135; Krick, *Lee's Colonels*, p. 392.

6. *OR*, vol. 25, pt. 1, p. 129; Krick, *Lee's Colonels*, 124.

7. *OR*, vol. 25, pt. 1, p. 134; Krick, *Lee's Colonels*, p. 180; Summers, *Borderland Confederate*, p. 56.

8. Robert J. Driver, *First & Second Maryland Cavalry, C.S.A.* (Charlottesville, VA: Rockbridge Publishing, 1999), p. 35 (hereafter cited as Driver, *First & Second Maryland Cavalry*); Krick, *Lee's Colonels*, p. 72; *OR*, vol. 25, pt. 1, p. 124.

9. *OR*, vol. 25, pt. 1, p. 127; Krick, *Lee's Colonels*, p. 167.

10. Scott C. Cole, *34th Virginia Cavalry* (Lynchburg, VA: H.E. Howard, Inc., 1993), pp. 38–39 (hereafter cited as Cole, *34th Virginia Cavalry*); Krick, *Lee's Colonels*, p. 404.

11. Roger U. Delauter, Jr., *McNeil's Rangers* (Lynchburg, VA: H.E. Howard, Inc., 1986), p. 38 (hereafter cited as Delauter, *McNeil's Rangers*).

12. *OR*, vol. 25, pt. 1, pp. 115–116; pt. 2, p. 711; William Williamson CSR, NA. After the raid, Williamson found time to complete his studies at VMI, graduating in 1864. He died at Pensacola in 1898 while helping construct coastal defenses during the Spanish-American War.

13. *OR*, vol. 25, pt. 1, pp. 115–116.

14. Charles T. O'Ferrall, *Forty Years of Active Service* (New York: Neale Publishing Co., 1904), p. 57 (hereafter cited as O'Ferrall, *Forty Years*); *Lee's Colonels*, p. 293.

15. George H. Moffett, "The Jones Raid Through West Virginia," *Confederate Veteran*, vol. 13, pp. 449–450 (hereafter cited as Moffett, "The Jones Raid Through West Virginia").

16. *OR*, vol. 25, pt. 1, pp. 115–116; John E. Divine, *35th Virginia Cavalry Battalion* (Lynchburg, VA: H.E. Howard, Inc., 1985), p. 23 (hereafter cited as Divine, *35th Virginia Cavalry Battalion*); Ball letter; Summers, *Borderland Confederate*, p. 58.

17. Frye, *12th Virginia Cavalry*, p. 23; George Neese, *Three Years in the Confederate Horse Artillery* (New York: Neale Publishing Co., 1911), pp. 155–156 (hereafter cited as Neese, *Three Years in the Confederate Horse Artillery*).

18. Ball letter.

19. *OR*, vol. 25, pt. 1, p. 116.

20. Ball letter.

21. Neese, *Three Years in the Confederate Horse Artillery*, p. 156.

22. *OR*, vol. 25, pt. 1, p. 116; Neese, *Three Years in the Confederate Horse Artillery*, p. 156.

23. Neese, *Three Years in the Confederate Horse Artillery*, pp. 156–157.

24. Frank M. Myers, *The Comanches: A History of White's Battalion, Virginia Cavalry* (Baltimore, 1871), p. 161 (hereafter cited as Myers, *The Comanches*).

25. Ball letter.

26. Neese, *Three Years in the Confederate Horse Artillery*, p. 156; Curry, *A House Divided*, pp. 49, 148.

27. *OR*, vol. 25, pt. 1, p. 116.

28. *Ibid.*; John C. Donahue Diary (Accession 28589, Miscellaneous Reel 519), Library of Virginia, Richmond (hereafter cited as Donahue diary).

29. *OR*, vol. 25, pt. 1, p. 116.

30. Myers, *The Comanches*, p. 161.

31. John Opie, *A Rebel Cavalryman with Lee, Stuart, and Jackson* (Dayton, OH: Morningside Press, 1972), p. 118 (hereafter cited as Opie, *A Rebel Cavalryman*); Michael P. Musick, *6th Virginia Cavalry* (Lynchburg, VA: H.E. Howard, Inc., 1990), pp. 31–32 (hereafter cited as Musick, *6th Virginia Cavalry*).

32. *OR*, vol. 25, pt. 1, p. 116; McDonald, *Laurel Brigade*, p. 120; Driver, *First & Second Maryland Cavalry*, p. 35; Richard Terrell Davis CSR, NA; Opie, *A Rebel Cavalryman*, p. 118.

33. Donahue diary.

34. George Wilson Booth, *Personal Reminiscences of a Soldier in the War Between the States* (Baltimore: Butternut & Blue, 1981), pp. 1–50, 82 (hereafter cited as Booth, *Personal Reminiscences*); George Booth CSR, NA.

35. Frye, *12th Virginia Cavalry*, p. 23; McDonald, *Laurel Brigade*, p. 120.

36. George Baylor, *Bull Run to Bull Run* (Richmond, VA: B.F. Johnson Publishing Co., 1900), pp.136–137 (hereafter cited as Baylor, *Bull Run to Bull Run*); George Baylor CSR, NA.

37. Frye, *12th Virginia Cavalry*, roster.

38. O'Ferrall, *Forty Years*, p. 57; Baylor, *Bull Run to Bull*, p. 137; Charles William Trussell CSR, NA.

39. O'Ferrall, *Forty Years*, p. 57; Frye, *12th Virginia Cavalry*, p. 24, and roster; James Henry Figgatt CSR, NA.

40. Driver, *First & Second Maryland Cavalry*, p. 35; French, "The Jones-Imboden Raid," p. 21; Fritz and Mark Haselberger, "The Battle of Greenland Gap," *West Virginia History*, vol. 28 (July 1967), p. 289 (hereafter cited as Haselberger, "The Battle of Greenland Gap"); Ball letter.

41. Ball letter; Booth, *Personal Reminiscences*, p. 82.

42. *OR*, vol. 25, pt. 1, p. 116; Kenneth Carvil, "Greenland Gap," *Wild, Wonderful West Virginia*, Sept. 1986, p. 28.

43. *OR*, vol. 25, pt. 1, p. 129; Krick, *Lee's Colonels*, p. 263.

44. *OR*, vol. 25, pt. 1, pp. 108–109.

45. Martin Wallace CSR, NA.

46. *OR*, vol. 25, pt. 1, pp. 108–109.

47. 14th West Virginia Infantry Record of Events and CSRs, NA; *OR*, vol. 25, pt. 1, p. 109; French, "The Jones-Imboden Raid," p. 24.

48. French, "The Jones-Imboden Raid," p. 25.

49. *OR*, vol. 25, pt. 1, pp. 108–109; French, "The Jones-Imboden Raid," p. 25.

50. *OR*, vol. 25, pt. 1, p. 109.

51. *OR*, vol. 25, pt. 1, pp. 116, 129.

52. Opie, *A Rebel Cavalryman*, pp. 118–119; John Opie CSR, NA.

53. *OR*, vol. 25, pt. 1, p. 129.

54. French, "The Jones-Imboden Raid," p. 25.

55. *OR*, vol. 25, pt. 1, pp. 109, 129; Goldsborough, *The Maryland Line*, p. 171.

56. *OR*, vol. 25, pt. 1, p. 121; William Alexander Buck CSR, NA.

57. *OR*, vol. 25, pt. 1, p. 129.

58. *OR*, vol. 25, pt. 1, pp. 116–117, 125, 129; Baylor, *Bull Run to Bull Run*, p. 137.

59. *OR*, vol. 25, pt. 1, p. 117; Frank A. Bond, "Storming A Blockhouse in Greenland Gap," *Confederate Veteran*, vol. 17 (Oct. 1909), p. 500 (hereafter cited as Bond, "Storming a Blockhouse in Greenland Gap"); Driver, *First & Second Maryland Cavalry*, p. 36.

60. *OR*, vol. 25, pt. 1, p. 109.

61. Bond, "Storming a Blockhouse in Greenland Gap," p. 500; Driver, *First & Second Maryland Cavalry*, p. 36; Goldsborough, *The Maryland Line*, p. 171.

62. *Ibid.*

63. Driver, *First & Second Maryland Cavalry*, p. 36; Edward Rich, *Comrades Four* (New York: Neale Publishing Co., 1907), pp. 54–55 (hereafter cited as Rich, *Comrades Four*); John Spencer CSR, NA.

64. *OR*, vol. 25, pt. 1, p. 109.

65. *OR*, vol. 25, pt. 1, pp. 117, 122.

66. *OR*, vol. 25, pt. 1, p. 125; Driver, *First & Second Maryland Cavalry*, p. 137; Divine, *35th Virginia Cavalry Battalion*, p. 24; Myers, *The Comanches*, pp. 163–164.

67. Booth, *Personal Reminiscences*, p. 84; *OR*, vol. 25, pt. 1, pp. 117, 125; Myers, *The Comanches*, pp. 163–164.

68. Booth, *Personal Reminiscences*, p. 84; Bond, "Storming a Blockhouse in Greenland Gap," p. 500.

69. Goldsborough, *The Maryland Line*, pp. 171–172.

70. Bond, "Storming a Blockhouse in Greenland Gap," p. 500.

71. Goldsborough, *The Maryland Line*, p. 172.

72. Bond, "Storming a Blockhouse in Greenland Gap," p. 500.

73. *OR*, vol. 25, pt. 1, pp. 109, 125; Henry C. Mettam, "Civil War Memories of the First Maryland Cavalry, C.S.A." *Maryland Historical Magazine*, vol. lviii, p. 148.

74. Goldsborough, *The Maryland Line*, p. 172.

75. Booth, *Personal Reminiscences*, p. 84.

76. "About Jones' Raid Into West Virginia," *Confederate Veteran*, vol. 15, p. 211; Goldsborough, *The Maryland Line*, p. 172; Bond, "Storming a Blockhouse in Greenland Gap," p. 500.

77. Bond, "Storming a Blockhouse in Greenland Gap," p. 500; *OR*, vol. 25, pt. 1, p. 135.

78. Divine, *35th Virginia Cavalry Battalion*, pp. 1–22; Myers, *The Comanches*, p. 164.

79. *OR*, vol. 25, pt. 1, p. 135.

80. Myers, *The Comanches,* p. 165.

81. *OR*, vol. 25, pt. 1, pp. 109–110, 135.

82. Bond, "Storming a Blockhouse in Greenland Gap," p. 500; Booth, *Personal Reminiscences*, p. 85; Edward Johnson CSR, NA.

83. Goldsborough, *The Maryland Line*, p. 172.

84. Divine, *35th Virginia Cavalry Battalion*, p. 24; *OR*, vol. 25, pt. 1, p. 135; Lang, *Loyal West Vir-*

ginia, p. 294; Haselberger, "The Battle of Greenland Gap," pp. 297–298.

85. Bond, "Storming a Blockhouse in Greenland Gap," p. 500.

86. Dan Oates, ed., *Hanging Rock Rebel: Lieutenant John Blue's War in West Virginia and the Shenandoah Valley* (Shippensburg, PA: Burd Street Press, 1994), p. 177 (hereafter cited as Blue, *Hanging Rock Rebel*).

87. Ball letter.

88. Blue, *Hanging Rock Rebel*, p. 177.

89. *Ibid.*; Bond, "Storming a Blockhouse in Greenland Gap," p. 500.

90. *Ibid.*; *OR*, vol. 25, pt. 1, pp. 125, 135; Kenneth Grogan CSR, NA.

91. *OR*, vol. 25, pt. 1, p. 121; Krick, *Lee's Colonels*, p. 72.

92. Haselberger, "The Battle of Greenland Gap," pp. 298–299.

93. Driver, *First & Second Maryland Cavalry*, p. 39; *OR*, vol. 25, pt. 1, pp. 110, 124; Haselberger, "The Battle of Greenland Gap," p. 298.

94. *OR*, vol. 25, pt. 1, p. 117.

95. *OR*, vol. 25, pt. 1, pp. 117, 135; Driver, *First & Second Maryland Cavalry*, p. 39.

96. Booth, *Personal Reminiscences*, pp. 85–86.

97. McDonald, *Laurel Brigade,* p. 123.

98. Homer Floyd Fansler, *History of Tucker County, West Virginia* (Parsons, WV: McClain Printing Co., 1962), p. 189 (hereafter cited as Fansler, *History of Tucker County*).

Chapter Five

1. Martin Wallace CSR, NA; Haselberger, "The Battle of Greenland Gap," p. 303.

2. Jacob Smith CSR, NA.

3. Driver, *First & Second Maryland Cavalry*, p. 39; *OR*, vol. 25, pt. 1, pp. 107–108.

4. *OR*, vol. 25, pt. 1, pp. 251, 253.

5. *OR*, vol. 25, pt. 1, p. 251.

6. *OR,* vol. 25, pt. 1, p. 252; 126th Ohio Infantry Record of Events, National Archives, Washington, D.C.

7. *OR*, vol. 25, pt. 1, p. 252.

8. French, "The Jones-Imboden Raid," p. 33.

9. Ball letter.

10. French, "The Jones-Imboden Raid," p. 33; Ball letter.

11. French, "The Jones-Imboden Raid," p. 40; *OR*, vol. 25, pt. 1, p. 117.

12. *OR*, vol. 25, pt. 1, p. 117; French, "The Jones-Imboden Raid," pp. 33, 40.

13. *OR*, vol. 25, pt. 1, p. 117; Stephen Schlosnagle, *Garrett County: A History of Maryland's Tableland* (Parsons, WV: McClain Printing Co., 1978), p. 229 (hereafter cited as Schlosnagle, *Garrett County*); Curry, *A House Divided*, pp. 49, 148.

14. *The Glades Star*, June 1961, p. 76 (hereafter cited as *Glades Star*).

15. French, "The Jones-Imboden Raid," p. 40; Samuel T. Wiley, *History of Preston County* (Kingwood, WV: The Journal Printing Co., 1882), p. 167 (hereafter cited as Wiley, *History of Preston County*).

16. Ball letter.

17. French, "The Jones-Imboden Raid," pp. 40–41.

18. John H. Showalter CSR and Sixth West Virginia Infantry Record of Events, NA.

19. French, "The Jones-Imboden Raid," pp. 41–42; Fansler, *History of Tucker County*, p. 195; Opie, *A Rebel Cavalryman*, pp. 121–122.

20. Opie, *A Rebel Cavalryman*, p. 122; French, "The Jones-Imboden Raid," p. 42.

21. Opie, *A Rebel Cavalryman*, pp. 121–122; Fansler, *History of Tucker County*, p. 195.

22. Wiley, *History of Preston County*, p. 167.

23. French, "The Jones-Imboden Raid," p. 43; *OR*, vol. 25, pt. 1, p. 117.

24. Wiley, *History of Preston County*, p. 167.

25. Lang, *Loyal West Virginia*, pp. 168–169; Johnston, *Virginia Railroads in the Civil War*, p. 289 fn.

26. Wiley, *History of Preston County*, pp. 167–168.

27. Wheeling *Intelligencer*, May 29, 1863; Opie, *A Rebel Cavalryman*, p. 122; *OR*, vol. 25, pt. 1, p. 127.

28. Opie, *A Rebel Cavalryman*, pp. 122–123.

29. *OR*, vol. 25, pt. 1, p. 127.

30. *OR*, vol. 25, pt. 1, p. 117.

31. Opie, *A Rebel Cavalryman*, p. 123.

32. *OR*, vol. 25, pt. 1, p. 117; John Shackleford Green CSR, NA.

33. *OR*, vol. 25, pt. 1, pp. 117–118; Wiley, *History of Preston County*, p. 168.

34. Wiley, *History of Preston County*, p. 169; Donohue diary.

35. Myers, *The Comanches*, p. 166.

36. Oren F. Morton, *History of Preston County, West Virginia* (Kingwood, WV: Preston Printing Co., 1911), p. 150 (hereafter cited as Morton, *History of Preston County*).

37. "About Jones's Raid Into West Virginia," *Confederate Veteran*, vol.15, p. 211.

38. Ball letter; Donohue diary.

39. Myers, The *Comanches*, p. 167.

40. *OR*, vol. 25, pt. 1, p. 118; Jacob Shoup CSR, NA.

41. French, "The Jones-Imboden Raid," pp. 47–48; *OR*, vol. 25, pt. 1, p. 118.

42. *OR*, vol. 25, pt. 1, p. 118.

43. Johnston, *Virginia Railroads in the Civil War*, p. 152; *OR*, vol. 25, vol. 25, pp. 118, 130.

44. *OR*, vol. 25, pt. 1, pp. 118, 130.

Chapter Six

1. *OR*, vol. 25, pt. 1, p. 134; Rich, *Comrades Four*, p. 57.

2. Rich, *Comrades Four*, pp. 1–10; Edward Rich CSR, NA.

3. *Glades Star*, p. 76.

4. *Glades Star*, pp. 75–76.

5. Patience W. Grant, "Episodes of Confederate Cavalry Raids of 1863," *The Glades Star*, June 1961, p. 87 (hereafter cited as Grant, "Episodes of Confederate Cavalry Raids of 1863").

6. Ruth and Iret Ashby, "Jones' Raid... It Aims and Results," *The Glades Star*, June 1961, pp. 84–85 (hereafter cited as Ashby, "Jones' Raid").

7. *Glades Star*, p. 75; Sixth West Virginia Infantry Record of Events, National Archives, Washington, D.C.; Joseph Godwin CSR, NA.

8. Ashby, "Jones' Raid," pp. 84–85; Cornelius Johnson CSR, NA.

9. Delauter, *McNeil's Rangers*, p. 39; *Glades Star*, p. 74; Summers, *Borderland Confederate*, p. 59; French, "The Jones-Imboden Raid," p. 35.

10. *Glades Star*, p. 74.

11. Joseph Godwin CSR, and Jackson Saucer CSR, NA; Baylor, *Bull Run to Bull Run*, p. 137.

12. Baylor, *Bull Run to Bull Run*, pp. 137–138.

13. Grant, "Episodes of Confederate Cavalry Raids of 1863," pp. 87–88.

14. Rich, *Comrades Four*, p. 57.

15. Grant, "Episodes of Confederate Cavalry Raids of 1863," p. 89.

16. *Ibid.*

17. *Glades Star*, p. 74.

18. *OR*, vol. 25, pt. 1, p. 134.

19. *Glades Star*, pp. 80–81.

20. *OR*, vol. 25, pt. 1, p. 134; Ashby, "Jones' Raid," and Grant, "Episodes of Confederate Cavalry Raids of 1863," pp. 84–88.

21. *Glades Star*, p. 75; Jackson Saucer CSR, NA; Wiley, *History of Preston County*, p. 168.

22. French, "The Jones-Imboden Raid," pp. 36–37.

23. *Ibid.*

24. Frye, *12th Virginia Cavalry*, pp. 25–26.

25. French, "The Jones-Imboden Raid," p. 37; Wiley, *History of Preston County*, pp. 170–173; Morton, *History of Preston County*, p. 150.

26. *Ibid.*

27. *Ibid.*; Wheeling *Intelligencer*, April 29, 1863.

28. French, "The Jones-Imboden Raid," p. 37; Wiley, *History of Preston County*, pp. 170–173; Morton, *History of Preston County*, p. 150.

29. *OR*, vol. 25, pt. 1, p. 134; Morton, *History of Preston County*, p. 151.

30. *OR*, vol. 25, pt. 1, pp. 126, 134; Morton, *History of Preston County*, p. 151; Frye, *12th Virginia Cavalry*, p. 26; Wiley, *History of Preston County*, p. 173.

31. Wheeling *Intelligencer*, April 29, 1863.

32. Morton, *History of Preston County*, p. 151.

33. Curry, *A House Divided*, pp. 49, 148; *OR*, vol. 25, pt. 1, p. 126; Goldsborough, *The Maryland Line*, pp. 172–173.

34. Wheeling *Intelligencer*, May 6, 1863; James Morton Callaghan, *History of the Making of Morgantown, West Virginia: A Type Study in Trans-Appalachian Local History* (Morgantown, WV: West Virginia University, 1926), pp. 204–206 (hereafter cited as Callaghan, *History of the Making of Morgantown*); Samuel T. Wiley, *History of Monongalia County, West Virginia, From Its First Settlements to the Present Time; With Numerous Biographical and Family Sketches* (Kingwood, WV: Preston Pub., 1883), p. 147 (hereafter cited as Wiley, *History of Monongalia County*).

35. Wiley, *History of Monongalia County*, p. 147.

36. *Ibid.*; Callaghan, *History of the Making of Morgantown*, pp. 204–205; *Fairmont Times*, April 29, 1934.

37. Wiley, *History of Monongalia County*, pp. 147–148; Sarah Jane Lough to "Dear Brother," May 3, 1863, West Virginia University (hereafter cited as Lough letter).

38. Driver, *First & Second Maryland Cavalry*, p. 41; Callaghan, *History of the Making of Morgantown*, p. 205; *OR*, vol. 25, pt. 1, p. 126.

39. *Ibid.*

40. Callaghan, *History of the Making of Morgantown*, p. 205; Wiley, *History of Monongalia County*, p. 148.

41. Frye, *12th Virginia Cavalry*, p. 26; Baylor, *Bull Run to Bull Run*, p. 138.

42. *Ibid.*

43. Callaghan, *History of the Making of Morgantown*, p. 205; Lough letter.

44. Callaghan, *History of the Making of Morgantown*, p. 205; Wheeling *Intelligencer*, May 2, 1863.

45. Callaghan, *History of the Making of Morgantown*, p. 205; John Bigelow, Jr., *The Campaign of Chancellorsville: A Strategic and Tactical Study* (New Haven, CT: Yale University Press, 1910), p. 465 (hereafter cited as Bigelow, *The Campaign of Chancellorsville*).

46. Lough letter.

47. *OR*, vol. 25, pt. 1, p. 134.

48. Edward McDonald, CSR, NA; Foxall A. Daingerfield CSR, NA.

49. Blue, *Hanging Rock Rebel*, p. 178.

50. *Ibid.*

51. *OR*, vol. 25, pt. 1, pp. 118, 134.

52. *Glades Star*, p. 73; Blue, *Hanging Rock Rebel*, p. 178.

53. Grant, "Episodes of Confederate Cavalry Raids of 1863," p. 88; Wheeling *Intelligencer*, May 16, 1863.

54. Blue, *Hanging Rock Rebel*, pp. 178–179.

55. Blue, *Hanging Rock Rebel*, p. 179.

56. *Ibid.*

57. Blue, *Hanging Rock Rebel*, pp. 179–180.

58. Blue, *Hanging Rock Rebel*, p. 180.

59. *OR*, vol. 25, pt. 1, p. 118.

60. Driver, *First & Second Maryland Cavalry*, p. 41; William Raisin CSR, NA.

61. Festus P. Summers, "The Jones-Imboden Raid," *West Virginia History*, vol. 47 (1988), p. 58; Wiley, *History of Monongalia County*, p. 149; Wheeling *Intelligencer*, May 6, 1863; William Raisin CSR, NA.

62. Wiley, *History of Monongalia County*, p. 149;

Wheeling Intelligencer, May 6, 1863; Glenn D. Lough, *Now and Long Ago: A History of the Marion County Area* (Fairmont, WV: Glenn D. Lough, 1969), pp. 643–645 (hereafter cited as Lough, *Now and Long Ago*).

63. Callaghan, *History of the Making of Morgantown*, p. 205.

64. *Ibid.*; Maxwell, *The History of Barbour County*, pp. 269–270.

65. Myers, *The Comanches*, p. 167.

66. Callaghan, *History of the Making of Morgantown*, p. 205; Myers, *The Comanches*, p. 167.

67. Musick, *6th Virginia Cavalry*, p. 33.

68. Blue, *Hanging Rock Rebel*, p. 180.

69. Wiley, *History of Monongalia County*, p. 149.

70. Rich, *Comrades Four*, p. 58.

71. Lough letter.

72. Wheeling *Intelligencer*, May 6, 1863.

73. Wheeling *Intelligencer*, May 29, 1863; Wiley, *History of Preston County*, pp. 174–176; Sixth West Virginia Infantry Record of Events, NA; Festus P. Summers, *The Baltimore and Ohio Railroad in the Civil War* (New York: G.P. Putnam's Sons, 1939), p. 159 (hereafter cited as Summers, *The Baltimore and Ohio*); *OR*, vol. 25, pt. 2, pp. 286–287.

74. *Ibid.*

75. Wheeling *Intelligencer*, May 4, 1863.

76. *Ibid.*

77. Wheeling *Intelligencer*, May 4 & May 29, 1863.

78. Wheeling *Intelligencer*, May 4, 1863.

79. Wheeling *Intelligencer*, May 6, 1863.

80. Wheeling *Intelligencer*, May 4 & 6, 1863.

81. *Ibid.*

82. *OR*, vol. 25, pt. 2, p. 373; Wheeling *Intelligencer*, May 4 & 6, 1863.

83. Wheeling *Intelligencer*, May 4 & 6, 1863.

84. Wheeling *Intelligencer*, May 4 & 6, 1863; *OR*, vol. 25, pt. 2, p. 375.

85. *OR*, vol. 25, pt. 2, p. 372.

86. *OR*, vol. 25, pt. 2, p. 415.

87. *OR*, vol. 25, pt. 2, p. 482.

88. *Ibid.*

89. *OR*, vol. 25, pt. 2, p. 283; French, "The Jones-Imboden Raid," pp. 49–50.

90. French, "The Jones-Imboden Raid," p. 50; *OR*, vol. 25, pt. 2, p. 430.

Chapter Seven

1. Bigelow, *The Campaign of Chancellorsville*, p. 465.

2. *Ibid.*

3. *OR*, vol. 25, pt. 2, pp. 278–279.

4. *OR*, vol. 25, pt. 2, p. 279.

5. *OR*, vol. 25, pt. 2, pp. 278–286. Mulligan's Fifth Brigade: Second Maryland Potomac Home Guards, Colonel Robert Bruce; Twenty-third Illinois Infantry, Lt. Colonel James Quirk; Fourteenth West Virginia Infantry, Major Daniel D. Johnson; First Illinois Artillery, Battery L, Captain John Rourke.

6. Wheeling *Intelligencer,* May 13, 1863.

7. *OR,* vol. 25, pt. 2, p. 298.

8. *OR,* vol. 25, pt. 2, pp. 296–297.

9. *OR,* vol. 25, pt. 2, p. 255.

10. *OR,* vol. 25, pt. 2, p. 270.

11. *OR,* vol. 25, pt. 2, pp. 279–280.

12. *OR,* vol. 25, pt. 2, pp. 280–281.

13. *OR,* vol. 25, pt. 2, pp. 281, 285.

14. *OR,* vol. 25, pt. 2, pp. 279, 286.

15. *OR,* vol. 25, pt. 1, p. 118; Curry, *A House Divided*, pp. 49, 148; Blue, *Hanging Rock Rebel*, p. 180; Bigelow, *The Campaign of Chancellorsville*, p. 467.

16. Lough, *Now and Long Ago*, p. 642.

17. *OR*, vol. 25, pt. 1, p. 118; *Times West Virginian*, March 13, 1997.

18. *OR*, vol. 25, pt. 1, p. 122; W.L. Balderson, *Fort Prickett and Marion County* (Fairmont, WV: Bicentennial Committee, 1976), p. 237 (hereafter cited as Balderson, *Fort Prickett and Marion County*).

19. *OR*, vol. 25, pt. 1, pp. 118, 130; Balderson, *Fort Prickett and Marion County*, p. 268.

20. Balderson, *Fort Prickett and Marion County*, p. 268.

21. Balderson, *Fort Prickett and Marion County*, p. 242; Lough, *Now and Long Ago*, p. 645.

22. Balderson, *Fort Prickett and Marion County*, pp. 236, 274; *Fairmont Times*, April 29, 1934.

23. Balderson, *Fort Prickett and Marion County*, p. 236; Fairmont *Times*, April 29, 1934.

24. Fairmont *Times*, April 29, 1934; Balderson, *Fort Prickett and Marion County*, p. 246.

25. Balderson, *Fort Prickett and Marion County*, pp. 249, 253.

26. Lough, *Now and Long Ago*, p. 650; Wheeling *Intelligencer*, May 6 & May 13, 1863; *Times West Virginian*, March 20, 1997; Balderson, *Fort Prickett and Marion County*, p. 239; Thomas Condit Miller and Hu Maxwell, *West Virginia and Its People*, 3 vols. (New York: Lewis Historical Publishing Co., 1913), vol. 1, p. 340 (hereafter cited as Miller, *West Virginia and Its People*).

27. Frederick Phisterer, comp., *New York in the War of the Rebellion 1861 to 1865*, 5 vols., (Albany, NY: F.B. Lyon Co., State Printers, 1912), vol. iv, p. 3242.

28. Sixth West Virginia Infantry Record of Events, NA.

29. *Ibid.*

30. Henry Solomon White diary, West Virginia University, Morgantown, WV (hereafter cited as White diary); Henry Solomon White CSR, NA.

31. White diary.

32. Balderson, *Fort Prickett and Marion County*, pp. 242, 249; White diary.

33. Balderson, *Fort Prickett and Marion County*, pp. 249–250.

34. Balderson, *Fort Prickett and Marion County*, p. 250.

35. *Ibid.*

36. *Ibid.*

37. *Ibid.*, pp. 250–251.

38. Balderson, *Fort Prickett and Marion County*, p. 242.

39. *Ibid.*

40. *Ibid.*

41. Blue, *Hanging Rock Rebel*, pp. 180–181.

42. Balderson, *Fort Prickett and Marion County*, p. 243.

43. Balderson, *Fort Prickett and Marion County*, p. 242.

44. Blue, *Hanging Rock Rebel*, p. 181.

45. *OR*, vol. 25, pt. 1, pp. 118, 130, 133–134.

46. Balderson, *Fort Prickett and Marion County*, p. 251.

47. Balderson, *Fort Prickett and Marion County*, pp. 254–255.

48. Balderson, *Fort Prickett and Marion County*, p. 255.

49. Balderson, *Fort Prickett and Marion County*, pp. 243, 251, 255.

50. Balderson, *Fort Prickett and Marion County*, p. 243; D.M. Santmyer CSR, NA; Lough, *Now and Long Ago*, p. 647.

51. Balderson, *Fort Prickett and Marion County*, pp. 251, 253, 255.

52. Balderson, *Fort Prickett and Marion County*, pp. 251–252.

53. Balderson, *Fort Prickett and Marion County*, pp. 255–256; Driver, *First & Second Maryland Cavalry*, p. 42.

54. Balderson, *Fort Prickett and Marion County*, pp. 251–252; Wheeling *Intelligencer*, May 8, 1863.

55. George Moffett, "The Jones Raid Through West Virginia," *Confederate Veteran*, vol. 13, pp. 449–451 (hereafter cited as Moffett, "The Jones Raid Through West Virginia"); Summers, *Borderland Confederate*, p. 60.

56. Balderson, *Fort Prickett and Marion County*, p. 256.

57. O'Ferrall, *Forty Years*, pp. 61–62.

58. Rich, *Comrades Four*, p. 58; Divine, *35th Virginia Cavalry Battalion*, p. 25.

59. Lough, *Now and Long Ago*, pp. 650–651; Balderson, *Fort Prickett and Marion County*, p. 245.

60. Ball letter.

61. Blue, *Hanging Rock Rebel*, p. 182.

62. Balderson, *Fort Prickett and Marion County*, p. 244; Lough, *Now and Long Ago*, pp. 649–650.

63. Balderson, *Fort Prickett and Marion County*, p. 237.

64. Balderson, *Fort Prickett and Marion County*, p. 241; Lough, *Now and Long Ago*, pp. 641, 650; Wheeling *Intelligencer*, May 6, 1863.

65. Balderson, *Fort Prickett and Marion County*, pp. 237, 240; Fairmont *Times*, April 29, 1913.

66. Balderson, *Fort Prickett and Marion County*, p. 252; Wheeling *Intelligencer*, May 6, 1863.

67. Blue, *Hanging Rock Rebel*, p. 182.

68. *OR*, vol. 25, pt. 1, pp. 128, 130, 133–134; Miller, *West Virginia and Its People*, vol. 1, p. 340.

69. *OR*, vol. 25, pt. 1, p. 119; Wheeling *Intelligencer*, May 6, 1863.

70. Fairmont *Times*, June 8, 1934; Balderson, *Fort Prickett and Marion County*, p. 256.

71. White diary; Balderson, *Fort Prickett and Marion County*, p. 262.

72. Balderson, *Fort Prickett and Marion County*, p. 256.

73. Balderson, *Fort Prickett and Marion County*, p. 252; Charles E. Primm CSR, NA.

74. Balderson, *Fort Prickett and Marion County*, p. 252.

75. *OR*, vol. 25, pt. 1, p. 128; Myers, *The Comanches*, p. 119; Wheeling *Intelligencer*, May 8, 1863.

76. Opie, *A Rebel Cavalryman*, p. 126.

77. *Ibid.*; Wheeling *Intelligencer*, May 8, 1863.

78. *OR*, vol. 25, pt. 1, pp. 118, 130.

79. Opie, *A Rebel Cavalryman*, p. 126.

80. Opie, *A Rebel Cavalryman*, p. 127.

81. *OR*, vol. 25, pt. 1, p. 118.

82. Opie, *A Rebel Cavalryman*, p. 127.

83. Wheeling *Intelligencer*, May 13, 1863.

84. *OR*, vol. 25, pt. 1, pp. 122–123.

85. *OR*, vol. 25, pt. 1, pp. 118, 123; Wheeling *Intelligencer*, May 6, 1863.

86. Balderson, *Fort Prickett and Marion County*, p. 252; Wheeling *Intelligencer*, May 8, 1863.

87. Balderson, *Fort Prickett and Marion County*, p. 257; *Wheeling Intelligencer*, May 6, 1863.

88. Wheeling *Intelligencer*, May 8, 1863.

89. Balderson, *Fort Prickett and Marion County*, pp. 266, 272–273; Fairmont *Times*, June 8, 1934.

90. Fairmont *Times*, June 8, 1934.

91. *OR*, vol. 25, pt. 1, p. 120.

92. White diary; Fairmont *Times*, February 28, 1904 & February 29, 1934.

93. *OR*, vol. 25, pt. 1, p. 120.

94. White diary.

95. Ball letter.

96. Fairmont *Times*, April 29, 1934.

97. Wheeling *Intelligencer*, May 5, 1863.

98. *Ibid.*

99. *Ibid.*

100. Wheeling *Intelligencer*, May 6, 1863.

101. Wheeling *Intelligencer*, May 8, 1863.

102. Balderson, *Fort Prickett and Marion County*, p. 274.

103. Balderson, *Fort Prickett and Marion County*, pp. 266–267; Fairmont *Times*, April 29, 1913.

104. *OR*, vol. 25, pt. 1, pp. 122, 126.

105. Balderson, *Fort Prickett and Marion County*, p. 245.

106. Balderson, *Fort Prickett and Marion County*, pp. 238, 244–245.

107. Lough, *Now and Long Ago*, p. 642.

108. Lough, *Now and Long Ago*, p. 643.

109. Lough, *Now and Long Ago*, pp. 643, 645.

110. Lough, *Now and Long Ago*, p. 649.

111. Wheeling *Intelligencer*, May 8, 1863; Fairmont *Times*, April 29, 1934.

112. *OR*, Vol. 25, pt. 2, pp. 283, 350, 376; Wheeling *Intelligencer*, May 4, 1863.

113. Wheeling *Intelligencer*, May 4, 1863.

Chapter Eight

1. Moffett, "The Jones Raid Through West Virginia," p. 450.

2. *Ibid*.

3. *OR*, vol. 25, pt. 1, p. 119; Lough, *Now and Long Ago*, p. 641.

4. Balderson, *Fort Prickett and Marion County*, p. 238.

5. Balderson, *Fort Prickett and Marion County*, pp. 246–247.

6. Opie, *A Rebel Cavalryman*, pp. 127–128.

7. *OR*, vol. 25, pt. 1, p. 130; Curry, *A House Divided*, pp. 49, 147.

8. Opie, *A Rebel Cavalryman*, pp. 129–130.

9. Clarksburg *Exponent*, April 29, 1990.

10. *Ibid*.

11. *Ibid*.

12. *Ibid*.

13. *Ibid*.

14. Opie, *A Rebel Cavalryman*, p. 131.

15. Clarksburg *Exponent*, April 29, 1990.

16. *Ibid*.

17. *OR*, vol. 25, pt. 1, pp. 119, 130, 136; Driver, *First & Second Maryland Cavalry*, p. 43; Frye, *12th Virginia Cavalry*, pp. 28–29.

18. Third West Virginia Cavalry Record of Events, NA.

19. Clarksburg *Exponent*, April 29, 1990.

20. *OR*, vol. 25, pt. 1, p. 96.

21. *OR*, vol. 25, pt. 1, pp. 96–97; Dorothy Davis, *History of Harrison County, West Virginia* (Parsons, WV: McClain Printing Co., 1970), p. 249 (hereafter cited as Davis, *History of Harrison County*); Ball letter.

22. Opie, *A Rebel Cavalryman*, pp. 133–134.

23. *OR*, vol. 25, pt. 1, p. 126; Myers, *The Comanches*, p. 170; Driver, *First & Second Maryland Cavalry*, p. 43.

24. *Ibid*.; Summers, *The Baltimore and Ohio*, p. 135.

25. *OR*, vol. 25, pt. 1, pp. 119, 123, 136; Summers, *The Baltimore and Ohio*, p. 135.

26. Curry, *A House Divided*, pp. 49, 147; Maxwell, *The History of Barbour County*, p. 270.

27. Shaffer, *Clash of Loyalties*, p. 112.

28. *OR*, vol. 25, pt. 1, p. 119; Dayton, *Samuel Woods*, p. 110.

29. Shaffer, *Clash of Loyalties*, pp. 112–113.

30. *OR*, vol. 25, pt. 1, pp. 119, 123, 128; Hornbeck, *Upshur Brothers*, p. 126.

31. *OR*, vol. 25, pt. 1, pp. 126, 131; Goldsborough, *The Maryland Line*, p. 173.

32. *OR*, vol. 25, pt. 1, p. 131; Summers, *Borderland Confederate*, p. 60.

33. Shaffer, *Clash of Loyalties*, pp. 99–100.

34. *OR*, vol. 25, pt. 1, p. 119.

35. Wheeling *Intelligencer*, April 27, 1863.

36. Curry, *A House Divided*, pp. 49, 148; Wheeling *Intelligencer*, April 28, 1863.

37. Wheeling *Intelligencer*, April 29 & 30, 1863.

38. Wheeling *Intelligencer*, April 30, 1863.

39. Wheeling *Intelligencer*, April 28, 1863.

40. *Ibid*.

41. Wheeling *Intelligencer*, May 2 & 11, 1863.

42. Wheeling *Intelligencer*, May 15, 1863.

43. Wheeling *Intelligencer*, April 30, 1863.

44. Wheeling *Intelligencer*, April 29, 1863.

45. Wheeling *Intelligencer*, May 2, 1863.

46. Wheeling *Intelligencer*, May 1, 1863.

47. Wheeling *Intelligencer*, April 29, 1863.

48. Shaffer, *Clash of Loyalties*, p. 77.

49. *OR*, vol. 25, pt. 1, p. 102; Armstrong, *25th Virginia*, p. 58.

50. *Ibid*.

51. *OR*, vol. 25, pt. 1, p. 102.

52. *OR*, vol. 25, pt. 1, pp. 102, 119; Curry, *A House Divided*, pp. 49, 147; Cook, *Lewis County*, p. 63.

53. Cook, *Lewis County*, pp. 63–64; Mortimer Johnson to "My Dear Wife," May 5, 1863, Johnson Family Papers, Manuscript #341, Virginia Military History Institute Archives, Lexington, Va. (hereafter cited as Johnson letter).

54. Johnson letter.

55. Cook, *Lewis County*, p. 64.

56. *Ibid*.

57. Cook, *Lewis County*, p. 65.

58. *Ibid*.

59. Smith, *History of Lewis County*, p. 312; Delauter, *18th Virginia Cavalry*, p. 5. O'Ferrall, *Forty Years*, pp. 58–59.

60. Tucker, *Brigadier General John D. Imboden*, p. 130; Summers, *Borderland Confederate*, p. 61.

61. *OR*, vol. 25, pt. 1, p. 115.

62. *OR*, vol. 25, pt. 1, p. 119; Donohue diary.

63. Henry Hayman, *History of Harrison County* (Morgantown, WV: Acme Publishing Co., 1910), p. 327 (hereafter cited as Hayman, *History of Harrison County*).

64. *OR*, vol. 25, pt. 2, p. 768; Tucker, *Brigadier General John D. Imboden*, p. 130.

65. *OR*, vol. 25, pt. 1, p. 102; Cook, *Lewis County*, pp. 63–64.

66. *OR*, vol. 25, pt. 1, p. 97.

67. Cook, *Lewis County*, p. 64.

68. *OR*, vol. 25, pt. 1, pp. 102–103.

69. *OR*, vol. 25, pt. 1, pp. 103, 119.

70. Delauter, *18th Virginia Cavalry*, p. 5.

71. *Ibid*.; Tucker, *Brigadier General John D. Imboden*, pp. 130–131: "Frank Imboden arranged for horses and eight wagons and loaded them with all their parents' possessions, but unfortunately the wagon train encountered a Union patrol, which seized the horses and the bulk of the personal property. Frank Imboden succeeded in getting away with the one wagon in which his parents were riding,

which carried only a few of their personal belongings.”); Woodward, *Defender of the Valley*, p. 74.

72. *OR*, vol. 25, pt. 1, p. 103; Cook, *Lewis County*, p. 65.

73. Hayman, *History of Harrison County*, pp. 328–329.

74. *OR*, vol. 25, pt. 2, p. 345.

75. *OR*, vol. 25, pt. 2, pp. 346, 372.

76. *OR*, vol. 25, pt. 2, p. 348.

77. *OR*, vol. 25, pt. 2, pp. 296, 318.

78. *OR*, vol. 25, pt. 1, p. 92.

79. *OR*, vol. 25, pt. 2, p. 376.

80. Wheeling *Intelligencer*, May 11, 1863.

81. *OR*, vol. 25, pt. 2, p. 376.

82. *OR*, vol. 25, pt. 2, pp. 374–375, 398.

83. *OR*, vol. 25, pt. 2, p. 399.

84. Polsley letters of April 25 & April 29, 1863.

85. Wheeling *Intelligencer*, May 5, 1863.

86. Hornbeck, Upshur Brothers, p. 121.

87. Smith, *History of Lewis County*, p. 313.

Chapter Nine

1. Summers, *Borderland Confederate*, p. 61.

2. O'Ferrall, *Forty Years*, pp. 58–59.

3. Reverend Richard T. Davis to "My Dear Wife," May 14, 1863, Davis-Preston-Saunders Papers, MSS 4951, Special Collections, University of Virginia Library, Charlottesville (hereafter cited as Davis letter).

4. *OR*, vol. 25, pt. 1, pp. 119–120, 134; Herman E. Matheny, *Wood County, West Virginia in Civil War Times* (Parkersburg, WV: Trans-Allegheny Books, Inc., 1987), p. 336 (hereafter cited as Matheny, *Wood County*).

5. *OR*, vol. 25, pt. 1, pp. 133–134; Matheny, *Wood County*, p. 336; Curry, *A House Divided*, pp. 49, 147.

6. *OR*, vol. 25, pt. 1, p. 111.

7. *OR*, vol. 25, pt. 1, pp. 111, 134; Summers, *Borderland Confederate*, p. 62.

8. *OR*, vol. 25, pt. 1, pp. 111, 134; Frye, *12th Virginia Cavalry*, p. 30.

9. O'Ferrall, *Forty Years*, p. 61.

10. Curry, *A House Divided*, pp. 49, 148; Matheny, *Wood County*, p. 337; Summers, *Borderland Confederate*, p. 62.

11. *OR*, vol. 25, pt. 1, p. 134; Summers, *Borderland Confederate*, p. 62.

12. Davis letter.

13. *OR*, vol. 25, pt. 1, p. 120.

14. *OR*, vol. 25, pt. 1, pp. 120, 126–127; 136.

15. *OR*, vol. 25, pt. 1, pp. 120, 123, 137; Myers, *The Comanches*, p. 171.

16. *OR*, vol. 25, pt. 1, p. 123.

17. *OR*, vol. 25, pt. 1, pp. 120, 134.

18. *OR*, vol. 25, pt. 2, p. 429.

19. *Ibid*.

20. *OR*, vol. 25, pt. 2, p. 431.

21. *OR*, vol. 25, pt. 2, p. 436.

22. *OR*, vol. 25, pt. 2, pp. 442–444.

23. *OR*, vol. 25, pt. 2, p. 446.

24. *OR*, vol. 25, pt. 2, p. 453.

25. *OR*, vol. 25, pt. 2, p. 447.

26. *OR*, vol. 25, pt. 2, pp. 454–455.

27. *OR*, vol. 25, pt. 2, p. 462.

28. Bernard L. Allen and David McKain, *Where It All Began: The Story of the People and Places Where the Oil & Gas Industry Began — West Virginia and Southeastern Ohio* (Parkersburg, WV: David L. McKain, 1994), pp. 1–35 (hereafter cited as Bernard, *Where It All Began*); Tucker, *Brigadier General John D. Imboden*, p. 131.

29. Bernard, *Where It All Began*, p. 37.

30. Howard B. Lee, *The Burning Springs: And Other Tales of the Little Kanawha* (Morgantown, WV: West Virginia University Press, 1968), p. 33 (hereafter cited as Lee, *The Burning Springs*); Parkersburg *News*, Dec. 29, 1968.

31. Lee, *The Burning Springs*, p. 33.

32. Lee, *The Burning Springs*, p. 43.

33. *Ibid.*, pp. 43–44.

34. Blue, *Hanging Rock Rebel*, pp. 183–184; Lee, *The Burning Springs*, p. 44.

35. Blue, *Hanging Rock Rebel*, pp. 183–184.

36. Myers, *The Comanches*, p. 172.

37. Lee, *The Burning Springs*, p. 35; Parkersburg *News*, Dec. 29, 1968.

38. *OR*, vol. 25, pt. 1, p. 120.

39. Lee, *The Burning Springs*, p. 37.

40. Lee, *The Burning Springs*, p. 43.

41. Myers, *The Comanches*, pp. 172–173.

42. O.P. Horn in the Rockingham *Register*, June 6, 1863.

43. Opie, *A Rebel Cavalryman*, p. 136.

44. Lee, *The Burning Springs*, p. 37.

45. Parkersburg *News*, Dec.29, 1968; Miller, *West Virginia and Its People*, vol. 1, p. 339.

46. Blue, *Hanging Rock Rebel*, p. 184.

47. Lee, *The Burning Springs*, pp. 38–39.

48. Lee, *The Burning Springs*, p. 37.

49. *OR*, vol. 25, pt. 1, p. 120.

50. Lee, *The Burning Springs*, p. 38; Parkersburg *News*, Dec. 29, 1968.

51. Rich, *Comrades Four*, p. 61.

52. Opie, *A Rebel Cavalryman*, p. 135.

53. Lee, *The Burning Springs*, p. 37.

54. Lee, *The Burning Springs*, pp. 40–42.

55. Lee, *The Burning Springs*, p. 45.

56. *OR*, vol. 25, pt. 1, p. 120; Bernard, *Where It All Began* p. 43.

57. Parkersburg *News*, Dec. 29, 1968.

58. Wheeling *Intelligencer*, May 13, 1863; Marietta *Intelligencer*, May 13, 1863.

59. Parkersburg *News*, Dec. 29, 1968.

Chapter Ten

1. *OR*, vol. 25, pt. 1, p. 103.

2. *Ibid.*; Hall diary; Cook, *Lewis County*, p. 64.

3. *Ibid.*; Snider journal.

4. McNeil, "The Imboden Raid and Its Effects," p. 310; Armstrong, *25th Virginia Infantry*, p. 59.

5. Snider journal.

6. Potts diary.

7. Lowry, *22nd Virginia Infantry*, p. 42.

8. Snider journal, Curry, *A House Divided*, pp. 49, 147.

9. Hall diary.

10. Curry, *A House Divided*, pp. 49, 148; *OR*, vol. 25, pt. 1.p. 103; Tucker, *Brigadier General John D. Imboden*, p. 132.

11. *OR*, vol. 25, pt. 1, p. 103; Tucker, *Brigadier General John D. Imboden*, p. 132; Potts diary.

12. Tucker, *Brigadier General John D. Imboden*, pp. 132–133; Snider journal.

13. *OR*, vol. 25, pt. 1, pp. 103, 120.

14. Wheeling *Intelligencer*, May 3, 1863; Curry, *A House Divided*, pp. 49, 148.

15. Wheeling *Intelligencer*, May 3, 1863.

16. Matheny, *Wood County*, pp. 327–328, 334.

17. Matheny, *Wood County*, pp. 335, 338; Marietta *Intelligencer*, May 29, 1861.

18. Matheny, *Wood County*, p. 334.

19. Matheny, *Wood County*, pp. 338–339.

20. Matheny, *Wood County*, pp. 337–338.

21. Matheny, *Wood County*, pp. 338–339.

22. Matheny, *Wood County*, p. 339.

23. Wheeling *Intelligencer*, May 13 & 15, 1863.

24. Matheny, *Wood County*, p. 340.

25. Matheny, *Wood County*, pp. 341–342.

26. Matheny, *Wood County*, p. 342.

27. Myers, *The Comanches*, p. 174; *OR*, vol. 25, pt. 1, pp. 133, 136.

28. *OR*, vol. 25, pt. 1, p. 133; Donohue diary.

29. Summers, *Borderland Confederate*, p. 63.

30. Davis letter.

31. *OR*, vol. 25, pt. 1, p. 133; Summers, *Borderland Confederate*, p. 63.

32. Donohue diary.

33. Myers, *The Comanches*, pp. 171–172.

34. Frye, *12th Virginia Cavalry*, p. 33; Summers, *Borderland Confederate*, p. 64.

35. Summers, *Borderland Confederate*, p. 64.

36. *OR*, vol. 25, pt. 2, p. 467.

37. *OR*, vol. 25, pt. 2, p. 468.

38. *OR*, vol. 25, pt. 2, p. 478.

39. White diary.

40. Polsley letter to wife, May 7, 1863.

41. Polsley letter to wife, May 14, 1863.

42. Polsley letter to a friend, May 15, 1863.

43. Wheeling *Intelligencer*, May 9, 1863.

44. Phillips journal.

45. Wheeling *Intelligencer*, May 8, 1863.

Chapter Eleven

1. *OR*, vol. 25, pt. 2, pp. 799–800.

2. Snider journal; *OR*, vol. 25, pt. 1, p. 104.

3. Snider journal; Curry, *A House Divided*, pp. 49, 148.

4. Snider journal; *OR*, vol. 25, pt. 1, p. 104; Armstrong, *25th Virginia Infantry*, p. 59.

5. Snider journal; *OR*, vol. 25, pt. 1, p. 104.

6. Hall diary.

7. Snider journal.

8. Armstrong, *19th and 20th Virginia Cavalry*, p. 10; Snider journal.

9. Snider journal; Hall diary.

10. *Ibid.*

11. *OR*, vol. 25, pt. 1, p. 120.

12. *OR*, vol. 25, pt. 1, pp. 120, 133; Moffett, "The Jones Raid Through West Virginia," p. 451; Blue, *Hanging Rock Rebel*, p. 184.

13. Blue, *Hanging Rock Rebel*, pp. 184–185.

14. Blue, *Hanging Rock Rebel*, pp. 185–186.

15. Moffett, "The Jones Raid Through West Virginia," p. 451.

16. *OR*, vol. 25, pt. 1, p. 133; Blue, *Hanging Rock Rebel*, p. 186.

17. *OR*, vol. 25, pt. 1, p. 131.

18. *Ibid.*; Davis letter.

19. *OR*, vol. 25, pt. 1, p. 131; O.P. Horn in Rockingham *Register*, June 6, 1863.

20. Musick, *6th Virginia Cavalry*, p. 34.

21. O'Ferrall, *Forty Years*, p. 62; *OR*, vol. 25, pt. 1, p. 131.

22. O'Ferrall, *Forty Years*, p. 59.

23. Davis letter.

24. Myers, *The Comanches*, p. 174; Summers, *Borderland Confederate*, p. 64.

25. Davis letter.

26. Summers, *Borderland Confederate*, pp. 64–65.

27. Summers, *Borderland Confederate*, p. 65; *OR*, vol. 25, pt. 1, p. 131.

Chapter Twelve

1. Tucker, *Brigadier General John D. Imboden*, pp. 136–137.

2. *OR*, vol. 25, pt. 1, pp. 120–121.

3. *OR*, vol. 25, pt. 1, pp. 104, 120; Boehm, "The Jones-Imboden Raid Through West Virginia," p. 20.

4. Boehm, "The Jones-Imboden Raid Through West Virginia," p. 20.

5. *OR*, vol. 25, pt. 1, pp. 104, 120, 133.

6. *OR*, vol. 25, pt. 1, p. 104.

7. *Ibid.*

8. *OR*, vol. 25, pt. 1, p. 102; Lowry, *22nd Virginia Infantry*, p. 42.

9. *OR*, vol. 25, pt. 1, pp. 104, 120.

10. Wheeling *Intelligencer*, May 16, 1863; Bigelow, *The Chancellorsville Campaign*, p. 466.

11. Grant, "Episodes of Confederate Cavalry Raids of 1863," p. 88; Johnston, *Virginia Railroads in the Civil War*, p. 155; Wheeling *Intelligencer*, May 1 & 5, 1863.

12. Wheeling *Intelligencer*, May 5, 1863.

13. Wheeling *Intelligencer*, May 16, 1863; Johnston, *Virginia Railroads in the Civil War*, p. 155; Summers, *The Baltimore and Ohio*, p. 139.

14. Bigelow, *The Chancellorsville Campaign*, pp. 471–472; Wheeling *Intelligencer*, May 19, 1863.

15. *OR*, vol. 25, pt. 1, pp. 104, 120; Bernard, *Where It All Began*, pp. 36–44; Tucker, *Brigadier General John D. Imboden*, p. 134; Goldsborough, *The Maryland Line*, p. 174. 11 Va. Cav. lost one killed, one wounded, and several captured; the 1st Md. Battalion lost 5 killed and 14 wounded, "more than any regiment in the command" — Goldsborough.

16. Summers, *The Baltimore and Ohio*, p. 138.

17. *OR*, vol. 25, pt. 2, p. 653.

18. Dayton, *Samuel Woods*, p. 108.

19. Wheeling *Intelligencer*, May 4, 1863.

20. Wheeling *Intelligencer*, May 6, 1863.

21. Clarksburg *Exponent*, April 29, 1990.

22. *OR*, vol. 25, pt. 1, p. 119.

23. *OR*, vol. 25, pt. 1, p. 105.

24. *OR*, vol. 25, pt. 1, p. 121.

25. see Tucker, *Brigadier General John D. Imboden*.

26. Davis, *The Confederate General*, vol. 3, pp. 217–218.

27. Faust, *Historical Times Illustrated Encyclopedia*, p. 465.

28. White diary; Wheeling *Intelligencer*, May 13, 1863.

29. Wheeling *Intelligencer*, May 15, 1863.

30. Wheeling *Intelligencer*, May 22, 1863.

31. *OR*, vol. 25, pt. 1, pp. 92–93.

32. Faust, *Historical Times Illustrated Encyclopedia*, pp. 636–637.

33. Wheeling *Intelligencer*, May 8, 1863.

Bibliography

Unpublished Primary Sources

Special Collections, University of Virginia Library, Charlottesville.
Reverend Richard T. Davis letters, Davis-Preston-Saunders Papers, MSS 4951.
Library of Virginia, Richmond.
John C. Donohue diary (Accession 28589, Misc. Reel 519).
Marshall University Library Special Collections, Huntington, WV.
James Potts diary (Accession 248)
Virginia Historical Society, Richmond.
Mottram Dulany Ball letter, from the William Selwyn Ball Reminiscences.
Virginia Military Institute Archives, Lexington, VA.
Mortimer Johnson letter, Johnson Family Papers (Manuscript #341).
West Virginia & Regional History Collection, West Virginia University Library, Morgantown, WV.
Sarah Lough letter, A&M #672.
Maria Louise Sumner Phillips journal, A&M #1846.
John Polsley letters, A&M #1601.
Joseph C. Snider, Journal of the Civil War 1861–1864, A&M #1504.
Henry Solomon White diary, A&M #1732.

Books

Allan, Bernard L., and McKain, David. *Where It All Began: The Story of the People and Places Where the Oil & Gas Industry Began—West Virginia and Southeastern Ohio.* Parkersburg, WV: David L. McKain, 1994.
Ambler, Charles H. *Francis H. Pierpont: Union War Governor of Virginia and Father of West Virginia.* Chapel Hill, NC: University of North Carolina Press, 1937.
Armstrong, Richard L. *25th Virginia Infantry.* Lynchburg, VA: H.E. Howard, Inc., 1990.
_____. *7th Virginia Cavalry.* Lynchburg, VA: H.E. Howard, Inc., 1992.
_____. *19th and 20th Virginia Cavalry.* Lynchburg, VA: H.E. Howard, Inc., 1994.
Ashcraft, John. *31st Virginia Infantry.* Lynchburg, VA: H.E. Howard, Inc., 1988.
Balderson, W.L. *Fort Prickett and Marion County.* Fairmont, WV: Bicentennial Committee, 1976.
Baylor, George. *Bull Run to Bull Run.* Richmond, VA: B.F. Johnson Publishing Co., 1900.
Bigelow, John Jr. *The Campaign of Chancellorsville: A Strategic and Tactical Study.* New Haven, CT: Yale University Press, 1910.
Booth, George Wilson. *Personal Reminiscences of a Soldier in the War Between the States.* Baltimore: Butternut and Blue, 1981.
Bosworth, A.S. *A History of Randolph County, West Virginia.* Parsons, WV: McClain Printing Co., 1975.
Callahan, James Morton. *History of West Virginia.* Chicago: The American Historical Society, Inc., 1923.
_____. *History of the Making of Morgantown, West Virginia: A Type Study in Trans-Appalachian Local History.* Morgantown, WV: West Virginia University, 1926.
Cohen, Stan. *The Civil War in West Virginia, A*

Pictorial History. Missoula, MT: Gateway Printing and Litho, 1976.

Cole, Scott C. *34th Virginia Cavalry*. Lynchburg, VA: H.E. Howard, Inc., 1993.

Cook, Roy Bird. *Lewis County in the Civil War*. Charleston, WV, 1924.

Curry, Richard. *A House Divided*. Pittsburgh: University of Pittsburgh Press, 1964.

Davis, Dorothy. *History of Harrison County, West Virginia*. Parsons, WV: McClain Printing Co., 1970.

Davis, William C., ed. *Confederate Generals*, 6 vols. The National Historical Society, 1991.

Dayton, Ruth Woods. *Samuel Woods and His Family*. Charleston, WV, 1939.

Delauter, Roger U., Jr. *18th Virginia Cavalry*. Lynchburg, VA: H.E. Howard, Inc., 1985.

_____. *McNeill's Rangers*. Lynchburg, VA: H.E. Howard, Inc., 1986.

_____. *62nd Virginia Infantry*. Lynchburg, VA: H.E. Howard, Inc., 1988.

Dickinson, Jack. *Tattered Uniforms and Bright Bayonets: West Virginia's Confederate Soldiers*. Huntington, WV: Marshall University Library Association, 1995.

Divine, John E. *35th Virginia Cavalry Battalion*. Lynchburg, VA: H.E. Howard, Inc., 1985.

Driver, Robert J. *First & Second Maryland Cavalry, C.S.A.* Charlottesville, VA: Rockbridge Publishing, 1999.

Fansler, Homer Floyd. *History of Tucker County, West Virginia*. Parsons, WV: McClain Printing Co., 1962.

Faust, Patricia, ed. *Historical Times Illustrated History of the Civil War*. New York: Harper & Row, 1987.

Frye, Dennis E. *12th Virginia Cavalry*. Lynchburg, VA: H.E. Howard, Inc., 1988.

Goldsborough, W.W. *The Maryland Line in the Confederate Army, 1861–1865*. Gaithersburg, MD: Olde Soldier's Books, Inc., 1987.

Hall, James E. *The Diary of a Confederate Soldier*. Philippi, WV: Elizabeth Teter Phillips, 1961.

Hardway, Ronald V. *On Our Own Soil: William Lowther Jackson and the Civil War in West Virginia's Mountains*. Quarrier Press, 2003.

Harris, Nelson. *17th Virginia Cavalry*. Lynchburg, VA: H.E. Howard, Inc., 1994.

Hayman, Henry. *History of Harrison County*. Morgantown, WV: Acme Publishing Co., 1910.

Hornbeck, Betty. *Upshur Brothers of the Blue and Gray*. Parsons, WV: McClain Printing Co., 1967.

Johnston, Angus James II. *Virginia Railroads in the Civil War*. Chapel Hill, N.C: University of North Carolina Press, 1961.

Jones, Virgil C. *Gray Ghosts and Rebel Raiders*. McClean, VA: EPM Publications, 1984.

Krick, Robert K. *Lee's Colonels: A Biographical Register of the Field Officers of the Army of Northern Virginia*. Dayton, OH: Morningside House, Inc., 1992.

Lang, Theodore F. *Loyal West Virginia From 1861 to 1865*. Baltimore: Deutch Publishing Company, 1895.

Lee, Howard B. *Burning Springs: And Other Tales of the Little Kanawha*. Parsons, WV: McClain Printing Co., 1968.

Lewis, Ronald. *West Virginia: Documents in the History of a Rural-Industrial State*.

Longacre, Edward G. *Mounted Raids of the Civil War*. Lincoln Neb.: University of Nebraska Press, 1972.

Lough, Glenn D. *Now and Long Ago: A History of the Marion County Area*. Fairmont, WV: Glenn D. Lough, 1969.

Lowry, Terry. *22nd Virginia Infantry*. Lynchburg, VA: H.E. Howard, Inc., 1991.

_____. *Last Sleep: The Battle of Droop Mountain*. Charleston, WV: Pictorial Histories, 1996.

McDonald, Capt. William N. *A History of the Laurel Brigade, Originally the Ashby Cavalry of the Army of Northern Virginia*. Baltimore, 1907.

McInnes, Hugh. *Civil War Letters of Hugh McInnes*. Parsons, WV: McClain Printing Co., 1981.

McKinney, Tim. *The Civil War in Fayette County, West Virginia*. Charleston, WV: Pictorial Histories Publishing Co., 1988.

Marshall, Fielding Lewis. *Recollections and Reflections of Fielding Lewis Marshall, A Virginian of the Old School*. Orange, Va., 1911.

Matheny, Herman E. *Major General Thomas Maley Harris*. Parsons, WV: McClain Printing Co., 1963.

_____. *Wood County, West Virginia in Civil War Times*. Parkersburg, WV: Trans Alleghany Books, Inc., 1987.

Maxwell, Hu. *The History of Randolph County, West Virginia*. Morgantown, WV: Acme Publishing Co., 1898.

_____. *The History of Barbour County, West Virginia*. Morgantown, WV: Acme Publishing Co., 1899.

Miller, Thomas Condit, and Hu Maxwell. *West Virginia and Its People*, 3 vols. New York: Lewis Historical Publishing Company, 1913.

Moore, George Ellis. *A Banner in the Hills: West*

Virginia's Statehood. New York: Appleton-Century Crafts, 1963.

Morton, Oren F. *History of Preston County, West Virginia*. Kingwood, WV: Preston Printing Co., 1911.

Musick, Michael P. *6th Virginia Cavalry*. Lynchburg, VA: H.E. Howard, Inc., 1990.

Myers, Frank M. *The Comanches: A History of White's Battalion, Virginia Cavalry*. Baltimore, 1871.

Neese, George. *Three Years in the Confederate Horse Artillery*. New York: Neale Publishing Co., 1907.

O'Ferrall, Charles T. *Forty Years of Active Service*. New York: Neale Publishing Co., 1904.

Oates, Dan, ed. *Hanging Rock Rebel: Lieutenant John Blue's War in West Virginia and the Shenandoah Valley*. Shippensburg, PA: Burd Street Press, 1994.

Opie, John. *A Rebel Cavalryman with Lee, Stuart, and Jackson*. Dayton, OH: Morningside Press, 1972.

Phisterer, Frederick, comp. *New York in the War of the Rebellion, 1861 to 1865*, 5 vols. Albany, NY: F.B. Lyon Co., State Printers, 1912.

Poe, Capt. David. *Personal Reminiscences of the Civil War*. Charleston, WV: The News-Mail Publishing Co., 1908.

Reader, Frank S. *History of the Fifth West Virginia Cavalry, Formerly the Second Virginia Infantry and of Battery G, First West Va. Light Artillery*. New Brighton, PA: F.S. Reader, 1890.

Report of the Adjutant General of the State of Illinois. Springfield, Ill., 1900.

Rice, Otis K. *West Virginia—The State and Its People*. Parsons, WV: McClain Printing Co., 1972.

Rich, Edward. *Comrades Four*. New York: Neale Publishing Co., 1907.

Roberts, Charles S. *The West End–Cumberland to Grafton 1848–1991*. Baltimore: Barnard, Roberts, and Co., Inc., 1991.

Robertson, James I. Jr. *Stonewall Jackson: The Man, The Soldier, The Legend*. New York: Macmillan Publishing, 1997.

Scharf, J. Thomas. *History of Western Maryland*, vol. 1. Baltimore: Clearfield Company & Family Line Pub., 1995.

Schlosnagle, Stephen. *Garrett County: A History of Maryland's Tableland*. Parsons, WV: McClain Printing Co., 1978.

Shaffer, John W. *Clash of Loyalties: A Border County in the Civil War*. Morgantown, WV: West Virginia University Press, 2003.

Sifakis, Stewart. *Compendium of the Confederate Armies*. New York: Facts on File, 1992.

Smith, Edward C. *History of Lewis County, West Virginia*. Weston, WV: pub. by author, 1920.

Stutler, Boyd Blynn. *West Virginia in the Civil War*. Charleston, WV: Education Foundation, 1966.

Summers, Festus P., ed. *A Borderland Confederate: The Civil War Letters and Diaries of William L. Wilson*. Pittsburgh: University of Pittsburgh Press, 1962.

_____. *The Baltimore and Ohio Railroad in the Civil War*. New York: G.P. Putnam's Sons, 1939.

Thacker, Victor L., ed. *French Harding: Civil War Memories*. Parsons, WV: McClain Printing Co., 2000.

Tucker, Spencer C. *Brigadier General John D. Imboden: Confederate Commander in the Shenandoah*. Lexington, KY: The University Press of Kentucky, 2003.

United States War Department. *The War of the Rebellion: A Compilation of the Official Records of the Union and Confederate Armies*, 70 volumes in 128 parts. Washington, D.C.: Government Printing Office, 1880–1901.

Wiley, Samuel T. *History of Preston County*. Kingwood, WV: The Journal Printing Co., 1882.

_____. *History of Monongalia County, West Virginia, From Its First Settlements to the Present Time; With Numerous Biographical and Family Sketches*. Kingwood, WV: Preston Pub., 1883.

William, C.R., comp. *Southern Sympathizers: Wood County Confederate Soldiers*. Parkersburg, WV: Inland River Books, 1979.

Woodward, Harold R. Jr. *Defender of the Valley: Brigadier John Daniel Imboden, C.S.A.* Berryville, Va.: Rockbridge Publishing, 1996.

JOURNAL & MAGAZINE ARTICLES

Boehm, Robert B. "The Jones-Imboden Raid Through West Virginia." *Civil War Times Illustrated*, 3 (May 1964).

Bond, Frank A. "Storming A Blockhouse in Greenland Gap." *Confederate Veteran*, 17 (Oct. 1909).

Bright, Semion. "The McNeil Rangers: A Study in Confederate Guerilla Warfare." *West Virginia History*, 12 (July 1951).

Carvil, Kenneth. "Greenland Gap." *Wild, Wonderful West Virginia*, Sept. 1986.

French, Stephen. "The Jones-Imboden Raid." *The Blue and Gray Education Society*, 10 (March 2002).

French, Steve. "Hurry Was the Order of the Day." *North & South*. Aug. 1999.

Haselberger, Fritz and Mack. "The Battle of Greenland Gap." *West Virginia History*, 28 (July 1967).

McNeil, John A. "The Imboden Raid and Its Effects." *Southern Historical Society Papers*, vol. 34.

Mettam, Henry C. "Civil War Memories of the First Maryland Cavalry, C.S.A." *Maryland Historical Magazine*, vol. lviii.

Moffett, George H. "The Jones Raid Through West Virginia." *Confederate Veteran*, 13 (Oct. 1905).

Summers, Festus P. "The Jones-Imboden Raid." *West Virginia History*, 47 (1988).

Young, T.J. "About Jones' Raid Into West Virginia." *Confederate Veteran*, 15 (May 1907).

NEWSPAPERS

Clarksburg Exponent
Fairmont Times
Glades Star
Marietta Intelligencer

Parkersburg News
Pittsburgh Gazette
Richmond Whig
Rockingham Register

Times West Virginian
Staunton Vindicator
Wheeling Intelligencer

INTERNET WEBSITES

www.gdg.org

www.generalsandbrevets.com

www.wikiipedia.org

Index

213